THE ARDEN SHAKESPEARE

THIRD EDITION
General Editors: Richard Proudfoot, Ann Thompson
and David Scott Kastan

OTHELLO

THE ARDEN SHAKESPEARE

*Second Series

THE ARDEN SHAKESPEARE

OTHELLO

Edited by

E. A. J. HONIGMANN

The general editors of the Arden Shakespeare have been
W. J. Craig and R. H. Case (first series 1899-1944)
Una Ellis-Fermor, Harold F. Brooks, Harold Jenkins and
Brian Morris (second series 1946-1982)

Present general editors (third series)
Richard Proudfoot, Ann Thompson and David Scott Kastan

This edition of *Othello,* by E. A. J. Honigmann,
first published by Thomas Nelson & Sons Ltd 1997
Reprinted 1999

Thomas Nelson & Sons Ltd
Nelson House Mayfield Road
Walton-on-Thames Surrey
KT12 5PL UK

I(T)P® Thomas Nelson is an International
Thomson Publishing Company
I(T)P® is used under licence

Editorial matter © 1997 E. A. J. Honigmann

Printed in Croatia

British Library Cataloguing in Publication Data
A catalogue record for this book is available from
the British Library

Library of Congress Cataloguing in Publication Data
A catalogue record has been applied for

ISBN 0-17-443465-0 (cased)
NPN 9 8 7 6 5 4 3
ISBN 0-17-443464-2 (paperback)
NPN 9 8 7 6 5

The Editor

E. A. J. Honigmann is the author of more than a dozen books on Shakespeare and his contemporaries, including *Shakespeare, Seven Tragedies: the Dramatist's Manipulation of Response* (1976) and *Myriad-Minded Shakespeare* (1989). He has taught as a lecturer at Glasgow University, as a Fellow of the Shakespeare Institute in Stratford-upon-Avon (Birmingham University), as Joseph Cowen Professor of English Literature in the University of Newcastle-upon-Tyne, and in Canada and the United States. His *The Texts of 'Othello' and Shakespearian Revision* (1996) is a companion volume to this Arden edition.

For

Elsie McConnachie Honigmann
(née Packman)

10.7.1929–6.12.1994

Only a sweet and virtuous soul
Like seasoned timber, never gives;
But, though the whole world turn to coal,
Then chiefly lives.
(George Herbert)

CONTENTS

THE TRAGEDY OF OTHELLO, THE MOOR OF VENICE 113

LIST OF
ILLUSTRATIONS

GENERAL EDITORS' PREFACE

The Arden Shakespeare is now nearly one hundred years old. The earliest volume in the first edition, Edward Dowden's edition of *Hamlet*, was published in 1899. Since then the Arden Shakespeare has become internationally recognized and respected. It is now widely acknowledged as the pre-eminent Shakespeare series, valued by scholars, students, actors, and 'the great variety of readers' alike for its readable and reliable texts, its full annotation and its richly informative introductions.

We have aimed in the third Arden edition to maintain the quality and general character of its predecessors, preserving the commitment to presenting the play as it has been shaped in history. While each individual edition will necessarily have its own emphasis in the light of the unique possibilities and problems posed by the play, the series as a whole, like the earlier Ardens, insists upon the highest standards of scholarship and upon attractive and accessible presentation.

Newly edited from the original quarto and folio editions, the texts are presented in fully modernized form, with a textual apparatus that records all substantial divergences from those early printings. The notes and introductions focus on the conditions and possibilities of meaning that editors, critics and performers (on stage and screen) have discovered in the play. While building upon the rich history of scholarly and theatrical activity that has long shaped our understanding of the texts of Shakespeare's plays, this third edition of the Arden Shakespeare is made necessary and possible by a new generation's encounter with Shakespeare, engaging with the plays and their complex relation to the culture in which they were – and continue to be – produced.

THE TEXT

On each page of the play itself, readers will find a passage of text followed by commentary and, finally, textual notes. Act and scene divisions (seldom present in the early editions and often the product of eighteenth-century or later scholarship) have been retained for ease of reference, but have been given less prominence than in the previous series. Editorial indications of location of the action have been removed to the textual notes or commentary.

In the text itself, unfamiliar typographic conventions have been avoided in order to minimize obstacles to the reader. Elided forms in the early texts are spelt out in full in verse lines wherever they indicate a usual late twentieth-century pronunciation that requires no special indication and wherever they occur in prose (except when they indicate non-standard pronunciation). In verse speeches, marks of elision are retained where they are necessary guides to the scansion and pronunciation of the line. Final -ed in past tense and participial forms of verbs is always printed as -ed, without accent, never as -'d, but wherever the required pronunciation diverges from modern usage a note in the commentary draws attention to the fact. Where the final -ed should be given syllabic value contrary to modern usage, e.g.

> Doth Silvia know that I am banished?
> (*TGV* 3.1.221)

the note will take the form

221 **banished** banishèd

Conventional lineation of divided verse lines shared by two or more speakers has been reconsidered and sometimes rearranged. Except for the familiar *Exit* and *Exeunt*, Latin forms in stage directions and speech prefixes have been translated into English and the original Latin forms recorded in the textual notes.

COMMENTARY AND TEXTUAL NOTES

Notes in the commentary, for which a major source will be the *Oxford English Dictionary*, offer glossarial and other explication of verbal difficulties; they may also include discussion of points of theatrical interpretation and, in relevant cases, substantial extracts from Shakespeare's source material. Editors will not usually offer glossarial notes for words adequately defined in the *Concise Oxford Dictionary* or *Webster's Ninth New Collegiate Dictionary*, but in cases of doubt they will include notes. Attention, however, will be drawn to places where more than one likely interpretation can be proposed and to significant verbal and syntactic complexity. Notes preceded by * involve readings altered from the early edition(s) on which the text is based.

Headnotes to acts or scenes discuss, where appropriate, questions of scene location, Shakespeare's handling of his source materials, and major difficulties of staging. The list of roles (so headed to emphasize the play's status as a text for performance) is also considered in commentary notes. These may include comment on plausible patterns of casting with the resources of an Elizabethan or Jacobean acting company and also on any variation in the description of roles in their speech prefixes in the early editions.

The textual notes are designed to let readers know when the edited text diverges from the early edition(s) on which it is based. Wherever this happens the note will record the rejected reading of the early edition(s), in original spelling, and the source of the reading adopted in this edition. Other forms from the early edition(s) recorded in these notes will include some spellings of particular interest or significance and original forms of translated stage directions. Where two early editions are involved, for instance with *Othello*, the notes will also record all important differences between them. The textual notes take a form that has been in use since the nineteenth century. This comprises, first: line reference, reading adopted in the text and closing square bracket; then: abbreviated reference, in italic, to the earliest edition to adopt the accepted reading, italic semi-colon and noteworthy alternative reading(s), each with abbreviated italic reference to its source.

Conventions used in these textual notes include the following. The solidus / is used, in notes quoting verse or discussing verse lining, to indicate line endings. Distinctive spellings of the basic text (Q or F) follow the square bracket without indication of source and are enclosed in italic brackets. Names enclosed in brackets indicate originators of conjectural emendations when these did not originate in an edition of the text, or when this edition records a conjecture not accepted into its text. Stage directions (SDs) are referred to by the number of the line within or immediately after which they are placed. Line numbers with a decimal point relate to centred SDs not falling within a verse line and to SDs more than one line long, with the number after the point indicating the line within the SD: e.g. 78.4 refers to the fourth line of the SD following line 78. Lines of SDs at the start of a scene are numbered 0.1, 0.2, etc. Where only a line number precedes the square bracket, e.g. 128], the note relates to the whole line; where SD is added to the number, it relates to the whole of a SD within or immediately following the line. Speech prefixes (SPs) follow similar conventions, 203 SP] referring to the speaker's name for line 203. Where a SP reference takes the form e.g. 38+SP, it relates to all subsequent speeches assigned to that speaker in the scene in question.

Where, as with *King Henry V*, one of the early editions is a so-called 'bad quarto' (that is, a text either heavily adapted, or reconstructed from memory, or both), the divergences from the present edition are too great to be recorded in full in the notes. In these cases the editions will include a reduced photographic facsimile of the 'bad quarto' in an appendix.

INTRODUCTION

Both the introduction and the commentary are designed to present the plays as texts for performance, and make appropriate reference to stage, film and television versions, as well as introducing the reader to the range of critical approaches to the plays. They discuss the history of the reception of the texts within the theatre and scholarship and beyond, investigating the interdependency of the literary text and the surrounding 'cultural text' both at the time of the original production of Shakespeare's works and during their long and rich afterlife.

PREFACE

'What I would now like to propose to you', the General Editor of the Arden Shakespeare wrote to me on 17 August 1982, 'is that you consider taking on the editing of the next Arden *Othello*.' He suggested 1988 as the completion date. I was tempted, but did I really want to give five or six years to a single play? After some soul-searching I signed a contract with Methuen & Co. to deliver the edition in 1988 in a form 'acceptable to the General Editor', with 'sufficient appendices' (whatever that means: is five sufficient?). I knew, of course, that *Othello* had received much less detailed editorial attention than *Hamlet* or *King Lear*, though not that so much editorial work still remained to be done. Five or six years have stretched to somewhat more, the Arden Shakespeare is no longer published by Methuen, its General Editor has been joined by two other General Editors, the edition of *Othello* needed a companion volume on *The Texts of 'Othello'* (Routledge, 1996) – much has changed, yet my gratitude to Richard Proudfoot has remained constant (or rather, has grown with the years). He chose the editor, he read through my drafts and always commented encouragingly (and, to my great advantage, critically). On almost every page I am indebted to him, and I gladly acknowledge this. At a later stage, in the last year or so, a second General Editor (David Scott Kastan) checked through the edition: I am grateful to him as well for many helpful comments.

Over the years innumerable offprints of articles on *Othello* have reached me, some from old friends, others from complete strangers. It was not possible to refer to all of them, the list of publications on the play being now so huge, but I hope that the edition has benefited, directly or indirectly. Other friends and colleagues have helped in different ways – sending books that were unobtainable in Britain, inviting me to give lectures or to write papers on *Othello*, or simply answering my questions: David Bevington, Helen Boden, Susan Brock, T. W. Craik, Katherine Duncan-Jones, R. A. Foakes, the late Charlton Hinman, Harold Jenkins, Holger Klein, Giorgio Melchiori, Sylvia Morris, Barbara Mowat, Elisabeth Orsten, Edward Pechter, Willem Schrickx, the late Terence Spencer, Marvin Spevack, Rosamond Kent Sprague and Stanley Wells. Mairi McDonald, Marian Pringle and Robert Smallwood of the Shakespeare Centre, Stratford-upon-Avon, were efficient and helpful in locating books, manuscripts and illustrations. In addition I am grateful to the librarians and officials of the Bodleian Library, the British Film Institute, the British Library, Cambridge University Library and Trinity College, Cambridge, Durham University Library, the Public Record Office, the Theatre Museum (London) and, last but not least, Newcastle University Library (the Robinson Library). To all, my sincere thanks: without their generous cooperation this edition would have had many more gaps and faults.

Jane Armstrong, a friend from the Methuen years and Arden 2, who took charge of the third Arden Shakespeare for the publisher, has been, as usual, understanding and supportive. Her colleagues, Penny Wheeler and Judith Ravenscroft, were equally tactful and efficient in dealing with the unforeseen quirks of an edition of Shakespeare – or should I say, of an editor of Shakespeare?

My greatest debt – for putting up with *Othello* uncomplainingly for so long, and for having so much else in common with the gentle Desdemona – is acknowledged in my dedication.

E. A. J. Honigmann
Newcastle upon Tyne

INTRODUCTION

The greatest tragedy?

Between about 1599 and 1608 Shakespeare wrote a series of tragedies, probably in the following order: *Julius Caesar*, *Hamlet*, *Othello*, *King Lear*, *Macbeth*, *Antony and Cleopatra*, *Coriolanus*, and
one less easy to date, *Timon of Athens*. By universal consent these
tragedies established him in the front rank of the world's dramatists, and, not a few would wish to say, in the very first place.
While the four or five tragedies that began with *Hamlet* are usually seen as the peak of his achievement, many critics have praised
either *Hamlet* or *King Lear* as his greatest tragedy.[1] Why not
Othello? This, the third of the mature tragedies, contains arguably
the best plot, two of Shakespeare's most original characters, the
most powerful scene in any of his plays, and poetry second to
none. We may fairly call it the most exciting of the tragedies –
even the most unbearably exciting – so why not the greatest? As
will emerge, there are reasons for this reluctance to recognize
Othello as Shakespeare's supreme masterpiece in tragedy, and also
reasons on the other side.

Date, text and principal source

For a discussion of the date of *Othello*, the play's textual history
and principal source, see Appendices 1–3. Here is a brief sum-
mary of conclusions.

    Date   (Late 1601–)1602. The traditional date is 1603 or 1604.

    Text   Arden 3 argues that the two early texts, called the Quarto
and Folio, or Q and F, derive from scribal transcripts copied from

---

1 See especially R. A. Foakes, *Hamlet versus Lear: Cultural Politics and Shakespeare's
Art* (Cambridge, 1993); also below, pp. 102ff.

1

two authorial manuscripts, and that some readings that differ in Q and F can be explained as Shakespeare's first and second thoughts. Yet both Q and F suffer from widespread misreading and other textual mishaps: often we cannot tell whether variant readings should be ascribed to authorial afterthoughts or to textual corruption.

Source   Shakespeare echoed his principal source, a short story in Giraldi Cinthio's *Hecatommithi* (1565), more closely and much more often than previous editors have indicated. To assist those who wish to compare the play and its source in detail, Appendix 3 prints a translation of Cinthio together with cross-references to the play.

Shakespeare and the Barbarians

Once we realize, following Alfred Hart,[1] that *Othello* should be dated (1601–)1602, we can answer a question that has received very little attention. What prompted Shakespeare to undertake the tragedy of 'The Moor of Venice'? We now know that he did not have to rely only on literary sources: not long before he began *Othello* he had the opportunity of observing a Moorish embassy at first hand. The ambassador of the King of Barbary arrived in England in August 1600, for a 'half year's abode in London' (the words of John Stow);[2] being Muslims and strange in their ways, he and his retinue caused a stir. Shakespeare's company, the Lord Chamberlain's Men, performed at court in the Christmas season (1600–1), before the ambassador's departure, and they attracted other foreign visitors to the theatre, so we may take it that the dramatist must have encountered 'the Barbarians', as they were called, and that the first audiences of *Othello* could compare Shakespeare's Moor with these much-discussed foreigners.

At a later point (p. 14) we shall have to return to an issue that has been hotly disputed, whether Othello is a black or an 'olive-coloured' north African Moor. The portrait of the Moorish ambassador to Queen Elizabeth (Fig. 1) settles the question of *this* Moor's ethnic background and, I think, has a bearing on Othello's.

---

1   Alfred Hart, 'The date of *Othello*', *TLS*, 10 October 1935, p. 631. Cf. Richmond Noble, 'The date of *Othello*', *TLS*, 14 December 1935, p. 859, and Honigmann, 'Date of *Othello*'.

2   See Bernard Harris, 'A portrait of a Moor', *SS*, 11 (1958), 89–97, and also Fig. 1.

1 The Moorish Ambassador to Queen Elizabeth, 1600–1: English School,
early seventeenth century

I would go further: the ambassador's intense and aristocratic face
seems to me right for Othello, and his age (42, inscribed on the

portrait together with the date, 1600) about right as well. Is it too fanciful to suppose that this very face haunted Shakespeare's imagination and inspired the writing of his tragedy?

Preliminary reading

In November 1600, John Pory published his translation of John Leo's *A Geographical Historie of Africa* which, said Geoffrey Bullough, 'Shakespeare almost certainly consulted' (Bullough, 208). Pory's dedication referred to the Moorish ambassador's presence in London. Leo, a Moor brought up in Barbary, wrote at length about his countrymen. 'Most honest people they are, and destitute of all fraud and guile', 'very proud and high-minded, and woonderfully addicted vnto wrath . . . Their wits are but meane, and they are so credulous, that they will beleeue matters impossible, which are told them' – like Othello? 'No nation in the world is so subiect vnto iealousie; for they will rather leese [lose] their liues, then put vp any disgrace in the behalfe of their women' (40–1).

Pory's biographical account of John Leo and his 'great Trauels' could also have influenced Othello's narrative of his own earlier life (1.3.129ff.):

> I maruell much how euer he should haue escaped so manie thousands of imminent dangers . . . For how many desolate cold mountaines, and huge drie, and barren deserts passed he? How often was he in hazard to haue beene captiued, or to haue had his throte cut . . . ?

Leo himself mentioned Africa's 'vast deserts', 'mighty caues', rocks, fountains, cisterns, as well as enchanters and Egyptian women who wear gowns 'curiously embroidered' (148–9, 205–6, 241–2; cf. 3.4.57–9: 'That handkerchief / Did an Egyptian to my mother give, / She was a charmer', and 3.3.437–8). It is hard to resist the feeling that John Leo, like the Moorish ambassador, stimulated Shakespeare's imagination.

A second encyclopedic book, on an even grander scale than John Leo's, seems to have had the same effect. Much of Shakespeare's information about the Mediterranean world is thought to come from Philemon Holland's translation of Pliny's *Historie of the World* (1601). In the words of Kenneth Muir (188ff.),

> Shakespeare used Holland's Pliny for many details . . . to suggest Othello's alien and exotic experience. Pliny mentions the medicinal gum of the Arabian trees, mines of sulphur, a statue made of chrysolite, mandragora, and coloquintida . . . There is no doubt that the simile of the Pontic Sea is based directly on Holland's translation, and is indeed a fusion of several different passages.

'Out of Pontus', said Pliny, 'the sea alwaies floweth, and *never ebbeth* againe.' 'The sea Pontus evermore floweth, and runneth out into Propontis . . . [and] *never retireth* backe'; '*pent and restrained* within those streights', at times it is 'frozen and *all an yce*' (Muir, 188–90). To such prosaic origins we owe the magnificence of

> Never, Iago. Like to the Pontic sea
> Whose *icy current* and *compulsive course*
> *Ne'er keeps retiring ebb* but keeps due on
> To the Propontic and the Hellespont . . .
> (3.3.456–9)

Pliny also described the 'Blemmyi', who 'have no heads, but mouth and eies both in their breast' (see Fig. 2) and cannibals called 'Anthropophagi, that feed of mans flesh' (Pliny 96, 154). Hence

> The Anthropophagi, and men whose heads
> Do grow beneath their shoulders.
> (1.3.145–6)

We have to concede, however, that just about all the items supposedly taken from Pliny, the most likely source, could also have come from other scattered publications.

It looks as though Shakespeare browsed through the translations of John Leo and Pliny. A third translation, one that he examined more closely, appeared more or less halfway between his two Venice plays – Sir Lewis Lewkenor's *The Commonwealth and Government of Venice* (1599), most of it translated from the Latin text of Cardinal Contarini. 'I have no doubt', Malone declared

2 One of the 'men whose heads / Do grow beneath their shoulders' (1.3.145–6), with a sciapod (man with one huge foot), a cyclops, Siamese twins and a wolf-man: from Sebastian Munster's *Cosmographia* (1572)

two hundred years ago, 'that . . . this treatise furnished our poet with the knowledge of those *officers* of night, whom Brabantio here [1.1.180] desires to be called to his assistance' (Malone, 1.1.180n.). In fact, a marginal gloss drew attention to the officers of night (p. 96); Lewkenor explained that 'out of euery tribe (for the city is deuided into six tribes,) there is elected an officer of the night . . . [whose duty] is, to keepe a watch euery other night by turn, within their tribes' – which may also have suggested Iago's 'Good God, the souls *of all my tribe* defend / From jealousy' (3.3.177–8).

Lewkenor analysed the complex power structure of Venice. The Duke (Shakespeare never calls him the Doge) presides over the Grand Council and any other council he joins; some editors think that Shakespeare misunderstood Lewkenor and therefore wrote that Brabantio has 'a voice potential / As double as the duke's' (1.2.13–14: see note). The Venetian Senate consists of many 'senators' (65: cf. 1.1.116, etc.), so the Council of Ten can be called together more quickly (78), by day or night, and deals with urgent business. The late gathering of the Duke and senators

6

3 Andrea del Verrocchio, equestrian statue of Bartolomeo Colleone, 1481–8

(1.2.94) may be intended as an emergency meeting of the Ten.
Shakespeare could have read of the 'signiory' (1.2.18) or Signoria
in Cinthio (cf. below, p. 385), and would know from hearsay about
gondoliers and magnificoes (1.1.123, 1.2.12). He could have seen
in Lewkenor that 'the Captaine Generall of our Armie . . . is alwaies
a straunger' (132), and may have thought of Othello as Venice's
supreme commander, like Bartolomeo Colleone, whose equestrian statue (Fig. 3) so superbly conveys the pride, pomp and
circumstance of success in war;[1] or, reading how Venice governs
subject cities (125ff.), he might have imagined Othello as merely a
local commander in Cyprus.

1 Lewkenor, *Commonwealth of Venice* (131–2), mentioned the statue of Colleone.

7

Lewkenor repeatedly alluded to the two social classes in Venice, the nobility and gentlemen, and 'the common and meaner people', observing significantly that the latter 'should also in sort haue their ambition satisfied, without hauing occasion either to hate or perturbe the estate of nobilitie' (146). Class distinctions seem to have been more rigid than in England. Iago's resentment against privilege and hankering to be treated as an equal by 'gentlemen' (cf. below, pp. 35–7) underlines these distinctions. The glover's son from Stratford-upon-Avon had acquired the title of 'gentleman' before he wrote *Othello*.

Venice in the sixteenth century

From long before Shakespeare's time until 1797 Venice was one of Italy's many sovereign states. In 1600 the city had a population somewhat like London's, 150,000 or a little more,[1] and attracted foreigners of many races, being Europe's most important trade link with north Africa and the East. By 1600, however, the ascendancy implied in Wordsworth's sonnet, 'On the extinction of the Venetian Republic', was already fading.

> Once did She hold the gorgeous east in fee;
> And was the safeguard of the west: the worth
> Of Venice did not fall below her birth,
> Venice, the eldest Child of Liberty . . .

The Turks took Cyprus from the Venetians in 1570–3 and, though heavily defeated by a Christian navy at the Battle of Lepanto (1571), henceforth dominated the eastern Mediterranean. Shakespeare may not have known it when he wrote *Othello*, but the loss of Cyprus signalled the decline of Venice; the Venetians ceded Crete to the Turks in 1669 and ceased to be a major force at sea.

In 1600, however, Venice was still viewed in London as a major

---

1 For the population of London *c.* 1600, see Alfred Harbage, *Shakespeare's Audience* (New York, 1941), 39; for Venice, David C. McPherson, *Shakespeare, Jonson, and the Myth of Venice* (Newark, 1990), 42.

trading rival.[1] A charter issued in 1592 to London's Venice Company and Levant merchants gave a twelve-year monopoly of English trade to Venice and Turkey to fifty-three merchants; another charter dated 31 December 1600 named eighty-three merchants – the scale of these operations must have been considerable. At the same time the Venetians had their representatives in London, being no less anxious to know of the other's activities. When Shakespeare wrote his two Venice plays he could therefore assume a greater local interest than when he placed comedies in such almost fictitious cities (from the English point of view) as Ephesus or Messina.

Students of *Othello* need to know one other fact that was taken for granted by Shakespeare – that Venice was the pleasure capital of Europe, especially in its sexual tolerance. Its courtesans were already celebrated. Byron, not the most shockable of men, wrote from Venice in 1817 that the state of morals

> is much the same as in the Doges' time; a woman is virtuous (according to the code) who limits herself to her husband and one lover; those who have two, three, or more, are a little *wild*; but . . . only those who are indiscriminately diffuse . . . are considered as overstepping the modesty of marriage.[2]

Rousseau admired the 'graceful manners of Venetian courtesans' and their charm. Sir Henry Wotton, visiting Venice in 1591, fled almost immediately, feeling that, 'not being made of stone', he could not trust himself 'among the famous Venetian courtesans'. Years later, now an ambassador in Venice, Wotton mentioned 'a decree in Senate against the courtesans . . . made at the suit of all the gentlewomen, who before were indistinguishable from those

---

1 For the background to England's trading relations with Venice, see Chew, and Alfred C. Wood, *A History of the Levant Company* (1964). For the history of Venice, see also William H. McNeill, *Venice: The Hinge of Europe 1081–1797* (Chicago, 1974); M. E. Mallett and J. R. Hale, *The Military Organization of a Renaissance State: Venice c. 1400 to 1617* (Cambridge, 1984). For Venice as seen by English dramatists, see McPherson, as on p. 8, n. 1.

2 *The Letters of Lord Byron*, ed. R. G. Howarth (1936), 151. See also Guido Ruggiero, *The Boundaries of Eros: Sex, Crime and Sexuality in Renaissance Venice* (Oxford, 1985).

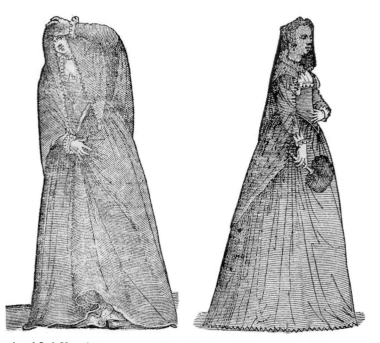

4 and 5 A Venetian courtesan (left) and fashionably dressed Venetian lady of 1550 (right): from C. Vecellio's *De Gli Habiti Antichi et Moderni* (Venice, 1590)

baggages'.[1] Histories of costume published in Venice, such as Cesare Vecellio's *De Gli Habiti Antichi et Moderni* (1590), might print different illustrations for 'Cortigiana' and 'Donna Venetiana' (Figs 4 and 5), but both ladies are expensively dressed and, as Wotton and others confirm, could be indistinguishable in clothes and manners.[2] This point, though not made in so many words in *Othello*, is used by Iago to deadly effect. Venetian wives look and behave like courtesans:

1 *The Life and Letters of Sir Henry Wotton*, ed. Logan Pearsall Smith, 2 vols (Oxford, 1907), 1.18; 2.114.
2 See also Lynne Lawner, *Lives of the Courtesans: Portraits of the Renaissance* (New York, 1987), 17.

> I know our country disposition well –
> In Venice they do let God see the pranks
> They dare not show their husbands . . .
> (3.3.204–6)

Why should Desdemona be any different? Othello begins to waver because she happens to be Venetian: the city's reputation[1] for sexual licentiousness helps to convince him.

> I took you for that cunning whore of Venice
> That married with Othello.
> (4.2.91–2)

Cyprus

Shakespeare saw Venice as part of his own world, but not so Cyprus. At the far end of the Mediterranean, Cyprus had passed into Turkish rule and, unlike Venice, seems not to have interested Shakespeare as a place, for it might be almost any one of many islands fortified by the Venetians. The play is quite specific about the Mediterranean background, mentioning Spain, Barbary, Egypt, Rhodes, the Pontic and Propontic seas, Mauretania, Jerusalem, Aleppo, Arabian trees, etc., and it reminds us some two dozen times of its location in Cyprus without really adding to the sketchy information given by Cinthio – namely, that the Venetians maintained forces there and sent out the Moor as their commander. Shakespeare identified the Turks as the threat to Cyprus (Cinthio no doubt took this for granted), but must have known other facts that he chose not to use: for example, that according to legend Aphrodite (or Venus) rose from the sea near Paphos, on the west coast of Cyprus. Poets celebrated Cyprus as the island of Venus, as in Sir John Harington's 'Of Cyprus' reprinted in Robert Allot's *England's Parnassus* (1600). Shakespeare referred to Paphos in *Venus and Adonis* 1193 and in *The Tempest* 4.1.93, though not in *Othello*. A strange oversight, in a tragedy of love? Desdemona is 'sport for Jove' (2.3.17), Othello talks of 'Jove's dread clamours' (3.3.359), and no one remembers Venus!

---

1 Shakespeare certainly knew of Venice's unsavoury reputation: cf. *MA* 1.1.271, 'if Cupid have not spent all his quiver in Venice'.

Cinthio

In 1601 or 1602, when Shakespeare started to think about *Othello*, he could assume that many theatre-goers had seen and perhaps conversed with Moors and Venetians in London. For his plot he turned to Cinthio's *Hecatommithi*, a collection of short stories, one of which supplied the outlines and not a little of the detail of the tragedy. We can learn so much about Shakespeare's working methods from a reading of Cinthio that I urge all serious students of the play to read and reread this 'source' (in Appendix 3), and promise that this will be a better investment of time than a perusal of my Introduction. Knowing, alas, that well-meant advice is often ignored, I offer, as a poor alternative to Appendix 3, a synopsis of Cinthio's story, necessary because I refer so frequently to Cinthio in this edition.

Synopsis A virtuous lady of Venice called Disdemona fell in love with a valiant Moor and married him, despite opposition from her relatives [= Brabantio]. They lived happily in Venice for some time, until the Venetian lords chose the Moor as their Commandant in Cyprus. She wanted to accompany him, and they sailed together. The Moor 'had in his company an Ensign of handsome presence but the most scoundrelly nature' [= Iago], who was married to a fair and honest young woman [= Emilia]. The Ensign fell in love with Disdemona; she took no notice of him, so he imagined that she loved a Corporal [= Cassio] who often visited the Moor's home; to revenge himself the Ensign decided to accuse Disdemona and the Corporal of adultery. Soon afterwards the Moor deprived the Corporal of his rank for wounding a soldier [= Montano] while on guard duty. Disdemona tried to reconcile the Moor and the Corporal; the Ensign hinted to the Moor that she did so for a good reason, but would not speak more explicitly, which tormented the Moor, who threatened his wife; she reacted humbly. The Ensign then told the Moor that his wife and the Corporal were lovers. Enraged, the Moor asked for proof. The Ensign had a three-year-old daughter; when Disdemona visited his wife, the Ensign handed the child to Disdemona and, as he did so, stole from her a treasured handkerchief. He left the handkerchief in the Corporal's room; then, having placed the

Moor where he could overhear them, the Ensign talked to the Corporal, laughing heartily, and afterwards told the Moor that the Corporal had confessed his adultery, and that Disdemona gave him the handkerchief. One day, after dinner, the Moor asked her for the handkerchief. She pretended to look for it, then said she could not find it. The Moor now thought about killing his wife. She noticed that he was greatly changed and asked her friend, the Ensign's wife, for advice; she, however, although she 'knew everything' (because the Ensign had tried to make her his accomplice), did not dare to speak plainly, for fear of her husband. The Corporal asked a woman who worked for him [= Bianca] to copy the embroidery of the handkerchief; she did so near a window, where the Ensign pointed out the woman with the handkerchief to the Moor, who now begged the Ensign to kill the Corporal. One night, as the Corporal left the house of a courtesan [= Bianca again], the Ensign cut his right leg through with his sword, then fled. The Ensign and Moor killed Disdemona by beating her with a stocking filled with sand, then made the ceiling fall to conceal her murder. After her death, realizing that the Ensign had caused it, the Moor hated him; the Ensign told the Corporal that it was the Moor who had cut off his leg and killed Disdemona. The Corporal informed the Signoria. The Moor, brought back to Venice, was tortured but did not confess; Disdemona's relatives later killed him in revenge.

Shakespeare's changes and additions to Cinthio's story are discussed in Appendix 3 and, in passing, in various parts of this Introduction.

Character criticism

The analysis of Shakespeare's 'characters' has become unfashionable and, in some quarters, discredited. Whether or not we agree with this modern trend we have to acknowledge that for more than three centuries the world admired 'our Shakespeare' (as he was called in his own lifetime) as a creator of character. 'O Shakespeare and Nature,' Hazlitt exclaimed, adapting a famous saying, 'which of you copied from the other?' This

Introduction, being intended – among other things – as a survey of some of the more stimulating criticism of the past, cannot simply ignore 'character criticism'. It will differ from Hazlitt and other good critics in emphasizing the contradictions in Othello and Iago, in arguing that readers and performers can interpret them in different valid ways and, more controversially, in suggesting that, when all is said, Othello and Iago defeat character criticism. We can learn much by looking closely at Shakespeare's complex characters, but we cannot pluck out the heart of their mystery.[1]

Othello

I begin with four points that all actors will want to ponder carefully, whereas readers may scarcely notice them.

(1) Should the Moor of Venice be played as a black, or as an 'olive-coloured' Moor of north Africa?

In 1957 J. Dover Wilson pronounced that 'Bradley was undoubtedly correct in his belief that Shakespeare intended us to think of him as a Negro. That is what "Moor" meant to Englishmen in the Middle Ages and at the time of Elizabeth and James.'[2] Yet whatever 'Moor' may have meant before 1600, would Londoners have expected a black 'Barbarian' after the Moorish ambassador's abode in their midst for half a year? Barbary was situated in north Africa, between Egypt and the Atlantic; the inhabitants were Arabs and Berbers (hence 'Barbary'), and mostly 'tawny' rather than black, as is confirmed by Figure 1.

One year after Dover Wilson had stated his opinion, Bernard Harris published 'A portrait of a Moor',[3] a less dogmatic contribution which reopened the possibility of a tawny Othello. Shakespeare, indeed, was better informed than Dover Wilson supposed, for he knew of both possibilities. In *Titus Andronicus* he made Aaron the Moor 'coal-black', with a 'fleece of woolly hair' and an

---

1 On character criticism, see also *SS*, 34 (1981), *passim*, and Peter Holland, 'The resources of characterization in *Othello*', *SS*, 41 (1989), 119–32.
2 J. Dover Wilson in Cam², ix. See also Jack D'Amico, *The Moor in English Renaissance Drama* (Tampa, Florida, 1991).
3 As on p. 2, n. 2.

infant son addressed as 'thick-lipp'd slave'.[1] He seems to have imagined Aaron as a black; Henry Peacham's sketch of Aaron, apparently based on a sixteenth-century production, depicts a coal-black Moor. Some years later the stage direction 'Enter *Morochus* a tawnie Moore all in white' (*MV* 2.1.0) proves that Shakespeare did not think that all Moors had to be black: those from north Africa could be 'tawnie'.

Iago refers to Othello as 'a Barbary horse' and 'an erring Barbarian' (1.1.110, 1.3.356). Coming so soon after the embassy of 'the Barbarians', do his remarks settle the question? Not entirely, because abuse makes for slippery evidence. So, too, Roderigo's word for Othello, 'the thicklips' (1.1.65), need not be literally true: had he called Othello 'the bastard' literal-minded critics might have had a field day explaining 3.4.57–70! Again, other characters describe Othello as black, and he himself says 'Haply for I am black' (2.3.29, 3.3.267) – does that settle it? No, because 'black' was often applied 'loosely, to non-European races, little darker than many Europeans' (*OED* black, 1c), as when Cleopatra speaks of being 'with Phoebus' amorous pinches black' (*AC* 1.5.28). Nor is it decisive that a number of black actors won acclaim as Othello – Ira Aldridge (Fig. 6) in the nineteenth century, and later Earle Hyman and Paul Robeson (Fig. 8) – for European actors made up as tawny Moors have had the same success. (Black make-up has the disadvantage that it obscures the performer's facial acting. Garrick, famous for his facial expressiveness, failed as Othello: choosing black, he sacrificed one of his greatest assets.)

Because of Shakespeare's vivid characterization and powerful effect on later writers, Othello perhaps impresses us now as a quintessential Moor, representative of his race (compare Shylock's 'Jewishness'). But what did Shakespeare know about Moors, over and above Cinthio's stereotype portrait? Not much, it used to be said, apart from watching stage Moors in many plays in the 1590s. (So familiar were stage Moors that a boy with theatrical pretensions in Jonson's *Poetaster* [autumn 1601] offers to 'do the Moor', adding 'master, lend me your scarf a little'[2] [for use as a turban?]).

---

1   *Tit* 3.2.78, 2.3.34, 4.2.175. For Peacham's sketch, see also Jonathan Bate's edition of *Titus Andronicus* (Ard³, 1995), 38ff.
2   *Poetaster* (Revels), 3.4.271.

6 Ira Aldridge as Othello

But we now realize that Shakespeare could observe the Moorish ambassador in London in 1600 and 1601, and also other north African Moörs that had 'crept into the realm' (cf. p. 29), and that changes the picture.

16

The majority of actors has chosen to emphasize Othello's race and colour as either Negro-black or north African tawny. We may wonder, finally, whether such a clear-cut distinction is really necessary in the theatre, as long as Othello's costume remains neutral.

(2) **Costume** Some actors of Othello have worn a turban – an error, I think, since he is so proudly Christian (see p. 22, and 5.2.353n.) and the turban counts as a symbol of the Muslim faith, like the Christian cross. Some have chosen to wear flowing oriental robes (Figs 6, 15 and 20) – another error, I believe, in view of Othello's urge to be assimilated as a Venetian (see p. 23). For the same reasons I would not equip him with a scimitar, even though Morocco in *The Merchant of Venice* and Aaron in *Titus Andronicus* both possess one.[1] An illustration in Rowe's Shakespeare of 1709 (Fig. 7) presents Othello in modern 'European' dress; Burbage, the first Othello, is likely to have worn European clothes of the early seventeenth century.[2] If so, only Othello's hands and face would have to indicate his ethnic background. I see him as a north African Moor, chiefly because the places he names are in the Mediterranean world and because of the Moorish embassy in London in 1600–1, but if he wears European clothes and has darkened skin of indeterminate hue, the question might well be left open in the theatre. Shakespeare, after all, wanted him to be a man of mystery.

(3) **Age** Othello's age is as puzzling as his race. He must be older than Desdemona (for whose youth see p. 41), but by how much? He speaks of youthful appetites now 'defunct' in him (1.3.261ff.), and later of being 'declined / Into the vale of years' (3.3.269–70); he wants to be 'free and bounteous to her mind' (1.3.266: does he mean 'to educate her'?); his travels, his military rank and other hints suggest a considerable age gap. He is almost a father figure, nearer to Brabantio than to·Desdemona in years. In the theatre his black or brown make-up will fudge the difference between 40 and 50 (this is where I tentatively place him).

(4) **Impaired vision?** In the theatre Othello's precise age cannot be determined. Yet in his very first scene Shakespeare makes a

---

1 See *MV* 2.1.24 and *Tit* 4.2.91; and Hankey, 201, for Othellos with scimitars.
2 According to Hankey (17), Othello usually wore an English general's uniform from the Restoration to the fourth quarter of the eighteenth century.

7 Frontispiece to *Othello* in Nicholas Rowe's edition of Shakespeare's works, 1709

point that could significantly affect the actor's performance, and our general interpretation. Othello asks 'But look, what lights come yond?' and Iago tells him 'Those are the raised father and his friends'. A moment later he asks again 'Is it they?', and twenty lines later, when Brabantio at last appears, Iago sees him first and reports 'It is Brabantio; general, be advised'. Shakespeare seems to suggest that Othello sees less clearly than Iago, that he depends on Iago's eyes. Here Iago might act as a look-out, but what of later scenes? Othello again appeals to Iago, 'Was not that Cassio parted from my wife?' (3.3.37) and, asked whether he had seen the very distinctive handkerchief 'Spotted with strawberries', he needs confirmation – 'Was that mine?' (3.3.438, 4.1.171). When Lodovico arrives unexpectedly, Iago helps again: ''Tis Lodovico, this, comes from the duke. See, your wife's with him' (4.1.214). If Burbage, the first Othello, was instructed to play the part as though suffering from weak or short sight, this could be visually reinforced in various ways. Let the duke and senators consult maps in 1.3: let Othello put on spectacles at line 211 or 222 to peer at a map, and again at 4.1.218 to read his letter. (Gloucester quite often puts on spectacles in *KL* 1.2.34–5 as he says 'Come, if it be nothing, I shall not need spectacles'). Othello's lines can be played straight, without any hint of defective eyesight; an ageing Moor with failing vision gives them added point, partly explains his general dependence on Iago, and puts more sting into taunts such as 'Look to her, Moor, if thou hast eyes to see' and 'Look to your wife, observe her well with Cassio' (1.3.293, 3.3.200: a deliberate echo?). Othello's own psychic need for ocular proof ('Make me to see't', 3.3.363ff.) may be related to his unacknowledged infirmity.

Othello's race, costume, age and impaired vision are all matters of opinion, not susceptible of proof. We have to admit that it is equally difficult to feel sure about his personality and motives. Is he confident, or secretly insecure? Does he love Desdemona's soul, or merely wish to possess her sexually? Is he a devout Christian, or is his Christianity only skin-deep? Pondering these questions we notice two difficulties. First, that as Iago's poison enters his mind he seems to change more completely than other tragic heroes: we must not confuse his earlier and later self. Second, that we cannot believe him when he speaks about himself, any more than we trust Iago's self-revelations. In *Othello* as in *Hamlet* many kinds of uncertainty coexist and interact. Some will disappear in the theatre (e.g. the actor may accept or reject the theory of

Othello's impaired vision) but we should not attempt to resolve all of them. In Shakespearian tragedy uncertainty is of the essence.

Not having the space to introduce Othello's character in much detail I want to concentrate on a few conflicting impressions that make him appear to be a mass of contradictions – in other words, a human being. Gentle himself, he loves 'the gentle Desdemona' (1.2.25), yet reacts savagely when he thinks himself betrayed. This is not a straightforward development from an earlier to a later self since we see him repeatedly switching from one to the other in 4.1.168ff. Trustful at first, he grows compulsively suspicious (4.2.1ff.), yet continues to trust Iago. Easily persuaded, he remains impervious to Desdemona's desperate pleading. I cannot help feeling that such contrary impressions are meant to intimate Othello's 'otherness', the volatile temperament that voyagers described as characteristic of non-European races, not least the 'Barbarians' (see Eldred Jones, 17–18; and p. 28). True, Shakespeare always delighted in human inconsistencies and exposed them in many plays. But in Othello, as in non-European Caliban, he linked emotional volatility with other 'racial' characteristics, looking from the civilized vantage-point of London. Gullibility, superstition, murderousness, a (primitive?) need to worship or abase oneself: 'colonial' Caliban and Othello, though not usually considered together, throw light on one another. Othello, therefore, is a representative but also a very special human being.

I cannot agree with those who say of Othello's race that 'in regard to the essentials of his character it is not important' (Bradley, 187). On the contrary, it seems to me as crucial as Shylock's Jewishness, or even more so, since Shylock appears in only five scenes whereas Shakespeare drew Othello on a bigger scale, with more fine detail. How many of the other tragic heroes weep as copiously as the Moor? Edwin Booth, not one of the most tempestuous Othellos, justified the frequent bouts of weeping in his performance: 'Remember how often he is moved to tears – therefore, I do not attempt to restrain them in the excess of passion here [5.2.20], in Act III, and elsewhere' (Rosenberg, 86). How many are reduced so often to near-meaningless roars, grunts, gasps (ha, hum, how, so so, pish, O, O, O)? How many roll their eyes and gnaw their lips (5.2.38, 43), and shake and tremble as he does

(4.1.266n.)? Such mannerisms occur individually in other tragic heroes, though not collectively as in Othello. Salvini and Olivier, who emphasized Othello's animal noises and panther-pacing, based their 'racist' interpretations on the firm evidence of the text.

A comparison of two other admired Othellos prompted a 'racial' observation in 1930 that is worth repeating. Godfrey Tearle, being English, made Othello more self-controlled than Paul Robeson, the famous black singer and actor: Mr Robeson, said a reviewer, 'comes of a race whose characteristic is to keep control of its passions only to a point and after that point to throw control to the winds' (Hankey, 223). Shakespeare, aware of this possibility, accentuated it by contrasting Othello with the in-human self-command of Iago.

Othello's exceptional sensuousness, though not necessarily 'racial', adds to our impression of his otherness.

> O thou weed
> Who art so lovely fair *and smell'st so sweet*
> *That the sense aches at thee* . . .
>
> (4.2.68ff.)

This is not just a passing thought, for he returns to the sense of smell immediately ('Heaven stops the nose at it') and again later as he contemplates Desdemona's sleeping body.

> I'll smell thee on the tree;
> O balmy breath, that dost almost persuade
> Justice to break her sword. Once more, once more . . .
>
> (5.2.15ff.)

Three times he inhales that 'balmy breath', savouring it, very nearly as if it were sexual congress, the third time ending with a kiss.[1] Olivier prepared for this climactic sequence at Othello's first appearance in 1.2. – 'He came on smelling a rose, laughing softly with a private delight' (Hankey, 147).

Compared with Shakespeare's other tragic heroes, Othello's sense of smell receives unusual emphasis. Desdemona's physical

---

1 In the past editors paid little attention to 'I'll smell thee on the tree', taking Othello's kiss or kisses as more important: see my notes on 5.2.16–19.

beauty and musical voice also have an overpowering effect on him.[1] What then are we to make of these lines?

> I had been happy if the general camp,
> Pioneers and all, had tasted her sweet body . . .
> (3.3.348–9)

Here 'taste' could mean handle or have carnal knowledge of (see commentary note at 3.3.349). Yet, given Othello's fury at being betrayed and his extraordinary sensuousness (smell, sight, sound), the word 'taste' is disturbing in its implications.

Let us now proceed to the Moor's Christianity. Iago, I note, cites or alludes to the Bible no less often than Othello (Noble, 216) – does that make him a good Christian? Yes, if we may trust Dr Johnson's judgement of John Campbell: 'Campbell is a good man, a pious man. I am afraid he has not been in the inside of a church for many years; but he never passes a church without pulling off his hat.' Christianity can be worn as a mask – consciously, as by Iago, and perhaps unconsciously by Othello, who adopts a militantly Christian tone as if to forestall criticism of him as an outsider, or even a pagan: 'For Christian shame put by this barbarous brawl' (2.3.168). He can guess how others are likely to speak of him behind his back – 'Bond-slaves and pagans shall our statesmen be' (1.2.99). Some critics think of him as a Christian convert[2] and ascribe his tone to this cause: he wants to be 'holier than the pope'. Others counter that by calling the malignant, turbanned Turk a 'circumcised dog' (5.2.351–3) he proves that he was not born into the Muslim faith, hence was born a Christian, since turbans were symbols of the Muslim religion and circumcision one of its rites.[3] Why, though, make the Muslim faith the

1 Compare 'O, the world hath not a sweeter creature . . . she will sing the savageness out of a bear!' and 'lest her body and beauty unprovide my mind again' (4.1.181ff., 202–3).
2 See p. 72. For Othello's conversion to Christianity, see also Greenblatt, 233, Bradshaw, 174. Bradley (186–7) rejected the 'mistaken view' that the play 'is primarily a study of a noble barbarian, who has become a Christian and has imbibed some of the civilisation of his employers'. While one cannot be certain about such matters I believe that Bradley for once misjudged the evidence.
3 It should be noted that a 'Moor' was usually thought to be a Mohammedan (*OED* Moor 1, 2). In his religion, however, as in other things Othello is a special case.

only alternative to Christianity? Could 'the Othello music' not point in another direction, to a more primitive worship of sun and moon and elemental forces of Nature, overlaid by later Christian imagery and attitudes? Othello's first account of the handkerchief (3.4.57–77) associates his parents with an undefined paganism, reminiscent of the witch doctors of north Africa (who were described by John Leo, 148–9: see above, p. 4).

We cannot prove Othello to be a Christian convert, but the play prompts us to speculate about his mysterious past and its effect on his multi-layered personality. Is there a connection between his Christianity, his choosing to serve Venice and his marriage to a white woman? Taking these probably consecutive steps he came ever closer to assimilation into an alien culture. The inner need for assimilation only grows clearly visible towards the end – pathetically, when he addresses Gratiano as 'uncle' ('I scarce did know you, uncle', 'Uncle, I must come forth', 5.2.199, 252), claiming a kinship that we knew nothing about and that has ceased to have meaning; tragically, when he recalls that in Aleppo once he killed a Turk who 'Beat a Venetian and traduced the state' (5.2.350ff.). In Aleppo this had signified his total identification with Venice, but now he is the killer and the killed, forever trapped in his divided loyalties.

More so than in most of the tragedies, the hero's past plays an integral part in the present, yet what do we know of Othello's past? We have access to it through his 'narrative self-fashioning',[1] unreliable as evidence. His longest narrative, placed in context, attempts to impress the Duke and senators by explaining how he impressed Desdemona (1.3.129ff.); the narrative within the narrative, allegedly the same story, had a different auditor and, one assumes, a less forensic presentation, so that in various ways it could not be the same story. The present inevitably reshapes the past, and in addition the narrator may reveal that he failed to understand events as they happened. 'Her father loved me, oft invited me' (1.3.129): whatever he may have said, Brabantio certainly did not love Othello as a prospective son-in-law. In his narratives of his father and mother (3.4.57ff.) and of the incident

---

1 Greenblatt, ch. 6. Compare Mack (132) on the play's 'moving retrospectives'.

in Aleppo, Othello's 'editing' of the past for an ulterior purpose is even more transparent.

So we can only guess about Othello's past and, by extension, about the man we see. His 'role-playing' increases our difficulties, not only in his narratives: the calm voice of authority as he responds to a crisis speaks for the senior officer, not necessarily for the inner man:

> Keep up your bright swords, for the dew will rust them.
>
> (1.2.59)

And when the mask slips, can we be certain that we then see 'the real Othello'?

> I do entreat that we may sup together.
> You are welcome, sir, to Cyprus. *Goats and monkeys!*
>
> (4.1.262–3)

A once famous attack on A. C. Bradley by F. R. Leavis centred in effect on 'the real Othello'. Leavis accused Bradley of misidentifying Othello as 'purely noble, strong, generous, and trusting, and as tragic hero . . . merely a victim'. 'He really is, beyond question, the nobly massive man of action', Leavis contended, but 'a habit of self-approving self-dramatization' is an essential element of his character, and this self-idealization turns out to be 'the disguise of an obtuse and brutal egotism. Self-pride becomes stupidity, ferocious stupidity, an insane and self-deceiving passion'.[1] Bradley and his followers located 'the real Othello' in the first half of the play, Leavis chiefly in the second half. A majority of critics sided with Bradley, while others argued that the truth lay between the two. If, however, we reject a 'fixed' view of character we may come closer to understanding Shakespeare's innovative psychology. Othello, then, is neither the 'noble Moor' nor 'the noble Moor later replaced by the brutal egotist': any formula along such lines omits too many of the complexities of his nature, as for instance the tensions between his Christianity and his more primitive or 'pre-Christian' drives (which may be ancestral voices heard from far, or

---

1 F. R. Leavis, 'Diabolic intellect and the noble hero', in Leavis, *The Common Pursuit* (1952). Earlier critics had anticipated both Bradley and Leavis on *Othello* (Honigmann, *Myriad-Minded Shakespeare*, 65).

his own personal past resurfacing). In short, it helps to think of 'the real Othello' as a time traveller, burdened like every human being with too much psychic luggage, a man hidden from us by slander, misunderstanding, idealization, self-deception and all the other mental manoeuvres with which we refuse to face the facts. Except that there are very few 'facts' where our knowledge of Othello is concerned, only impressions, intuitions, surmises, most of which have to be cancelled or modified as the play proceeds. Desdemona, who believed that she knew 'the real Othello', who saw his visage 'in his mind' (1.3.253), misrepresents him as confusingly as Iago, from a different angle – albeit, we may like to think, from one that gives her a better insight. But it remains a too narrow angle, occluding important parts of Othello that are visible to the audience – hence 'My lord is not my lord' (3.4.125). She has never fully known him; perhaps no one properly 'knows' him.

'Iago ruins Othello by insinuating into his mind the question, "How do you know?"' said Helen Gardner in her defence of 'the Noble Moor'.[1] John Bayley, writing of 'Love and Identity', widened the issue by focusing on an incomprehension that haunts the whole play. 'No one in *Othello* comes to understand himself or anyone else',[2] and Shakespeare repeatedly draws attention to these failures.

> IAGO   My lord, you *know* I love you.
>
> OTHELLO
> I *think* thou dost.
> And for I *know* thou'rt full of love and honesty . . .
> (3.3.119ff.)

While Othello and Iago, both initially so confident, become more and more uncomprehending, the same failure involves other characters – and also the audience. How can Othello *not* recognize Desdemona's sincerity, we ask ourselves, and instead trust Iago's lies? In short, the play was so devised that its characters and the theatre audience cannot explain all that happens, and consequently the 'need to know' survives to the end.

---

1 'The Noble Moor', *Proceedings* of the British Academy (1955); reprinted in *Interpretations of Shakespeare*, ed. Kenneth Muir (Oxford, 1985): see p. 170.
2 John Bayley, *The Characters of Love* (1960), 146. Compare Adamson, 225, 231–2, 253.

> Will you, I pray, demand that demi-devil
> *Why* he hath thus ensnared my soul and body?
> (5.2.298–9)

Does this mean that *Othello* is a cheat, a puzzle without a solution? Because we cannot explain the motivation of hero and villain as clearly as we would like, so that every critic offers a different solution? Not really: after all, we cannot explain as clearly as we would like the motivation of many living men and women that we think we know. Such explanations are found in old-fashioned Shakespeare criticism, where Othello figures as 'the jealous man' or 'the noble Moor', etc., fixed in a formulated phrase, but are of little use when we try to understand the puzzling behaviour of our contemporaries. We 'know' Othello in this other way – by intuition rather than verbal definition.

Some readers will think my account of Othello reprehensible, since it appears to confuse a character in a play with a living person. A dramatic character has no life, we have been told, beyond the words of the play. Precisely: in the case of Othello it is the words of the play that require us to ponder the relationship of his Christianity and his possible paganism, his peripatetic past and his need to come safely to rest 'here', in the 'fountain from the which my current runs'(4.2.58–65). The words of the play dwell insistently on Othello's past and its relationship to the present; in comparison we know very little about Iago's past, and we 'know' Iago less satisfyingly than his general. When Othello first enters we may miss the 'time traveller' dimension as he speaks of 'My services which I have done the signiory' and 'men of royal siege', taking this as conventional exposition. When the play ends and the past once more leaps into the present –

> I took by th' throat the circumcised dog
> And smote him – *thus*!

– we marvel at the symbolic truth of the image he chooses, the instant that stretches across years, the life compressed into an instant. Is it a pure coincidence that in *Othello* Shakespeare makes so much of a double time scheme (see pp. 68–72)?

Otherness

Of late, Shakespeare critics have looked more closely at cultural tension and assimilation, an important factor in several of the plays, not least in *Othello*. Cinthio's story of the Moor who marries a beautiful white wife, and who arouses a deadly grudge in his ensign, must have appealed to Shakespeare partly because it allowed him to grapple with an emerging social problem, one that many critics of *Othello* have passed over in silence. I mean racism, Europe's response to the 'other'.

Be he a black or a north African Moor (see pp. 14–17), Othello's otherness remains. He is more than a stranger, he comes from a mysteriously 'other' world, a world that lies beyond our reach, hinted at rather than defined. Despite his self-identification with Venice and Christianity the Moor cannot shake off this mystery, a by-product of his dark skin and of the associations this had in European minds.

It was probably G. K. Hunter's 'Othello and colour prejudice' (1967)[1] that moved the play's racism more centrally into critical discussion. This was followed by Leslie A. Fiedler's *The Stranger in Shakespeare* (1972), and then by detailed explorations of the culture clash of European and non-European in the Renaissance period, notably Tzvetan Todorov's *The Conquest of America: The Question of the Other* and Anthony Pagden's *The Fall of Natural Man: The American Indian and the Origins of Comparative Ethnology*, both published in 1982. We are indebted to the New Historicism, however, and in particular to Stephen Greenblatt,[2] for bringing together ethnology and Shakespeare criticism. Miscegenation, some will say, but a stroke almost as bold and imaginative as the writing of *Othello* itself.

While Todorov, Pagden and Greenblatt focused chiefly on the New World, the attitudes they record as Europeans encounter the

---

1   In the *Proceedings of the British Academy* (1967); reprinted in *Interpretations of Shakespeare*, ed. Muir, and in G. K. Hunter's *Dramatic Identities and Cultural Tradition* (Liverpool, 1978). See also Edward Berry, 'Othello's alienation', *SEL 1500–1900*, 30 (1990), 315–33, and Arthur L. Little, Jr on 'The primal scene of racism in *Othello*', *SQ*, 44 (1993), 304–24.
2   See Stephen Greenblatt, *Shakespearean Negotiations* (Berkeley and Los Angeles, 1988); *Learning to Curse* (1990); *Marvelous Possessions* (Oxford, 1991).

'other' are repeated more generally in both place and time. Edward W. Said's *Orientalism* (1978), a study of the 'Anglo-French-American experience of the Arabs and Islam, which for almost a thousand years together stood for the Orient', contained anecdotes not unlike those of European condescension and incomprehension in the New World when face to face with the non-European. Thus A. J. Balfour and Lord Cromer regarded Europeans as rational, virtuous, mature and 'normal', and Orientals as irrational, depraved, childlike, 'different'.[1] They reaffirmed age-old prejudices, to which Iago also subscribes: 'These Moors are changeable', Othello is gross and lascivious, will be easily led by the nose, and so on (1.3.347, 1.1.110, 124, 1.3.400).

Todorov, Pagden and Greenblatt wrote illuminatingly about 'cross-cultural communication', the inevitable misunderstandings when two races lack a common language and communicate by signs, which may mislead. Similar misunderstandings are possible, I believe, when different races share the same language because, at a deeper level than language, they do not properly know one another – as we can see in modern cities, where a foreign accent can add to the complications.

Should Othello, the Moor of Venice, speak with a 'foreign' accent? Or in beautifully correct English (this being understood as the equivalent of correct Italian)? Either way, his speaking can accentuate his otherness, as in Olivier's outlandish vocal performance, and a too perfect command of an acquired language can have the same effect (compare the writings of Nabokov or Joseph Conrad). Othello's longer speeches are, as rhetoric, almost too self-consciously measured – Iago would call them bombastic – another instance of cultural assimilation gone wrong or overdone (see p. 23).

We may note in passing that Othello's account of 'antres vast and deserts idle', of cannibals and 'men whose heads / Do grow beneath their shoulders' (1.3.141ff.) refers to a time before he entered the service of Venice, for Venice had not attempted to colonize inland Africa or Asia. Indeed, the opening of his speech –

> Her father loved me, oft invited me,
> Still questioned me the story of my life

1   Edward W. Said, *Orientalism* (1978), 17, 40.

– also implies that Othello was a newcomer in Venice, one who had spent most of his life elsewhere. Being a Moor and a fairly recent arrival he was twice an outsider.

From an Elizabethan viewpoint, Othello's rank as governor of Cyprus would magnify his otherness. It is as if Caliban, smartly dressed, were to reappear as Prospero, king of the island. That a black man lords it over Europeans, let alone marries an upper-class white wife, upsets all contemporary notions of decorum, until at least the end of the seventeenth century, as we learn from Thomas Rymer's hysterical criticism. Rymer announced the moral of the play to be 'a caution to all Maidens of Quality how, without their Parents consent, they run away with Blackamoors'.[1]

If Shakespeare never left the shores of England, as is widely assumed (we do not know it for certain), how could he experience the racism that growls and snarls in so many scenes – the racism that (*pace* Rymer) he seems to have set himself to challenge in *Othello*? The Moorish ambassador's presence in London (see p. 2) provided a model of an aristocratic Barbarian. Contrary to popular belief, other black men had 'crept into the realm' in sufficient numbers to be designated a public nuisance.

> 1601. Negroes and Blackamoors. – Whereas the Queen's Majesty is discontented at the great number of 'negars and blackamoores' which are crept into the realm since the troubles between her Highness and the King of Spain, and are fostered here to the annoyance of her own people . . . In order to discharge them out of this country, her Majesty hath appointed Caspar Van Zeuden, merchant of Lubeck, for their transportation . . . This is to require you to assist him to collect such negroes and blackamoors for this purpose.[2]

The 'annoyance' lingered for some time. On 12 July 1602 Dr Julius Caesar wrote to Sir Robert Cecil:

---

1 Thomas Rymer, *A Short View of Tragedy* (1693), for which see Vickers, vol. 2, and Nigel Alexander, 'Thomas Rymer and *Othello*', *SS*, 21 (1968), 67–77.
2 HMC, Hatfield House, Part XI (1601) (1906), 569. I have modernized the spelling. Eldred Jones reproduces the document.

> I have persuaded the merchants trading to Barbary, not without some difficulty, to yield to [i.e. pay for] the charges of the Moors lately redeemed out of servitude by her Majesty's ships, so far as may concern their lodging and victuals, till some shipping may be ready to carry them into Barbary.

On 5 August Lord Buckhurst wrote to Cecil on the same subject.[1]

One of the consequences of being a sceptred isle, a 'precious stone set in the silver sea' (*R2* 2.1.40, 46), can be xenophobia. Iago and Emilia (she calls Desdemona's marriage a 'most filthy bargain', 5.2.153) represent something worse, a racism that probably traces back to the streets of London, not just to the other plays about Moors that flourished at the same time.[2] Leslie Fiedler thought that Elizabethan racism differed from later kinds.

> It would be a mistake to think of *Othello* as trading on the kinds of horror at the mating of a black male and a white female commonly felt by, say, American audiences of the late nineteenth and early twentieth centuries . . . since the whole notion of miscegenation had not yet been invented.
>
> (Fiedler, 172)

Racism is bound to have different implications in different historical contexts, yet consider Prospero's words to Caliban –

> I have us'd thee
> (Filth as thou art) with human care, and lodg'd thee
> In mine own cell, till thou didst seek to violate
> The honor of my child.
>
> (*Tem* 1.2.345–8)

'Filth', again: it could almost be Brabantio or Emilia addressing

---

1 HMC, Hatfield House, Part XII (1602) (1910), 222, 284. For Moors who became residents in London, see Roslyn L. Knutson, 'A Caliban in St. Mildred Poultry', in *Shakespeare and Cultural Traditions*, ed. Tetsuo Kishi *et al.* (Newark, 1994).

2 The other plays about Moors shown in London shortly before *Othello* included Peele's *The Battle of Alcazar* (apparently revived *c.* 1601), *The Spanish Moor's Tragedy* (for which Henslowe paid Dekker, Day and Haughton in February 1600: this may be *Lust's Dominion*, printed in 1657); *Captain Thomas Stukeley* (SR, 11 August 1600, printed 1605); *King Sebastian of Portugal* (for which Henslowe paid Dekker and Chettle in April–May 1601).

Othello. At the start of his career Shakespeare reflected similar attitudes in the reaction to white Tamora's child sired by black Aaron.

> A joyless, dismal, black, and sorrowful issue!
> Here is the babe, as loathsome as a toad.
>
> (*Tit* 4.2.66–7)

In *Othello*, though, such racism coexists with the play's essentially sympathetic portrait of the Moor, a more wonderful insight into otherness than is afforded by Shylock or Caliban.

Shakespeare knew more about racism than modern critics have cared to admit. And we, living in multi-racial societies in the twentieth century, differ less from earlier centuries than we like to pretend. In the 1930s some reviewers of *Othello* were 'shocked that [black] Paul Robeson should be allowed to kiss [white] Peggy Ashcroft'; in the 1960s Olivier said of the play 'it's tremendously, highly sexual because it's a black man. I'm sure Shakespeare meant there to be a great splash of shock' (Hankey, 100, 18). Who will dare to say, in the more liberal 1990s, that we have changed so completely that Othello's 'otherness' no longer affects us in the theatre?

Iago

For many years critics have treated Othello and Iago as somehow equal and opposite, even more so than Richard and Bolingbroke or other yoked characters. This view has much to recommend it (see pp. 98–9), and is also misleading. In the theatre they may seem equally 'big' as parts, and one influential critic has actually praised Iago as the more 'wonderful' of the two (Bradley, 208). Greatly as I admire Iago as a dramatic character, I think Othello the grander achievement. First, because Shakespeare took the trouble to tell us so much more about him. Next, Othello's emotional range is huge, Iago's definitely more limited. We see Othello under greater pressure, wavering, going to pieces, whereas Iago keeps his self-control; we get to 'know' Othello more intimately in his defeats than Iago in his victories. Again, Othello's relationships are more open and varied than Iago's; even when Iago appears to enter a free-wheeling relationship, as with Cassio (2.3.255ff.) or Lodovico

8 Paul Robeson (Othello) and Peggy Ashcroft (Desdemona): Savoy Theatre,
   1930

(4.1.264ff.), we notice a certain repetitiveness, his need to win the
upper hand. Finally, Iago was modelled on many predecessors:
Aaron in *Titus Andronicus*, Richard of Gloucester in *3 Henry VI*
and *Richard III*, Lorenzo in *The Spanish Tragedy* and other stage

Machiavels; the Devil and Vice of pre-Shakespearian drama; the clever slave of classical comedy.[1] So far as we know, Othello was based on no models closer than Titus Andronicus or the Brutus of *Julius Caesar*.[2] For these and similar reasons I regard Othello as the more original, the character who stimulated Shakespeare most profoundly and stretched him to the limits.

Othello and Iago are in some ways opposites or complementaries, yet Elizabethans would also have thought them curiously alike. According to the psychology of humours, jealousy and envy were closely related, jealousy being 'a species of envy, which is in turn a species of hatred'.[3] So Othello and Iago suffer from the same disease, and can be seen as parallel studies in so far as both are professional soldiers who take their wives abroad on active service, feel betrayed by them, kill them, and thus in effect destroy themselves. Both are outsiders, Othello as a Moor, Iago as a malcontent with a grudge against privilege (see pp. 35–6); both stand apart from their fellow men, both want to be accepted. Some of these similarities were added by Shakespeare, who liked symmetry in his plots (Cinthio's Ensign does not resent 'Cassio's' upper-class advantages, since the Corporal is not his superior, and he does not kill his wife), but of course Othello and Iago differ more than they mirror one another.

Iago talks to Roderigo and speculates privately concerning his own motives, much to the confusion of commentators, who disagree about him as strangely as about Othello. The most celebrated interpretation of Shakespeare's most interesting villain, it is often forgotten, has reached us only in shortened form, as a note on the last speech of Act 1, not meant for publication. 'The last Speech, the motive-hunting of motive-less Malignity – how awful! In itself

---

1   For Iago's predecessors, see also Bernard Spivack, *Shakespeare and the Allegory of Evil* (1958), and Leah Scragg, 'Iago – vice or devil?', *SS*, 21 (1968), 53–65.
2   Titus, Brutus and Othello are high-minded idealists who kill one they love on principle, as it were: Lavinia and Desdemona are thought to be sexually polluted, therefore have to die, Caesar may corrupt the political system; Brutus and Othello are tricked by 'friends' (Cassius, Iago), impress us at times as simpletons, speak of themselves grandly in the third person and suffer from an inflated self-image. See also Jones, *Scenic Form*, 139–40. But Shakespeare may also have modelled Othello on Moors in plays now lost (see above, p. 30, n. 2).
3   Lily B. Campbell, *Shakespeare's Tragic Heroes: Slaves of Passion* (Cambridge, 1930; 1960 edn), 148.

fiendish – while yet he was allowed to bear the divine image, too fiendish for his own steady View.'[1] So Coleridge, in his copy of Shakespeare, a note that he probably expanded upon in his lecture of 1819. Yet Coleridge, a voracious reader, was almost certainly indebted to others for the idea, perhaps to E. H. Seymour's *Remarks . . . upon the Plays of Shakespeare*:

> This part of Iago's conduct [the soliloquy at the end of 2.1] has always appeared to me to have been either mismanaged or neglected by the poet, there are no sufficient motives apparent for this excess of malignity.[2]

Or he may have owed the idea to Wordsworth, who wrote a 'short essay, illustrative of that constitution and those tendencies of human nature, which make the apparently motiveless actions of bad men intelligible to careful observers'.[3] Wordsworth wrote the essay while composing *The Borderers*, a tragedy influenced by *Othello*, in the very year (1795) when he and Coleridge met for the first time.

Others refined on 'the motive-hunting of motive-less Malignity' by claiming that Iago has too many motives. 'Certainly he [Iago] assigns motives enough; the difficulty is that he assigns so many . . . And this is not all. These motives appear and disappear in the most extraordinary manner.'

> Resentment at Cassio's appointment is expressed in the first conversation with Roderigo, and from that moment is never once mentioned again in the whole play. Hatred of Othello is expressed in the First Act alone. Desire to get Cassio's place scarcely appears after the first soliloquy, and when it is gratified Iago does not refer to it by a single word.

(Bradley, 225)

On the contrary: these motives do not disappear completely. To

---

1   S. T. Coleridge, *Lectures 1808–1819 On Literature*, ed. R. A. Foakes, 2 vols (1987), 2.315.
2   E. H. Seymour, *Remarks*, 2 vols (1805), 2.320. Compare also Thomas Wilkes: Iago's wish for promotion is his only motive – 'He has no other real motive for his villainy' (1759, reprinted in Vickers, 4.360).
3   *The Prose Works of William Wordsworth*, ed. A. B. Grosart, 3 vols (1876), 3.13.

take them in turn: (1) Resentment at Cassio's appointment. See 1.3.391–2 ('To get his place'), 2.1.171–2 ('strip you out of your lieutenantry'), 3.3.250 ('Although 'tis fit that Cassio have his place'). Iago's 'How do you now, *lieutenant?*' (4.1.104), after Cassio has been dismissed and he himself promoted, cannot be entirely innocent. (2) Hatred of Othello. See 'Doth like a poisonous mineral gnaw my inwards' (2.1.295); again, when Iago torments Othello with degrading sexual images of Desdemona (3.3.205ff., 4.1.2ff.), is his hatred not perfectly visible? (3) Desire to get Cassio's place. See (1), above. Othello's unexpected 'Now art thou my lieutenant' (3.3.481) confirms that he knew of Iago's wish to get Cassio's place, and Iago's reply, 'I am your own for ever', acknowledges that his wish has been granted. In brief, neither Shakespeare nor Iago loses sight of these stated motives: glancing reminders later ensure that we, too, remain conscious of them, even though we realize that unstated motives may play a part as well.

Hidden or unconscious motives are important in all of Shakespeare's tragedies, nowhere more so than in *Othello*.[1] Long before Freud he took an interest in dreams and the inner life, and this helps to explain the fascination of both Iago and Othello. Iago, indeed, invents Cassio's dream of adultery (3.3.416–30) because he knows that the significance of such unconscious self-revelation will be understood.[2] And Iago's own unconscious motives are equally transparent – his resentment of social privilege; his contemptuousness; his artistic delight in power and in manipulating others[3] – linked by his high regard for himself and his grievance at being undervalued. He may not express these motives in so many words but they can be sensed even when he appears to speak respectfully (e.g. when he repeatedly fawns on Othello as 'my lord', or secretly hugs himself at the joke that Othello 'would be satisfied' by seeing Desdemona 'topped': 3.3.36ff., 396ff.). In the theatre his body language reinforces these impressions.

His resentment of privilege comes through unmistakably in the

---

1 See 'Secret motives in *Othello*', in Honigmann, *Seven Tragedies*, ch. 6.
2 See also Lancelot Law Whyte, *The Unconscious before Freud* (1959). Whyte, I think, understated his case: 'self-conscious European man discovering his unconscious' should have had more to say about Shakespeare and his contemporaries.
3 See Bradley, 222–32; Honigmann, *Seven Tragedies*, 78–88.

brilliant opening scene. The 'bookish' Cassio has been promoted and he himself, an experienced soldier, passed over – 'And I, God bless the mark, his Moorship's ancient!' In a world of masters and servants he is one of the servants, though not 'his master's ass'. Brabantio tells him 'Thou art a villain', he snarls back 'You are . . . a senator!' Resentment of privilege binds such episodes together, and, triggered so easily and so often, may impress us as a more potent motive than hatred of Cassio or Othello. Hence his otherwise excessive anger when Cassio plays *noblesse oblige* with Desdemona: 'Ay, smile upon her, do: I will gyve thee in thine own courtesies . . . well kissed, and excellent courtesy.' Cassio had patronized him –

> Let it not gall your patience, *good Iago*,
> That I extend *my manners*; 'tis *my breeding*
> That gives me this bold show of *courtesy*
>   (2.1.97–9, my italics)

– and Iago cannot stand it. Another instance of 'class feeling' throws light on his bitterness at losing the lieutenancy: when he encounters the two noble Venetians, Gratiano and Lodovico, they recognize him as Othello's ancient, 'a very valiant fellow'; he knows their names, they have forgotten his.

> IAGO
>   Signior Lodovico?
> LODOVICO
>   He, sir.
>   (5.1.67–8)

And later,

> IAGO
>   Signior Gratiano? I cry you gentle pardon:
>   These bloody accidents must excuse *my manners*
>   That so neglected you.
> GRATIANO   I am glad to see you.
>   (5.1.93–5, my italics)

Now it is Iago who draws attention to 'my manners', aping the 'courtesy' that he ridiculed in soliloquy. He wants to be accepted as an equal, therefore addresses Cassio as 'brother' (71) and, guessing that Roderigo's 'class' will be known, claims him as 'my friend and my dear countryman' (89, 102). He caresses the Venetians with the word 'gentlemen' ('Light, gentlemen'; 'Gentlemen all, I do suspect this trash'; 'Stay you, good gentlemen'; 'Do you see, gentlemen?'; 'Kind gentlemen . . .'), hoping that they will accept him as one of themselves, and achieves the very opposite: a gentleman does not behave like this. His bitterness when Cassio won the lieutenancy (1.1.7ff.) sprang not so much from disappointment on this one occasion as from his general sense that he is not acceptable as 'officer material'. Triumphing over the hapless Roderigo, a member of the upper class, he compensates for these humiliations, the daily beauty of privilege 'That makes me ugly' (5.1.20).

Iago as artist is sometimes seen as a matador toying with Othello, the bull, or as a dramatist, the creator of much of the plot, who finds fulfilment in it. 'Pleasure and action make the hours seem short' (2.3.374)! His dramatic skills may not strike us, at first, as exceptional: he spins his yarn to master Roderigo's rebelliousness, then switches to obscenity to infuriate Brabantio, a representative of privilege. His exploitation of Roderigo and cold contemptuousness become clearer in 1.3 ('Put money in thy purse'); on landing in Cyprus his skills are put on display as he takes control of the conversation, and are shown in dangerous action, fully in command, as he engineers the drunken riot in 2.3. The long speech that explains what has happened (2.3.216–42), and his 'comforting' of Cassio thereafter, sharpens our awareness of his manipulative skills: pretending honesty and goodwill, he persuades others to accept *his* version of events – a dangerous gamble, from his own point of view. The temptation scene (3.3), perhaps the most breath-taking scene in the whole of Shakespeare, has been prepared for by the gradual revelation of Iago's outstanding dramatic talents – his Shakespearian talents, we may say, in so far as Iago's creator endowed him with his own verbal dexterity and psychological insight.

'My mistress is power', Napoleon once remarked, 'but it is as an artist that I love power. I love it as a musician loves his violin'.[1]

---

1 F. M. H. Markham, *Napoleon and the Awakening of Europe* (1954), 92.

Roderigo, Cassio and Othello are Iago's violins. He finds it more difficult to 'play' on Desdemona and Emilia because, for all his cleverness, he fails to understand women, and in the end this destroys him. He thinks of women as sex objects and sexual predators, and nothing more – an attitude that could be understood as merely humorous, the stance of the traditional male satirist (2.1.100ff.), yet, by sheer repetition, it betrays itself as a kind of hang-up ('the beast with two backs', 'when she is sated with his body', 'Lechery, by this hand', 1.1.115, 1.3.351, 2.1.255). When he torments Othello with obviously fabricated images of Desdemona's sexual activity I feel that Iago gives himself away: he cannot resist the voyeuristic satisfaction of imagining other people's sex lives, and he entraps himself by supplying Othello with more and more detail. There are many hints that his own marriage has gone dead long before he and Emilia turn on each other in 5.2; she means little or nothing to him (3.3.304ff.) and she seems to think that he prefers other sexual partners (4.3.85ff.). Some critics deduce that Iago must be a latent homosexual (see p. 50) – a possibility, though not one that worked in the theatre when Olivier tried it out (see p. 51).

Liar, betrayer, mental torturer of Othello and Desdemona, murderer: if Iago were a straightforward villain he would arouse little fellow feeling in audiences, yet of course he is anything but straightforward and audiences have responded to him in different ways, depending on the actor. Readers, too, have disagreed. 'The character of Iago is so conducted, that he is from the first scene to the last hated and despised.' Dr Johnson's verdict[1] was echoed by Bradley, who reacted to 4.2.112ff. with 'burning hatred and burning tears' (197). Not so Charles Lamb: 'while we are reading any of [Shakespeare's] great criminal characters – Macbeth, Richard, even Iago, – we think not so much of the crimes which they commit, as of the ambition, the aspiring spirit, the intellectual activity which prompts them to overleap those moral fences.'[2]

---

1 *Johnson on Shakespeare*, ed. Walter Raleigh (1908), 201. Compare Adamson (101), who writes of her 'violent antipathy' to Iago, who arouses 'hatred and fear'.
2 *The Works of Charles Lamb*, ed. Charles Kent (1904), 568. Compare Mack, 136: 'Hazlitt gets it right, it seems to me, when he says that Iago's fascination for us combines equal parts of admiration and horror.'

There is much to be said on both sides. In the theatre our reactions are unlikely to remain the same 'from the first scene to the last'; they fluctuate, and may come close to sympathizing with a villain. Dramatic perspective can even make us the villain's accomplices: he confides in us, so we watch his plot unfolding from his point of view. This happens in the novel as well: in *Crime and Punishment* we tremble with Raskolnikov, the murderer. A good actor grips the audience more completely, being in control of timing: he dictates the mode of impact of his wickedness and can whirl the audience off its feet, whereas a reader controls his own timing.

Iago enjoys another important advantage, that he is the play's chief humorist. Most of Shakespeare's major characters are endowed with their own brand of humour (Falstaff, Touchstone, Hamlet, Lear; Rosalind, Viola, Cleopatra); Iago's, though related to the humour of Aaron and Richard III, is also quite distinctive. W. H. Auden called him 'the joker in the pack', a 'practical joker of a peculiarly appalling kind', partly because Emilia speaks of him as her 'wayward husband' and 'she must know Iago better than anybody else does'.[1] Yet *wayward* does not mean joker (see 3.3.296n.), and Auden's loose label really identifies one of Iago's convenient masks, not the inner man, and may blind readers to Iago's essential sadism. His humour either intends to give pain or allows him to bask in his sense of his own superiority; very rarely is it at his own expense (contrast Falstaff, Cleopatra, etc.), and it is never merely delightful, as is Rosalind's or Puck's. When Iago says 'Well: happiness to their sheets!' (2.3.26) he deliberately defiles Cassio's image of Desdemona; deciding whimsically that it scarcely matters who kills whom –

> Now, whether he kill Cassio
> Or Cassio him, or each do kill the other,
> Every way makes my gain
>
> (5.1.12–14)

– he enjoys a godlike sense of power. In 2.1.100–60 we see Iago at his most playful; the impression that he *simply* enjoys himself, having

1   W. H. Auden, *The Dyer's Hand and Other Essays* (1975 edn), 253.

fun and being sociable, is overshadowed by our awareness that he 'crowds' his companions, and then suddenly cancelled when he reveals, in soliloquy, that he hates the social games he took part in.[1]

Nevertheless, since his victims lack humour, Iago appeals to us as more amusing: dramatic perspective compels us to see with his eyes, and to share his 'jokes'. His humour also makes him seem cleverer than his victims. His cleverness, however, should not be exaggerated, as by Harold Goddard, an otherwise perceptive critic, who thought that Shakespeare bestowed 'the highest intellectual gifts' on Iago.[2] This might be Iago's opinion, but hardly Shakespeare's. Iago excels in short-term tactics, not in long-term strategy. The possibility that his own despised wife may accuse him publicly of 'a lie, an odious, damned lie' (5.2.176) and send him to his death has not occurred to him. This is because, despite his cleverness, he has neither felt nor understood the spiritual impulses that bind ordinary human beings together, loyalty, friendship, respect, compassion – in a word, love. Emilia's love (of Desdemona) is Iago's undoing.

Though emotionally stunted, Iago impresses me as a dramatic version of a human being, not as a mere monster. Many human beings are underdeveloped on one side of their personality and overdeveloped on another, not unlike Iago; his dummy, Roderigo, is also an emotional cripple, and that may be why they make such an effective twosome, almost a music-hall turn. Some of Balzac's and Dostoevsky's 'Shakespearian' villains are grotesques, not Iago: as long as the actor resists the temptation to play him as a villain of melodrama (see p. 98) we no more question his humanity than that of an at least equally extraordinary dramatic character, the Moor of Venice.

How was it done? Two contrasting Iagos first catch our attention, the bluff 'honest soldier' role that he adopts in society,

---

1   Compare Snyder, 79–80: 'Iago is a clown without good humour.' He lacks *good* humour, yet delights in many kinds of biting humour.

2   Goddard, 2.78. Compare Snyder, 76: 'Iago is the most intelligent character in the play'; Bradley, 236: 'to say that [Iago's] intellectual power is supreme is to make a great mistake'. The practical intelligence of the Duke in 1.3 is surely more rational and far-sighted than Iago's blinkered cleverness, which often degenerates into wishful thinking; the Duke avoids disaster, Iago seems drawn to it like a sleep-walker.

and the malcontent revealed in soliloquy and in his scenes with Roderigo and, less fully, with Emilia. Iago wears his honesty as a mask, but that does not mean that the malcontent represents 'the real Iago', the complete man, for, as we have seen, at a less self-conscious level he functions as an artist, a voyeur, a humorist, and so on.[1] Shakespeare took care to bind these roles together: whichever one sits nearer the surface, Iago's deeper attitudes and ingrained speech habits remain much the same. His heartiness, his gusto, his man-to-man voice ('Come, be a man!' to Roderigo; 'Good sir, be a man' to Othello: 1.3.336, 4.1.65), his animal imagery, his improvisatory skills; or, again, his mask as well-meaning adviser, with Roderigo, Cassio, Othello, even with Montano and Lodovico (2.3.117ff., 4.1.270ff.), his tendency to congratulate or scold his victims – all these and many similar characteristics hold together the conflicting impulses known as Iago. His motives, too, help to make him a credible human being, provided that we refrain from searching for a master motive, one that unlocks all the rest. His motives, like his roles, interpenetrate one another, somewhat like the different instruments that play together in a symphony.

It is best, I think, to take leave of Othello and Iago on this note: they speak to us, as does music, from their own self-consistency. They have their own humanity, limited but convincing, as only Shakespeare could imagine it. We feel it, even if criticism cannot translate it into words. 'The words of Mercury are harsh after the songs of Apollo.'

Desdemona

Though too often played by mature actresses, there are many hints that Desdemona is meant to be very young, almost childlike; for instance, Emilia's remark about the handkerchief, 'she reserves it evermore about her / To kiss and talk to' (3.3.299–300), and

---

1 For 'character and role' problems, see particularly Peter Ure's 'Shakespeare and the inward self of the tragic hero' and 'Character and role from *Richard III* to *Hamlet*', both reprinted in Ure's *Elizabethan and Jacobean Drama*, ed. J. C. Maxwell (Liverpool, 1974); Philip Edwards, 'Person and office in Shakespeare's plays', *Proceedings of the British Academy* (1970).

Iago's 'She that so young could give out such a seeming' (3.3.212; see also p. 55, and 4.2.113ff., 4.3.82). Her relationship with Emilia resembles that of Juliet and the Nurse, yet her emotional dependence on Emilia is greater. We should imagine her as perhaps 15 or 16, not as a 'lady' in the modern sense. (She is addressed as 'lady', but so is Juliet.) Just about every character misunderstands her. Brabantio calls her 'A maiden never bold' (1.3.95); Iago thinks that 'she must have change' (1.3.352), Roderigo that she can be bought with presents. Some feminist critics (see below, n. 3) think Cassio equally mistaken – 'She is indeed perfection' (2.3.25). Like Cassio, Othello idealizes her; we may deduce from his quite general reflection

> O curse of marriage
> That we can call these delicate creatures ours
> And not their appetites!
>
> (3.3.272–4)

that her awakened sexuality took him by surprise.[1] Such misjudgements tell us more about the speakers than about Desdemona.

Several critics find Desdemona's 'cheap backchat with Iago' in 2.1.100ff. distasteful – 'one of the most unsatisfactory passages in Shakespeare'.[2] (Does this tell us more about the critics or about Desdemona?) Victorian producers omitted some of the 'indelicate' dialogue. John Quincy Adams, sixth President of the USA, reacted even more strongly. 'Who can sympathise with Desdemona?' he said. 'She falls in love and makes a runaway match with a blackamoor . . . She not only violates her duties to her father, her family, her sex, and her country, but she makes the first advances'![3] Producers and presidents are the creatures of their time.

---

1 I assume that Othello and Desdemona consummate their love before Act 3 begins (see 2.3.9n.); others argue – unconvincingly, I think – that it is never consummated. See, for instance, T. G. A. Nelson and Charles Haines, 'Othello's unconsummated marriage', *Essays in Criticism*, 33 (1983), 1–18; Bradshaw, 163ff.; also R. N. Hallstead, 'Idolatrous love', *SQ*, 19 (1968), 107–24, esp. 113.

2 M. R. Ridley in Ard², 54. Compare Cressida's backchat in *TC* 1.2.37ff., which is quite different in its overall effect.

3 Quoted by Rosenberg, 207. Some critics (including feminist critics) still find plenty of faults in Desdemona. For balanced replies, see W. D. Adamson, 'Unpinned or undone?' and Ann Jennalie Cook, 'The design of Desdemona: doubt raised and resolved', both in *SSt*, 13 (1980, 169–86 and 187–96 respectively).

The purpose of 2.1.100ff., we today would say, is to portray Desdemona as aware of the way of the world. The passage also suggests, as Iago's banter becomes more risqué and she persists, that she does not know when to stop – as, again, when she asks Othello to recall Cassio (3.3.41–83, 3.4.90ff.). Overconfidence, in the first half of the play, reflects an essential innocence, which remains with her to the end.

In the second half of the play she is sometimes criticized as too passive. Fanny Kemble's and Helen Faucit's Desdemona surprised contemporaries by making a fight of it in the death scene; Ellen Terry, who also objected to the 'passive' interpretation, thought Desdemona strong, not weak (see p. 110, and Rosenberg, 138–9). Her strength, we should remember, partly depends on Othello's love: only when he rejects her handkerchief (see p. 48) is her self-confidence checked. Thereafter she may seem passive; it would be kinder to describe her as bewildered, out of her depth, not as defeated. True, she bows to Othello's anger, which a modern wife might refuse to do; it is possible, though, to see Desdemona as the strongest, the most heroic person in the play (see pp. 56–8).

Emilia

Less complicated than her husband, Emilia is often simplified and misrepresented in the theatre. Should she be made up as middle-aged and unattractive, more or less like the Nurse in *Romeo and Juliet*?[1] If so, one wonders why Iago married her, and the thought that Othello may be her lover (2.1.293ff.) becomes ludicrous. Iago has 'looked upon the world for four times seven years' (1.3.312–13), consequently Cinthio's account of the Ensign's wife might also apply to Emilia – 'a fair and honest young woman' (see p. 373). She must be older than Desdemona, let us say in her mid-twenties, and definitely attractive. Hence Iago's sexual possessiveness: he may not love her, but the possibility that she has a lover 'Doth like a poisonous mineral gnaw my inwards'. Different as

1 See Hankey on 'the unfortunate custom, apparently a law of our stage, of assigning Emilia to a lady old enough to be Desdemona's mother' (183).

they are, Iago and Othello experience a similar torment, a monster of the imagination in both cases.

Cinthio's narrative throws light on a related problem, Emilia's feeling for her husband. Cinthio's 'Emilia' knew of the Ensign's plot to kill Disdemona, refused to help him, but 'did not dare, for fear of her husband, to tell her anything. She said only: "Take care not to give your husband any reason for suspicion . . ."' (see p. 381). Fear of Iago, though not expressed explicitly, explains Emilia's attitude as Shakespeare's tragedy unfolds. When they are first seen alone (3.3.304–23) his derision and her resentment prove that all is not well between them. This is a relationship more sharply focused than in Cinthio, one that proceeds quite naturally – given their characters in the play – to the wife's later defiance of her husband and his murderous revenge, both added by Shakespeare.

How guilty is Emilia of acting as a passive accomplice in Iago's plot? The question arises when Desdemona asks 'Where should I lose that handkerchief, Emilia?' and she lies, 'I know not, madam' (3.4.23–4). Just four words, yet momentous in their implications. Had she not been afraid of Iago the truth might have come out and Iago's plot would have collapsed. How typical of Shakespeare that the most passionate indictment of untruthfulness is later addressed to Emilia ('She's like a liar gone to burning hell', 5.2.127), and that Emilia then feels obliged to 'report the truth'. Her 'I know not, madam' may not deserve to be punished in burning hell, yet what of her silence when Othello so insistently demands the handkerchief (3.4.52–99)? Shakespeare took care to have Emilia present during this painful confrontation and, hearing what she hears, she can hardly fail to understand that her lie has had serious consequences. But, being afraid, she tries to warn Desdemona without accusing Iago directly (exactly like the Ensign's wife in Cinthio) – 'Is not this man jealous?' (3.4.100).

We must now attend to a statement thrice repeated by Emilia. Iago 'hath *a hundred times* / Wooed me to steal it [the handkerchief]'; she calls it 'That which *so often* you did bid me steal', and asks 'What will you do with't that *you have been so earnest* / *To have me filch it?*' (3.3.296–7, 313, 318–19; my italics). Shakespeare wants us to know, just before Othello makes such an issue of it in the next scene, that the handkerchief was of special interest to

9 Ralph Richardson (Iago) and Edith Evans (Emilia): Old Vic, 1932

Iago and that Emilia had noticed this – a point repeated once more in the final scene, where it leads immediately to her death.

> For often, with a solemn earnestness
> – More than indeed belonged to such a trifle –
> He begged of me to steal't.
>
> (5.2.225–7)

Emilia therefore should have suspected her 'wayward husband' of being somehow connected with Othello's fury in the handkerchief scene (3.4.51ff.). And perhaps she does. Perhaps in her outburst against Desdemona's slanderer –

> I will be hanged if some eternal villain . . .
> Have not devised this slander, I'll be hanged else!
>
> (4.2.132–5)

– she voices her suspicion as directly as she dares.[1] But now the consequences would be so frightening, should her suspicion prove correct, that she takes the easy way out, accepting Iago's cool disclaimer, 'Fie, there is no such man, it is impossible'. Emilia later refers back to this exchange, just as Iago's guilt becomes absolutely clear.

> Villainy, villainy, villainy!
> I think upon't, I think I smell't, O villainy!
> I thought so then: I'll kill myself for grief!
>
> (5.2.187–9)

'I thought so then': she may mean that she thought in 4.2.132ff. that some villain had slandered Desdemona, or that she thought 'then' that Iago was responsible. The alternatives are to suppose either that Shakespeare wants us to consider Emilia exceptionally dimwitted or that he made her (like the Ensign's wife in Cinthio) too afraid of Iago to wish to challenge him, until it is too late.[2]

What did Shakespeare gain if, as I think, he followed the hint in

---

1 In one production Emilia spoke 'suspiciously eyeing Iago'; Booth thought that Emilia speaks 'without intended reference to Iago' (Sprague, 206). Hart, in his Ard[1] edition of *Othello* (148), noted 'Emilia's fear of her husband'.

2 In 1964 one reviewer thought Emilia's 'O God, O heavenly God!' (5.2.216), 'when she realizes the mischief she has unwittingly done . . . the strongest moment of the evening' (Hankey, 321). 'Unwittingly' may be the wrong word.

Cinthio? First, he heightened suspense: Iago's plot hangs by a thread once Emilia's suspicions are aroused, even if he manages to bluff it out in 4.2. Second, he reinforced 'the human will to see things as they are not' to which T. S. Eliot drew attention (see p. 83). Emilia, already disillusioned with her husband, prefers not to ask too many questions, fearing to discover things as they really are.

> what he will do with it
> Heaven knows, not I,
> I nothing, but to please his fantasy.
> (3.3.301–3)

Emilia repays some attention: her developing relationship with her husband and her developing moral involvement illustrate Shakespeare's remarkable control of detail, which in turn justifies those critics who think it their duty to peer into the recesses of character and motive.

Relationships

Although criticism has been slow to recognize it, Shakespeare observed the dynamics of relationships as penetratingly as the development of character. In our play the relationship of Othello and Iago has received more comment, yet that of Othello and Desdemona is psychologically no less interesting. We may think of it as an older writer's *Romeo and Juliet*, except that in *Othello* the marriage of two idealists covers so much more emotional ground. At first, to 3.3, the ecstasy of romantic love; then the relationship comes under pressure and we realize belatedly that Othello and Desdemona scarcely know one another. How could they, differing as they do in age, race, experience of life?

Shakespeare traces the crumbling of this relationship back to its origins, to Desdemona's generous impulsiveness, a factor prior to Iago's plot. She takes a bold step in the wooing scene, as described by Othello, and again in demanding to accompany him to Cyprus, two unconventional moves. When we first see them together in a more private situation she again wants to lead him, requesting the reinstatement of Cassio (3.3.41ff.). She does so very prettily, ascribing her interference to wifely solicitude; his unease is not lost upon her, yet she persists. Here, for the first time, she chooses a collision course, since he had said to Cassio, publicly and decisively, 'never more be officer of mine' (2.3.245): she entered at this very point (see the textual notes: Q and F differ by one line) and no doubt heard his words. Even before this she had corrected Othello, on his arrival in Cyprus. To his 'not another comfort like to this / Succeeds *in unknown fate*', she replied '*The heavens* forbid / But that our loves and comforts should increase' (2.1.191–2, my italics); she rejected his notions of diminishing love and of 'fate', and semi-consciously he registered her dissent as minor 'discords' (196).

Desdemona's pleading on behalf of Cassio (3.3.41ff.), a domestic clash partly engineered by Iago (2.3.331ff.), follows on quite naturally from her previous relationship with Othello as we have seen it evolve. Next, when she calls him to dinner (3.3.284), he, unable to respond lovingly, pretends he has a headache. She again tries to take charge, beginning to bind his head: the gesture with which he rejects the handkerchief – and Desdemona – should be a significant turning point in the play (Goddard, vol. 2, 85–6). (Perhaps neither of them later remembers how the handkerchief was lost because they are so blinded to everything else by the pain of this rejection.) At their next meeting she ignores all the danger signals and again asks for the recall of Cassio; even when he more or less commands her to fetch the handkerchief she continues to plead for Cassio. From Othello's point of view her behaviour must be intolerable, quite apart from Iago's lies about her, since yet again she attempts to lead him.[1] Unintentionally she appears to question his manly prerogatives; he cannot outtalk her so he falls back, like some other husbands, on physical violence. She, in turn, realizing that her impulsiveness has had such unforeseen consequences, suppresses it and thus denies her own nature, almost becoming another person in the last two acts. The husband and wife chained together may be quite unique, yet we are not unfamiliar with the dynamics of their relationship: many another

---

1 See Adamson, 138, on the 'matrimonial power-struggle' in the play.

marriage has similar rhythms. Othello and Desdemona speak for themselves, and for all husbands and wives.

Two other 'domestic' relationships are found in the play, both with signs of strain invented by Shakespeare, both fast-moving. Those of Iago–Emilia and of Cassio–Bianca include mutual suspicion, sudden resentment, contests for mastery, defiance, and (in one case) a second wife-murder, counterpointing the Othello–Desdemona relationship. Each relationship grows naturally out of the development of two characters and at the same time proceeds in step with every other developing relationship. The same is true of non-domestic relationships, which also merit attention: for example, Iago–Cassio, Cassio–Desdemona, Desdemona–Emilia (see pp. 54–5).

Sex and love

One of Shakespeare's most original achievements in *Othello* is his exploration of the psychology of sex. We can trace a progression from *Julius Caesar* (1599), where an interest in sex is minimal, to *Hamlet* (*c.* 1600), where it becomes important, to *Othello*, his most wide-ranging and deeply probing study of various kinds of sexuality. Comparing *Othello* with earlier work in which sex had played a significant part, such as *Romeo and Juliet* or the two narrative poems, we must acknowledge an extraordinary advance towards realism: for all its physical frankness, *Venus and Adonis* remains a traditional 'literary' text, like Spenser's *Epithalamion*, whereas *Othello* seems to escape from the literary past and to chart completely new territory. In this Shakespeare may have been helped by a recent reading of Rabelais; Iago's gusto when he talks about sex – which he does rather often, straining compulsively in this direction – might be called Rabelaisian (with this proviso, that the Frenchman keeps at a joky distance from uro-genital events and Iago seems as if mesmerized by them, their slave and not their master). The play closest to *Othello* in its preoccupation with sex is *Troilus and Cressida*, and Chaucer's Pandare, a voyeur who manipulates the sex drive of others, perhaps also gave Shakespeare ideas for Iago.

Iago's sexual hang-ups, the first we encounter in the play, later contribute much of the spice of the great temptation scene. Othello's own problems – his apparent sexual inexperience and emotional immaturity[1] – are at least as complicated as Iago's and as mysterious, even if we tend to think of him as psychologically more transparent. The admixture of racial difference and the curious rhythms of his passion ('O, Iago, the pity of it, Iago! . . . I will chop her into messes!', 4.1.193–7) make his sexual behaviour as unique as Iago's and at the same time do not disqualify him as, surprisingly, a representative 'everyman' figure. Several others in the play are also thwarted or divided in their sex drive (who isn't?): Emilia cannot understand her husband and seems to feel sexually cheated (3.3.296, 4.3.85ff.); Bianca has a crush on Cassio, her 'customer' (4.1.120); Cassio makes use of Bianca, and worships 'The divine Desdemona' (2.1.73). Only Desdemona herself appears to be sexually uncomplicated, as unaware as a child – until too late.

And what of Iago's relationship with Othello? 'Dr Ernest Jones has pointed out to me', wrote J. I. M. Stewart in 1949, 'that, from the psycho-analytic point of view, *Othello* . . . turns upon sexual inversion, there being no possible motive for Iago's behaviour in destroying Othello and Desdemona except the rancour of the rejected and jealous lover of the Moor.'[2] No possible motive? Readers are cordially invited to turn back to pp. 33ff. A decade earlier the same Ernest Jones, a disciple of Freud, assisted Laurence Olivier with the same diagnosis. Iago's 'deep affection' for Othello explained his actions, said Jones, a 'subconscious affection' the homosexual foundation of which Iago did not understand. Olivier, delighted to have found a new interpretation, played Iago opposite Ralph Richardson as Othello – one of their few disasters. 'Hardly anyone could tell what Olivier's Iago was doing and why' (Rosenberg, 158). Years later Marvin Rosenberg asked leading actors,

---

1 I say emotional immaturity because it seems that Othello has not loved before, and because his idealizing of the beloved is in some ways as 'adolescent' as Desdemona's.

2 See J. I. M. Stewart, *Character and Motive in Shakespeare: Some Recent Appraisals Examined* (1949), 143, n. 68; compare F. L. Lucas, *Literature and Psychology* (1951), 76. Leslie Fiedler, on the other hand, believes that Iago's 'ambivalent passion . . . is directed not toward Othello, but toward one whom Othello has preferred to him, Michael Cassio' (152).

including Olivier, whether homosexuality should 'be stipulated visually as Iago's central motivation'.

> The six modern Othellos I questioned rejected the theory. Olivier thought it was worth a try – and it still would be for an actor who sensed such a motive in Iago strongly enough. Certainly Olivier does not now [1971]; and apparently never did.
>
> (Rosenberg, 182)

Yet, perhaps inevitably, the homosexual lobby has grown. David Suchet, who played Iago with the Royal Shakespeare Company in 1985 and 1986, wrote in 1988 that

> Othello replies with 'I greet thy *love*' [3.3.472] and then suggests putting Cassio to death. Fairly straightforward, I thought, until Iago's reply caught me unawares by its homosexual suggestion, 'My *friend* is dead' – homosexual in the context of 'I lay with Cassio lately' [3.3.416].[1]

Suchet built on 'the fact that Cassio went to bed with Iago', but of course it is not a fact. (We cannot rule it out as an impossibility; why, though, take Iago's statement as more trustworthy than the later one (3.3.442) that he has seen Cassio 'wipe his beard' with Desdemona's handkerchief?) As for 'love', in this context it need not mean more than the dutiful affection of a servant for his master, as often elsewhere in Shakespeare.

Despite the presence of one significant instance of male bonding, that of Cassio and Othello,[2] we must beware of making too much of Iago's supposed homosexuality for, as Olivier subsequently accepted, if it exists entirely in the subconscious 'there is no object in touching on it in any detail of performance' (Rosenberg, 182); moreover, had Shakespeare really wished to push our thoughts towards homosexuality, why should he be so much

---

1 David Suchet, 'Iago in *Othello*', in *Players of Shakespeare 2*, ed. Russell Jackson and Robert Smallwood (Cambridge, 1988), 194.

2 Cf. 'Cassio, I love thee, / But never more be officer of mine', 'Dear general, I never gave you cause' (2.3.244–5, 5.2.296), and 'he loves you', 'You do love my lord', 'one that truly loves you' (3.1.49, 3.3.10, 48). This, however, suggests nothing more than the non-sexual bonding of males who 'play in the same team' (here, military service): cf. *OED* love 4b, 'to be fond of'.

more secretive than in depicting the relationship of Achilles and Patroclus? That said, it remains true that Iago's perverted nature sets him apart from the more 'normal' men and women of the tragedy.

Whether or not we believe in Iago's latent homosexuality, the play's preoccupation with sex is reinforced in many other ways. Othello and Desdemona have to give up their wedding-night in Venice (1.3.278–9). No sooner do they retire in Cyprus to consummate their marriage (2.3.9–10) than Iago stirs up the brawl that interrupts them, and dares to say to Othello, 'friends all . . . like bride and groom / Divesting them for bed' (2.3.175–7), whereupon Othello speaks as if Desdemona had just been roused from 'balmy slumbers'! Thus Shakespeare reminds us of the off-stage bridal bed, as also by means of Iago's voyeuristic witticisms, 'You rise to play, and go to bed to work', 'happiness to their sheets!' (2.1.115, 2.3.26). The imagined bed becomes more and more solid as we hear Othello tell Desdemona 'Get you to bed' and she asks Emilia to 'Lay on my bed my wedding sheets' (4.2.107, 4.3.5, 20). The bed itself, when it finally appears in 5.2,[1] completes a movement from mental to physical image that repeats Othello's from his 'whore of Venice' fixation to the smothering of Desdemona.[2]

Appropriately, in this sex-drenched play, we observe sexual activity from many angles: 'making the beast with two backs' (Iago, 1.1.115); 'The rites for which I love him' (Desdemona, 1.3.258); 'Make love's quick pants in Desdemona's arms' (Cassio, 2.1.80); 'tasted her sweet body' (Othello, 3.3.349) (the second and third suggest sexual rites and pants, but could be interpreted as less specific). The smothering of Desdemona may even go through the motions of orgasm: a struggle, indistinct cries, a paroxysm, 'the moment of total stillness and privacy . . . here is a subtle transfer of terms . . . As Empson puts it, "It is as a sort of parody of the wedding night . . . that the scene is given its horror"' (Heilman, 192).

Many critics have written about Othello's 'sexual anxiety',

---

1 The bed is sometimes introduced before 5.2, in 4.2 or 4.3 (M. Neill, 'Unproper beds', *SQ*, 40 (1989), 383ff.). Compare the Orson Welles film. I think it best to leave the bed unseen until 5.2.

2 Heilman (189) wrote illuminatingly about the bed imagery in *Othello*.

which was fuelled, it has been said,[1] by theologians who condemned immoderate sexual pleasure within marriage. To love
one's wife too ardently, according to St Jerome, is to commit
adultery. Despite his many biblical allusions I do not see Othello
as a theologian,[2] and I doubt whether his intense sexual feeling
for Desdemona *on its own* would strike Shakespeare's audience as
sinful, any more than Romeo's. But this feeling must be related to
Othello's tendency to overvalue the things of this world – the
pride, pomp and circumstance of war, skin white as snow and
smooth as monumental alabaster – and compared with Christ's
teaching that we only attain eternal life by rejecting the world. 'It
is easier for a camel to go through the eye of a needle . . .' (Matthew
19.24). While Othello's 'perdition catch my soul / But I do love
thee!' (3.3.90–1) may be no more than figurative speaking, it implies a willingness to give 'all for love', a worship of God's creature rather than of God.

Othello talks of love, not of sex. We may think it excessive love,
from the point of view of Christian eternity, and react to it uneas-
ily. But what does love mean in this play? We must not suppose
that there is only one kind of love, or even that Othello's exactly
matches Desdemona's. Lovers tend to assume this equivalence, as
indeed do bystanders who commend the intercourse that 'soul to
soul affordeth' (1.3.115). Othello and Desdemona use the same
language of love, as if intending theirs to be a mating of souls; yet,
as Virginia Woolf once remarked, when one wants to concentrate
on the soul 'life breaks in'.[3] Desdemona's soul burns steadily;
when life breaks in, in the form of a husband who strikes and kills
her, this cannot extinguish her love. Othello's burns with a more
flaring flame, at times so intensely that he gasps for breath
(2.1.194); it switches easily to its opposite, an equally unbearable
hatred. *She* goes on loving despite the evidence of his mental and

1   Greenblatt is perhaps the most committed spokesman for Othello's 'sexual anxiety'
    (232, 250, etc.). On the other side, Mack refuses 'to believe that Othello is a sexual
    cripple, or has a narcissistic incapacity to love any but himself, or is emotionally
    underdeveloped' (140). Cf. above, p. 42, n. 1.

2   Others have questioned Greenblatt's theology. Catherine Belsey found 'a new legiti-
    mation of married sexual pleasure' in Puritan theologians ('Desire's excess and the
    English Renaissance theatre', in *Erotic Politics: Desire on the Renaissance Stage*, ed.
    Susan Zimmerman [1992]); compare Bradshaw, 196ff.

3   Virginia Woolf, *The Diary*, ed. Anne Olivier Bell, 5 vols (1979–85), 2.234.

physical cruelty, *he* stops loving without having any real proof against her. I do not say that his love is shallow compared with hers, only that it turns out to be utterly different, contrary to the impression of likeness generated in the play's first scenes.

Feminism

In *Romeo and Juliet* Shakespeare had already portrayed Juliet as emotionally more mature than Romeo – equally ardent, yet more far-sighted and resolute in the pursuit of love. Two comedies written just before *Othello*, *As You Like It* and *Twelfth Night*, developed this 'feminist' bias, assigning less sense and less sensibility to the heroes than to the heroines. The women in *Othello* are used to make a similar point. Desdemona, Emilia and Bianca are all cast aside by their menfolk, the first two being treated as disloyal, though we know them to be more loyal than their husbands; and all three give themselves to love more unstintingly than the self-centred men, who have other preoccupations. One wonders, indeed, whether the men are capable of unselfish love. Is Othello not deflected too easily? Bianca feels more for Cassio than he for her; and if Emilia has learned not to love Iago, her devotion to Desdemona – which compels her to accuse her husband – is one of the most powerful and genuine emotions in the play.[1]

The Willow Song scene (4.3), drastically cut in many productions (Sprague, 203), is essential for our understanding of this emotion, and underpins the play's feminism. It becomes clear from Emilia's great speech on double standards (4.3.85ff.) that both wives have suffered from the emotional brutality and blinkered vision of their husbands: their quiet fellow feeling unleashes moral forces that later challenge and defeat the masculine values of Othello and Iago. The song itself introduces a pause – or, let us say, continues a slow-motion sequence that begins with Desdemona's 'unpinning'. This, the unpinning either of her hair or of her dress (4.3.19n.), necessitates gentle personal contact and accompanying silences.

---

1   In John Barton's 1971 production one reviewer thought 4.3 (the Desdemona–Emilia scene) 'the emotional peak of the evening' (Hankey, 297).

DESDEMONA   No, unpin me here. [*Emilia begins.*]
EMILIA   [*after a silence*] This Lodovico is a proper man.
   [*Another silence*] A very handsome man.
DESDEMONA   [*not interested*] He speaks well.
EMILIA   I know a lady in Venice . . .

$$(4.3.33-7)^1$$

So a modern performance-script might present the text. The silences, like the physical contact, suggest an intimate togetherness, and yet each of the two pursues her own thoughts. Desdemona's musing breaks out as the Willow Song, where she has in mind her own plight and bemoans it so movingly that Emilia answers in a new voice (prepared for by 'Come, come, you talk', 23) –

DESDEMONA
   Doth that bode weeping?
EMILIA   'Tis neither here nor there.

– no longer an attendant, more a mother speaking protectively to her child. The song, and the seemingly inconsequential gossip that precedes and follows, is an emotion-packed climax of feminine tenderness and communion unparalleled until Cordelia addresses her awakening, bewildered father in *King Lear* 4.7.

Tenderness may not be the hallmark of feminism as understood today. Yet Shakespeare, who helped to bring about many cultural changes, including feminism, saw feminine tenderness, quite unsentimentally, as a moral force to be reckoned with. In *Othello* it embraces not only the three women who appear on stage but also the unhappy Barbary of the Willow Song and the account of Othello's mother and her need of the talismanic handkerchief.

   if she lost it
Or made a gift of it, my father's eye
Should hold her loathed, and his spirits should hunt
After new fancies.

$$(3.4.62-5)$$

The feminism of *Othello*, though less visible than in *All's Well*

---

1   I assign 'This Lodovico is a proper man' to Emilia, the Folio to Desdemona (see t.n. and commentary). Q omits these speeches, as well as the Willow Song.

That Ends Well,[1] has advanced far beyond *Romeo and Juliet*. In the military environment of Cyprus feminine values are

> Not less but more heroic than the wrath
> Of stern Achilles on his foe pursued
> Thrice fugitive about Troy wall . . .

because they represent 'the better fortitude / Of patience'.[2] This traditional Christian view assigns a far from passive role to Desdemona: in the play's moral struggle she affirms and radiates Christian virtues (love, patience, forgiveness). The angel defeats the devil (see p. 107); her moral strength partakes of 'the grace of heaven' (2.1.85), nowhere more so than when she 'lies' to protect her husband, one of Shakespeare's most sublime touches.

> Nobody. I myself. Farewell.
> Commend me to my kind lord – O, farewell!
> (5.2.122–3)

In different centuries the feminine ideal (like the notion of what it means to be a gentleman) will change, according to the conventions of the time. We today would not react to Charlotte Vandenhoff's Desdemona as did one reviewer in 1851.

> It is an unalloyed delight . . . to see her sad, fearful, yet gentle as a bruised dove, bend meekly to the implacable jealousy of the swart Othello, and receive her death while kissing the hand which gives it.
>
> (Hankey, 315)

Here Victorian attitudes grotesquely misrepresent Shakespeare's psychology. Some feminist critics, marching under a more modern banner, may equally misunderstand Shakespeare's purposes when they denounce Desdemona as too good to be true, woman as man likes to reinvent her. They overlook Shakespeare's general probing of stereotypes in the play (see pp. 60–1), and the necessary polarization of good and evil in its metaphysical conflict (pp. 107ff.). And if 'the gentle Desdemona' irritates feminist

1 See '*All's Well That Ends Well*: a "feminist" play?', in Honigmann, *Myriad-Minded Shakespeare*, 130–46.
2 *Paradise Lost*, 9.13ff.

10 Tony Britton (Cassio) and Barbara Jefford (Desdemona): Shakespeare
Memorial Theatre, Stratford-upon-Avon, 1954

critics, who mutter (like Iago) 'Ay, too gentle!' (4.1.193), let us not overlook the strength in Desdemona, unmistakable even in her most subdued replies[1] – the strength of a 'sweet soul' (5.2.50) as defined by George Herbert.

> Only a sweet and virtuous soul,
> Like seasoned timber, never gives;
> But, though the whole world turn to coal,
>   Then chiefly lives.[2]

Morality and 'the moral'

Inevitably, feminism poses moral questions. In the tragedies Shakespeare's moral sense is a gift as precious as his psychological insight; the two, of course, are intimately related – criticism may have had more to say about the latter, yet, like it or not, readers and theatre-goers are caught up in the play's morality and respond to it, at first uncertainly and then, as the action unfolds, more positively, a process carefully controlled by the dramatist.

As we have seen, even secondary characters and apparently minor or fill-in episodes may suddenly thrust moral questions upon us. We react morally to Emilia's 'I know not, madam' (see p. 44), and to Desdemona's similar 'lie' in the same scene ('It is not lost', 3.4.85, 87). In a play so centrally concerned with honesty and lying, even half-lines can have a function in the total design. Emilia's lie prepares for Desdemona's, and Desdemona's must be related to the 'lie' that almost sanctifies her and becomes her crowning glory – her dying need to prove her love of Othello (5.2.122–3). Shakespeare seems to be making a point about deception and intent, distinguishing between different kinds of culpability, as also in many other lines in the play: 'O, she deceives me / Past thought!', 'She has deceived her father, and may thee', 'She did

---

1 I am thinking of lines such as 'Whate'er you be, I am obedient', 'I' faith, you are to blame', 'I will not stay to offend you' (3.3.89, 3.4.98, 4.1.246).
2 George Herbert, 'Virtue'. Barbara Jefford, the best Desdemona I have seen (Stratford, 1954, with Anthony Quayle as Othello, see Fig. 10, p. 57), managed to combine exceptional sweetness with exceptional moral strength. Hazlitt put it differently: 'The truth of conception, with which timidity and boldness are united in the same character, is marvellous' (in *The Characters of Shakespeare's Plays* (1869 edn), 37).

deceive her father', 'She's like a liar gone to burning hell' (1.1.163–4, 1.3.294, 3.3.209, 5.2.127). Our sense of Desdemona's goodness and essential truthfulness ('O, she was heavenly true!', 5.2.133) survives this bombardment of accusations and, paradoxically, may be strengthened by it. There is no Richter scale for moral indignation – not, at least, in Shakespeare's theatre, where we are asked to exercise moral awareness more often than moral judgement.

In the theatre a dramatist's moral awareness need not commit him to moral judgement. Shakespeare was less inclined to offer such judgement than Jonson, Webster or Middleton, usually leaving it to the audience to decide for itself. So it is probably significant that he makes one character after another denounce Iago in the final scene as a slave, villain, viper, devil, demi-devil, dog, and Iago's actions as odious, damned, monstrous, pernicious, most heathenish and most gross, etc. (5.2.168ff.). Perhaps Shakespeare felt that Iago's special relationship with the audience had unbalanced the play's morality, had come close to turning the villain into a villain-hero, as in the case of Shylock. A change of emphasis, and might the play not be called *The Tragedy of Iago?* Indirectly these denunciations of Iago also help to rehabilitate Othello, whose smothering of Desdemona comes close to turning the hero into a villain.

While we have no time in the theatre to judge every moral issue as it arises, what of the play as a whole? We must not shirk the most difficult question, whether or not the play has a moral. When Othello and Desdemona decided to marry was that a terrible mistake, one condemned by the play? Even if Shakespeare had not heard of Aristotle's *hamartia*, i.e. the notion that a tragic hero's 'error of judgement' causes his fall,[1] several of his mature tragedies seem to accord with Aristotle's formula, so we must ask the racist question: was it a tragic 'error of judgement' that a black man marries a white wife? Some critics have argued along these lines, encouraged by the fact that Cinthio made this the moral of his novella. In a preliminary discussion (Bullough, 240) Cinthio argued that those who wish to marry must 'use judgement', choosing partners of the same 'nature and quality'.

1   See Humphry House, *Aristotle's Poetics* (1964 edn), 93–6.

Cinthio's Disdemona later speaks quite explicitly. 'I fear greatly that . . . Italian ladies will learn by my example not to tie themselves to a man whom Nature, Heaven and manner of life separate from us' (see p. 380).

To apply this 'moral' to the play seems to me entirely wrong-headed. Shakespeare was not bound to adopt Cinthio's moral, any more than to take over Cinthio's characters as he found them. He chose to dramatize Cinthio's story for the opportunities it gave him – to do what? If we may judge from results, to challenge popular stereotypes; not only the stereotype of 'the Moor' but, equally, received thinking about love and marriage. Does Shakespeare condemn the love of Romeo and Juliet, or of Antony and Cleopatra? As in these other tragedies of love, the feeling of the play supports the lovers; although love leads to death, the choice of love does not impress us as an error of judgement when Othello, like Romeo and Antony, finds it so fulfilling ('when I love thee not / Chaos is come again', 3.3.91–2). If *Othello* has a moral it cannot be Cinthio's which, let us not forget, differs little from the most notorious misreading of the play, that of Thomas Rymer (see p. 29).

Perhaps, though, the implications of a play that makes so much of good and bad judgement can be summarized in other ways: that knowing others, and oneself, is not easy; that love is a form of knowledge. Mere platitudes? Not necessarily, if these thoughts are made to rise as naturally from sharply observed behaviour as odour from a rose. Rather than functioning as a moral tagged on afterwards they are part of the deeply rooted suggestiveness that we admire in most of Shakespeare's best work.

Stereotypes

We may take it as certain that an Elizabethan dramatist who chose to write about a Moor's marriage with a white wife did not do so merely to peddle platitudes. Moors and other non-Europeans might be seen in London, but a black man's marriage to a white woman would have been far less of an everyday occurrence than today – would have been undreamed of, except in works of fiction. It follows that the marriage of Othello and Desdemona overturns all preconceived notions of normal behaviour.

Shakespeare's determination to question 'the normal' emerges from the large number of stereotypes that he sets up only to knock them down. We first hear of Othello as a 'black ram', a 'lascivious Moor', i.e. the stereotypical lustful Moor, a damaging misrepresentation of the man we meet in scenes 2 and 3. We hear of Desdemona 'making the beast with two backs', and expect a Venetian lady of easy virtue, a possibility kept alive, if only just, by her participation in the 'cheap backchat' of 2.1.109ff. (see p. 42; at this point we scarcely know her). Cassio, a Florentine, might well be a 'slipper and subtle knave' (2.1.239–40), this being how others perceived the fellow citizens of Machiavelli. Iago, disguised as an 'honest soldier', would be thought straightforward and reliable like Antony's Enobarbus or the sentinels in *Hamlet* ('O, farewell, honest soldier', 1.1.16); Emilia reminds us of the bawdy serving woman, Bianca of the aggressive prostitute. We are encouraged to expect these stereotypes, which Shakespeare had used in other plays, and find that each one fails to conform to our expectations. Othello himself takes the process even further: first his civilized voice and deportment contradict Iago's account of him as a lustful barbarian, then, reacting to Iago's lies, he slides into just such a role, that of a cruel, sex-driven savage, finally recovering his 'civilized' manner and yet standing apart from the Europeans and his former self ('O thou Othello, that wert once so good', 5.2.288), weeping unashamedly. As we get to know him and the other characters we realize that all stereotypes are misleading. The dramatist challenges us to locate the man beneath the mask – contrast Ben Jonson's comedy of humours – and to reconsider society's stereotype thinking more generally. Is it unnatural for a white woman to love and marry a Moor? Brabantio seems to think so, Iago agrees, even Emilia speaks of the marriage as a 'filthy bargain' (1.3.63, 2.1.231ff., 5.2.153). In *Othello* Shakespeare asks us to think the unthinkable, and in passing touches on many of the stereotypical judgements that society takes for granted.[1]

1   In his brief discussion of stereotypes, Mack (136) suggests that a reversal of a stereotype is purposeful: 'it required the audience to discover how easily it could be led into mistaken judgments'. I suggest that the stereotypical judgement that a wife's adultery deserves death is also questioned in *Othello*: Honigmann, 'Social questioning in Elizabethan and Jacobean plays, with special reference to *Othello*', in *Jacobean Drama as Social Criticism: Salzburg University Studies*, ed. James Hogg (1995), 3–11.

Plot

Just about every other component has to be taken into account when a dramatist thinks out his plot – the development of character, of language and imagery, of 'themes', morality, the structure and relationship of scenes, and so on. I deal with most of these concerns in other sections, and here offer short notes on additional plotting problems that deserve some attention.

Act 1   Shakespeare very nearly created Act 1 *ex nihilo*. Cinthio informed him that Disdemona's relatives 'did all they could to make her take another husband', and that she and the Moor nevertheless lived happily together, until 'the Venetian lords' chose the Moor as their commander in Cyprus (see p. 371). From this hint of family opposition grew Brabantio and two and a half of the three scenes that make up Act 1. Since this act seems almost detachable, being divided from the closely knit four acts that follow by a time gap and by a change of supporting characters and location, one wonders why Act 1 was necessary. Verdi's opera *Otello* omitted it[1] – why did Shakespeare choose to blow up Cinthio's hint as he did, into so lengthy an introduction?

My guess is that, in a play in which psychology becomes all-important, Shakespeare wanted the audience to see Othello and Desdemona before they succumb to pressure. She, spirited and independent initially, is shocked into seeming passivity, against her nature; he, monumentally calm and self-confident in Act 1, later loses all self-control. Dwelling on the first phase of the story Shakespeare makes the two of them travel a greater psychological distance. We also hear at length of Othello's romantic past, to which the play returns several times, as when he speaks of his experience 'in Aleppo once' (5.2.350). Characteristically he remembers himself as alone and threatened. The stage images in Act 1 present other threats visually: in scene 2 he, with Iago and perhaps a couple of attendants, has to face Brabantio, who no doubt brings a larger band of supporters; in scene 3 Othello is the

---

1   Though for different reasons, Dr Johnson would have preferred Shakespeare to omit Act 1 (*Johnson on Shakespeare*, 201): 'Had the scene opened in *Cyprus* . . . there had been little wanting to a drama of the most exact and scrupulous regularity.'

accused, almost a prisoner in the dock, and only the fact that Venice needs his services tips the balance. These threats are reinforced by the racial antagonism that repeatedly flares up in all three scenes. 'Racism' receives its heaviest emphasis in Act 1, and combines with Iago's hatred of privilege (see pp. 35–7) and Brabantio's anger – all directed against Othello – to create a sense of lurking dangers, an atmosphere of foreboding.

Act 1 contributes to the emotional 'atmospherics' in other ways. Many critics have explained the purpose of the council scene (1.3.1–50), in strangely similar terms – as in the *Critical Essays* of W. Watkiss Lloyd, an underrated Victorian.

> The consideration, by the Duke and Senators, of the news from Cyprus is no mere surplusage; it strikes a tone of dispassionate appreciation of evidence and opinion that dominates all the succeeding scenes of agitation . . . From inconsistent intelligence, the main point of agreement is carefully adopted for further examination . . . intelligence, otherwise of good authority, is condemned as fallacious from collateral indications . . . thus prepared for the last courier has full credence, and the critical circumstances once understood, action follows at once.[1]

Equally Brabantio, told of his daughter's elopement, 'is obstinately incredulous; in the disposition of the rejected suitor he sees a probable cause of the disturbance, and is satisfied to look no further . . . [He disbelieves the unceremonious shouting of] wretches and ruffians; yet when a more sober assertion gains attention, he becomes at once alarmed.' In between these critical reactions in 1.1 and 1.3 comes Othello's unquestioning acceptance of Iago's story (1.2.1–10), which we know to be distorted. Such implied comparisons are characteristic of Shakespeare, as again when the feinting of the Turkish fleet indirectly prepares for Iago's favourite manoeuvre, retreating in order to attack. We marvel at

---

1   W. Watkiss Lloyd, *Critical Essays on the Plays of Shakespeare* (1892 edn), 463. For other useful discussions of 1.3, see Goddard, 2.81, and Wolfgang Riehle, 'Strukturprobleme in Shakespeares "Othello"', *GRM*, 25 (1975), 1–11.

Shakespeare's economy: below the surface of cause-and-effect events one senses other connections.

Tempo   All three scenes of Act 1 begin abruptly, in mid-action as it were, as do several later ones, notably 4.1. At the start of 1.1 we know neither what has angered Roderigo nor the identity of 'him' – 'Thou toldst me / Thou didst hold him in thy hate.' The dialogue rushes on, we are left to sink or swim. From 1.1.80, Brabantio's first appearance, we witness a verbal mugging not unlike the one we have just experienced, and we can assume that the dramatist planned the first no less consciously than Iago thinks out the second. By the time he wrote *Othello* Shakespeare had mastered all the tricks of scenic form[1] and of the modulation of tempo.

Despite the attention-tangling speed of the opening, with a major speech as early as line 6, *Othello* only slips into top gear in Act 3; then, however, the audience has to brace itself for climax after climax, the most tightly plotted three acts in Shakespeare, more gripping than any similar sequence of scenes except for the first three acts of *Macbeth*. In *Macbeth* readers and actors feel that the plotting then falters; in *Othello* no one complains of the first two acts, so conscious are we of the controlled build-up of momentum.

We can sample Shakespeare's control by examining the play's songs, mood-regulators inserted in mid-scene for quite specific reasons. Iago's drinking-songs have an ulterior motive (2.3.65ff.), to press wine upon Cassio and make him drunk. We observe Cassio's tipsiness in his thickening speech and in his movements (Garrick once called out to a colleague who was supposed to be playing a drunk man, 'Your legs are sober!'). Iago, having twice forced Cassio to give way to a less senior officer in a protracted verbal contest (lines 13, 40), probably addresses Cassio directly as he sings 'And *thou* art but of low degree, / 'Tis *pride* that pulls the country down' (90–1, my italics), to provoke him, and rank-conscious Cassio rises to the bait – 'The lieutenant is to be saved before the ancient' (105–6)! Below the surface of the song and of the 'all boys together' atmosphere Iago's plot pushes relentlessly forward.[2]

---

1   See particularly Jones, *Scenic Form*, ch. 5, and M. J. B. Allen in *Stratford-upon-Avon Studies*, 20 (1984).
2   For the Willow Song, see pp. 54–5.

The temptation scene (3.3) displays Shakespeare's most astonishing control of tempo. Just as car manufacturers describe performance in terms of 'acceleration, 0–60 m.p.h., 9 secs' or the like, this one scene travels in record time from a standing start (Othello still loves Desdemona) to a faraway emotional point (he vows to kill her). Yet the scene dawdles at first, quite unlike a racing car that shoots away from the starting grid. First it focuses on Desdemona, who tries to persuade Othello to recall Cassio: the artless impulsiveness of her attack contrasts with Iago's deviousness. Iago's tempo will differ in any two productions, with many hesitations, pauses, criss-crossing stage movements: here a reader is at a great disadvantage compared with a spectator, the body language being so important (see the account of Salvini's 'business', p. 93). The speed of the scene may also puzzle readers because reading time and performance time obey different rules. In the theatre Othello's soliloquy (262–81) and his absence (293–332) both affect our sense of time's passing: off stage his mood may change more rapidly. Placing Emilia and Iago on stage alone and together (294–332), and thus bisecting the two Othello–Iago sequences, Shakespeare in effect 'stretches' the scene and thus reduces its speed, making Othello's emotional change more credible.

Why did Shakespeare write the two clown scenes (3.1.3–29, 3.4.1–22), probably the feeblest clown scenes in his mature work? It will be noticed that they come shortly before and just after the temptation scene, introducing jolting changes of tone and tempo. The clown's habit of verbal analysis, applying his own irrepressible criticisms to the matter in hand, contrasts with Othello's overpowering imagination, which incapacitates his reasoning faculties. Shakespeare no doubt had other motives for writing the two scenes, but producers often omit them.

So far I have considered tempo from the reader's and spectator's point of view – what of the actor's? Of all Shakespeare's major roles Othello is the most exhausting (with one possible exception: King Lear). From Act 3 he has to switch on extremes of passion repeatedly, and to oscillate between different extremes. He has to go through the motions of an epileptic fit, which can be as draining as a genuine fit, and in some productions he screws up

11 Paul Scofield (Othello) and Felicity Kendal (Desdemona): National
    Theatre, 1980

his eyes at later moments as if about to fall again. Edmund Kean,
one of the greatest Othellos, whose performance was 'a series of
explosions', was once found in his dressing-room 'stretched out

12 Portrait of Richard Burbage, the first actor of Othello

on a sofa, retching violently and throwing up blood' (Rosenberg, 62, 68). I fancy that more than one actor has said, like Henry Irving, 'Never again!' (Rosenberg, 79). Shakespeare pushed Burbage, the first Othello, to the very limit: all actors of the part must therefore pace themselves with care. In the long final scene

Shakespeare perhaps took pity on Burbage, writing weariness into his speeches (5.2.198–303).[1]

The double plot   Many of Shakespeare's plays contain a sub-plot that mirrors the main plot. In *Othello* this is reduced to the minimum, revolving round Roderigo (Shakespeare's addition to Cinthio's story). It is sometimes said that Roderigo, hovering on the edge of things, scarcely amounts to a subplot. Possibly so, yet Shakespeare took some trouble to integrate him, making him more than merely a ventriloquist's dummy. Roderigo, the rejected suitor of Desdemona who twice waylays his supposed rival in cowardly fashion, personifies the degenerate sexuality of Venice, the male counterpart of Venice's female unchastity, which the play takes for granted (see pp. 9–11). In addition Roderigo activates poisonous impulses in Iago that are concealed from everyone else; Roderigo's overmastering, self-destructive desire for Desdemona mirrors Othello's; and Iago's manipulation of Roderigo, as of Cassio, prepares for his more skilful handling of his third gull, the Moor. What economy, devising so many different uses for a non-entity called Roderigo! If the play lacks the 'density' provided by a more fully developed double plot, perhaps its double time compensates to some degree.

Double time   The discovery of a 'double time scheme' in *Othello* is now commonly ascribed to John Wilson's articles in *Blackwood's Magazine* (1849, 1850), and dismissed as academic nit-picking. Yet Theobald, Dr Johnson and Malone already worried about it much earlier;[2] double time, I want to suggest, is neither a purely modern discovery nor a critical irrelevance.

We are indebted to Wilson and his followers for identifying double time as a general problem in Shakespeare, not just a curiosity in one play. In *Othello* we have the prize exhibit, for here the two time schemes are more intricately interwoven than elsewhere and affect

---

1   Garrick, it was felt, failed as Othello partly 'in being too *early*, or too frequent, in that violence of emotion' (quoted Rosenberg, 41). Compare Hazlitt's fine perception that the 'movements of passion in Othello resemble the heaving of the sea in a storm . . . but Mr Macready goes off like a shot' (Rosenberg, 72).
2   Compare Vickers, 2.525 (Theobald); 5.163, 165 (Dr Johnson); and Malone (1821), 9.220: 'In several other instances beside this, our poet appears not to have recollected that the persons of his play had only been one day at Cyprus.'

our response to character. According to the short time scheme, Othello and Desdemona leave Venice for Cyprus the day after they marry; they meet in Cyprus and, in the words of M. R. Ridley,

> The represented time from then to the end of the play is some thirty-three hours. They land somewhere about four o'clock on Saturday (2.2.9); the scene of the cashiering of Cassio begins just before ten o'clock (2.3.13) and lasts . . . till early on Sunday morning (2.3.373, 3.1.32 and 3.3.57–61). Cassio makes up his mind to petition Desdemona 'betimes in the morning' (2.3.324). He does so, and there follows the long 'temptation' scene (3.3). It is then just possible to assume some interval, but I think very awkward, since 3.4.18–20, 23 seem to indicate continuity. Desdemona has become immediately aware of the loss of the handkerchief . . .
>
> Between Acts 3 and 4 is the one place, so far as I can see, where an interval can be credibly inserted . . . [But] when once Iago has Othello on the rack it would be undramatic to allow a respite. From the beginning of Act 4 there is no possibility of an interval.[1]

As will be clear from this extract, a multitude of detail knits together the 'short' time scheme. Ridley, indeed, missed one point that rules out an interval between Acts 3 and 4 – that Bianca says 'What did you mean by that same handkerchief you gave me *even now?*' (4.1.147–9, my italics, referring to 3.4.179ff.). Leaving

---

1 See Ridley in Ard², lxvii–lxx. I have changed Ridley's line references to agree with Ard³. Several critics have tried to explain one series of long-time allusions by arguing that Desdemona might have committed adultery with Cassio between her betrothal and marriage with Othello (see Arthur McGee, 'Othello's motive for murder', *SQ*, 15 (1964), 45–54; K. P. Wentersdorf in *SJW* (1985), 63–77; Arthur L. Little, ' "An essence that's not seen": the primal scene of racism in *Othello*', *SQ*, 44 (1993), 317); nevertheless, the other long-time allusions remain even if one accepts this explanation. I cannot accept it: it disregards the play's many hints as to Desdemona's innocence (e.g. 4.3.59ff., her refusal to 'do such a wrong / For the whole world', 77–8). In his subtle analysis of time and continuity, Emrys Jones contended that in *Othello* 'the Long Time part of the [double-time] theory is more or less acceptable' but not short time, because 'the prime concern is not duration but continuity' (*Scenic Form*, ch. 2). I think that this underrates the number and pressure of short-time allusions. Bradshaw, on the other hand, preferred to keep to short time and dismissed the long-time and double-time theories as unnecessary (128, 148ff.).

aside Act 1, which is separated from Act 2 by a sea voyage, the rest of the play seems to rush to its conclusion in 'short' time – except for a series of countersignals, less fully worked out, pointing in the opposite direction.

What then is the evidence for 'long' time? Iago persuades Othello that Desdemona and Cassio have 'the act of shame / A thousand times committed' (5.2.209–10); Emilia recalls that Iago 'hath a hundred times' asked her to steal the handkerchief (3.3.296); Bianca complains that Cassio deserted her for a whole week (3.4.173); Roderigo, having just reached Cyprus, has squandered his money (4.2.174ff.); and so on. These indicators of 'long' time are incompatible with 'short' time – how can we explain this inconsistency?[1] In the first place let us note that Cinthio's narrative, Shakespeare's source, operates mostly in 'long' time: the 'short' scheme was grafted on by the dramatist, for good reasons. To return to Ridley, 'short' time

> is not only, from the point of view of dramatic tension, desirable, but also, from the point of view of credibility, imperative. If Iago's plot does not work fast it will not work at all. If Othello meets Cassio and asks him the question which he asks too late, in the last scene, the plot will be blown sky high . . . And Iago is acutely aware of this – 'the Moor / May unfold me to him – there stand I in much peril' (5.1.20–1).

Yet Shakespeare actually increased the risk of discovery in various ways – by making Desdemona ask Emilia 'Where should I lose that handkerchief?' (3.4.23); by introducing Roderigo, who knows of Iago's plot and threatens to denounce him; above all, by amplifying Iago's lies ('stolen hours of lust', 3.3.341; Cassio's erotic

---

1 See also Ned B. Allen, 'The two parts of *Othello*', *SS*, 21 (1968), 13–29, who argued that two time schemes exist separately in the play's two parts, Acts 1 and 2, Acts 3 to 5. The second part was probably written before Acts 1 and 2, and '*all* the references to a longer time can be explained' if we assume that when Shakespeare wrote Acts 3 to 5 he 'thought of all the characters, not as having arrived in Cyprus on the previous day, but as having long been there – as in Cinthio'. Even those who disagree with Allen will still find that he sharpens their understanding of time in the play.

dream, 3.3.416ff.; 'naked with her friend in bed', 4.1.3), offered as proofs of Desdemona's guilt, any one of which, if tested, might have wrecked his plot. The double time scheme therefore allowed Shakespeare to transform Cinthio's Ensign into a much more daring gambler, one who revels in risk-taking.[1] Equally it allowed him to make his Moor both more and less gullible than Cinthio's, and thus more psychologically intriguing: more, because the more circumstantial Iago's 'proofs' the flimsier they seem to the audience; less, because Iago is so much more fiendishly clever than the Ensign.

It follows that the double time scheme is intricately bound up with Shakespeare's reshaping of his material. Despite attempts to deny its existence or to explain it as the result of exceptional methods of composition,[2] I see double time as important in *Othello* and believe that, though more elaborately worked out, it functions very much as in a number of other plays. Once again I cannot resist quoting my Arden 2 predecessor, M. R. Ridley.

> I cannot agree with the critics who hold that any examination of the double time scheme is an idle waste of time, on the grounds that no one in the theatre notices the discrepancies. In the first place any such examination of small points puts a keener edge on one's appreciation of the play as a whole; but apart from that it throws light on Shakespeare's astonishing skill and judgement as a practical craftsman. He knew to a fraction of an inch how far he could go in playing a trick on his audience, and the measure of his success is precisely the unawareness of the audience in the theatre that any trick is being played. What Shakespeare is doing is to present, before our eyes,

1 Shakespeare must have been aware of the risks he himself took in resorting to 'double time': see 4.2.140n. Again, Emilia knows that Desdemona keeps the handkerchief 'evermore about her / To kiss and talk to' (3.3.299–300), so Cassio – who 'came a-wooing' with Othello (3.3.71) – might be expected to recognize it as hers. In Cinthio the Corporal (= Cassio) found the handkerchief 'and *knowing that it was Disdemona's*, he determined to give it back to her' (my italics: see p. 378). Evidently Shakespeare decided that if Cassio recognized the handkerchief, this – together with the play's double time – would later multiply too many improbabilities. In the theatre we do not see how many threads link the handkerchief to alternative possibilities but we feel that Iago builds his plot on the flimsiest foundations, a feeling also prompted by Iago's lies and the use of double time.

2 See p. 69, n. 1; p. 70, n. 1.

an unbroken series of events happening in 'short time', but to present them against a background, of events not presented but implied, which gives the needed impression of 'long time'.

Christianity, fate, chance   Iago thinks every man the master of his own destiny ("'tis in ourselves that we are thus, or thus', 1.3.320–1). Othello believes in the Christian God and also in fate, destiny, the stars and similar external powers. 'Amen to that, sweet powers!' (2.1.193): the curious combination of 'Amen' and 'sweet powers' highlights the coexistence of incompatibles in his mind. Since Christian providence and fate carry different implications, Othello's tendency to invoke non-Christian powers lends support to those who see him as a Christian convert (see pp. 22–3), even though he sometimes refers to such powers partly to escape from responsibility for his actions.[1] His confusion also raises the question of the 'ultimate power' in the world of the play.

Who or what is in charge? Many readers have noticed that blind chance repeatedly favours Iago's plots, perhaps more often than is probable. The full extent of the intervention of chance – a convenient plot mechanism, from the dramatist's viewpoint – is still easily overlooked. Consider the handkerchief: Desdemona loses it just when Iago needs proof to convince Othello, later fails to remember where she lost it, and Cassio fails to recognize it as hers (see p. 71, n. 1). In addition Cassio asks Bianca to copy it, and she throws it back at him just when Othello, in hiding, can witness this 'proof' (4.1.148–76). It is also an unlucky chance that Desdemona refuses to admit that the handkerchief is lost (she may think of it as merely mislaid), and then insists on Cassio's reinstatement as Othello, more and more furiously, requests to see it. Chance seems to have stacked the cards against Desdemona (Cinthio mentioned that her father had given her an unlucky name – it meant 'unfortunate' – see p. 386). As we watch the play we are perhaps more conscious of Iago's brilliance in making the most of his opportunities, yet not all of Desdemona's misfortunes are engineered directly by Iago. Her unlucky words, 'for the love I bear to

---

1   Compare 'It is the very error of the moon', 'Who can control his fate?', 'O, ill-starred wench' (5.2.108, 263, 270).

Cassio' and 'By my troth, I am glad on't' (4.1.232, 237), and her equally innocent exclamations on her deathbed, again misunderstood by Othello (5.2.75–6), contribute to our sense that a malign force, not simply Iago, acts against her. Having done its worst, it ceases with her death. Now the handkerchief serves as proof of Iago's guilt, papers found in Roderigo's pocket confirm it, and the 'slain Roderigo' accuses Iago: after a run of bad luck these fortunate discoveries adjust the balance, the world rights itself. It is a world, though, in which chance plays a decisive part, and Othello's vision –

> Blow me about in winds, roast me in sulphur,
> Wash me in steep-down gulfs of liquid fire!
> (5.2.277–8)

– proves not so much that divine justice is 'in charge' as man's need to believe in divine justice, a less comforting conclusion.[1]

It may be that Shakespeare invented the storm at sea and unexpected annihilation of the Turkish fleet (2.1.1–201) because he foresaw how heavily the plot would depend on chance. Again an external force intervenes: such things can happen, as we know from the Spanish Armada. We may not notice, however, that the chance destruction of the Turkish fleet indirectly validates another plot mechanism, the fateful handkerchief.

Genre

Othello is sometimes described as a 'domestic tragedy'.[2] At least two representatives of this subgenre of tragedy preceded Shakespeare's play, both anonymous: *Arden of Faversham* (1592) and *A*

---

1 Cf. Elliott, ch. 3, on Fate, and Katherine S. Stockholder, 'Egregiously an ass: chance and accident in *Othello*', *SEL 1500–1900*, 13 (1973), 256–72. For the 'damnation' of Othello, see Robert H. West, 'The Christianness of *Othello*', *SQ*, 15 (1964), 333–43, and Roy Battenhouse, *Shakespearean Tragedy: Its Art and Christian Premises* (Bloomington, Indiana, 1969).

2 Dympna Callaghan described *Othello* as 'embarrassingly domestic' (*Woman and Gender in Renaissance Tragedy* (1989), 35) and, while she makes a different point, it is true that Othello's domestic affairs get in the way of his official duties embarrassingly (somewhat like Antony's in *Antony and Cleopatra*). See also Henry H. Adams, *English Domestic or Homiletic Tragedy 1575 to 1642* (New York, 1943), and Leanore Lieblein, 'The context of murder in English domestic plays, 1590–1610', *SEL 1500–1900*, 23 (1983), 177–96.

Warning for Fair Women (1599), the latter performed by Shakespeare's own company. While *Othello* differs from these plays and from Heywood's *A Woman Killed with Kindness* (written 1602–3) in not having an English middle-class husband and wife at its centre, Shakespeare was clearly aware of *Arden* and *Warning*, and adapted some of the most inspired touches in *Othello* from these predecessors. In *Arden* and *Warning* a young wife and her lover are guilty of the murder of her husband; a series of chance events saves the victim initially, and later brings the murderers to justice; in the end the murderers confess and are led off to execution. The chance events, 'strange and miraculous', are heavily emphasized,[1] and in *Warning* a handkerchief becomes a significant instrument in the plot, helping to reveal the murderers' guilt.[2] In *Othello* the plot is similar, except that the husband murders his wife and his accomplice tries to murder the wife's 'lover'; chance, and a handkerchief, once more play a part before the murder, and in bringing the truth to light at the end; and Othello's death speech serves as his confession. Many details confirm Shakespeare's indebtedness. (1) The husband in *Arden* complains that his wife called out her lover's name in her sleep and suddenly 'Instead of him, caught me about the neck' (1.65–70). This must be connected with Cassio's erotic dream and embrace, invented by Iago (3.3.416–28). (2) Much is made in *Arden* of the husband's being a gentleman, whereas the lover is basely born;[3] the lover naturally resents being treated as an inferior (8.135), as does Iago (see pp. 35–7), and class feeling stirs up passion on both sides. (3) *Warning* contains two scenes in which victims, left for dead, regain consciousness and speak before they die; in one a servant manages to identify the murderer. By contrast, Desdemona, left for dead, tries to shield her murderer instead of accusing him. (4) The murderer's tool villain in *Warning* has the name Trusty Roger,[4] a misnomer as ironic as 'honest Iago'.

---

1 Cf. *Arden* (Revels), 3.51 SD, 9.133: 'Arden, thou hast wondrous holy luck', etc.; *Warning* (1599), D3a: 'Except by miracle, thou art deliuered as was neuer man', E2b, etc.
2 *Warning*, F1a, F3a, I2a.
3 *Arden*, 1.26ff., 36, 198ff., 304–5, etc.
4 'Trusty Roger' seems to have been a cant name for a rogue as early as 1593: see Katherine Duncan-Jones, 'Much ado with red and white: the earliest readers of Shakespeare's *Venus and Adonis*', *RES*, 44 (1993), 487.

Minor threads also link *Othello* to the two earlier plays. In both, murderers waylay their victims in dark places, as in *Othello* 5.1.1ff.; in *Arden* they repeatedly fail to kill (compare Roderigo and Iago). Black Will '*kneels down and holds up his hands to heaven*' (*Arden*, 9.36), a blasphemous invocation not unlike Iago's promise to revenge (3.3.465ff.). Jealousy, more often a theme for comedy, is seen as tragic.[1] A wife holds out her palm to be read, and we know that the 'reader' wants to influence her actions.[2] The same thoughts are repeated: for instance, that men fear the world's judgements more than God's.[3] Such thoughts and episodes are not unique to these plays but prove, I think, that Shakespeare's mind looked back to the routines of domestic tragedy, as was only natural in a dramatization of domestic strife and murder.

Othello could also be called a tragedy of intrigue. Without Iago's originating plot, and resourcefulness in pushing it forward, the outcome would have been different. Iago, though, as the dramatist or plotter inside the play, is a direct descendant of the intriguing slave of classical comedy (with this difference: the slave more often than not solves the problems of his master's family, whereas Iago creates them). Like Iago, the *servus* soliloquizes about ways and means, cries '*habeo!*' when he sees how to proceed ('I have't, it is engendered!', 1.3.402), treats others – including his master – as dimwits, and helps out as universal adviser, 'friend' and joker. Shakespeare added the darker hues of Iago's character, yet owed much to the deceitful, gleeful slaves of Plautus and Terence.

Classical comedy and its derivatives influenced *Othello* in other ways.[4] The *meretrix* and angry *senex* became Bianca and Brabantio. Shakespeare's early *Comedy of Errors* has in it a Courtesan

1 *Arden*, 1.48, 370ff.; 4.39, etc.
2 *Warning*, C3a; *Oth* 3.4.36ff.
3 *Warning*, F3b, 'Shall I feare more my seruants, or the world, / Then God himselfe?'; *Oth* 3.3.205ff.
4 See p. 33, n. 1, and also Susan Snyder's useful but too short *The Comic Matrix of Shakespeare's Tragedies* (Princeton, New Jersey, 1979). Also Barbara Heliodora C. de Mendonça, '*Othello*: a tragedy built on a comic structure', *SS*, 21 (1968), 31–8, and Jones, *Scenic Form*, who demonstrates how closely some scenes in *Othello* were modelled on Shakespeare's own comedies. Many others have discussed the comedy in *Othello*. Russ McDonald is useful on the popular comic figure of the 'imaginary cuckold' ('Othello, Thorello, and the problem of the foolish hero', *SQ*, 30 (1979), 51–67).

very like the classical stereotype – how far he had developed by the time he created Bianca! And how much more individuality he conjured up for Brabantio compared with Egeus, the *senex* in *A Midsummer Night's Dream*. In addition some of the locations of *Othello* are borrowed from classical comedy (the street scene, the seaside scene).[1] As for Shakespeare's play's dominant emotions, Othello's jealousy and Iago's envy, they featured prominently in Ben Jonson's recent *Every Man* comedies (performed by Shakespeare's company in 1598 and 1599). *Every Man in His Humour* presents the jealous Thorello as well as an intriguing servant, a gull and a *senex*; *Every Man out of His Humour*, prompted by the contemporary fashion for satire, has Macilente, a malcontent who, 'wanting that place in the world's account that he thinks his merit capable of, falls into . . . an envious apoplexy'. Iago's sneering contemptuousness owes not a little to Macilente and to the snarling satirists at the turn of the century.[2]

To understand how comedy enriched the tragedy of *Othello* we must look beyond stage comedy. Othello, no longer young, marries a much younger wife (see p. 17); such marriages were not uncommon but were thought ridiculous and risky – as in Chaucer's *Merchant's Tale*, where old January 'is ravished in a trance' whenever he gazes at his wife, the lady May, or in Spenser's account of old Malbecco and the fair Hellenore.[3] Both January and Malbecco suffer what was thought appropriate punishment: each goes through agonies as he spies on his wife committing adultery with a young lover. Thanks to Iago's graphic narratives (3.3.400ff., 4.1.1ff.) Othello in effect also spies on his wife's 'adultery', and his agony and fury again carry comic potential, the more so since we see Iago, the puppet-master, twitching the strings. And even if Othello were not an older and almost doting husband, jealousy – especially causeless jealousy – was thought ridiculous in itself, a folly deserving laughter, as the bystanders tell us in *The Winter's Tale* (2.1.198, 2.3.128). We do not laugh at either Leontes or

1 See Barbara Everett, '"Spanish" Othello', *SS*, 35 (1982), 101ff.
2 For the satirists at the turn of the century, see Oscar J. Campbell, *Comicall Satyre and Shakespeare's 'Troilus and Cressida'* (San Marino, California, 1938).
3 *The Faerie Queene*, Book III, cantos 9 and 10.

Othello, yet the dramatist, a master of emotional chiaroscuro, knew that the conventions of comedy can tone in with tragedy, a 'mingle' that enriched his work in many plays.[1]

In *Othello* the debt to comedy is pervasive, since Shakespeare so frequently falls back on comic routines. Iago arranges that Othello, his dupe, overhears what he wants him to hear, to mislead him (4.1.76ff.): compare Plautus, *Miles Gloriosus*, 1210ff. The episode in which Othello demands 'The handkerchief!' three times and Desdemona continues to plead for Cassio's recall (3.4.87–99) is a comic 'cross-purposes' routine used several times in *The Comedy of Errors*, as when the Goldsmith repeatedly demands 'the chain', in mounting fury, from the twin brother of the man he gave it to (4.1.40ff.). Brabantio's distracted lamentations after Desdemona's elopement (1.1.158ff.) are disturbingly similar to Shylock's after Jessica's flight (*MV* 2.8.12ff.). Iago's milking of Roderigo ('Put money in thy purse') repeats Sir Toby's preying on Sir Andrew ('Send for money, knight', *TN* 2.3.186), a double echo if the same two actors played Toby and Andrew, Iago and Roderigo (see p. 346). Even Othello's fit, which ends with a splutter of disconnected words, may owe something to the vomiting of words by Jonson's pseudo-poets, a pill-induced fit staged in the autumn of 1601 (4.1.36–44n.).

But, as I said, we do not laugh. Nor do we consciously identify these routines as borrowed from comedy as we watch *Othello*. Such information is only useful if it helps us to track down the unique feeling of every episode, and this will be more complicated than in the equivalent one in comedy. When the Goldsmith demands the chain, confusing one twin with another, the absurdity of the situation is all-important, and we pay little attention to the inner state of those involved. When Othello calls for the handkerchief, his inner state and Desdemona's preoccupy us, while the absurdity of their mutual misunderstanding is pushed into the background. Actors and readers may argue about details but will agree, I hope, that this explosive episode in *Othello* is packed with implications, amongst others with potentially comic implications.

1 Cf. Honigmann, 'Shakespeare's mingled yarn and *Measure for Measure*', in the *Proceedings of the British Academy* (1981), 101–21.

Language

Imagery   The study of Shakespeare's imagery has been one of the success stories of our century. Others had prepared the way, then the books of G. Wilson Knight, Caroline Spurgeon and Wolfgang Clemen established Shakespeare's imagery as a technical resource that no critic can afford to ignore.[1]

Wilson Knight's 'The Othello music' (1930)[2] became an anthology favourite, and deservedly so. It analysed Othello's two styles, one 'diffuse, leisurely, like a meandering river', which 'radiates a world of romantic, heroic, and picturesque adventure', and is characterized by the use of resonant proper names, Anthropophagi, Ottomites, the Pontic Sea, the Propontic and Hellespont, Arabian trees, the turbanned Turk. This style expresses itself in terms of the 'machinery of the universe', the sun and moon, the ebb and flow of the sea, perceived in wonder:

> If heaven would make me such another world
> Of one entire and perfect chrysolite . . .
>
> (5.2.140–1)

The second style Wilson Knight described, less illuminatingly, as 'blatantly absurd, ugly'. He identified it with the spirit of Iago, a poison that invades Othello when he speaks in anger. Iago 'is the spirit of denial, wholly negative. He never has visual reality'. Wilson Knight's ideas are highly suggestive, though not always accurate. 'Awake the snorting citizens with the bell', 'And will as tenderly be led by th' nose / As asses are' – no visual reality? Again, Iago like Othello has a weakness for resonant names ('as acerb as coloquintida', 'Not poppy nor mandragora': 1.3.349–50, 3.3.333). Hero and villain differ, certainly, yet also resemble each other (see p. 33).

Imagery critics chose to dwell on the differences. 'Othello and Iago', said Clemen, 'have entirely different attitudes towards their

---

1   See particularly G. Wilson Knight, *The Wheel of Fire* (Oxford, 1930); Caroline F. E. Spurgeon, *Shakespeare's Imagery and What It tells Us* (Cambridge, 1935); Wolfgang Clemen, *The Development of Shakespeare's Imagery* (1951). Clemen's book was a revised version of his much earlier *Shakespeares Bilder* (Bonn, 1936).
2   In *The Wheel of Fire* (as in n. 1).

images. Iago is consciously looking for those which best suit his purpose. With Othello, however, the images rise naturally out of his emotions.'[1] When Iago thinks of love 'the image of rutting animals always makes its appearance in his imagination' (1.1.87, 110; 3.3.399);[2] from 3.3 'the imagery portrays Othello's inner alteration . . . [his] fantasy is filled with images of repulsive animals such as were up to that point peculiar to Iago'.[3] Iago speaks of 'the *trade* of war' (1.2.1, my italics), Othello sees war as his *occupation* (3.3.360), and so on. Clemen and Morozov,[4] both eager to demonstrate 'the individualization of Shakespeare's characters through imagery', significantly advanced our understanding but did so by way of sweeping generalization, as if Iago has only a single voice and Othello only two (his own, then his own transformed by Iago's).

It is also a weakness that imagery critics concentrated on nouns. Had they considered verbal action as well their emphasis might have been different. Verbal imagery, however, lends itself less readily to tabulation, even though an underlying picture or idea may be repeated. Take the imagery of entrapment: 'serve my turn upon him' (1.1.41), 'show out a flag' (154), 'practised on her with foul charms' (1.2.73), 'To keep us in false gaze' (1.3.20), 'gyve thee in thine own courtesies' (2.1.170), 'have our Michael Cassio on the hip' (303), 'They do suggest at first with heavenly shows' (2.3.347), or single verbs such as encave, enfettered, enmesh, ensnare, ensteeped. Such verbal imagery, less prominent than noun images, can have a similar function in defining character and 'the world of the play'.[5]

Othello and Iago Othello's language changes as he reacts to pressure, not only in its use of imagery. The fluidity and confident

1 Clemen, *Development* (as on p. 78, n. 1), 120.
2 Ibid., 128.
3 Ibid., 131–2.
4 See Mikhail Morozov, 'The individualization of Shakespeare's characters through imagery', *SS*, 2 (1949), 83–106.
5 Compare Catherine Bates, 'Weaving and writing in *Othello*', *SS*, 46 (1994), 51–60, and Madeleine Doran, 'Iago's "if": an essay on the syntax of *Othello*', in *The Drama of the Renaissance: Essays for Leicester Bradner*, ed. Elmer M. Blistein (Providence, Rhode Island, 1970), 69–99.

expansiveness of his narrative voice give way in Act 3 to shorter sentences, questions, exclamations, hesitations – 'Ha!', 'O misery!', 'Dost thou say so?', 'Nay, stay, thou shouldst be honest', 'Would? nay, and I will!', 'Death and damnation! O!' (3.3.167, 173, 208, 384, 396, 399). In the next scene this staccato voice changes even more, compared with his beautifully controlled speaking earlier, as he begins to shout at Desdemona ('The handkerchief! . . . The handkerchief!', 3.4.94ff.), and in the following one it breaks down altogether in the jumble of words before he falls in a trance. Thereafter a habit of repetition sets in, his mind seems to lose its grip, like that of a punch-drunk boxer: 'A fine woman, a fair woman, a sweet woman!' (4.1.175–6); 'Good, good, the justice of it pleases; very good! . . . Excellent good' (4.1.206ff.); 'you, you, ay you!' (4.2.94); 'O fool, fool, fool!' (5.2.321). This tendency begins in 3.3 ('O blood, blood, blood!', 454), and affects our response to one of his most mysteriously moving speeches, 'But yet the pity of it, Iago – O, Iago, the pity of it, Iago!' (4.1.192–3). He grieves for Desdemona, we grieve for Othello as well as his mind swings back and forth, out of control. In Acts 4 and 5 he appears to recover his earlier voice at times, though not without some signs of a willed performance. Beneath the rhetorical surface of 'It is the cause' and 'Soft you, a word or two' (5.2.1ff., 336ff.) we ought to sense tremendous strain[1] – after all, he steels himself in each case to deliver a death stroke. These language changes, indeed, may suggest that Othello's 'trance' is more than a brief attack of *petit mal*: it could be seen as a mental collapse from which he never fully recovers.

Iago's language likewise has its own characteristics. M. R. Ridley noticed its slipperiness. It often appears to say more than it does, or to mean very little, acting as a verbal smokescreen.

> He's that he is: I may not breathe my censure
> What he might be; if what he might, he is not,
> I would to heaven he were!
>
> (4.1.270–2)

---

1 Compare Adamson, 270: 'the surface calm of [Othello's] speech stretches over an abyss of quite other feelings'.

Iago's use of unfamiliar Latinate words has a similar bamboozling effect, the more so when these words are followed immediately by less opaque language.

> It was a violent commencement in her, and thou shalt see an answerable sequestration – put but money in thy purse.
>
> (1.3.345–7)

> unless his abode be lingered here by some accident – wherein none can be so determinate as the removing of Cassio.
>
> (4.2.227–9)

Iago, a connoisseur of language, comments on the speaking habits of other characters[1] and expertly switches his own voice as the occasion requires, from false courtesy to the most brutal directness.

Dislocated language   Throughout *Othello* Shakespeare is interested in what we may call dislocated language, which culminates in the verbal and physical breakdown of the epileptic fit (4.1.35–43n.). Brabantio's distracted questions (1.1.160–75) are perfectly natural in the circumstances, and have the added advantage of underlining Othello's calm in the next scene. Iago's nonsensical songs (2.3.65–92) exacerbate Cassio's drunkenness, which in turn leads to the confused shouting of the brawling soldiers. After the fit Othello again collapses into distracted speech at 4.1.253ff. ('Sir, she can turn, and turn, and yet go on'), he shouts at Emilia (4.2.94), and Desdemona's stunned reaction to the brothel scene introduces dislocating pauses, in the theatre if not in a reading text (4.2.99ff.). The night scene, with its various confusions, causes a more general breakdown (5.1.23ff.). Almost all of these incidents are engineered by Iago, repeating the successful formula of 1.1.66ff.

---

1   'Horribly stuffed with epithets of war' (1.1.13, of Othello); 'She puts her tongue a little in her heart / And chides with thinking' (2.1.106–7, of Emilia); 'He takes her by the palm; ay, well said, whisper' (2.1.167–8, of Cassio); 'I'll pour this pestilence into his ear' (2.3.351, of himself).

> Call up her father,
> Rouse him, make after him, poison his delight,
> Proclaim him in the streets, incense her kinsmen . . .

A different kind of dislocation occurs when two speakers pursue quite distinct trains of thought. Othello and Desdemona do so at 3.4.32–99, 4.1.225ff., 4.2.24ff., and, their most tragic dislocation, when he prepares to kill her (5.2.23ff.): each sequence ends with a form of breakdown, when all speaking stops. The dislocated language in *Othello* points to Shakespeare's wider interest in breakdown, which developed from *Julius Caesar* to *Hamlet* to *Othello* to *King Lear*.

Disbelieving the speaker   Should we believe what we are told? This is a nagging question in each of Shakespeare's tragedies. Must we believe Brutus' stated reasons for the necessity of killing Caesar, or Hamlet's for not killing Claudius? May dramatic characters deceive themselves in soliloquy? Yes, say some, because in Shakespeare's mature plays soliloquies enact thought processes, and we are all capable of deceiving ourselves. If so, how do we know for certain that we should not believe them? The answer is that in a play we know very little for certain: we have to evaluate what we hear in the light of the available evidence and we reach provisional conclusions, which may have to be modified later.

At the beginning of *Othello* we know nothing about antecedent events and we evaluate more tentatively than later, when we get our bearings. Is it really true that 'Three great ones of the city' off-capped to Othello, in support of Iago? And that Iago should have been promoted? Various signals warn us to be on our guard. Iago protests too vigorously (''Sblood . . . If ever I did dream / . . . abhor me') and refers to his enemies so sarcastically that one senses that he exaggerates; his grievance at being undervalued reinforces this impression. Then his account of himself ('not I for love and duty . . .') prepares us for Brabantio's assessment ('Thou art a villain!') and we come to the provisional conclusion that Iago is not to be trusted. His blatant lie that he was greatly tempted to stab Roderigo (1.2.1ff.) confirms these early impressions, which are all of a piece.

From the start Shakespeare establishes that we should not believe Iago when he talks to others; later we learn to distrust him even when he soliloquizes.[1] For different reasons the statements of other characters also need to be evaluated. Othello says 'Her father loved me' (1.3.129: see p. 23) – how correctly? Both Desdemona and Othello claim that theirs was a love of the mind (1.3.253, 266), and he actually disclaims physical 'appetite': his later agonized references to 'her sweet body', and the sensuousness of

> Who art so lovely fair and smell'st so sweet
> That the sense aches at thee

prove that he misjudged the importance of appetite,[2] underrating it just as Iago overrates it (2.1.219ff.).

It is particularly when Othello speaks of himself that we learn to distrust him. T. S. Eliot, in an influential paragraph, disbelieved Othello's final self-justification, 'Soft you, a word or two' (5.2.336ff.), and many critics agreed with him.

> What Othello seems to me to be doing in making this speech is *cheering himself up*. He is endeavouring to escape reality, he has ceased to think about Desdemona, and is thinking about himself . . . nothing dies harder than the desire to think well of oneself. Othello succeeds in turning himself into a pathetic figure, by adopting an *aesthetic* rather than a moral attitude, dramatizing himself against his environment. He takes in the spectator, but the human motive is primarily to take in himself. I do not believe that any writer has ever exposed this *bovarysme*, the human will to see things as they are not, more clearly than Shakespeare.[3]

Other characters, not only Othello, deceive themselves, but he has a special aptitude for self-deception, even when Iago is not directly responsible. Consider 'It is the cause' (5.2.1ff.), where he takes in a sharp-eyed critic. The speaker, said Bradley (197),

1 See Honigmann, *Seven Tragedies*, 78–88.
2 See 3.3.349, 4.2.69–70; also 4.1.176ff., 5.2.15–20.
3 T. S. Eliot, 'Shakespeare and the Stoicism of Seneca', in his *Selected Essays* (1953 edn), 130–1.

is not the man of the Fourth Act. The deed he is bound
to do is no murder, but a sacrifice. He is to save Desdemona from herself, not in hate but in honour; in honour,
and also in love. His anger has passed; a boundless sorrow
has taken its place.

Here Bradley accepts Othello's self-justification too readily, for
Othello relapses into anger almost immediately (73), re-enacting
the emotional seesaw of 'O, Iago, the pity of it, Iago . . . I will chop
her into messes' (4.1.190ff.). In 'It is the cause' he wants to persuade himself, committed as he thinks himself to noble action, yet
by this time we know how completely he is capable of surrendering
to illusions. The idea that Desdemona's death can be a sacrifice,
not a murder (5.2.65), repeats Brutus' self-deception – 'Let's be
sacrificers, but not butchers, Caius' (*JC* 2.1.166) – and this shows
that Shakespeare saw through Othello, even if Bradley didn't.

Othello's simplistic distinction between murder (or revenge)
and sacrifice resembles the other one that I have just mentioned,
between appetite and spiritual love, and brings us back to the
debate about his nobility (see p. 24). Othello divides all human
activity into higher and lower, and thinks of himself as invariably
committed to the higher, just as Iago always chooses the lower.
Othello sees himself as a Christian and Venetian, not as a pagan
Turk (2.3.165ff., 5.2.351), as clear running water, not as a foul
cistern (4.2.60ff.). At a definitive moment, as he tries to sum up
his life, he speaks of war:

> Farewell the neighing steed and the shrill trump,
> The spirit-stirring drum, th'ear-piercing fife,
> The royal banner, and all quality,
> Pride, pomp and circumstance of glorious war!
>
> (3.3.354ff.)

He recalls the 'higher' war, its glory and pageantry, and omits the
other, 'feats of broil and battle', 'being taken by the insolent foe /
And sold to slavery' (1.3.88, 138–9). 'Broil' – how evocative, how
different from the 'higher' view! In his idealizing speeches Othello
does not set out to deceive,[1] as Iago might, but he presents only

---

1 Cf. Adamson, 200: when Othello says of his love ''Tis gone' many critics 'seem
(rather credulously) to take him at his word'.

one kind of truth, not the whole truth. A reader may find it difficult to resist him, to disbelieve; in the theatre, however, we observe a battle-hardened soldier listening to Othello's glamorized retrospect – and what does Iago make of pride, pomp and circumstance?

General Many of the words used by Shakespeare almost four hundred years ago have changed their connotations, often by a process of narrowing. The commentary draws attention to the richer suggestiveness of the most ordinary words (e.g. blood, foul, put), and to the special meanings of seemingly familiar words (battle, knave, owe). In addition repeated words in a play need careful attention, especially elastic abstractions[1] (heaven, love, nature, soul) and deceptively straightforward words, such as 'black' in *Othello*. William Empson's essay on 'Honest in *Othello*' indicates some of the difficulties.[2] 'Honest', said Empson, 'carried an obscure social insult as well as a hint of stupidity', and 'good' (as in 'good Iago', 2.1.97, 2.3.30) was 'apparently a less obtrusive form of the same trick of patronage'. Hence Iago's resentment ('as honest / As I am': 2.1.199–200), and Cassio's when called 'good lieutenant' (2.3.101). Empson was not the first to comment on the social implications of these words. Simon Daines, in a book of 1640 'teaching the art of right speaking', recommended that 'gentlemen of quality' should address their social inferiors as '*Honest Thom. Kinde Ieffrey, Good Will*',[3] and in Richardson's *Clarissa* a servant objects to being called 'honest Joseph'.[4]

To understand the special flavour of Shakespeare's language we

---

1   Adamson often notes how words in *Othello* slide and skid from one sense to another. See also M. M. Mahood, *Shakespeare's Wordplay* (1957).
2   William Empson in *The Structure of Complex Words* (1964 edn), 219, 222n.
3   Simon Daines, *Orthoepia Anglicana* (1640), 90.
4   Samuel Richardson, *Clarissa*, Shakespeare Head edn, 8 vols (Oxford, 1930), 2.371. See also Toni Morrison on the hidden attitudes embedded in language: 'I am a black writer struggling with and through a language that can powerfully evoke and enforce hidden signs of racial superiority, cultural hegemony, and dismissive "othering" of people and language which are by no means marginal' (*Playing in the Dark: Whiteness and the Literary Imagination* (1992), x). I assume that Shakespeare was equally sensitive to attitudes 'hidden' in the language he used.

need to know the social implications of words, and their history – e.g. whether he coins a new word or uses one recently introduced into English. We need to recognize proverbial and semi-proverbial phrases, many of them no longer familiar, as well as echoes of the Bible and of classical texts. Readers who compare Arden 3 with earlier editions will find that the commentary offers many scores of new notes that attempt to convey the contemporary flavour of Shakespeare's language with greater precision. At the same time Arden 3 often glosses a word as 'could =' or 'perhaps =', to draw attention to possible meanings that other editors have ignored. Yet, strangely, even though the 'hinterland' of Shakespeare's language gives it a unique potency, making it differ in so many ways from modern English, readers can still enjoy the play without once glancing at the commentary – a sobering reflection for that well-intentioned drudge, the humble editor.

Stage imagery

The study of verbal imagery led inevitably to a reconsideration of stage imagery (objects and actions shown on the stage) and to the interconnections of the two.[1] R. B. Heilman[2] observed how innumerable allusions to the bridal bed prepare for its physical appearance in 5.2. This scene is dominated in many productions by a curtained four-poster, a thing of pomp and circumstance that becomes something like a cage from which Desdemona cannot escape (like her marriage). Her unpinned hair, flimsy nightdress and her position in bed, towered over by Othello, bring out her helplessness visually; her desperate verbal scurrying has a similar effect.[3]

The whole of Act 5, like the whole of Act 1, takes place by

---

1 See Clemen (as on p. 78, n. 1), 99–102, and R. A. Foakes, 'Suggestions for a new approach to Shakespeare's imagery', *SS*, 5 (1952), 89–90.

2 Heilman, 188–93. Later critics have rediscovered the importance of the bridal bed: e.g. Michael Neill ('Unproper beds', *SQ*, 40 [1989], 383–412), who notes (390) that in some productions the bed was introduced before 5.2.

3 Desdemona usually remains in the bed throughout 5.2, sometimes kneeling in it in prayer or to plead for mercy (Hankey, 315). In a few productions she has dashed across the stage to escape Othello.

night, and 2.3 is another night scene. Torches, tapers and candles would normally signal darkness to the audience; if there was any danger of sudden attack, as in 1.2, 2.3 and 5.1, the actors would move about in the 'darkness' with special caution. Iago chooses darkness for several of his planned attacks (1.1, 2.3, 5.1), and sees himself as a creature of 'Hell and night' (1.3.402); in darkness he can generate confusion, raising a 'dire yell / As when by night and negligence the fire / Is spied in populous cities' (1.1.74–6), 'cry a mutiny' (2.3.153), make more noise while pretending to quell it or while pretending that silence is somehow dangerous ('How silent is this town! Ho, murder, murder!', 5.1.64). Defeated in the end, the apostle of noise and confusion opts for silence (5.2.301) – an explosive silence, we may guess, not mere passivity (see p. 98).

In *Othello* there is a special emphasis on arrivals and awakenings. Before Desdemona's first appearance in the play we hear several conflicting accounts of her (1.1.85ff., 1.2.62ff., 1.3.60–170); she crosses the stage in silence, and we await her first words to find out which was right. Her measured sentences immediately modify previous impressions: she is neither headstrong nor bewitched, nor merely the impulsive, romantic and apparently motherless girl described by Othello. On the contrary, she confronts her angry father and later the Duke with complete presence of mind, not unlike her efficiency in the wooing scene. A series of carefully spaced arrivals follows in 2.1: Cassio, Desdemona and her party, Othello, each with elaborate greetings. No one pays much attention to Iago, a mere ensign, who none the less takes charge of the situation with astonishing speed (as in 1.1, 2.3, 3.3, 5.1). In the theatre Othello's and Desdemona's arrivals are tension-fraught as his moods change.

> Look where she comes:
> If she be false, O then heaven mocks itself
> (3.3.281–2)

> Look where he comes. Not poppy nor mandragora . . .
> (333)

Different kinds of awakening climax in two that are particularly theatrical. First, Othello recovers from his fit, on the ground, helpless, with Iago looking down upon him; next, Desdemona wakes up in bed to face her executioner, who also looks down upon his unconscious victim. In addition Brabantio, Othello and Desdemona are aroused at night (1.1.66ff., 2.3.159, 244), and Iago appears 'in his shirt' (5.1.47), as if from his bed. Cassio awakes from drunkenness, Othello from his belief in Desdemona's innocence, and they have to adjust to a new world. So, too, Desdemona, when Othello strikes her, treats her as a whore and tells her to prepare for death; Othello, when he learns the truth; Emilia, when she hears that her husband instigated the murder; Iago, when he realizes that the game is up. In a play in which confusion and mental readjustment are so important these awakenings are all connected, like theme and variations in music.[1]

Whether or not *Othello* qualifies as a domestic tragedy (see pp. 73ff.), verbal and stage imagery make much of the domestic side of life. Eating together, the basic ritual of every home, is frequently alluded to. Othello invites the islanders to dinner (3.3.284) and Lodovico to supper (4.1.263, 4.2.171); Bianca invites Cassio to supper, as Iago later remembers (4.1.158–63, 5.1.117–19). This never-ending domestic activity locks into the plot when Desdemona asks for Cassio's recall.

> Shall't be tonight, at supper? – No, not tonight. –
> Tomorrow dinner then? – I shall not dine at home.
> (3.3.57ff.)

Not tomorrow night, not Tuesday morn, nor Tuesday 'noon or night': she chooses meal times, when one sees one's friends, and he will have none of it. With Shakespeare's 'unlocalized stage' we cannot always know where each scene occurs, yet modern producers sometimes make 3.3 a domestic interior, even though people come and go as in a more public place. From 3.4 several scenes are progressively more domestic: 4.2, 4.3 and 5.2. Without 4.3 the play's homely dimension would be seriously diminished. The scene adds nothing to the plot, and yet how crucially it affects

---

1 Mack (138) defined 'the play's fundamental dramatic rhythm' as 'calm – sleep, in fact – invaded by uproar'.

pace and mood and our sense of domestic privacy, not to mention the relationship of Desdemona and Emilia and the suppressed 'feminism' that now breaks out! Only an insane producer would omit it.[1]

Many other stage directions deserve attention. I select one, the kneeling required by stage directions and 'implied stage directions' (i.e. implied by the dialogue). Nevill Coghill noted that Othello's kneel at 3.3.454 prepares for 'a still more important kneel that is to come', Desdemona's

> Here I kneel:
> If e'er my will did trespass 'gainst his love . . .
> (4.2.153ff.)

Othello and Desdemona are both brought to their knees before their trusted tormentor in 'a stroke of stage-craft of great visual force and point, a double demonstration of Iago's triumph'.[2] Presumably Desdemona kneels when she first appears, to Brabantio, or when she first addresses him, knowing that she has given offence.[3] When she next appears the islanders kneel to her ('You men of Cyprus, let her have your knees!'), no doubt led by Cassio, who worships 'the divine Desdemona' (2.1.84, 73). She kneels to Othello in the brothel scene ('Upon my knees, what doth your speech import?', 4.2.31), and perhaps elsewhere. Ceremonial kneeling (1.3, 2.1) is succeeded by more passionate vows and entreaties; it may be that she kneels before Othello kills her, that he smothers her as she makes a final, desperate appeal on her knees to God, an attempted prayer.

> DESDEMONA   [*kneeling*]
> But while I say one prayer!
> OTHELLO   It is too late.
> DESDEMONA
> O Lord! Lord! Lord! [*He*] *smothers her.*
> (5.2.82–3)

---

1   In previous centuries 4.3 was heavily cut, often losing all or part of its discussion of sexual morality (59–end). Sprague noted (400, n. 85) that Winter, in his long career as a playgoer, heard the Willow Song only once.
2   Nevill Coghill, *Shakespeare's Professional Skills* (Cambridge, 1964), 188–90.
3   'From early in the nineteenth century, Desdemona has knelt to her father on his exit [1.3.294]' (Sprague, 188).

The play in the theatre

This section is not intended as a 'stage history'. It deals with some representative and some unusual interpretations of *Othello* in the theatre, what actors, audiences and reviewers have liked and disliked in almost four hundred years of almost non-stop performance and comment. As the section is short, interested readers are advised to consult specialist studies of *Othello* in the theatre, and should keep in mind that around ninety prompt-books of the play dating from the nineteenth century or earlier still survive.[1]

Expurgation   From the Restoration to the present day *Othello* has been performed more often than not in a cut text. The cuts were often dictated by fashionable notions of 'refinement' and decorum, and point back to the supposed sensitivity of female members of the audience: the expurgation of Shakespeare's plays tells us much about the history of taste, and about the history of misunderstanding Shakespeare, less about the strengths and weaknesses of the plays as we today see them. It is now a matter of mainly historical interest to find that at Dublin's Smock Alley Theatre, Othello

> is not allowed to wish that housewives make a skillet of his helm or for his nature to be exchanged for that of a goat. It is beneath his dignity to set Emilia to spy on Desdemona . . . Gone too is the obsessive visual sexuality of

---

1   I have found Rosenberg, Sprague and Hankey particularly valuable. See also Charles H. Shattuck, *The Shakespeare Promptbooks: A Descriptive Catalogue* (Urbana, Illinois, 1965), and Carol J. Carlisle, *Shakespeare from the Greenroom: Actors' Criticisms of Four Major Tragedies* (Chapel Hill, North Carolina, 1969). Kenneth Tynan's *Othello: The National Theatre Production* (1966) is generously illustrated and explains how a production develops before and after the first night. Micheal MacLiammóir (in *Put Money in Thy Purse*, 1952) had previously given an account of the filming of the Orson Welles *Othello* (in which MacLiammóir played Iago. This film version juggled more than most theatre productions with the text). Martin L. Wine's *Othello* in the Text and Performance series (1984) comments usefully on several more recent productions (Olivier at the National Theatre; John Barton's Royal Shakespeare Company *Othello*, 1970–1; Peter Coe's American Shakespeare Theatre *Othello*, 1981–2; and Jonathan Miller's BBC *Othello*, with Anthony Hopkins and Bob Hoskins). In *Shakespeare in Performance: An Introduction through Six Major Plays* (New York, 1976) John Russell Brown expertly analyses the play's stage business line by line.

13 Still from the film *Othello*, directed by Orson Welles, 1951

his lines at the beginning of 4.1; and he goes to his death
without his tears like Arabian gum.[1]

By the middle of the eighteenth century 4.1 was cut even more
drastically. 'Gone are the delirium and the trance . . . gone the
humiliating eavesdropping on Cassio, Iago and Bianca' (Rosenberg, 35). Still dissatisfied, Francis Gentleman, an editor of acting
texts, preferred to eliminate all of 4.1.1–202, up to 'I'll not

1 Norman Sanders, ed., *Othello* (Cam³, 1984), 39, referring to the Smock Alley
Theatre, Dublin, in the later seventeenth century.

expostulate with her'. Starting here, he said, 'would save delicacy a blush or two'. J. P. Kemble and nineteenth-century 'theatrical' editors accepted his advice; enemies of lowness and indecency sanitized *Othello* in these and other ways. Bianca disappeared completely from many productions, a major amputation of supposedly infected matter (Hankey, 263); the two clown scenes and much else also disappeared.

Violence   More interesting from our point of view, taking us into a more dispute-worthy area, is the reaction to violence – in particular violence to women, such as Othello's striking of Desdemona (4.1.239; curiously, Iago's stabbing of Emilia caused less uproar amongst reviewers, perhaps because less attractive women are less important ... ?). Some Othellos struck Desdemona with the letter, and this was thought 'a shade better than the back-handed blow which Salvini delivers full on those sweet lips'.[1] The smothering of Desdemona, if violence was emphasized, filled many audiences and reviewers with indignation. In France the great Talma started 'a universal tumult. Tears, groans and menaces resounded from all parts of the theatre' (Rosenberg, 159); in England and America the even more sensational Salvini pounced upon Desdemona,

> lifted her into the air, dashed with her . . . across the stage and through the curtains, which fell behind him. You heard a crash as he flung her on the bed, and growls as of a wild beast over his prey.
>
> (Rosenberg, 113)

He was reviled for his pains – 'he arouses only horror in his audience'. One Desdemona, Helen Faucit, surprised audiences by fighting for her life. 'How could I be otherwise than "difficult to kill"?' she asked. 'I would not die dishonoured in Othello's esteem. This was bitterer than fifty thousand deaths' (Rosenberg, 114, 137–8). Shakespeare's women, we must remember, were played by boy actors until the Restoration. Whether he would have required actors to strike actresses we do not know: the boy

---

1   See Sprague (203), who adds 'Salvini struck her only with the paper'.

14 Edmund Kean as Othello

actors gave him opportunities for physical and mental violence that actresses might have inhibited.

Actors of Othello Recorded performers of Othello fall into two groups, those who stressed his thoughtful, noble, tender and grieving side and others who excelled in explosive acting. The former included Betterton ('serious, venerable, and majestic', Rosenberg, 20), J. P. Kemble, the American Edwin Booth, Henry Irving, and more recently Godfrey Tearle. The explosive Othellos won more acclaim, especially Kean and Salvini, although both also antagonized some reviewers by going to extremes; Garrick, however, attempted violence and was not a success.[1] Kean's Othello was described as 'the most terrific exhibition of human passion that has been witnessed on the modern stage' (Rosenberg, 62). Hazlitt, initially critical of Kean as 'too often in the highest key of passion, too uniformly on the verge of extravagance', later surrendered to his magic: Kean's Moor was 'the finest piece of acting in the world'.[2] Salvini, a specialist in 'animal fury', tiger-pacing and tiger-springs, comes to life in this account of 3.3.362ff.

> He rushes upon Iago, clutches him by the throat, and forces him down upon his knees . . . at times seeming almost to twist Iago's head from his body . . . [then] flings him prostrate upon the stage . . . Then, with clenched hands upraised, and distended eyes and passion-contorted face, he raises one foot, as if to stamp out Iago's life. He restrains himself . . . He then advances again quickly to the prostrate Iago, who raises his left hand, as if to ward off a fresh attack upon him. Othello grasps Iago's hand and raises him to his feet, with an inarticulate sound, expressive of grief, shame, regret . . .
>
> (Rosenberg, 110)

Like several other Othellos, Salvini could burst into convulsive tears (after 'Farewell: Othello's occupation's gone', after 'away, away, away!' and elsewhere). Killing himself in 5.2 he used a short scimitar: he 'literally cut and hacked at his throat and fell to

---

1 Cf. p. 68, n. 1.
2 Rosenberg, 66. For Hazlitt's criticism, see also Jonathan Bate, *Shakespearean Constitutions* (Oxford, 1989), 160–1.

TOMMASO SALVINI.*

15 Tommaso Salvini as Othello

16 Laurence Olivier (Othello) and Frank Finlay (Iago): National Theatre, 1964

the ground, gasping and gurgling' (Rosenberg, 114). Laurence Olivier owed much to reports of Salvini's very 'African' Othello, his ferociousness, primitivism, animal noises and modulations of mood. According to Henry James, an unlikely admirer, Salvini's tremendous force also made itself felt when he became 'magnificently quiet' (Rosenberg, 103).

Actors of Iago Actors of Iago come vividly to life in accounts of their stage business. Irving, at 1.3.393 ('How? How? let's see:'), covered his face with his two hands, then, after a long pause, 'slowly drew down his hands, revealing a face all alive with the devilish scheme which had come into his mind'. Watching Desdemona and Cassio at 2.1.167 he plucked and slowly ate a bunch of

17 Laurence Olivier (Othello) and Maggie Smith (Desdemona): National Theatre, 1964

grapes, 'spitting out the seeds, as if each one represented a worthy virtue'. When Cassio and Montano clash at 2.3.147ff., Irving's Iago enjoyed 'a mischievous sense of mastery by flicking at them with a red cloak, as if they were bulls in the arena'. Having run Roderigo through at 5.1.61, Irving turned over the body 'with his foot, in indolent and mocking curiosity . . . to see if life were extinct' (Sprague, 189, 191, 209). Some of these touches were widely imitated. The elder Booth, urging Roderigo to call up Brabantio (1.1.66), spoke with 'devilish unconcern . . . playing meanwhile with his sword-hilt'; John Ryder 'actually sat on the council table and coolly swung his leg' (1.3.302ff.); Fechter made a two-finger 'gesture of contempt' at Othello at 3.3.245 (Sprague, 185, 196). It will be noticed that in these various ways actors of Iago deliberately slowed down the action for their own benefit or accentuated Iago's diabolical inhumanity.

Actors have to resist two temptations: they tend to give Iago either too little or too much humanity. Some have turned him into a music-hall villain, with fiendish smiles of triumph over his victims, even at the very end of the play, pointing to the corpses (Kean, J. B. Booth and his son, Edwin Booth). John Vandenhoff advanced to the front of the stage at 4.2.136, as Emilia seems about to unmask him, 'and his features disclosed alternate emotions of rage and fear; at length, overpowering both, cunning resumes its sway' (Sprague, 196, 222–3, 206). At the other extreme, several actors have made Iago too gay, too jolly, too agreeable.[1] The best Iago that I remember, Antony Eustrel (Stratford, 1945, with George Skillan as Othello), managed to combine magnetic good looks and frightening glimpses of evil, indolence and lightning thrusts, but most actors overplay in one direction. That may be why Brian Vickers writes that 'there is no one in the world whose confidence I would rather share less than Iago's, and that is one of the reasons for the discomfort I feel each time I experience this play'.[2] Could it be that we are meant to feel discomfort – as also, perhaps, at the idea of miscegenation – or is Iago too difficult a part for actors to get just right?

Nevertheless, whether or not they get it right, Iago is an easier part than Othello to succeed in. Unless the actor of Othello has a commanding presence, Iago can unbalance and steal the play (this is not a question of physical size: Kean was a small man and a great Othello). The actors of Othello and Iago, often two 'stars', engage in a kind of tug of war, competing with one another professionally – an extra-dramatic contest that adds another dimension to the dramatic action. This extra-dramatic interest is heightened when the same two actors alternate as Othello and Iago – most famously in the case of Irving and Booth (1881). In addition,

---

1   Edwin Booth made Iago as 'unvillain-like' as possible; Kean transformed him into a 'flippant comedian' (Rosenberg, 128; Hankey, 177). Cf. Richardson, Fig. 9, p. 45.
2   Brian Vickers, *Returning to Shakespeare* (1989), 110.

18 Antony Eustrel as Iago: Shakespeare Memorial Theatre, Stratford-upon-Avon, 1945

some of the greatest actors have attempted both parts at different times (Kean, Macready, Forrest, Irving, Olivier), for the simple

19 Edwin Booth as Iago: painting by Thomas Hicks, 1863

reason that these are two of the most challenging parts in Shakespeare, offering totally different opportunities.

Audience reaction   I have stressed Salvini's uniqueness as a tempestuous Othello because, although Kean, Olivier and perhaps one or two others may have equalled him in theatricality, Salvini always spoke his lines in Italian, even when his fellow actors spoke English. This tells us something about the play. Unsurpassed in its poetry, it can still function without Shakespeare's words (Salvini assumed of course that the words were known). From Act 3 a storm of passion whirls the audience along; or, more accurately, words melt together with sound and movement and emotion and other rhythms that become irresistible, sympathy for the hero and heroine generates a momentum that overwhelms us, and these invisible reserves buoyed up Salvini's *Othello* despite a language barrier. The intensity of this special audience response is attested by spectators from the very first eye-witness account onwards.

In 1610 Shakespeare's King's Men 'drew tears not only by their speech but also by their action. Indeed, Desdemona, though always excellent, moved us especially in her death when, as she lay on her bed, her face itself implored the pity of the audience' (Rosenberg, 5). After Richard Burbage died in 1619 an anonymous elegy named 'the grieved Moor' as one of his outstanding roles. Shakespeare's friend and admirer Leonard Digges again noted the extraordinary audience reaction achieved by Burbage and his colleagues.

> oh how the Audience,
> Were ravish'd, with what wonder they went thence,
> When some new day they would not brooke a line,
> Of tedious (though well laboured) *Catiline[s]*;
> *Sejanus* too was irkesome, they priz'de more
> Honest *Iago*, or the jealous Moore.[1]

Mrs Siddons as Desdemona (in the late eighteenth century) aroused 'the most intense sympathy'. Addressing Iago ('Am I that name, Iago?', 4.2.120), she 'quite electrified the house' (Rosenberg, 52). When, in the nineteenth century, Macready as Othello took Iago by the throat, a gentleman in the audience cried 'Choke the devil! choke him!' (Sprague, 199).

---

1   Chambers, *Elizabethan Stage*, 2.309, and *William Shakespeare*, 2.233.

According to A. C. Sprague (199), anecdotes that show that spectators were completely swept away by the play 'are particularly numerous in the case of *Othello*, and furnish a curious tribute to its tragic intensity'.

Reading and seeing *Othello* As will be clear from this section, theatrical productions can transform a play. Not always for the better: that depends on the producer's tact. A badly cut text must change the rhythms of the play, and Shakespeare's sensitivity to the local and larger rhythms of a speech, a scene, or the 'echoing' of one episode by another, cannot be easily improved upon.

Two kinds of innovation are customary in the theatre – deliberate changes of the text (cuts, additions, or the changing of words), and new interpretations of roles and lines. I find the former inexcusable, except where words have lost all meaning for modern audiences; the latter offers opportunities for genuine creativeness, and can suddenly lift an average production, reanimating all that surrounds it. To illustrate: (1) We read that after he stabs himself at the end, the American Edwin Booth 'cries simply "O, Desdemona!", makes an effort to reach the bed, clutching (not much) for the curtains as he falls back dead' (Rosenberg, 87). (2) Another great American actor of the nineteenth century, Edwin Forrest, spoke 3.3.434 as never before. He 'began furiously, "I will tear her" – when his love came over it [i.e. returned], and he suddenly ended with pitying softness – "all to pieces"' (Rosenberg, 98). The first seems to me wrong; inserting 'O, Desdemona!' (from 5.2.279), it attempts a more tear-jerking death, 'better than Shakespeare'. The second, whether we like it or not, is a legitimate interpretation, one that refrains from changing the words, and it brings out the ding–dong of Othello's changes of mood. In a good production one can hope to experience many similar flashes of insight.

Again: the greatest tragedy?

We may now return to the question with which I began: why not place *Othello* with *Hamlet* and *King Lear*, why not give it its due as a tragedy unexcelled even by Shakespeare? Both *Hamlet* and

20 Edwin Forrest as Othello

King Lear are too long, it is often said; they sag under their own weight (this remains true even if we refuse to conflate the Quarto and Folio versions of *King Lear*), whereas no one complains of the length of *Othello*. And does *Othello* not surpass the other tragedies in many ways? *King Lear* peaks in three powerful episodes, the blinding of Gloucester, the reunion and deaths of Lear and Cordelia (3.7, 4.7, 5.3). In *Othello* we have to endure a greater number of episodes of at least equal power, the temptation scene, Othello's fit, his striking of Desdemona, the brothel scene, the murder of Desdemona – sustained without much lessening of tension throughout the second half of the play. The killing of Cordelia, moreover, is merely reported, that of Desdemona is enacted on the stage. It is not unfair to add that the tragic effect at the end of *King Lear* depends largely on pathos whilst in *Othello* it includes pity and also terror, as the mad conviction grips Othello that Desdemona has sinned and must die. The extraordinary momentum of *Othello* and the audience response it generates place it, in these respects, ahead of its nearest rivals, *Hamlet* and *King Lear*.

So why has this not been generally conceded? Bradley, who agreed that 'of all Shakespeare's tragedies . . . not even excepting *King Lear*, *Othello* is the most painfully exciting and the most terrible', must be held partly responsible. He argued that in *King Lear* 'the conflict assumes proportions so vast that the imagination seems, as in *Paradise Lost*, to traverse spaces wider than the earth. In reading *Othello* the mind is not thus distended.'[1] In reading – yes, perhaps. Should we not counter, though, that *Hamlet* and *King Lear* are particularly successful as reading plays, not easy to stage, and that *Othello* scores as a theatre play? Bradley went on to analyse 'the comparative confinement of the imaginative atmosphere' in *Othello*, a 'partial suppression of that element in Shakespeare's mind which unites him with the mystical poets and with the great musicians and philosphers'. *Othello*, he said,

> leaves an impression that . . . we are not in contact with the whole of Shakespeare. And it is perhaps significant in this respect that the hero himself strikes us as having, probably, less of the poet's personality in him than many

1 See Bradley, 176, 181. For Bradley on *Othello* see also Mark Gauntlett, 'The perishable body of the unpoetic: A. C. Bradley performs *Othello*', *SS*, 47 (1994), 71–80.

characters far inferior both as dramatic creations and as men.

(Bradley, 185, 186)

A strange view, coming from Bradley – for in an essay on 'Shakespeare the man' written at much the same time[1] he observed that Ben Jonson's tribute to Shakespeare 'almost quotes' Iago's words about Othello.

> The Moor is of a free and open nature
> That thinks men honest that but seem to be so.
> (1.3.398–9)

Shakespeare, said Jonson, 'was indeed honest, and of an open and free nature': consciously or unconsciously Jonson chose to describe his friend and fellow dramatist in terms originally applied to Othello, not to Hamlet or King Lear. Although Othello must not be seen as his creator's self-portrait, we may take it that Jonson's echo points to a significant resemblance between the Moor's personality and the poet's.

In a quite different way, Iago also speaks for Shakespeare. Attempting to manipulate the other characters, Iago is the dramatist inside the play; in soliloquy he weighs the options for his plot, as Shakespeare must have done, and no doubt his delight in his creative brilliance was shared by his only begetter. Iago's humour, too, though by no means identical with Shakespeare's (see p. 39), intersects with his creator's. For Shakespeare, writing the words of Iago was partly a voyage of self-discovery.

Returning now to Bradley's opinion that Othello has 'less of the poet's personality' than some of Shakespeare's inferior creations, we may answer that in this tragedy Shakespeare divided himself between the hero and villain.[2] Othello draws on

---

1 'Shakespeare the man', in A. C. Bradley, *Oxford Lectures on Poetry* (1909).

2 J. I. M. Stewart (as on p. 50, n. 2) thought that we find in Othello and Iago 'such an imaginative "splitting" as myth and poetry often employ to express violent polarities and ambivalences in the mind. The true protagonist of the drama . . . [should be apprehended] as interlocked forces within a single psyche . . . Iago is unreal . . . Othello is unreal . . . But the two together and in interaction are not unreal. The two together make your mind, or mine' (109–10). Equally we may say that 'the two together' make Shakespeare's mind (though Desdemona, Roderigo, etc., are also components). Cf. Hugh Kingsmill, *The Return of William Shakespeare* (1929), 168: '*Othello* expresses the struggle between two opposing forces in Shakespeare himself.'

Shakespeare's own emotional nature – the openness of his response to love and beauty (witness Ben Jonson and the *Sonnets*) – whereas Iago, like two other superlative characters, Falstaff and Cleopatra, has in common with Shakespeare an unflagging inventiveness, his skills in improvisation. In Iago, Falstaff and Cleopatra this expresses itself, among other things, in their habitual lying; in Shakespeare, in the invention of the plays and in contemporary anecdotes about his quickness in repartee.[1] Because Shakespeare divided himself *Othello* strikes us as less personal than *Hamlet*, where the prince sometimes seems to speak directly for the dramatist (e.g. in his advice to the players); on the other hand, the mysterious togetherness of Iago and Othello may be seen as no less personal, an outward manifestation of interior impulses – indeed, of a potential interior split.[2] For the Iago–Othello relationship is one of a series that stretches from Proteus–Valentine through Bolingbroke–Richard, Cassius–Brutus as far as Octavius–Antony, and represents something deeply embedded in the dramatist. He did not *have* to return to this formula again and again, since he could succeed without it – he chose to, and the locking together of Iago and Othello, of opportunist and idealist, the most intensely realized instance of this conflict, makes their tragedy quite as personal as *Hamlet*, even if less transparently so.

As for the 'partial suppression' of elements of Shakespeare's mind in *Othello*, we may admit that Hamlet and Lear have minds – very different minds – that seem to peer more successfully into 'the mystery of things' (*KL* 5.3.16; cf. *Ham* 3.2.366) and to range more widely than either Othello or Iago. Yet Othello and Iago *together* release energies and insights unattempted in the other tragedies: again we must beware of false comparisons. And 'the comparative confinement of the imaginative atmosphere' in *Othello*? If we try to judge from specific examples the danger of invalid comparisons is once more obvious. Take Shakespeare's visions of death and annihilation: how does Othello compare with the other tragic heroes? Perhaps his view is more confined, less 'universal', than Lear's 'Blow, winds, and crack your cheeks'

---

1 For Shakespeare's quickness in repartee and composition, see Chambers, *William Shakespeare*, 2.212, 230, 232, 245, etc.

2 See p. 105, n. 2.

(3.2.1) or Macbeth's 'pity, like a naked new-born babe / Striding the blast' (1.7.21). Othello's

> Blow me about in winds, roast me in sulphur,
> Wash me in steep-down gulfs of liquid fire!
> (5.2.277–8)

is more personal than universal. Might we not say the same, though, of Hamlet's 'To be or not to be'? And should *Hamlet* count as inferior for that reason?

Othello differs from *Hamlet*, *King Lear* and *Macbeth* in being more insistently time-bound, concerned with the here and now rather than with eternal verities. In *Othello* the philosophizing habit belongs to Iago, whose thinking we quickly learn to distrust. But do we really rate the other tragedies so highly because of the truth of their philosophizing? Or could it be that we admire the intensity of their truth-seeking rather than the profundity of their ideas? And if intensity is our criterion, who is more intense than Othello?

A further alleged difference between *Othello* and the other great tragedies is this: the others stretch and enrich the 'imaginative atmosphere' by their use of the supernatural (the gods in *King Lear* are almost physically present. Do we not hear their thunder?). Once more *Othello* seems to suffer in the comparison, though again only if we seek for exact parallels. As in the other tragedies we should be aware of a metaphysical or cosmic contest between Good and Evil. Welcoming the 'divine Desdemona' to Cyprus, Cassio kneels and salutes her, 'Hail to thee, lady, and the grace of heaven . . . Enwheel thee round!' (2.1.85–7). This, I have said, comes close to being a 'Hail Mary', and her identification with heaven continues to the end of the play. 'If she be false, O then heaven mocks itself', 'O, the more angel she . . . O, she was heavenly true!' (3.3.282, 5.2.128–33). Iago, her opposite, speaks for hell. He thinks of himself as supported by 'all the tribe of hell', by 'Hell and night' (1.3.358, 402).

> Divinity of hell!
> When devils will the blackest sins put on
> They do suggest at first with heavenly shows . . .
> (2.3.345–7)

Although the dramatic conflict centres on Othello and Iago, the principals of what we may call the metaphysical conflict are Iago and Desdemona. They compete for Othello's soul almost like Mephistopheles and the Good Angel for Faustus's, continuing an earlier dramatic tradition in which the 'Everyman' figure's love–hate relationship with his tempter sometimes anticipates that of Othello and Iago. At the end Othello, like Faustus, foresees his own damnation.

The devil will come, and Faustus must be damned.[1]

When we shall meet at compt
This look of thine will hurl my soul from heaven
And fiends will snatch at it.

(5.2.271–3)

Some critics think 'the damnation of Othello' as certain as that of Faustus.[2] Must this follow? Desdemona and Iago are not literally an angel and a devil; Othello, sentencing himself to an eternity of suffering 'in steep-down gulfs of liquid fire' (5.2.278), may err as grievously as in sentencing Desdemona to death.

The metaphysical conflict which, *pace* Bradley, distends the play's 'imaginative atmosphere' and the viewer's mind, must be understood as both internal and external – internal within Desdemona and Iago, as well as within Othello. Whenever Desdemona checks herself under extreme provocation we are conscious of the unconquerable strength of Goodness. Othello cries 'Devil!', strikes her – and? – 'I have not deserved this' (4.1.240). There is a question here, an effort to comprehend, no anger. Reacting to his virulence in the brothel scene she appeals repeatedly to heaven, without once throwing accusations back at him; her last words before death are an act of forgiveness, in the spirit of 'Father, forgive them; for they wot not what they do' (Luke 23.34). And just as Iago's poison invades Othello, a spiritual 'flow' from Desdemona enters into and strengthens Emilia in Acts 4 and 5.

Externalized, the same forces confront each other in the persons of Desdemona and Iago. We already sense that they obey

1 *Doctor Faustus* (Revels, 1993), 5.2.76.
2 Cf. p. 73, n. 1.

different moral imperatives when he tries to get under her skin with sexual innuendo (2.1.109ff.), his characteristic mode of attack – a light preliminary skirmish with as yet undefined implications. Later they are brought face to face and engage in a life-and-death struggle (4.2.112–73) that can only be fully appreciated in the theatre. Merely reading the play we notice that neither Desdemona nor Iago seems to know what to do, and we can misjudge the episode as a pause, a diminuendo. Nothing could be farther from the truth. Desdemona, appealing to Iago for help, too stunned for tears, actually forgives her unknown enemy when Emilia so very nearly unmasks him.

> IAGO
> Fie, there is no such man, it is impossible.
> DESDEMONA
> If any such there be, heaven pardon him.
>   (4.2.136–7)

Her anguish is almost unbearable. In the theatre we wonder how Iago can resist it and reconcile himself to her 'heavenly' forgiveness – the opposite of all he stands for – and her kneeling insistence on the purity of her love. Between them, Desdemona and Emilia put Iago under tremendous moral pressure, without knowing it: we watch him, to see what Evil can say for itself. Wilson Knight suggested that the actor should keep his own counsel.

> Let Iago turn up-stage after Desdemona's exit and stand with his back to the audience. Iago must not be shown as positively callous of her pathetic position, nor as deeply moved by it. He speaks courteously enough to her. It is just outside his inhuman attention. I do not think that the producer should commit himself.[1]

In the Globe theatre Iago could not 'stand with his back to the audience', as it more or less surrounded the stage. Harold Goddard (vol. 2, 98) came closer to the mark: Iago's thoughts may remain a secret, yet Desdemona's effect on him is perfectly visible.

---

1   G. Wilson Knight, *Shakespearian Production* (1964), 102.

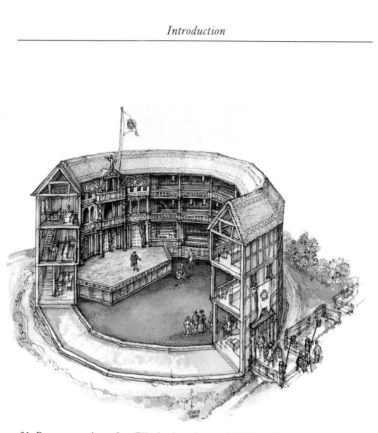

21 Reconstruction of an Elizabethan theatre (the Rose theatre): by
    C. Walter Hodges

When Desdemona goes out, Roderigo enters, and in the
first part of what ensues we see Iago for the first time at
his wit's end, unable to devise anything by way of answer
to Roderigo's importunities. In his brief and stalling replies to his dupe's reiterated complaints Shakespeare is
plainly registering the profound and disturbing effect
that Desdemona – and incidentally Emilia – has just had
on him. She has sapped his power.

Love and Goodness defeat Evil; not absolutely, at this point, yet
anticipating Iago's collapse in 5.2. There again he keeps his own

counsel ('From this time forth I never will speak word'), though once more the effect on him must be discernible.

Is it a little old-fashioned to write of Good and Evil in Shakespeare? If it seems so, let us not forget that he lived four hundred years ago, wrote unashamedly in this old-fashioned vein, perhaps even achieved pre-eminence partly because of his interest in the metaphysical world. We must accept him on his own terms. Critics as different as A. C. Bradley, Terence Hawkes, Norman Rabkin, Elias Schwartz[1] and many more have found it necessary to comment on the fierce dispute of Good and Evil in *Othello* – justifiably, since this less visible conflict is somehow connected with the human drama that we observe in the foreground, much as in the other tragedies.

Othello, though it differs from the other tragedies, has more in common with them than Bradley and his followers allowed. Yet in *Othello* Shakespeare also set himself new targets: to explore, from the inside, human nature on the very verge of its confine, man as devil, woman as angel. In the centre, between them, he placed human nature mysteriously right and not right, familiar and yet unknown – a non-European. The artistic daring of this choice is now easily missed. Shakespeare, at the height of his powers, exerting himself to the utmost, achieved perfect command of his material and – let us put it unaggressively – gave the world a tragedy as magnificently Shakespearian as any in the canon.

1 Bradley, 35; Terence Hawkes, *Shakespeare and the Reason* (1964), 100; Norman Rabkin, *Shakespeare and the Common Understanding* (New York, 1967), 67–9; Elias Schwartz, *SEL 1500–1900*, 10 (1970), 297–313.

THE TRAGEDY OF

OTHELLO,
THE MOOR OF
VENICE

LIST OF ROLES

OTHELLO	*the Moor [a general in the service of Venice]*
BRABANTIO	*father to Desdemona [a Venetian senator]*
CASSIO	*an honourable lieutenant [who serves under Othello]*
IAGO	*a villain [Othello's ancient or ensign]*
RODERIGO	*a gulled gentleman [of Venice]*
DUKE	*of Venice*
SENATORS	*[of Venice]*
MONTANO	*governor of Cyprus [replaced by Othello]*
GENTLEMEN	*of Cyprus*
LODOVICO *and* GRATIANO	*two noble Venetians [Desdemona's cousin and uncle]*
SAILOR	
CLOWN	
DESDEMONA	*wife to Othello [and Brabantio's daughter]*
EMILIA	*wife to Iago*
BIANCA	*a courtesan [and Cassio's mistress]*

[Messenger, Herald, Officers, Gentlemen,
Musicians and Attendants
Scene: Act 1, Venice; Acts 2–5, Cyprus]

THE TRAGEDY OF OTHELLO, THE MOOR OF VENICE

[1.1]   *Enter* RODERIGO *and* IAGO.

RODERIGO

    Tush, never tell me, I take it much unkindly

    That thou, Iago, who hast had my purse

    As if the strings were thine, shouldst know of this.

IAGO

    'Sblood, but you'll not hear me. If ever I did dream

    Of such a matter, abhor me.

RODERIGO   Thou told'st me   5

    Thou didst hold him in thy hate.

IAGO   Despise me

    If I do not. Three great ones of the city,

LIST OF ROLES. See LN.

1.1 For the act and scene divisions, see p. 352, and *Texts*, 31. Location: a street outside Brabantio's house in Venice. Shakespeare is vague about many details (*this*, 3, *him*, 6, *her*, 73): we have to piece them together. Iago and Roderigo, it seems, have been arguing for some time. It is night (*Awake*, 78).

  1 **Tush** a mild oath, removed from some play-texts as 'profanity' (Marlowe, 2, 247). Such exclamations (cf. *'Sblood*, 4) could be treated as extra-metrical. **much unkindly** with much dissatisfaction

  2 **thou** might be misread as *you* (cf. Q; *Texts*, 83)

    Iago three syllables

  3 **strings** 'threaded strings by drawing

which the mouth of a purse is closed' (*OED*); hence, to hold the purse strings

  4 **'Sblood** God's blood, an oath expurgated in F (see p. 352)

4–5 **If ... matter** semi-proverbial (Dent, D592, 'He never dreamed of it')

4–6 For the scansion, see *Texts*, 122–3.

  5 **abhor** '*Abhor* retains the literal sense of the Latin *abhorreo*, "shrink from me in horror" ' (Kittredge).

  6 **him** Othello: not identified until 32, and persistently misrepresented by Iago in 1.1

  7 **great ones** Did Shakespeare know of Venice's *Savii Grandi* (elected by the Senate to superintend boards beneath it, in effect ministers of state)? See Wotton, 1.413n.

1.1] *Actus Primus. Scoena Prima. F; not in Q* 0.1 RODERIGO *and* IAGO] *as* F *(Rodorigo) throughout; Iago* and *Roderigo Q (Roderigo) throughout* 1 Tush] *Q; not in* F 2 thou] F; you *Q* hast] F; has *Q* 3 the] ẙ F 4–7] *as* F; *Q lines* heare me, / abhorre me. / hate. / Citty 4 'Sblood] *Q; not in* F you'll] you'l F; you will *Q*

115

In personal suit to make me his lieutenant,
Off-capped to him, and by the faith of man
I know my price, I am worth no worse a place.   10
But he, as loving his own pride and purposes,
Evades them, with a bombast circumstance
Horribly stuffed with epithets of war,
And in conclusion
Nonsuits my mediators. For 'Certes,' says he,   15
'I have already chose my officer.'
And what was he?
Forsooth, a great arithmetician,
One Michael Cassio, a Florentine,
A fellow almost damned in a fair wife   20
That never set a squadron in the field

8 **lieutenant** In *H5* Ancient Pistol is also 'lieutenant' (2.1.26, 39): Cassio is a different kind of lieutenant, hence the sharp distinction in 31, 32. See LN.

9 **Off-capped** took off their caps (any headdress for men, not a modern cap), as a sign of respect

10 **price** worth; suggesting 'the price by which my support may be purchased' (*OED* 4), i.e. the lieutenancy

12 **Evades** avoids giving a direct answer, puts off (a questioner) (*OED* 3b, first here)
bombast (cotton or cotton wool, used as stuffing for clothes): bombastic (language)
circumstance circumlocution; formality (*OED* 6, 7)

13 **stuffed** padded; crammed (of speech: *OED* 9)
epithets terms, expressions. Cf. *MA* 5.2.66, 'Suffer love! a good epithite!' (Q)

15 **Nonsuits** stops the suit of, refuses (legal: causes the voluntary withdrawal of the petition) (unique in Shakespeare)
mediators suitors, go-betweens

Certes truly (an 'upper-class' word; could be monosyllabic). As QF use no quotation marks, we could read ' "For, certes," says he'.

16 **my officer** The captain appoints and dismisses his own officers (see LN, 1.1.8), hence is their *master* (41ff.).

17 **And ... he?** seems to complete 14 as one pentameter (cf. 5.2.81ff.). Perhaps Iago raises his voice at *And* (14, 17), suggesting an interrupted line.

18 **Forsooth** sneering at 'genteel' oaths: cf. Iago's *'Sblood*, 4, Othello's *Certes*, 15.
arithmetician sneering at Cassio's lack of experience of battle (cf. *bookish theoric*, 23). Yet others think differently, appointing Cassio to succeed Othello (4.1.237).

19 **Florentine** Machiavelli was seen as the quintessential Florentine, hence 'a crafty devil'. Cf. 3.1.41n., 2.1.235–46.

20 **A ... wife** unexplained. Perhaps a line deleted by Shakespeare: an unmarried Cassio suits his plot better (*Texts*, 36). See LN.

21 **squadron** a body of soldiers drawn up in square formation

9 Off-capped] *F;* Oft capt *Q*   11 purposes] *QF;* purpose *Theobald*   14] *Q; not in F*   16–17] *one line QF*   16 chose] *F;* chosen *Q*   20 damned] dambd *Q;* damn'd *F*

Nor the division of a battle knows
More than a spinster – unless the bookish theoric,
Wherein the toged consuls can propose
As masterly as he. Mere prattle without practice   25
Is all his soldiership – but he, sir, had th'election
And I, of whom his eyes had seen the proof
At Rhodes, at Cyprus and on other grounds,
Christian and heathen, must be be-leed and calmed
By debitor and creditor. This counter-caster   30
He, in good time, must his lieutenant be
And I, God bless the mark, his Moorship's ancient!
RODERIGO

By heaven, I rather would have been his hangman.
IAGO

Why, there's no remedy, 'tis the curse of service:

22 **division** methodical arrangement
battle a body of troops or the main
body of an army (*OED* 8, 9)
23 **unless** but for
24 **toged** togèd. Both Q and F are possible, *toged* from Lat. *togatus*, wearing
the toga (the garb of peace), *tongued*
as in *Cym* 3.2.5, 'as poisonous
tongued as handed'. Tongue could be
spelled *tong* (*R2* 5.5.97, Q), so this
may be misreading (*Texts*, 83), as in
Q *MV* 1.1.112 (togue) and F *Cor*
2.3.115 (*tongue* for *toge*).
consuls councillors
propose hold forth
25 **prattle ... practice** Cf. Dent,
P550.1, 'more prattle than practice'
(first recorded 1611; echoing *Oth*?).
26 **election** formal choosing of a person
for an office, usually by a vote (*OED* 1a,
c). Whether or not others voted, Iago
believes that it was Othello's decision.
27 **his** i.e. Othello's
28 **on ... grounds** in ... lands
29 **be-leed** left without wind (of ships),
left high and dry
calmed becalmed

30 **By ... creditor** by a mere book-
keeper. Or is it hinted that Cassio was
promoted to pay back a favour? Cf.
Cym 5.4.168.
counter-caster a coinage; 'one who
counts with the assistance of counters
or an abacus, but here much the same
as the *arithmetician* [18]' (Ridley)
31 **in good time** indeed (ironical, ex-
pressing amazement, incredulity:
OED time 42c). Cf. *Forsooth*, 18.
32 **God ... mark** Dent, G179.1, 'God
bless (save) the mark': cf. *RJ* 3.2.53.
'An apologetic or impatient exclamation when something horrible or disgusting has been said' (*OED* mark 18).
Moorship's Shakespeare's coinage,
on the analogy of kingship, general-
ship, worship (sarcastic)
ancient a standard-bearer, ensign.
'Our "colour-sergeant" or perhaps
"regimental sergeant-major" would
be an approximation' (Ridley).
34 **no remedy** no help for it, no alternative. Cf. *TN* 3.4.296, 305, 333.
service public or military service;
serving a master

24 toged] *Q ;* Tongued *F* 26 th'] *F ;* the *Q* 28 Cyprus] *F (*Ciprus*); Q (Cipres) throughout*
other] *Q ;* others *F* 29 Christian] *Q ;* Christen'd *F* be be-leed] *F ;* be led *Q* 32 God] *Q ; not in*
F ; Sir *Q2 (*Sir (blesse the marke) *...)* Moorship's] *as F ;* Worships *Q* 34] *QF lines* remedy,
/ seruice, / Why] *F ;* But *Q*

Preferment goes by letter and affection   35
And not by old gradation, where each second
Stood heir to th' first. Now sir, be judge yourself
Whether I in any just term am affined
To love the Moor.

RODERIGO   I would not follow him then.

IAGO

O sir, content you!   40
I follow him to serve my turn upon him.
We cannot all be masters, nor all masters
Cannot be truly followed. You shall mark
Many a duteous and knee-crooking knave
That, doting on his own obsequious bondage,   45
Wears out his time much like his master's ass
For nought but provender, and, when he's old,
    cashiered.
Whip me such honest knaves! Others there are

35 i.e. promotion comes if you have supporting letters and the goodwill of
friends, viz. by favouritism. Cf. 7: did
three great ones really plead for Iago?
36 **old gradation** advancing step by
step, according to seniority, as of old
38 **Whether** could be monosyllabic
('whe'er')
term respect; footing. Usually plural,
'in . . . terms'.
affined bound
39 **follow** serve
40 **content you** don't worry about that!
41 **serve my turn** common (= to serve
my purpose), less usual with *upon*.
Hinting at 'to turn the tables upon
him'?
42 **We . . .¹ masters** Dent, M107: 'Every
man cannot be a master' (from 1592).
43 **truly** faithfully
shall mark i.e. may observe
44 **duteous** subservient
knee-crooking bowing, making a
leg, as in *Ham* 3.2.61, 'crook the

pregnant hinges of the knee' (Ridley)
(unique in Shakespeare)
knave servant; anyone of low status
45 **obsequious** obedient, dutiful; cring-
ing (*OED* 1, 2)
bondage slavery; subjection (*OED* 2,
3)
46 **Wears out** passes, spends
time life-time (*OED* 7). Cf. *AYL*
2.7.142, 'one man in his time plays
many parts'.
47 **provender** food; fodder (for animals). Apprentices and servants often
received board and lodging in their
master's house.
cashiered i.e. he's cashiered. But
this word, hanging loose in the sentence, could be an exclamation: 'and
when he's old – cashiered! –'
48 **me** as far as I'm concerned (ethic
dative, 'for me'). Almost 'for my
sake'. Petty offenders (usually *dis-
honest knaves*) were whipped.

36 And . . . by] *F;* Not by the *Q*   37] *as F; two lines Q* first: /   to th'] to' th' *F;* to the
Q   38 affined] *F;* assign'd *Q*   42 all be] *F;* be all *Q*   47 nought] noughe *Q;* naught *F*   48–51]
as F; Q lines knaues: / formes, / hearts, / throwing / Lords, /

118

Who, trimmed in forms and visages of duty,
Keep yet their hearts attending on themselves   50
And, throwing but shows of service on their lords,
Do well thrive by them, and, when they have lined
    their coats,
Do themselves homage: these fellows have some soul
And such a one do I profess myself. For, sir,
It is as sure as you are Roderigo,   55
Were I the Moor, I would not be Iago.
In following him I follow but myself:
Heaven is my judge, not I for love and duty
But seeming so, for my peculiar end,
For when my outward action doth demonstrate   60
The native act and figure of my heart
In complement extern, 'tis not long after

---

49 **trimmed** dressed up
   forms images; customary ways; set
   methods of behaviour (*OED* 2, 11,
   14)
   visages assumed appearances (*OED*
   8); i.e. faces like masks, concealing
   their feelings
50 Cf. the 'clever slave' of classical
   comedy who boasts 'My dependence
   is wholly on myself' (e.g. Terence,
   Phormio, 139).
51 **throwing** directing (*OED* 15, 16)
52 elide: *by⌐m, they⌐ve* (see *Texts*,
   121)
   lined their coats Dent compares 'to
   line one's purse' (P664; from 1521).
53 **Do ... homage** i.e. pay themselves
   their due, serve their own interests.
   Here we begin to see two Iagos.
   soul i.e. spirit. Cf. Othello's use of
   the word!
54 **For, sir** extra-metrical
56–7 **Were ... myself*: F follows Q's
   colon and full stop, but this punctuation is probably without authority

(*Texts*, 127ff.). Reversing the colon
and stop we make the lines slightly
less baffling. 'Were I the Moor, I
would not wish to be Iago. [But,
being Iago,] I only follow him to
follow my own interests.'
58 **Heaven ... judge** Dent, G198.1,
   'God (Heaven) is my judge.'
   not ... love I do not follow him out
   of love.
59 **peculiar end** private purpose
60 **demonstrate** (probably stressed on
   second syllable) manifest, exhibit
61 **native** innate, i.e. secret
   act activity or active principle (*OED*
   3; Hulme, 288)
   figure appearance; design
62 **complement extern** outward show
   or completeness. Complement and
   compliment were not distinguished:
   Iago implies outward 'civility' or
   'complement' to the inner. 'When his
   actions exhibit the real intention and
   motives of his heart *in outward completeness*' (Knight, in Furness).

52–3] *QF lines* 'em, / coates, / homage, / soule, /   52 them] *F;* 'em *Q*   53 these] *F;* Those
Q   54 For, sir] *as QF; om.* Pope   56–7 Iago. . . . myself:] *this edn;* Iago: . . . my selfe. *QF*   60 doth]
F; does *Q*

But I will wear my heart upon my sleeve
For daws to peck at: I am not what I am.

RODERIGO

What a full fortune does the thicklips owe   65
If he can carry't thus!

IAGO   Call up her father,
Rouse him, make after him, poison his delight,
Proclaim him in the streets, incense her kinsmen,
And, though he in a fertile climate dwell,
Plague him with flies! Though that his joy be joy   70
Yet throw such changes of vexation on't
As it may lose some colour.

RODERIGO

Here is her father's house, I'll call aloud.

IAGO

Do, with like timorous accent and dire yell
As when by night and negligence the fire   75

---

63 **wear … sleeve** 'I will expose my feelings to everyone' (*OED* heart 54f). Cf. Greene's *Planetomachia* (1585), E1b, 'they weare their hearts in their handes … their thoughts in their tongues end'; Dent, F32, 'He pins his faith (etc.) on another man's sleeve.' Servants wore their master's badge on their sleeve.

64 **daws** jackdaws, proverbially foolish
I … am appears to mean 'I am not what I seem' (cf. *TN* 3.1.141). Profanely alluding to God's 'I am that I am' (Exodus 3.14: cf. 1 Corinthians 15.10).

65 **full fortune** perfect good fortune
thicklips unique in Shakespeare (but cf. *Tit* 4.2.175, the Moor to his child, 'you thick-lipp'd slave', and pp. 14–15 above)
owe own, possess

66 **carry't** carry it off, win the day (*OED* 15). Cf. *MW* 3.2.69–70.

67 **him … him … his** i.e. Brabantio. Some editors think 'the "him" throughout is Othello' (Walker), because of F's punctuation: yet F's punctuation has little authority (*Texts*, 127ff.).
make after pursue

69 **though** even though (he already dwells in a fertile climate, plague him with more flies)

70–2 **Plague … colour** plague him with further irritations; though his delight be (unalloyed) delight, yet direct such harassments against it that it may lose some reason for its existence (*OED* colour 12b). Some editors prefer F *chances* (*OED* 2: mischances, accidents).

70 **Though that** i.e. though

74 **timorous** fear-inspiring, terrible
accent tone, voice

75 elliptical: as when a fire which gained hold by negligence at night

64 daws] *F*; Doues *Q*   65 full] *Q*; fall *F* thicklips] *Q*; Thicks-lips *F*   66 't] *F*; 'et *Q*
68 streets, incense] streete, incense *Q*; Streets. Incense *F*   71 changes] *Q*; chances *F* on't] *F*; out *Q*   74 timorous] timerous *QF*

Is spied in populous cities.

RODERIGO

What ho! Brabantio, Signior Brabantio ho!

IAGO

Awake, what ho, Brabantio! thieves, thieves, thieves!
Look to your house, your daughter and your bags!
Thieves, thieves!   80

BRABANTIO [*appears above*] *at a window.*

BRABANTIO

What is the reason of this terrible summons?
What is the matter there?

RODERIGO

Signior, is all your family within?

IAGO

Are your doors locked?

BRABANTIO   Why? Wherefore ask you this?

IAGO

Zounds, sir, you're robbed, for shame put on your
     gown!   85
Your heart is burst, you have lost half your soul,
Even now, now, very now, an old black ram

78, 80 **thieves** Iago's repetitions generate hysteria: cf. 87.

79 **bags** money bags

80.1 ***window*** Some Elizabethan play-
houses had an upper stage or balcony
and/or upper windows.

81 **What is** scan *what's*
terrible stronger than today:
terrifying

85 **Zounds** = by God's (or Christ's)
wounds
for shame fie. How characteristic of
Iago to accuse Brabantio of shame-

lessness just when he himself speaks
so shamelessly!
gown coat; or, senator's gown

86 **burst** broken

87 **very** (intensive) i.e. at this very
moment
old the first hint as to Othello's age
ram Cf. *OED* rammish: lustful, lascivious. An old husband with a young
wife was a traditional butt of comedy
(Plautus, *Miles Gloriosus*, 965; see p.
76 above).

---

77 Signior] Seignior *Q (throughout)*; Siginor *F*   78 ³thieves] *Q*; *not in F*   79 ²your] *F*; you
Q   80.1] *this edn;* Brabantio *at a window. Q*; *Bra. Aboue. F(SP)*   81 terrible summons?] *Q*; *F*
lines terrible / there? /   84 your ... locked] *F*; all doore lockts *Q*   Why?] *F*; Why,
Q   85 Zounds] *Q*; *not in F*   you're] y'are *F*; you are *Q*   87 ²now] *F*; *not in Q*

Is tupping your white ewe! Arise, arise,
Awake the snorting citizens with the bell
Or else the devil will make a grandsire of you,   90
Arise I say!

BRABANTIO   What, have you lost your wits?

RODERIGO
Most reverend signior, do you know my voice?

BRABANTIO
Not I, what are you?

RODERIGO   My name is Roderigo.

BRABANTIO
The worser welcome!
I have charged thee not to haunt about my doors: 95
In honest plainness thou hast heard me say
My daughter is not for thee; and now in madness,
Being full of supper and distempering draughts,
Upon malicious bravery dost thou come
To start my quiet?   100

RODERIGO
Sir, sir, sir –

BRABANTIO   But thou must needs be sure
My spirit and my place have in them power
To make this bitter to thee.

---

88 **tupping** (of rams) copulating with.
Cf. 3.3.399, *topped*.
white white (as opposed to black);
pure, unstained; precious, beloved
(*OED* 7, 9)

89 **snorting** snoring, sleeping heavily;
or, snorting like animals
bell alarm bell

90 **devil** monosyllabic. Othello, because
devils were thought to be black. Cf.
1.2.63, 'Damned as thou art', 5.2.129.

92 **reverend** respected
know my voice It is too dark to see
him.

94 **worser** double comparative, not unusual (Abbott, 11)

98 **distempering draughts** intoxicating
liquor

99 **Upon . . . bravery** in bravado, in defiance (*OED* 1). F *knauerie* 'is slightly
redundant after *malicious*' (Ridley).

100 **start** startle

101 **Sir . . . sir** extra-metrical. Brabantio's two half-lines really make a
pentameter: Roderigo attempts to interrupt, perhaps several times, as Brabantio speaks on (cf. Hankey, 143).
But . . . sure You had better be clear
about this.

102 **spirit . . . place** character . . . social
position

103 **bitter** painful

90–1 Or . . . say!] *F; one line Q*   94 worser] *F* (worsser*); worse *Q*   99 bravery] *Q; knauerie
F*   100 quiet?] *Q;* quiet. *F*   102 spirit] *Q;* spirits *F*   them] *Q;* their *F*

RODERIGO   Patience, good sir!

BRABANTIO

What tell'st thou me of robbing? This is Venice:

My house is not a grange.

RODERIGO   Most grave Brabantio,   105

In simple and pure soul I come to you –

IAGO   Zounds, sir, you are one of those that will not

serve God, if the devil bid you. Because we come to

do you service, and you think we are ruffians, you'll

have your daughter covered with a Barbary horse;   110

you'll have your nephews neigh to you, you'll have

coursers for cousins and jennets for germans!

BRABANTIO   What profane wretch art thou?

IAGO   I am one, sir, that comes to tell you your daughter

and the Moor are now making the beast with two backs.   115

BRABANTIO

Thou art a villain!

---

103 **Patience, good sir**! could be 'Patience! good sir –'

105 **grange** country house or outlying farmhouse, i.e. more vulnerable than a house in a city
grave respected

106 **simple** free from duplicity, honest (*OED* 1)
pure unblemished, sincere

110 **covered** Cf. *OED* cover 6: of a stallion, to copulate with a mare.
Barbary Barbary, the home of Berbers or Moors (see pp. 2, 14), could refer to all Saracen countries along the north coast of Africa (*OED* 4). Barbary horse = barb, Arab horse, i.e. Othello.

111 **nephews** grandsons, descendants
neigh Notice the alliteration in 111, 112: and *neigh* would echo *neph*[ews] if *-gh-* was sounded as in enough, laugh, etc. Cf. Jeremiah 5.8, 'In the desire of uncleanly lust they are become like the stoned horse, every man neigheth at his neighbour's wife'; 13.27, 'Thy adulteries, thy neighings . . . thy abominations have I seen.'

112 **coursers** could be a powerful horse, ridden in battle, or a racehorse
jennets small Spanish horses. (He chooses this word because the Moors had settled in Spain?)
germans close relatives

113 **profane wretch** foul-mouthed despicable person

115 **making . . . backs** copulating. Cf. Dent, B151, 'the beast with two backs' (Fr. and It. proverb); Rabelais, 1.3, '*faisoient . . . la beste a deux doz*', and 5.30. Shakespeare seems to have known the works of Rabelais: see p. 49. Cf. *AYL* 3.2.225, 'Gargantua's mouth'.

116 **Thou . . . You** *Thou* is contemptuous or familiar, *You* is (usually but not here) respectful.

104–5] *as Q ; F lines* Robbing? / Grange. /   104 What] *F;* What, *Q*   107 Zounds] *Q ; not in F*
109 and] *F; not in Q*   112 jennets for germans] Iennits for *Iermans Q ;* Gennets for Germaines *F*   114 comes] *F;* come *Q*   115 now] *Q ; not in F*

IAGO   You are a senator!

BRABANTIO

This thou shalt answer. I know thee, Roderigo!

RODERIGO

Sir, I will answer anything. But I beseech you,
If't be your pleasure and most wise consent,
As partly I find it is, that your fair daughter   120
At this odd-even and dull watch o'th' night,
Transported with no worse nor better guard
But with a knave of common hire, a gondolier,
To the gross clasps of a lascivious Moor –
If this be known to you, and your allowance,   125
We then have done you bold and saucy wrongs.
But if you know not this, my manners tell me
We have your wrong rebuke. Do not believe
That from the sense of all civility
I thus would play and trifle with your reverence.   130
Your daughter, if you have not given her leave,
I say again, hath made a gross revolt,
Tying her duty, beauty, wit and fortunes

---

116 **a senator** contemptuous (perhaps he
spits as he speaks). Pause after *You* or
are or *a*? Notice the class feeling. Between equals, the epithet *villain*
would lead to a duel.

117 **answer** answer for. Brabantio knows
Roderigo, not Iago.

119 **pleasure** delight; will (sarcastic)
wise fully aware, as in modern 'he's
wise to that one' (Ridley)

120 **As ... is** 'as, by your refusal to
listen to us, I am half inclined to believe it *is*' (Kittredge)

121 ***odd-even** a coinage = (?)neither
one thing nor the other, neither night
nor day. Cf. 'What is the night? /
Almost at odds with morning, which
is which' (*Mac* 3.4.125–6).
dull drowsy, lifeless
o'th' so F. Perhaps a scribal contrac-

tion of *o' the* (see *Texts*, 140).

122–3 elliptical (Roderigo stumbles,
speaking hastily): he means 'your
daughter *has been* transported ...
than with a knave'.

123 **But** One expects 'Than'.
knave male servant
gondolier F *Gundelier* suggests two
syllables, accent on first.

124 **clasps** embraces

125 **and your allowance** and has your
approval

126 **saucy** insolent

127 **manners** good breeding

129 **from** away from, without
civility civilized behaviour

130 **your reverence** a respectful form of
address, in general use

132 **gross** great (Folger); or, disgusting

119–35] *F; not in Q*   121 odd-even] *Malone;* odde Euen *F*

In an extravagant and wheeling stranger
Of here and everywhere. Straight satisfy yourself: 135
If she be in her chamber or your house
Let loose on me the justice of the state
For thus deluding you.
BRABANTIO   Strike on the tinder, ho!
Give me a taper, call up all my people.
This accident is not unlike my dream,   140
Belief of it oppresses me already.
Light, I say, light!   *Exit above.*
IAGO   Farewell, for I must leave you.
It seems not meet, nor wholesome to my place,
To be produced, as, if I stay, I shall,
Against the Moor. For I do know the state,   145
However this may gall him with some check,
Cannot with safety cast him, for he's embarked
With such loud reason to the Cyprus wars,
Which even now stands in act, that for their souls
Another of his fathom they have none   150

---

134 **In** i.e. to. Could be corrupt.
   extravagant roaming, vagrant, as in *Ham* 1.1.154, the 'extravagant and erring spirit hies / To his confine': cf. 'erring Barbarian' (1.3.356)
   wheeling (?)reeling, hence giddy, unstable. Though first recorded 1661, *wheedling* (= using soft flattering words) is not impossible (cf. *Per* 5, chor. 5, *neele* for *needle*).
135 **Of ... everywhere** of uncertain background
138 **Strike ... tinder** strike a light with the tinderbox
139 **taper** candle; light
140 **accident** occurrence, (unforeseen) event
143 **meet** fitting, proper
   place i.e. as Othello's ensign (lightly ironic)
144 ***produced** F may be correct but would be meaningless today.
146 **gall** vex
   check reprimand
147 **cast** discharge
   for the third *for* in six lines. A copyist's error? Omit?
   embarked involved (*OED* 2); or, loosely speaking, his belongings are embarked
148 **loud** urgent
148–9 **wars ... stands** Shakespeare sometimes has the plural verbal *-s* (Abbott, 338), but these could be misprints (*Texts*, 85).
149 **act** action, i.e. have started
   for their souls to save their souls
150 **fathom** ability (*OED* 2b)

---

134 wheeling] *F;* wheedling *Collier²*   138 thus ... you] *F;* this delusion *Q*   142 SD] *F; not in Q*   143 place] *F;* pate *Q*   144 produced] *Q;* producted *F*   146 However] How euer *Qu, F;* Now euer *Qc*   147 cast him] *Q;* cast-him *F*   150 fathom] *Q;* Fadome *F*   none] *F; not Q*

To lead their business – in which regard,
Though I do hate him as I do hell-pains,
Yet for necessity of present life
I must show out a flag and sign of love,
Which is indeed but sign. That you shall surely find
　him,　　　　　　　　　　　　　　　　　　155
Lead to the Sagittary the raised search,
And there will I be with him. So farewell.　　　　*Exit.*

Enter BRABANTIO *in his night-gown and Servants with torches.*

BRABANTIO

It is too true an evil, gone she is,
And what's to come of my despised time
Is nought but bitterness. Now Roderigo,　　　　160
Where didst thou see her? – O unhappy girl! –
With the Moor, say'st thou? – Who would be a
　father? –
How didst thou know 'twas she? – O, she deceives
　me

151 **business** three syllables
　　in which regard for which reason.
　　Notice how loosely this speech hangs
　　together.
152 ***hell-pains** the torments of hell (cf.
　　hell-fire, hell-hound, etc.)
153 i.e. because it is necessary for my
　　livelihood
154 **sign** Lat. *signum* = (1) token, sign;
　　(2) military standard, banner. Iago is
　　Othello's ancient or standard (sign)-
　　bearer.
155 **sign** show, pretence
156 **Sagittary** an inn or house with the
　　sign of Sagittarius (= the Centaur: a
　　mythological figure, with head, trunk,
　　arms of a man and lower body and
　　legs of a horse. Alluding to Othello's

'divided nature'?). Cf. *CE* 1.2.9.
Either Q or F may be correct (*Texts*,
85), but cf. *TC* 5.5.14, 'the dreadful
Sagittary' (Q and F).
search search party
157.1 *night-gown* dressing-gown
159 and what lies ahead in my despised
　　life: despised because a father whose
　　daughter has eloped suffers from loss
　　of face (like a cuckolded husband)
160–5 Cf. Shylock's reported distrac-
　　tion after Jessica's elopement (*MV*
　　2.8.15ff.), a comedy routine; see p. 77
　　above. 'O treason of the blood' =
　　Shylock's 'My own flesh and blood to
　　rebel!' (3.1.34).
161 **unhappy** miserable, wretched cf. p.
　　386

152 hell-pains] hells paines *Q*; hell apines *F*　155–6] *as F*; *Q lines* surely / search, /
156 Sagittary] Sagittar *Q*; Sagitary *F*　157.1] *as Q* (Barbantio); *Enter Brabantio, with Seruants and
Torches. F*　160 nought] *Q*; naught *F*　bitternesse. Now] *F*; bitternesse now *Q*　161–4] *F uses
brackets:* (Oh vnhappie Girle) . . . (Who . . . Father?) . . . (Oh she . . . thought:)　163 she deceives] *F*
(deceaues); thou deceiuest *Q*; she deceaued (*Furness*)

Past thought! – What said she to you? – Get more
   tapers,
Raise all my kindred. Are they married, think you?   165
RODERIGO
   Truly I think they are.
BRABANTIO
   O heaven, how got she out? O treason of the blood!
   – Fathers, from hence trust not your daughters'
      minds
   By what you see them act. – Is there not charms
   By which the property of youth and maidhood   170
   May be abused? Have you not read, Roderigo,
   Of some such thing?
RODERIGO   Yes sir, I have indeed.
BRABANTIO
   Call up my brother. – O, would you had had her!
   Some one way, some another. – Do you know
   Where we may apprehend her and the Moor?   175
RODERIGO
   I think I can discover him, if you please
   To get good guard and go along with me.
BRABANTIO
   Pray you lead on. At every house I'll call,
   I may command at most: get weapons, ho!
   And raise some special officers of night.   180
   On, good Roderigo, I'll deserve your pains.   *Exeunt.*

---

164 **Past thought!** beyond compre-
   hension
   more F *moe* = more
167 **O heaven** extra-metrical
   treason . . . blood (1) betrayal of her
   father and family; (2) rebellion of the
   passions (Folger)
169 **Is . . . charms** are there not magical
   powers
170 **property** nature

171 **abused** perverted; deceived; violated
173 **brother** Cf. 5.2.199n.
176 **discover** expose to view, find
180 **officers of night** Cf. pp. 5–6.
   Discussed by Lewkenor, who prints
   'Officers of night' in the margin (p.
   96).
181 **deserve your pains** requite the
   trouble you take

164 more] *Q;* moe *F*   167] *as Q; F lines* out? / blood. /   170 maidhood] *F;* manhood *Q*
172 thing] *QF;* things *Q3*   Yes . . . indeed] *F;* I haue sir *Q*   173 would] *F;* that *Q*   178 you lead]
F; leade me *Q*   180 night] *Q;* might *F*   181 I'll] *Q;* I will *F*

[1.2]   *Enter* OTHELLO, IAGO *and Attendants with torches.*

IAGO

Though in the trade of war I have slain men
Yet do I hold it very stuff o'th' conscience
To do no contrived murder: I lack iniquity
Sometimes to do me service. Nine or ten times   .
I had thought t'have yerked him here, under the   5
   ribs.

OTHELLO

'Tis better as it is.

IAGO   Nay, but he prated
And spoke such scurvy and provoking terms
Against your honour,
That with the little godliness I have
I did full hard forbear him. But I pray, sir,   10
Are you fast married? Be assured of this,
That the magnifico is much beloved
And hath in his effect a voice potential

1.2 Location: a street outside the Sagittary (cf. 1.1.156n.)

1 **trade** business (cf. Othello's *occupation*, 3.3.360)

2 **stuff** (?)stock-in-trade (*OED* 1j); (?)alluding to 'the stuffs of war', the munitions of an army (*OED* 1c)

3 **contrived** còntrived. Cf. *H5* 4.1.162, 'premeditated and contriv'd murther'.

4 **Nine ... times** With Iago's pretended indecisiveness, cf. 2.3.149ff.

5 **yerked** to yerk or yark = strike, esp. with rod or whip; Iago means with a dagger. Q *ierk'd* (jerked) is possible (facetious understatement).
him Roderigo (hence 58)? But could refer to Brabantio.

6 **prated** chattered foolishly

7 **scurvy** contemptible

10 **I ... him** I put up with (or spared) him with great difficulty.

11 **fast** firmly (*OED* 4: firmly tied). So

MM 1.2.147, 'she is fast my wife'. Sometimes a couple could be divorced (cf. 14) if the marriage was not consummated: that may be Iago's point. See p. 42, n. 1.

12 **magnifico** 'The chief men of Venice are by a peculiar name called *Magnifici*, i.e. Magnificoes' (Tollet, quoted Ridley). So *MV* 3.2.280.
is ... beloved has many good friends

13 **effect** i.e. power
potential potent; possible as opposed to actual, latent (*OED* 1, 2)

13–14 **a ... duke's** Shakespeare 'supposed (erroneously) that the "duke" had a casting vote, and so, on an equal division, two votes'; Iago says Brabantio is so popular that he can 'get his own way as effectively as if he also had two votes' (Ridley).

1.2] *Scena Secunda. F; not in Q* 0.1 *and*] *Q; not in F* 2 stuff o'th'] *F;* stuft of
Q 4 Sometimes] *Q;* Sometime *F* 5 t'] *F; to Q* yerked] *F;* ierk'd *Q* 10 pray] *Q;* pray you
F 11 Be assured] *F;* For be sure *Q*

As double as the duke's: he will divorce you
Or put upon you what restraint or grievance   15
The law, with all his might to enforce it on,
Will give him cable.
OTHELLO   Let him do his spite;
My services, which I have done the signiory,
Shall out-tongue his complaints. 'Tis yet to know –
Which, when I know that boasting is an honour,   20
I shall promulgate – I fetch my life and being
From men of royal siege, and my demerits
May speak unbonneted to as proud a fortune
As this that I have reached. For know, Iago,
But that I love the gentle Desdemona   25
I would not my unhoused free condition
Put into circumscription and confine
For the sea's worth. But look, what lights come
    yond?

Enter CASSIO, *with Officers and torches.*

15 **grievance** infliction, oppression
16 **his** could refer to Brabantio or to the law (*his* = modern *its*)
    enforce it on press it home
17 **cable** i.e. scope. For Iago's nautical metaphors, cf. 1.1.29, 150, 2.3.59, etc.
    do his spite do his spiteful worst
18 **signiory** the governing body (Signoria) of Venice
19 **out-tongue** outspeak, i.e. get the better of (unique in Shakespeare)
    'Tis . . . know i.e. it is not yet known (Folger)
21 **promulgate** make publicly known. Q *provulgate* means the same but was a rarer word, and could well be Shakespeare's (Lat. *promulgare, provulgare*).
22 **siege** rank (lit. seat); Q *height* (= high rank, *OED* 7) is possible

demerits merits; deficiencies
23 **speak . . . to** appeal to (*OED* 13c); or (loosely), claim
    unbonneted Fr. *bonneter* = to put off one's bonnet (headdress), out of respect; *unbonneted* seems to mean 'without removing my bonnet', but some editors prefer 'having removed my bonnet'. Cf. 1.1.9.
    proud high, grand
26 **unhoused** unhousèd. Othello had lived in tents (1.3.86).
    free unmarried
27 i.e. restrict and confine (*confine* = confinement)
28 **For . . . worth** for all the treasures buried in the sea
    But . . . yond? Here and elsewhere Othello seems to suffer from failing eyesight: see pp. 17–19.

14 duke's] *QF;* Duke *Q3*   15 or] *F;* and *Q*   16 The] *F;* That *Q*   17 Will] *F;* Weele *Q*   18 services] *QF;* service *Q3*   20 Which . . . know] *F; not in Q*   21 promulgate] *F;* provulgate *Q*   22 siege] *F (*Seige*);* height *Q*   28 sea's] *Theobald;* seas *QF;* seas' *Cam (anon.)*   yond] *F;* yonder *Q*   28.1] *Enter* Cassio *with lights, Officers, and torches. Q opp. 28; Enter Cassio, with Torches. F*

129

IAGO

  Those are the raised father and his friends,
  You were best go in.

OTHELLO   Not I, I must be found.   30

  My parts, my title and my perfect soul
  Shall manifest me rightly. Is it they?

IAGO

  By Janus, I think no.

OTHELLO

  The servants of the Duke? and my lieutenant?
  The goodness of the night upon you, friends.   35
  What is the news?

CASSIO   The duke does greet you, general,

  And he requires your haste-post-haste appearance,
  Even on the instant.

OTHELLO   What's the matter, think you?

CASSIO

  Something from Cyprus, as I may divine;
  It is a business of some heat. The galleys   40
  Have sent a dozen sequent messengers
  This very night, at one another's heels,
  And many of the consuls, raised and met,

---

29 **raised** raisèd = roused, for attack or
defence; roused from sleep
30 **I ... found** it is fitting that I be
found
31 **parts** (good) qualities; actions
title legal right or claim
perfect flawless, blameless; 'fully
prepared for what may occur' (Hart)
32 **manifest me rightly** reveal me correctly as I am
33 **Janus** Roman god with two faces, at
front and back of the head. Iago,
himself 'two-faced', may mean 'by
the god who sees what others cannot
see', because it is dark.
34 This line could be *either* one or two
questions, *or* one or two exclamations

('!' was often printed '?'). For F's
punctuation, see *Texts*, 127ff.
35 May the goodness of the night
(peace? rest?) light upon you.
36 **general** Cf. 53, *captain*; see LN,
1.1.8.
37 **haste-post-haste** urgent. Often written as a command on letters, here
used as an adjective. Cf. 1.3.47.
40 **heat** i.e. urgency
galleys still used in Venice in the
seventeenth century, not in England
41 **sequent** successive
43 **consuls** Cf. 1.1.24n.
raised roused (from sleep), or gath-
ered (*OED* 4, 26)

---

29 Those] *F;* These *Q*   32 Is ... they?] *F;* it is they. *Q*   34 Duke *Q;* Dukes *F*   Duke? ...
lieutenant?] *as Q; F lines* Dukes? / Lieutenant? /   35 you, friends.] you (Friends) *F;* your friends,
Q   38 What's] *Q;* What is *F*   41 sequent] *F;* frequent *Q*

Are at the duke's already. You have been hotly called
    for,
When, being not at your lodging to be found,   45
The Senate hath sent about three several quests
To search you out.

OTHELLO   'Tis well I am found by you:
I will but spend a word here in the house
And go with you.   [*Exit.*]

CASSIO   Ancient, what makes he here?

IAGO

Faith, he tonight hath boarded a land carrack: 50
If it prove lawful prize, he's made for ever.

CASSIO

I do not understand.

IAGO   He's married.

CASSIO   To whom?

IAGO

Marry, to –

Enter OTHELLO.

Come, captain, will you go?

OTHELLO   Ha' with you.

44 **hotly** urgently
45 **When** whereupon; inasmuch as, since
46 **about** around, in the city
    quests searches
48 **spend** utter (cf. *R2* 2.1.7, *Ham* 5.2.131). It may be that Othello does not exit and re-enter but speaks to someone in the doorway.
49 **makes he** is he doing
50 **boarded** gone on board of, entered (a ship), often with sexual implications: Paris 'would fain lay knife aboard' (*RJ* 2.4.202), 'board her, woo her, assail her' (*TN* 1.3.57)
    carrack treasure ship (usually Spanish)
51 **lawful prize** i.e. if he's legally mar-

ried (*prize* = capture, booty). Cf. 11n.
52 ***To whom?** Cf. 3.3.94ff., where Cassio seems to know all that has happened. Some think he feigns ignorance here. The 'inflection of *who* is frequently neglected' (Abbott, 274, citing also 2.3.15, 4.2.101); yet *whom* might be misread as *who* (*Texts*, 89).
53 **Marry** (originally) by the Virgin Mary, a mild exclamation
    captain Cf. 36n., 2.1.74.
    ***Ha' with you** = I'm ready (cf. *AYL* 1.2.256). Q mistook *Ha* as an exclamation, so *Ha* must have stood in the Q manuscript; F modernized to *Haue.*

46 hath . . . about] *F;* sent aboue *Q*   48 I will but] *F;* Ile *Q*   49 Ancient] *F (*Aunciant*)*   SD] *Rowe; not in QF*   50 carrack] Carrick *Q;* Carract *F*   51 he's made] *Q;* he' made *F*   52 whom] *Q2;* who *QF*   53 SD] *Rowe (after* go?*); not in QF*   Ha' with you] Ha, with who? *Q;* Haue with you. *F*

CASSIO

Here comes another troop to seek for you.

Enter BRABANTIO, RODERIGO, *with Officers and torches and weapons.*

IAGO

It is Brabantio: general, be advised,   55
He comes to bad intent.

OTHELLO   Holla, stand there!

RODERIGO

Signior, it is the Moor.

BRABANTIO   Down with him, thief!

[They draw on both sides.]

IAGO

You, Roderigo! come sir, I am for you.

OTHELLO

Keep up your bright swords, for the dew will rust
    them.

Good signior, you shall more command with years   60
Than with your weapons.

BRABANTIO

O thou foul thief, where hast thou stowed my
    daughter?

54.1–2 Cf. John 18.1–11. Like Jesus, Othello is challenged by enemies in the dark (*officers*, with *torches* and *weapons*), and is led off to a higher authority. Compare 59 and John 18.11, 'Jesus said unto Peter, Put up thy sword into the sheath' (Mrs Rosamond K. Sprague, private communication). Note that the SD differs in Q and F. Just a coincidence?

55 **advised** careful

56 **to bad intent** with bad intention
Holla stop! or, a shout to excite attention (*OED* 1, 2)

58 **You ... you** Iago picks on Roderigo

as if to confirm that Roderigo *prated* (6) and was the cause of Othello's trouble. Perhaps 'I'm for you!'

59 Cf. 54 SD n., *KJ* 4.3.79, 'Your sword is bright, sir, put it up again.' When Kean spoke this famous line, it was as if his voice 'had commanded where swords were as thick as reeds', according to John Keats; Salvini's voice was 'touched with gallant laughter' (Rosenberg, 62–3, 105).

60 **you** Cf. 62, *thou*!

62 **foul** loathesome; wicked; ugly (*OED* 1, 7, 11)
stowed placed, i.e. hidden

54.1–2] *Enters* Brabantio, Roderigo, *and others with lights and weapons.* Q *(after* To who *52); Enter Brabantio, Rodorigo, with Officers, and Torches.* F   55 Brabantio: general,] *subst.* F   57 SP BRABANTIO] F; *Cra.* Q   SD] *Rowe; not in QF*   58 You ... come] *as Q*; You, *Rodorigo*? Cme F   59–61] *as Q; prose* F   59 them] F; em Q   62] *as Q; F lines* Theefe, / Daughter? /

132

Damned as thou art, thou hast enchanted her,
For I'll refer me to all things of sense,
If she in chains of magic were not bound,   65
Whether a maid so tender, fair and happy,
So opposite to marriage that she shunned
The wealthy, curled darlings of our nation,
Would ever have, t'incur a general mock,
Run from her guardage to the sooty bosom   70
Of such a thing as thou? to fear, not to delight.
Judge me the world if 'tis not gross in sense
That thou hast practised on her with foul charms,
Abused her delicate youth with drugs or minerals
That weakens motion: I'll have't disputed on,   75
'Tis probable and palpable to thinking.
I therefore apprehend and do attach thee
For an abuser of the world, a practiser
Of arts inhibited and out of warrant.
Lay hold upon him; if he do resist   80
Subdue him at his peril!

---

63 **Damned ... art** Devils were
thought to be black, so black implied
damnation ('his soul may be as
damn'd and black / As hell', *Ham*
3.3.94; 'the complexion of a devil',
said of Morocco, *MV* 1.2.130).
enchanted cast a spell on
64 **refer me** submit my case
things of sense persons (*OED* 10)
66 **tender** delicate; gentle; sensitive
fair unblemished (of character or
reputation)
happy contented; perhaps = successful (?conventional) in doing what the
circumstances require (*OED* 5)
67 **opposite** opposed
68 **curled** curlèd. May imply artificial
curls, worn by men.
69 **mock** mockery
70 **guardage** guardianship (first recorded here)

71 **thing** (contemptuous)
to ... delight *either* 'run ... to fear,
not to delight' (two nouns), *or* 'a
thing ... to fear (frighten) not to delight' (two infinitives)
72 **gross in sense** obvious in meaning
73 **practised on** plotted against
74 **minerals** mineral medicines or poisons (*OED* 4c)
75 **weakens** Hanmer's *waken* is attractive (*Texts*, 88).
motion desire, inclination (so
1.3.331); or, inward impulse or
prompting (i.e. against Othello)
disputed on looked into (lit.
debated)
77 **attach** arrest
78 **abuser** deceiver
79 **inhibited** prohibited
out of warrant illegal
81 **Subdue** overpower

64 things] *F*; thing *Q*   65] *F; not in Q*   68 darlings] *Q ;* Deareling *F*   69 t'] *F;* to *Q*   72–7] *F;*
not in Q   75 weakens] *F;* waken *Hanmer*   78 For] *F;* Such *Q*

133

OTHELLO   Hold your hands,
  Both you of my inclining and the rest:
  Were it my cue to fight, I should have known it
  Without a prompter. Where will you that I go
  To answer this your charge?
BRABANTIO   To prison, till fit time   85
  Of law, and course of direct session
  Call thee to answer.
OTHELLO   What if I do obey?
  How may the duke be therewith satisfied,
  Whose messengers are here about my side
  Upon some present business of the state,   90
  To bring me to him?
OFFICER   'Tis true, most worthy signior,
  The duke's in council, and your noble self
  I am sure is sent for.
BRABANTIO   How? the duke in council?
  In this time of the night? Bring him away:
  Mine's not an idle cause, the duke himself,   95
  Or any of my brothers of the state,
  Cannot but feel this wrong as 'twere their own.
  For if such actions may have passage free
  Bond-slaves and pagans shall our statesmen be.   *Exeunt.*

---

81 **Hold** i.e. don't move
82 **my inclining** my side ('you who incline towards me')
83 **cue** Q's *Qu.* is Shakespeare's spelling
   elsewhere (*Texts*, 160).
84 **Where** F *Whether* is a variant spelling
   of whither, where.
86 **direct session** 'normal process of
   law' (Ridley)
90 **present** immediate, urgent
93 **I am** read 'I'm'
94 **In** at (Abbott, 161)
95 **idle** groundless; frivolous
   cause (legal) case

96 **brothers ... state** fellow Senators
   (Sanders)
97 **as** as if
98 **passage** the fact of 'passing current'
   or being generally accepted (*OED* 6)
99 **Bond-slaves** Cf. 1.3.139: Othello was
   once a slave. Brabantio's *pagans* implies (rightly or wrongly) that he was
   or is a heathen (see pp. 22, 72). For
   slaves as their masters' masters in a
   topsy-turvy world, the same sarcasm,
   see Cicero, *Letters to Atticus*, 2.1: 'Are
   we to be slaves of freedmen and
   slaves?'

83 cue] *F* *(Cue); Qu. Q*   84 Where] *Q;* Whether *F*   85 To] *F;* And *Q*   87 I] *Q; not in*
F   91 bring] *F;* beare *Q*

[1.3]   *Enter* DUKE *and* Senators, *set at a table, with lights and Attendants.*

DUKE

There is no composition in these news
That gives them credit.

1 SENATOR   Indeed, they are disproportioned.
My letters say a hundred and seven galleys.

DUKE

And mine a hundred forty.

2 SENATOR   And mine two hundred.
But though they jump not on a just account –   5
As in these cases, where the aim reports,
'Tis oft with difference – yet do they all confirm
A Turkish fleet, and bearing up to Cyprus.

DUKE

Nay, it is possible enough to judgement:
I do not so secure me in the error   10
But the main article I do approve
In fearful sense.

SAILOR   (*within*)   What ho, what ho, what ho!

1.3 Location: a council chamber. For the importance of this scene, see p. 63.

1.3.0.1 DUKE i.e. the Doge (a word not used in *Oth* or *MV*)

1 **composition** consistency
  news reports

2 **credit** credibility
  disproportioned out of proportion

3–4 Cf. *JC* 4.3.175ff.

5 **jump** agree
  just account exact estimate. For the same QF variants, cf. 2.1.288.

6 **aim** guess, conjecture. Before modern methods of communication were invented the movements of foreign armies and navies were reported to the Privy Council (or guessed at) exactly as here: cf. HMC, Hatfield

House, Part 12 (1602), 386.

8 **bearing up** proceeding

9 **to judgement** i.e. when you think about it

10 **secure** feel overconfident (because of the discrepancy of the numbers)

11–12 But I believe the chief point (that a Turkish fleet is making for Cyprus) to be true, with frightening implications (for us).

12–17 In F the 'sailor shouts "within" and is then introduced by the officer. In Q "one within" [the sailor?] shouts and the sailor then introduces himself' (Ridley). This passage, and others in this scene, may have been rewritten by Shakespeare (*Texts*, 16–18).

1.3] *Scoena Tertia.* F; *not in Q*   0.1–2] *Q; Enter Duke, Senators, and Officers. F*   1 There is] *Q;* There's *F*   these] *Q;* this *F*   4 forty] *Q;* and forty *Q*   5 account] *Q;* accompt *F*   6 the aim] *F;* they aym'd *Q*   10 in] *F;* to *Q*   11 article] *F;* Articles *Q*   12] *as F;* In fearefull sense. *Enter a Messenger. / One within.* What ho, . . . *Q*

135

Enter Sailor.

OFFICER
    A messenger from the galleys.
DUKE
    Now? what's the business?
SAILOR
    The Turkish preparation makes for Rhodes,   15
    So was I bid report here to the state
    By Signior Angelo.
DUKE
    How say you by this change?
1 SENATOR   This cannot be,
    By no assay of reason: 'tis a pageant
    To keep us in false gaze. When we consider   20
    Th'importancy of Cyprus to the Turk,
    And let ourselves again but understand
    That as it more concerns the Turk than Rhodes
    So may he with more facile question bear it,
    For that it stands not in such warlike brace   25
    But altogether lacks th'abilities
    That Rhodes is dressed in. If we make thought of
        this

15 **preparation** force, or fleet (prepared
    for action)
17 **By . . . Angelo** The 'governor of
    Cyprus' (cf. 2.1.0.1n.) would be the
    appropriate person to report 'to the
    state': Shakespeare could have con-
    fused Angelo and Montano. A de-
    leted half-line, printed in error by F?
18 **by** about
19 **assay** trial, judgement
    pageant show; trick (*OED* 1c)
20 **in false gaze** 'looking in the wrong
    direction, with our attention di-
    verted' (Sanders); 'a specific meta-
    phor from hunting' (Ridley)
21 **importancy** importance; import,

significance
22 **again** moreover
24 'carry it (in the military sense of "win
    it") with less arduous fighting'
    (Ridley, adding 'but question is not
    elsewhere used in Shakespeare in that
    sense'). Perhaps *question* = a subject
    of debate or strife (*OED* 4), viz.
    physical 'argument', fighting.
25 **For that** because
    brace state of defence (*OED* 1c, the
    only entry); or a coinage from the
    verb (*OED* brace 4: to brace oneself),
    i.e. 'bracedness', resoluteness
26 **abilities** power, means
27 **dressed in** prepared with

13 galleys] *F;* Galley *Q*   14] *as F;* Now, the businesse? *Q*   17 By . . . Angelo] *F; not in Q*   18–
19 This . . . pageant] *F; Q lines* reason – / Pageant, /   21 Th'] *F;* The *Q*   25–31 For . . .
profitless.] *F; not in Q*

. We must not think the Turk is so unskilful
   To leave that latest which concerns him first,
   Neglecting an attempt of ease and gain   30
   To wake and wage a danger profitless.

DUKE
   Nay, in all confidence, he's not for Rhodes.

OFFICER
   Here is more news.

Enter a Messenger.

MESSENGER
   The Ottomites, reverend and gracious,
   Steering with due course toward the isle of Rhodes,   35
   Have there injointed with an after fleet –

1 SENATOR
   Ay, so I thought; how many, as you guess?

MESSENGER
   Of thirty sail; and now they do re-stem
   Their backward course, bearing with frank
       appearance
   Their purposes toward Cyprus. Signior Montano,   40
   Your trusty and most valiant servitor,
   With his free duty recommends you thus

28 a more respectful view of non-Europeans than Iago's (346, 356, 399ff.)
31 **wage** risk, hazard (*OED* 5)
34 **Ottomites** Turks, Ottomans
   reverend and gracious respected
   and gracious (senators)
35 **due** appropriate
36 **injointed** joined. Why did F insert
   them? Perhaps intending *enjoined
   them*. 'Injoint' is first recorded by
   OED in *Oth*. Cf. *AC* 1.2.92, 'jointing
   their force 'gainst Caesar'.
   after fleet unexplained. Perhaps 'a
   following fleet'. In 1570 a Turkish
   fleet sailed towards Rhodes, then

joined another fleet to attack Cyprus,
as here: Shakespeare must have
known this (see Honigmann, 'Date of
Othello', 218–19).
38–9 **they … course** they navigate
   back again (*stem* = to keep on a fixed
   course, of a ship)
39 **frank** unchecked; open
41 **servitor** servant. He is the governor
   of Cyprus (*Texts*, 37), hence *relieve
   him* (43).
42 **free duty** willing service (Walker);
   'unstinted devotion' (Kittredge)
   recommends you reports to you

32 Nay] *F;* And *Q* 33.1 *a* Messenger *F; a* 2. *Messenger Q* 34 Ottomites] *Ottamites
QF* 36 injointed] *as Q;* inioynted them *F;* injoin'd *Rowe* 37] *F; not in Q* 38 re-stem] *F;*
resterine *Q* 40 toward] *F;* towards *Q*

And prays you to relieve him.

DUKE

'Tis certain then for Cyprus.
Marcus Luccicos, is not he in town?   45

1 SENATOR

He's now in Florence.

DUKE

Write from us to him; post-post-haste, dispatch.

1 SENATOR

Here comes Brabantio and the valiant Moor.

Enter BRABANTIO, OTHELLO, CASSIO, IAGO, RODERIGO
and Officers.

DUKE

Valiant Othello, we must straight employ you
Against the general enemy Ottoman.   50
[*to Brabantio*] I did not see you: welcome, gentle
    signior,
We lacked your counsel and your help tonight.

BRABANTIO

So did I yours. Good your grace, pardon me,
Neither my place nor aught I heard of business

---

43 *relieve QF *beleeue* is feeble, in such a situation, and *relief* is sent immediately.

45 **Marcus Luccicos** a strange name, probably a misreading (but with the same spelling in Q and F). Some think it alludes to Paulo Marchi Luchese, master of an Italian inn in London: unlikely.
in town *OED* town 4b: in the town (pre-Shakespearian)

47 **post-post-haste** a variant of *haste-post-haste* (1.2.37)
dispatch send (*OED*: 'the word regularly used for the sending of official messengers')

48–9 **Moor ... Othello** Others mostly speak *of* him as the Moor, *to* him as Othello.

50 Against the general enemy (of all Christians), the Turk. *Ottoman* is oddly placed, if an adjective: perhaps we should read *Ottoman enemy*, or *enemy, Ottoman* (transpose, or insert comma).

51 **gentle** a polite form of address to a gentleman

54 **place** (official) position or rank
aught anything

---

43 relieve] *Johnson (T. Clark);* beleeue *QF*   45 Luccicos] *QF; Lucchese / Capell*   he] *F;* here *Q*   47] *as Q; F lines* vs, / dispatch. /   to] *F;* wish *Q*   48.1–2] *as F; Enter* Brabantio, Othello, Roderigo, Iago, Cassio, Desdemona, *and Officers. Q (after 47)*   51 SD] *Theobald; not in QF*   52 lacked] *F;* lacke *Q*

Hath raised me from my bed, nor doth the general
    care   55
Take hold on me, for my particular grief
Is of so flood-gate and o'erbearing nature
That it engluts and swallows other sorrows
And it is still itself.

DUKE   Why? What's the matter?

BRABANTIO
    My daughter, O my daughter!

1 SENATOR   Dead?

BRABANTIO   Ay, to me: 60
    She is abused, stolen from me and corrupted
    By spells and medicines bought of mountebanks,
    For nature so preposterously to err
    Being not deficient, blind, or lame of sense,
    Sans witchcraft could not.   65

DUKE
    Whoe'er he be, that in this foul proceeding
    Hath thus beguiled your daughter of herself,
    And you of her, the bloody book of law
    You shall yourself read, in the bitter letter,
    After your own sense, yea, though our proper son   70

---

55 **from my bed** an afterthought, hence extra-metrical?
care anxiety, concern
56 **particular** private
57 **flood-gate** (sluice-gate; hence, of the water held back) torrential
58 Dent, G446, 'The greater grief drives out the less.'
engluts devours
59 **And . . . itself** i.e. it is unaffected by other sorrows
61 **abused** wronged; cheated, deceived. Notice how Brabantio surrenders to a fixed idea, as Othello does later.
62 **mountebanks** quacks, charlatans. Sidney referred scornfully to 'the mountebanks at Venice' (*Apology*, ed.

G. Shepherd [1965], 131); cf. Jonson, *Volpone*, 2.2.4ff.
63–5 Confusing, because of a change of construction: 64 and 65 need *err*, not *to err*, in 63. 'For, without witchcraft, nature – as long as it is not deficient, blind or defective in sense – could not err so preposterously.'
67 i.e. made her act so unlike herself
68–70 **the . . . sense** 'you shall yourself pronounce the sentence (from) the death-decreeing book of law, (taking it) in its (most) severe interpretation, according to your own judgement'. Witchcraft (65) was a capital crime (Sanders).
70 **our proper** i.e. my own

56 hold on] *F;* any hold of *Q* grief] *F;* griefes *Q*   59 Why?] *F;* Why, *Q*   60 SP 1 SENATOR] *Sen. F; All. Q*   64] *F; not in Q*   65 Sans] *F;* Since *Qu (*Saunce *Qc)*   70 your] *F;* its *Q*   yea] *F; not in Q*

Stood in your action.

BRABANTIO   Humbly I thank your grace.
Here is the man, this Moor, whom now it seems
Your special mandate for the state affairs
Hath hither brought.

ALL   We are very sorry for't.

DUKE [*to Othello*]
What in your own part can you say to this?   75

BRABANTIO
Nothing, but this is so.

OTHELLO
Most potent, grave, and reverend signiors,
My very noble and approved good masters:
That I have ta'en away this old man's daughter
It is most true; true, I have married her.   80
The very head and front of my offending
Hath this extent, no more. Rude am I in my speech
And little blest with the soft phrase of peace,
For since these arms of mine had seven years' pith
Till now some nine moons wasted, they have used   85
Their dearest action in the tented field,
And little of this great world can I speak
More than pertains to feats of broil and battle,

---

71 **Stood ... action** were (the other)
party in your legal action (*OED* stand
95)
74 SP ALL Probably one senator speaks,
others indicate agreement (see Honigmann, 'Stage direction').
75 **in** i.e. on
76 **but** except
78 **approved** proved (by experience);
esteemed
79 **this old man's** A tactless way of
speaking of his new father-in-law,
perhaps triggered by 72, 'Here is the
man'.
81 **head and front** (*OED* head 41, first
here) height, highest extent
82 **Rude** Lat. *rudis*, rough, unskilled

83 **soft** pleasing; gentle; quiet
phrase style of expression, language
84 **pith** strength. He has helped in
battles from the age of 7 (cf. 133,
'from my boyish days'), like the Boy
in *H5*.
85 **wasted** gone; with a hint of squandered, as he devotes his life to war
(Adamson, 62)
86 **dearest** worthiest
tented Cf. 1.2.26n.
87 **this great world** Perhaps he bows to
the senators. Venice was an independent state and cultural centre in
1600.
88 **broil** confused disturbance, tumult,
turmoil

---

75 SD] *Theobald; not in QF*   82 extent, no more.] extent no more. *Q ;* extent; no more.
F   83 soft] *F;* set *Q*   88 feats of broil] feate of broyle *Q ;* Feats of Broiles *F*

140

And therefore little shall I grace my cause
In speaking for myself. Yet, by your gracious patience,   90
I will a round unvarnished tale deliver
Of my whole course of love, what drugs, what
     charms,
What conjuration and what mighty magic –
For such proceeding I am charged withal –
I won his daughter.

BRABANTIO   A maiden never bold,   95
Of spirit so still and quiet that her motion
Blushed at herself; and she, in spite of nature,
Of years, of country, credit, everything,
To fall in love with what she feared to look on?
It is a judgement maimed and most imperfect   100
That will confess perfection so could err
Against all rules of nature, and must be driven
To find out practices of cunning hell
Why this should be. I therefore vouch again
That with some mixtures powerful o'er the blood   105
Or with some dram conjured to this effect
He wrought upon her.

DUKE   To vouch this is no proof,

---

91 **round** honest, plain
    unvarnished unpolished (unique in
    Shakespeare)
92–5 Note the change of construction:
    either 'with what drugs . . . I won', *or*
    'what drugs . . . won'. Perhaps *with*
    was dropped because of *withal* (=
    with), 94.
95 **never bold** How well does he know
    his daughter?
96 **motion** (any) inward impulse or
    desire (*OED* 9)
97 **in . . . nature** i.e. in spite of *differ-*
    ences of nature
98 **credit** reputation

100 **maimed** F *main'd* is a variant
    spelling.
101 **err** go astray
102 **and . . . driven** i.e. and *sound judge-*
    ment must be driven
103 **practices** intrigues, treacheries
104 **vouch** affirm
105 **blood** (the supposed seat of) pas-
    sion; sexual appetite (*OED* 5, 6)
106 **dram** a small draught of medicine
    conjured (accent on second syllable)
    made by magic
107 **wrought upon** worked on, influ-
    enced (*OED* work 30)
    To . . . proof Dent, S1019, 'Suspi-
    cion (Accusation) is no proof.'

---

91 unvarnished] *as Q;* vn-varnish'd u *F*   92] *as Q; F lines* Loue. / Charmes, /   94 proceeding]
F; proceedings *Q*   I am] *F;* am I *Q*   95–6 bold . . . so] *F subst.;* bold of spirit, / So *Q*   99 on?] *Q;*
on; *F*   100 maimed] *Q;* main'd *F*   101 could] *F;* would *Q*   107 SP] *Q; not in F*   vouch] *F;*
youth *Q*

Without more certain and more overt test
Than these thin habits and poor likelihoods
Of modern seeming do prefer against him. 110

1 SENATOR
But, Othello, speak:
Did you by indirect and forced courses
Subdue and poison this young maid's affections?
Or came it by request and such fair question
As soul to soul affordeth?

OTHELLO   I do beseech you, 115
Send for the lady to the Sagittary,
And let her speak of me before her father.
If you do find me foul in her report
The trust, the office I do hold of you
Not only take away, but let your sentence 120
Even fall upon my life.

DUKE
Fetch Desdemona hither.

OTHELLO
Ancient, conduct them, you best know the place.
And till she come, as truly as to heaven
                    Exeunt [*Iago and*] *two or three.*

---

108 **overt** manifest. An overt act (in law) was 'an outward act, such as can be clearly proved to have been done, from which criminal intent is inferred' (*OED* 2b).
test proof; trial; witness; evidence (*OED sb.* 1, 3)
109 **thin** implausible
habits (clothes; appearances, hence) suggestions
poor likelihoods weak probabilities
110 **modern seeming** commonplace appearance. Is this an appeal against racial prejudice?
prefer bring
112 **indirect** devious

forced forcèd: constraining
113 **poison** pervert morally (*OED* 3)
114 **question** talk; questioning. 'Or did it come about by (your or her) request and such blameless talk as one soul can grant another?' Hinting that (1) Desdemona took the initiative, (2) it was a 'soul to soul' relationship.
116 **Sagittary** Cf. 1.1.156n.
117 **before** in the presence of
118 **foul** wicked; guilty
119 **office** position (as general)
122 **Desdemona** He knows her name without being told. The leading Venetians are a closed circle; Othello is very much an outsider.

---

108 certain . . . overt] *Q* (ouert); wider . . . ouer *F*   109 Than these] *F*; These are *Q*   110 seeming do] *F*; seemings, you *Q*   111 SP] *Q*; *Sen. F*   116 Sagittary] Sagittar *Q*; Sagitary *F*   119] *F*; not in *Q*   123] as *Q*; *F* lines them: / place. / Ancient] *Q*; Auuciant *F*   124 till] *Q*; tell *F*   truly] *F*; faithfull *Q*   SD] *Exit two or three. Q*; not in *F*

I do confess the vices of my blood   125
So justly to your grave ears I'll present
How I did thrive in this fair lady's love
And she in mine.
DUKE   Say it, Othello.
OTHELLO
Her father loved me, oft invited me,
Still questioned me the story of my life   130
From year to year – the battles, sieges, fortunes
That I have passed.
I ran it through, even from my boyish days
To th' very moment that he bade me tell it,
Wherein I spake of most disastrous chances,   135
Of moving accidents by flood and field,
Of hair-breadth scapes i'th' imminent deadly
      breach,
Of being taken by the insolent foe
And sold to slavery; of my redemption thence

---

125 **vices** depravities; or, faults ('with-out implication of serious wrong-doing': *OED* 4)
      blood Cf. 105n.
126 **justly** faithfully
      present (legal) lay before a court
128 **And ... mine** perhaps read 'And she *did thrive* in mine' (Proudfoot, private note)
      Say it an unusual turn of phrase, not quite the same as 'Speak'. Also, a short line: something missing (see previous note)?
129 **Her ...¹me** Did Othello or Brabantio deceive himself? How does Brabantio react to this line?
      oft i.e. the lovers took their time (cf. 85, *nine moons*)
130 **Still** constantly
131 **From ... year** This half-line adds nothing essential; perhaps cancelled, and printed in error (*Texts*, 36–7)?

132 **passed** gone through; escaped
135 **spake** for *o:a* misreading, see *Texts*, 83.
      disastrous ill-starred, unlucky (*OED* 1)
      chances 'Chance' seems to have been against Othello from an early age, so he thinks: pp. 72–3, and cf. 5.2.339, 'these unlucky deeds'.
136 **moving** changeful; affecting (the feelings)
      accidents occurrences
      flood and field by water and by land; or, by sea (fight) and on the (battle) field
137 **scapes** escapes
      imminent hanging over one's head, ready to fall
      breach a gap in a fortification made by battery
138 **insolent** overbearing; insulting; exulting

125] *F; not in Q*   131 battles] *Q; Battaile F*   fortunes] *Q; Fortune F*   134 To th'] Toth' *QF*   135 spake] *Q; spoke F*   136 accidents by] *F; accident of Q*   139 of] *F; and Q*

143

And portance in my travailous history; 140
Wherein of antres vast and deserts idle,
Rough quarries, rocks and hills whose heads touch
   heaven
It was my hint to speak – such was my process –
And of the cannibals that each other eat,
The Anthropophagi, and men whose heads 145
Do grow beneath their shoulders. This to hear
Would Desdemona seriously incline,
But still the house affairs would draw her thence,
Which ever as she could with haste dispatch
She'd come again, and with a greedy ear 150

---

140 **portance** bearing, behaviour. Cf.
Cor 2.3.224.
  ***travailous** toilsome, wearisome. Q
trauells perhaps resulted from the
phonetic spelling of *-ous* as *-es* or *-s*,
as in *Ham* 2.1.3, 'meruiles [F
'maruels'] wisely' (Q2); *TC* 1.2.136,
'a maruel's white hand' (QF).

141 **antres** caves (Lat. *antrum*); *OED*
first records here.
  vast . . . idle Both words could mean
empty (Lat. *vastus*).
  deserts See pp. 28–9. As Venice did
not possess (or wage war in) deserts
he refers to a time before he entered
the service of Venice.

142 **quarries** perhaps = large masses of
stone or rock (*OED* 2); or in the
modern sense, places where men
(?slaves) hew rocks

143 **hint** occasion, opportunity. Could
be *hent* in the seventeenth century (so
Q).
  process proceeding (cf. 94); drift; story

145 **Anthropophagi** 'man-eaters', cannibals. With Q's *-ie* ending, cf. '*An-
dronicie*' (*TA* 2.3.189).

145–6 **men . . . shoulders** See p. 5 and
Fig. 2; cf. *Tem* 3.3.44ff., 'Who would

believe . . . that there were such men
/ Whose heads stood in their
breasts?', *Patient Grissill*, 5.1.25
(Dekker, 1.278). The F reading is
possible if there is a heavy pause after
'Grew—' (Shakespeare's revision?).

146 **This to hear** *Either* hearing this
would make Desdemona incline earnestly, *or* in order to hear this
Desdemona would incline (towards
me) earnestly. Incline = physical or
mental inclination (bend towards, or
bend mind or heart towards). For the
QF variants, see *Texts*, 35–6.

148 Desdemona seems to be a motherless girl, in charge of household
affairs, partly because her mother is
not mentioned (except as a memory,
4.3.24).

149 **Which** A Latin construction: '(And)
ever as she could dispatch them
(which), she'd come again'.

150 **greedy ear** Cf. *Faerie Queene*,
6.9.26, 'Whylest thus he talkt, the
knight with greedy eare / Hong still
upon his melting mouth attent'
(Malone). But *greedy . . . Devour* has
stronger implications (cf. *MA* 3.1.28,
'greedily devour the treacherous bait').

---

140 portance in] *F;* with it all *Q* travailous] *(R. Proudfoot (N&Q, NS 21 [1974], 130–1));* trauells
Q; Trauellours *F* 141 antres] Antrees *Q;* Antars *F* 142 and hills] *Q;* Hills *F* heads] *Q;* head
F 143 hint] *F;* hent *Q* ²my] *F;* the *Q* 144 other] *Q;* others *F* 145 Anthropophagi] *Anthro-
pophagie Q; Antropophague F* 146 Do grow] *Q;* Grew *F* This] *Q;* These things *F* 148 thence]
Q; hence *F* 149 Which] *F;* And *Q* 150 She'd] *as Q;* She'l *F*

Devour up my discourse; which I, observing,
Took once a pliant hour and found good means
To draw from her a prayer of earnest heart
That I would all my pilgrimage dilate,
Whereof by parcels she had something heard   155
But not intentively. I did consent,
And often did beguile her of her tears
When I did speak of some distressful stroke
That my youth suffered. My story being done
She gave me for my pains a world of sighs,   160
She swore in faith 'twas strange, 'twas passing
    strange,
'Twas pitiful, 'twas wondrous pitiful;
She wished she had not heard it, yet she wished
That heaven had made her such a man. She thanked
    me
And bade me, if I had a friend that loved her,   165
I should but teach him how to tell my story
And that would woo her. Upon this hint I spake:
She loved me for the dangers I had passed
And I loved her that she did pity them.

151–4 **which . . . dilate** i.e. Othello took the very first step
152 **pliant** suitable (*OED* 2c); or, an hour when she was easily influenced (transferred epithet)
153 **earnest** intense, ardent
154 **pilgrimage** i.e. life's journey, implying that his was a dedicated life
    dilate relate
155 **by parcels** in bits and pieces (parcel = part). Cf. *2H4* 4.2.36, 'the parcels and particulars of our grief'.
156 **intentively** attentively, with steady application
157 **often** implying that the story was told more than once or over a period of time
    beguile A smiling allusion to 'practices of cunning hell' (103)?
158 **distressful** 'A literary and chiefly poetical word' (*OED*). Of how many other words in Othello's longer speeches could the same be said?
    stroke blow; calamitous event (*OED* 3b, first entry 1700)
161 **swore** affirmed emphatically
    passing very, surpassingly
164 **made her** Romance heroines sometimes wish they were men (*MA* 4.1.317), but this could also mean 'made such a man *for her*'.
166 **but** only
167 **hint** occasion, opportunity; a suggestion conveyed indirectly (first here)
168–9 How well does he understand her love, or his own?
169 **that** because

155 parcels] *F;* parcell *Q*   156 intentively] *Q;* instinctiuely *F*   158 distressful] *F;* distressed *Q*   160 sighs] *Q;* kisses *F*   161 in faith] *F;* Ifaith *Q*   167 hint] *F;* heate *Q*

This only is the witchcraft I have used: 170

Enter DESDEMONA, IAGO, *Attendants.*

Here comes the lady, let her witness it.

DUKE

I think this tale would win my daughter too.

Good Brabantio, take up this mangled matter at the
best:

Men do their broken weapons rather use

Than their bare hands.

BRABANTIO   I pray you, hear her speak. 175

If she confess that she was half the wooer,

Destruction on my head if my bad blame

Light on the man. Come hither, gentle mistress:

Do you perceive, in all this noble company,

Where most you owe obedience?

DESDEMONA   My noble father, 180

I do perceive here a divided duty.

To you I am bound for life and education:

My life and education both do learn me

How to respect you; you are the lord of duty,

---

170 Shakespeare probably recalled Pliny's
account of a former bondslave, C.
Furius Cresinus, who, accused of
acquiring wealth by 'indirect means,
as if he had used sorcery', pointed to
his plough and farm implements
and said 'Behold, these are the sor-
ceries . . . and all the enchantments
that I use' (E. H. W. Meyerstein,
quoted Bullough, 211).
only alone

171 **lady** For her age, see pp. 41–2.
witness furnish evidence concerning, bear witness to

173 **Good Brabantio** extra-metrical
mangled mutilated; i.e. 'accept this
less than perfect business in the best
possible way'. Cf. Dent, B326, 'Make

the best of a bad bargain'.
177 **bad** incorrect, mistaken (*OED* 2,
first entry 1688)
178 **Light on** fall or descend on
gentle mistress This is not how a
father normally addressed his daughter.
179 **noble** perhaps an error, anticipating
noble, 180 (Walker)
182 **bound** tied, united; obliged; sub-
jected
education upbringing
183 **learn** teach
184 **lord** master. She distinguishes two
kinds of *lord* (cf. 189) and duty: 'you
are the master of my duty hitherto,
but now I owe a wife's duty to the
Moor, my new lord'. Cf. *KL* 1.1.91ff.

170.1 *Attendants*] *F*; *and the rest. Q; SD follows 171 QF*   177 on my head] *F*; lite on me
Q   184 the lord of] *F*; Lord of all my *Q*

I am hitherto your daughter. But here's my
    husband: 185
And so much duty as my mother showed
To you, preferring you before her father,
So much I challenge that I may profess
Due to the Moor my lord.

BRABANTIO

God be with you, I have done.   190
Please it your grace, on to the state affairs;
I had rather to adopt a child than get it.
Come hither, Moor:
I here do give thee that with all my heart
Which, but thou hast already, with all my heart   195
I would keep from thee. For your sake, jewel,
I am glad at soul I have no other child,
For thy escape would teach me tyranny
To hang clogs on them. I have done, my lord.

DUKE

Let me speak like yourself, and lay a sentence   200
Which as a grise or step may help these lovers
Into your favour.

---

185 **hitherto** implying that her new identity as wife now supersedes the previous one as daughter
187 **preferring** placing; loving (you more than)
188 **challenge** claim (as a right). In effect she also challenges her father (and later Othello: 3.3.60ff.).
189 **the Moor** Cf. 48–9n., 249, 253.
    my lord the male head of a household, as in the Bible (e.g. Matthew 24.45)
190 probably four syllables originally, 'God bye (= God be with you), I've done', making a complete verse line with 189
191 **Please it** may it please
192 **get** beget
194 i.e. in the circumstances he is glad to be rid of her

195 **but thou hast** except that thou hast it
196 **For your sake** because of you
198 **escape** elopement; outrageous transgression (*OED* 7)
199 **clogs** blocks of wood, etc., attached to the neck or legs of man or beast to prevent escape
200–2 Could be prose.
200 **like yourself** i.e. by giving advice; or, as ideally you would speak
    lay expound
    sentence opinion; decision (of a court); pithy saying or maxim. He adopts the conventional wisdom that 'What cannot be eschew'd must be embrac'd' (*MW* 5.5.237).
201 **grise** stairway; step

190] *F;* God bu'y, I ha done *Q*   195] *F; not in Q*   199 them] *F;* em *Q*   200] *as Q ; F lines* selfe: / Sentence, /   202 Into your favour] *Q ; not in F*

When remedies are past the griefs are ended
By seeing the worst which late on hopes depended.
To mourn a mischief that is past and gone   205
Is the next way to draw new mischief on.
What cannot be preserved when fortune takes,
Patience her injury a mockery makes.
The robbed that smiles steals something from the
    thief,
He robs himself that spends a bootless grief.   210

BRABANTIO

So let the Turk of Cyprus us beguile,
We lose it not so long as we can smile;
He bears the sentence well that nothing bears
But the free comfort which from thence he hears.
But he bears both the sentence and the sorrow   215
That, to pay grief, must of poor patience borrow.
These sentences to sugar or to gall,
Being strong on both sides, are equivocal.
But words are words: I never yet did hear
That the bruised heart was pierced through the ear.   220

---

203 Cf. Dent, R71.1, 'Where there is no remedy it is folly to chide'; i.e. 'when it is too late for remedies'.
  griefs suffering; sorrows
204 i.e. because we have seen the worst happen, which formerly was subject to hopes (that it would not happen); or, *hope* = expectation 'of ill as well as of good, and so is sometimes practically equivalent to "fear"' (Kittredge)
205 **mischief** evil; misfortune; injury
206 **next** nearest
207–8 When fortune takes away what cannot be saved, (your) patience makes a mockery of (= mocks, defeats) fortune's wrongful action.
210 **spends** expends; wastes
  bootless pointless
213–14 He bears your *sentence* (200) well who suffers only the free (?cheap)

consolation which he hears (and not the grief that occasioned it). *Bears the sentence* 'plays on the meaning, "receives judicial sentence"' (Bevington).
216 **pay** pacify
217 **gall** (bile, hence) bitterness
218 **equivocal** equally appropriate
219 **words are words** Dent, W832, 'Words are but words'.
220 **bruised** crushed, battered (a stronger word than today)
  pierced piercèd: 'That the crushed heart was relieved by mere words that reach it through the ear.' *Through* could be disyllabic (*thorough*) but probably isn't here. F has two errors, *eares* (the rhyme supports Q *eare*), and *pierc'd*. Kittredge preferred 'piecèd' (= mended, cured).

206 new] *F;* more *Q*   211 So let] *QF;* So, let *Theobald*   220 pierced] *Q;* pierc'd *F;* pieced *Warburton*   ear] *Q;* cares *F*

148

I humbly beseech you, proceed to th'affairs of state.

DUKE   The Turk with a most mighty preparation makes
for Cyprus. Othello, the fortitude of the place is best
known to you, and, though we have there a substitute
of most allowed sufficiency, yet opinion, a sovereign   225
mistress of effects, throws a more safer voice on you.
You must therefore be content to slubber the gloss of
your new fortunes with this more stubborn and
boisterous expedition.

OTHELLO

The tyrant custom, most grave senators,   230
Hath made the flinty and steel couch of war
My thrice-driven bed of down. I do agnize
A natural and prompt alacrity
I find in hardness, and do undertake

222–9 The switch to prose is all the more jolting after two speeches of rhymed couplets. We move from private to public business, and this makes Othello's verse rhythms (230ff.) sound self-indulgent.

222 **preparation** Cf. 15n.

223 **fortitude** physical or structural strength; ?fortification

224 **substitute** deputy. This seems to refer to Montano, the 'governor of Cyprus': see *Texts*, 37.

225 **allowed** praised. The sense 'acknowledged' is not recorded before 1749 (*OED* 3).
sufficiency ability; qualification
opinion Lat. *opinio* (feminine, hence *mistress*, 226). 'General opinion, which finally determines what ought to be done, will feel safer with you in command' (Ridley).

226 **effects** purposes; results
voice preference; vote

227 **slubber** obscure; smear, sully
gloss lustre; fair semblance

228 **stubborn** difficult; rough ('more' so

than the 'gloss of . . . new fortunes')

229 **boisterous** (painfully) rough, violent
expedition military enterprise; haste (cf. 277)

230 **custom** Dent, C933, 'Custom makes all things easy'. Cf. Henry Howard in *A Defensative* (1583), 'That irregular and wilfull tyraunt Custome' (Kittredge); *Ham* 3.4.161, 'that monster custom'.

231 **flinty and steel** He refers to sleeping on the ground in armour (Sanders).

232 **thrice-driven** 'softest possible; a current of air drifted the finer and lighter feathers away from the coarser and heavier' (Ridley)
agnize acknowledge. 'I acknowledge (that) I find a natural and ready eagerness (in myself) in (situations of) hardship.'

233 **natural** inherent, innate
alacrity cheerful readiness

234 **hardness** difficulty; (sleeping on) the hard ground
undertake take in charge

221] *as* F; Beseech you now, to the affaires of the state. *Q*   222 a most] *F*; most *Q*   225 a] *Q*; a more *F*   230 grave] *F*; great *Q*   231 couch] *Pope*; Cooch *Q*; Coach *F*   233 alacrity] *Q*; Alacartie *F*   234 do] *F*; would *Q*

This present war against the Ottomites.   235
Most humbly therefore, bending to your state,
I crave fit disposition for my wife,
Due reverence of place, and exhibition,
With such accommodation and besort
As levels with her breeding.   240

DUKE

Why, at her father's.

BRABANTIO   I'll not have it so.

OTHELLO

Nor I.

DESDEMONA   Nor would I there reside
To put my father in impatient thoughts
By being in his eye. Most gracious duke,
To my unfolding lend your prosperous ear   245
And let me find a charter in your voice
T'assist my simpleness.

DUKE

What would you, Desdemona?

DESDEMONA

That I did love the Moor to live with him

---

235 *war For the QF plural, 'common errors' and final -*s* errors, see *Texts*, 85, 89, 90.

236 bending ... state submitting to your high office. He may bow respectfully as he speaks.

237 crave request
disposition arrangements

238 proper respect for her place (as my wife) and maintenance

239 accommodation room and suitable provision (*OED* 7, first here); supply of necessities
besort suitable company (*OED*, first

here). A coinage: cf. the verb, *KL* 1.4.251, 'Such men as may besort your age' (first here).

240 levels with equals, is on a par with
breeding upbringing

242 Removing Q's first *I*, F softens Desdemona's refusal (*Texts*, 16–18).

244 eye sight. So *Ham* 4.4.6, 'We shall express our duty in his eye.'

245 unfolding what I shall unfold (say)
prosperous favourable

246 charter privilege; pardon
voice   expressed   judgement
(*OED* 3)

---

235 war] *Q2;* warres *QF* Ottomites] *Ottamites QF*   238 reverence] *Q;* reference *F*   239 With] *F;* Which *Q* accommodation] *Q (*accomodation?*)*   241 Why, ... father's.] Why at her Fathers? *F;* If you please, bee't at her fathers. *Q* I'll] *as Q;* I will *F*   242 Nor would I] *F;* Nor I, I would not *Q*   245 your prosperous] *F;* a gracious *Q*   247 T'assist] *F;* And if *Q* simpleness.] *F;* simplenesse. – *Q*   248 you, Desdemona?] *F;* you – speake. *Q*   249 did] *Q; not in F*

150

My downright violence and scorn of fortunes   250
May trumpet to the world. My heart's subdued
Even to the very quality of my lord:
I saw Othello's visage in his mind,
And to his honours and his valiant parts
Did I my soul and fortunes consecrate,   255
So that, dear lords, if I be left behind,
A moth of peace, and he go to the war,
The rites for which I love him are bereft me,
And I a heavy interim shall support
By his dear absence. Let me go with him.   260

250 **downright** positive, absolute
violence i.e. violent rupture with
conventional behaviour
scorn Both *scorn* and *storm* of fortune
were commonplaces (cf. Q and F):
thus Heywood, *Edward the Fourth*
(1600), 'stormes of fortune' (Part 1,
B3b), 'ouerthrowne, / By fortunes
scorne' (Part 2, I6a). Also *TC* 1.3.47,
'storms of fortune' (classical in
origin: Seneca, *Agamemnon*, 594: *pro-
cella Fortunae*). Both are possible
here; each could be misread as the
other.

250 **fortunes** So QF: a misreading of
fortune?

251 **trumpet** proclaim (*OED*, here first
with this sense)

252 **quality** profession (Malone);
nature, moral and mental identity
(Cowden-Clarke, quoted Furness).
The thought is as in *Son* 111, 'My
nature is subdued / To what it works
in, like the dyer's hand': her inmost
being (*OED* heart 6) has been assimilated to Othello's nature (and
military profession). Q *vtmost pleasure*
looks like a first thought, changed
because it might suggest sexual
pleasure.

253 'I saw (the colour of) Othello's face
in (the quality of) his mind', i.e. his
face was transformed, in her eyes, by
his mind. She does not refer to his

colour directly but seems to be half
apologizing for it.

254 **parts** personal qualities or attributes
(*OED* 12), as in *MA* 5.2.60–1, 'For
which of my bad parts didst thou first
fal in loue with me?' (Q).

256 **dear** worthy, honoured

257 **moth** *either* drone, idler; *or* alluding
to the moth's attraction to light: if he
goes away to war, she, deprived of his
honours and *valiant parts*, will be like
a moth in the dark. Cf. *Cor* 1.3.82ff.,
'You would be another Penelope: yet
they say, all the yarn she spun in
Ulysses' absence did but fill [Ithaca]
full of moths.'

258 **rites** *Right* and *rite* were interchangeable spellings. Probably both
are intended here: *right* = enjoyment
of privileges, 'sharing his life and
dangers' (Walker); *rite* as in *rites of
love*, a cliché (cf. *R3* 5.3.101, *AW*
2.4.41).
bereft ('with double object: to be-
reave *any one a possession*', *OED* 1c),
i.e. the rights–rites are taken from
me. So *2H6* 3.1.84–5, 'all your interest in those territories / Is utterly
bereft you'.

259 **heavy** distressful
support endure (with quibble on
propping up something heavy)

260 **dear** grievous (cf. *Son* 37, 'Fortune's
dearest spite')

250 scorn] *Q ;* storme *F, Q2*   252 very quality] *F;* vtmost pleasure *Q*   258 which] *Q ;* why *F*

OTHELLO

Let her have your voice.
Vouch with me, heaven, I therefore beg it not
To please the palate of my appetite,
Nor to comply with heat, the young affects
In me defunct, and proper satisfaction,   265
But to be free and bounteous to her mind.
And heaven defend your good souls that you think
I will your serious and great business scant
When she is with me. No, when light-winged toys
Of feathered Cupid seel with wanton dullness   270
My speculative and officed instrument,
That my disports corrupt and taint my business,

261 **voice** support, approval
262 **Vouch** bear witness (*OED* 5b, first here)
263 **palate** taste; liking
    appetite (sexual) desire
264 **comply with** act in accordance with; satisfy
    heat passion; sexual excitement in animals, esp. females
    affects appetites, lusts
265 **defunct** extinct, dead (Hulme, 153–4)
    ***proper** in conformity with rule (*OED* 4, 10), permissible; correct. 'Nor to satisfy sexual passion – the youthful appetites that are extinct in me – and permissible gratification of desire.' Many editors feel that the passage is corrupt. For the misreading of final -*e*/-*y* (as apparently in *me*/*my* here), see *Texts*, 85.
266 **free** generous, liberal
    her mind Cf. *his mind*, 253. They both almost repudiate the body: how well do they know themselves?
267 **defend** forbid
268 **scant** stint, neglect

269 **light-winged** (?)insubstantial, trifling (a coinage)
    toys amorous sport, dallying; light caresses; trumpery, rubbish (*OED* 1, 2, 5)
270 **feathered** referring to Cupid's wings or arrows
    seel close (the eyes), alluding to blind Cupid. In falconry, young hawks were trained by having their eyes seeled (hooded).
    wanton dullness drowsiness, resulting from amorous dalliance
271 'my organ of sight, which has this particular function (i.e. to see clearly)'. *Speculative* (of faculties), exercised in vision; *officed*, having a particular office or function; *instrument*, a part of the body with a special function, an organ. Q's *foyles* = overthrows; *active instruments* = hands and feet (Malone).
272 **disports** (sexual) sports
    taint injure
    business diligence; care; official duties (*OED* 1, 6, 12)

261–2 Let … heaven] *F;* Your voyces Lords: beseech you let her will, / Haue a free way *Q* 265 me] *Capell (Upton);* my *QF* defunct] *QF;* distinct *Theobald* 266 ²to] *F;* of *Q* 268 great] *F;* good *Q* 269 When] *F;* For *Q* 270 Of] *F;* And *Q* seel] *F;* foyles *Q* 271 officed instrument] *F;* actiue instruments *Q*

Let housewives make a skillet of my helm
And all indign and base adversities
Make head against my estimation.   275

DUKE

Be it as you shall privately determine,
Either for her stay or going: th'affair cries haste
And speed must answer it.

1 SENATOR   You must away tonight.

DESDEMONA

Tonight, my lord?

DUKE   This night.

OTHELLO   With all my heart.

DUKE

At nine i'th' morning here we'll meet again.   280
Othello, leave some officer behind
And he shall our commission bring to you,
And such things else of quality and respect
As doth import you.

OTHELLO   So please your grace, my ancient:
A man he is of honesty and trust.   285

---

273 **housewives** Perhaps 'hussies'?
  skillet cooking pot, a metal container
  similar in shape to a helmet but lacking its dignity (Elliott, 15)
  helm helmet
274 **indign** shameful (unique in Shakespeare)
275 **Make head** advance, rise up
  estimation the way I am valued;
  reputation. Five syllables.
277 **cries** calls for (*OED* 7: first here)
278 **answer it** i.e. be answerable (corresponding) to it; with quibble on
  cries and *answer*
  tonight viz. their wedding night
279 **With . . . heart** 'Othello gazes long-

ingly, even despairingly, at his new
wife . . . then says with a sigh . . .
"With all my heart"' (Mack, 141).
Or he pretends, covering up his disappointment, or to persuade Desdemona.
280 **we'll meet** The Duke and senators
will meet; Othello will have sailed.
Note that Iago leaves later but arrives
in Cyprus before Othello: hence
2.1.67ff.
283–4 'and such other things as concern
your rank and the respect due to
you'; import = relate to
285 **honesty** could = honour; integrity;
good reputation

---

273 housewives] *F;* huswiues *Q* skillet] *F;* skellet *Q* 275 estimation] *F;* reputation *Q*
277 her] *F; not in Q* th'affair cries] *F;* the affaires cry *Q* 278–9] And speede must answer, you
must hence to night, / *Desd.* To might my Lord? / *Du.* This night. / *Q;* And speed must answer it.
/ *Sen.* You must away to night. / *F* 280 nine] *F;* ten *Q* i'th'] *F;* i'the *Q* 283 And] *F;* With
Q and] *F;* or *Q* 284 import] *F;* concerne *Q* So please] *F;* Please *Q*

To his conveyance I assign my wife,
With what else needful your good grace shall think
To be sent after me.

DUKE   Let it be so.
Good-night to everyone. And, noble signior,
If virtue no delighted beauty lack   290
Your son-in-law is far more fair than black.

1 SENATOR
Adieu, brave Moor, use Desdemona well.

BRABANTIO
Look to her, Moor, if thou hast eyes to see:
She has deceived her father, and may thee.

> *Exeunt [Duke, Brabantio, Senators, Officers].*

OTHELLO
My life upon her faith. Honest Iago,   295
My Desdemona must I leave to thee:
I prithee, let thy wife attend on her
And bring them after in the best advantage.
Come, Desdemona, I have but an hour
Of love, of worldly matter and direction   300
To spend with thee. We must obey the time.

> *Exeunt Othello and Desdemona.*

---

286 **conveyance** escort(ing)
287 'with whatever else your good grace shall think needful'
290 **delighted** delightful
291 **fair** fair-skinned; free from moral stain (*OED* 9), after *virtue*, 290
294 Cf. Dent, D180, 'He that once deceives is ever suspected.'
 SD As Brabantio turns to leave, Desdemona 'is often directed to kneel to him for a blessing, and his rejection is another shock to her' (Rosenberg, 213).
295 **My . . . faith** '(I would wager) my life on her good faith.'
 Honest 'a vague epithet of appreciation or praise, esp. as used in a patron-

izing way to an inferior' (*OED* 1c); cf. 'good Iago' (2.1.97), and pp. 85, 74.
297 He does not ask Desdemona whether this arrangement suits her. As she has just eloped, this will be the first time Emilia attends on her.
298 **in . . . advantage** as opportunity best serves (Ridley)
300 **love** (?)loving talk; not 'love-making' (cf. 2.3.9)
 direction instruction. He is in charge.
301 **obey the time** i.e. 'we must comply with the needs of this emergency'. In effect *she* must obey. Cf. Dent, T340.2, 'To obey the time' (probably Shakespeare's coinage).

---

293 if . . . see] *F;* haue a quicke eye to see *Q*   294 and may] *F;* may doe *Q*   SD *Exeunt*] *Q; Exit*
F   298 them] *F;* her *Q*   300 worldly] *Q;* wordly *F*   matter] *F;* matters *Q*   301 the] *Q;* the the
F   SD] *Exit Moore and* Desdemona. *Q; Exit. F*

RODERIGO Iago!

IAGO What sayst thou, noble heart?

RODERIGO What will I do, think'st thou?

IAGO Why, go to bed and sleep.   305

RODERIGO I will incontinently drown myself.

IAGO If thou dost, I shall never love thee after. Why,
thou silly gentleman?

RODERIGO It is silliness to live when to live is torment;
and then have we a prescription to die, when death is   310
our physician.

IAGO O villainous! I have looked upon the world for
four times seven years, and since I could distinguish
betwixt a benefit and an injury I never found a man
that knew how to love himself. Ere I would say I   315
would drown myself for the love of a guinea-hen I
would change my humanity with a baboon.

303 **thou** Iago's ascendancy has grown since 1.1, where he addressed Roderigo as *you* and *sir*; *noble heart* (drawled?) is close to insolence.

304 **What ... do** Cf. Terence, *Phormio*, 540, '*Geta*. Quid faciam? *Antiph*. Invenias argentum' (*G*. What am I to do? *A*. You must raise the money), and 'Put money in thy purse', 340.

306 **incontinently** immediately; with unconscious quibble on sexual incontinence, since he cannot control his 'love'

drown myself clearly not a heroic death. Cf. the Clown in *Mucedorus* (1598), B2a, 'I wil go home & put on a cleane shirt, and then goe drowne my selfe.'

307–8 **Why ... gentleman?** could be a question or an exclamation

310 **prescription** doctor's prescription; ancient custom (*OED* 4c)

310–11 **death ... physician** Cf. Dent, D142.3, 'Death is a physician' (could be post-Shakespearian).

312 **villainous** shameful

313 **four ... years** Why does Shakespeare make such a point of Iago's precise age? Cf. *Ham* 5.1.143–62; *Oth* 3.4.173ff. (a similar round-about calculation). Iago is younger than Othello and older than young Roderigo (5.1.11).

316 **guinea-hen** a showy bird with fine feathers (Johnson); (?)prostitute (*OED* 2b, 'slang': but not recorded in this sense before *Oth*). Since *hen* could = female, and *ginny* = cunning, ensnaring, seductive (*OED*, first recorded 1615), perhaps 'cunning female'. Pliny mentions 'Ginnie or Turkey Hens ... in great request' in Numidia (p. 296).

317 **change** exchange

baboon sometimes glossed as simpleton, i.e. a fitting victim for a 'ginny hen'. Baboons were thought to be particularly lecherous (*TNK* 3.5.132, 'the bavian [baboon] with long tail and eke long tool').

304 think'st] *F*; thinkest *Q*   307 If] *F*; Well, if *Q*   after] *F*; after it *Q*   307–8 Why, thou ... gentleman?] Why, thou ... Gentleman. *Q*; Why thou ... Gentleman? *F*   309 torment] *F*; a torment *Q*   310 have we] *F*; we haue *Q*   312 O villainous! I have] *as F*; I ha *Q*   314 betwixt] *F*; betweene *Q*   a man] *Q*; man *F*

RODERIGO What should I do? I confess it is my shame
to be so fond, but it is not in my virtue to amend it.

IAGO Virtue? a fig! 'tis in ourselves that we are thus, or   320
thus. Our bodies are gardens, to the which our wills
are gardeners. So that if we will plant nettles or sow
lettuce, set hyssop and weed up thyme, supply it with
one gender of herbs or distract it with many, either to
have it sterile with idleness or manured with industry   325
– why, the power and corrigible authority of this lies
in our wills. If the balance of our lives had not one
scale of reason to poise another of sensuality, the
blood and baseness of our natures would conduct us
to most preposterous conclusions. But we have   330
reason to cool our raging motions, our carnal stings,
our unbitted lusts; whereof I take this, that you call
love, to be a sect or scion.

319 **fond** infatuated; foolish
   virtue power; moral excellence
320 **a fig!** contemptuous exclamation (cf.
   2H4 5.3.118); an obscene gesture
   'which consisted in thrusting the
   thumb between two of the closed fingers or into the mouth' (*OED* fig 2)
   in ourselves i.e. in our own power
320–1 **thus, or thus** Cf. *STM*, 'It is in
   heaven that I am thus and thus' (Addition III.1, sometimes ascribed to
   Shakespeare).
321 **gardens** alluding to Galatians 6.7,
   'whatsoever a man soweth, that shall
   he also reap'. Iago's speech is a mock
   sermon, using theological commonplaces: cf. St Teresa on the good
   Christian as a gardener (*The Life*, ch.
   18), or Robert Mason, *Reasons Mon-
   archie* (1602), 71–3, on the 'motions
   of lust . . . against Reason'.
322 See LN.
323 **set** plant
324 **gender** kind
   distract it with divide it among
325 **sterile with idleness** unproductive

because of our inactivity
   manured managed; cultivated; enriched with manure; worked upon by
   hand (*OED* 1–4)
326 **power** control (of oneself)
   corrigible **authority** corrective
   power to influence others (*OED*
   authority 4)
327 **balance** scales; equilibrium. F *braine*
   could be a misreading of *beame* (= the
   bar from the ends of which the scales
   of a balance are suspended; or, 'the
   balance itself' [*OED* 6]).
328 **poise** hold in equilibrium, counter-
   poise
329 **blood** (the supposed seat of) animal
   appetite, fleshly nature
330 **preposterous** perverse, irrational
   (placing last what should be first)
   conclusions results
331 **motions** impulses
332 **unbitted** i.e. unrestrained
   lusts pleasures; appetites; sexual
   desires
333 **sect** cutting
   scion graft; sucker

321 gardens] *Q*; our Gardens *F*   323 hyssop] *F* (Hisope); Isop *Q*   327 balance] *Q*; braine *F*; beam *Theobald*   332 our] *Q*; or *F*   333 sect] *QF*; Set *Johnson*   scion] syen *Q*; Seyen *F*

RODERIGO   It cannot be.

IAGO   It is merely a lust of the blood and a permission of   335
the will. Come, be a man! drown thyself? drown cats
and blind puppies. I have professed me thy friend,
and I confess me knit to thy deserving with cables
of perdurable toughness. I could never better stead
thee than now. Put money in thy purse, follow thou   340
the wars, defeat thy favour with an usurped beard;
· I say, put money in thy purse. It cannot be that
Desdemona should long continue her love to the
Moor – put money in thy purse – nor he his to her. It
was a violent commencement in her, and thou shalt   345
see an answerable sequestration – put but money in
thy purse. These Moors are changeable in their wills
– fill thy purse with money. The food that to him
now is as luscious as locusts shall be to him shortly as

335 **permission** perhaps alluding to
God's 'permissive will', which toler-
ates the existence of evil (see *Paradise
Lost*, 3.685)
336 **be a man** Cf. 4.1.66.
337 **blind** i.e. new-born, therefore helpless
338 **deserving** desert, worthiness
cables strong ropes. Cf. Polonius,
'Those friends thou hast, and their
adoption tried, / Grapple them unto
thy soul with hoops of steel' (*Ham*
1.3.62–3).
339 **perdurable** imperishable
stead help, serve the needs of
340 **Put ... purse** Cf. 304n. He means
'sell your assets to raise money' and
Roderigo understands (380).
follow i.e. as a hanger-on, not as a
soldier
341 **defeat** destroy the beauty of,
disfigure
favour appearance; face
usurped false, counterfeit; i.e. make
yourself less pretty by wearing a false
beard (Roderigo is too young to have

a beard of his own: see 313n.,
5.1.11n.). Cf. *TN* 5.1.250, 'my masculine usurp'd attire' (Ridley). Kittredge thinks 'spoil thy pretty face by
growing a beard to which it has no
right'.
344–7 The dashes come from Q. I suspect that Iago is 'otherwise engaged'
as he speaks – tying a lace? fencing
with his shadow? – and throws out
'Put money . . .' as if it's no concern
of his. Cf. Rosenberg, 126.
346 **answerable** corresponding
sequestration (lit. an act of seques-
tering or cutting off); here probably
= cessation, or sequel (Lat. *sequor*, I
follow). Cf. Dent, B262, 'Such beginning such end'; N321, 'Nothing
violent can be permanent.'
347 **wills** desires; whims; wilfulness
349 **locusts** 'The carob groweth in
Apulia . . . so full of sweet juice that
it is used to preserve ginger . . . [This
is] thought to be that which is translated *locusts*' (Gerard's *Herball*,
1597, quoted Ridley).

337 have professed] *F;* professe *Q*   340 thou the] *F;* these *Q*   342 be] *Q;* be long *F*
343 should long] *Q;* should *F*   to] *F;* vnto *Q*   344 his] *F; not in Q*   345 in her] *F; not in Q*

acerb as coloquintida. She must change for youth;   350
when she is sated with his body she will find the
error of her choice: she must have change, she must.
Therefore, put money in thy purse. If thou wilt
needs damn thyself, do it a more delicate way than
drowning – make all the money thou canst. If sanc-   355
timony, and a frail vow betwixt an erring Barbarian
and a super-subtle Venetian, be not too hard for my
wits and all the tribe of hell, thou shalt enjoy her –
therefore make money. A pox of drowning thyself, it
is clean out of the way: seek thou rather to be hanged   360
in compassing thy joy than to be drowned and go
without her.

RODERIGO   Wilt thou be fast to my hopes, if I depend
on the issue?

IAGO   Thou art sure of me – go, make money. I have   365
told thee often, and I re-tell thee again and again, I

---

350 **acerb** bitter (from Cinthio's *acerbis-simo*: see p. 374)
coloquintida colocynth, a bitter apple. Its bitterness and use as a purgative were noted in herbals.
for youth for a younger man than Othello
351 **sated** satiated
353–4 **wilt needs** must
354 **delicate** (ironical) delightful; finely sensitive
355 **make** raise
355–6 **sanctimony** lit. holiness; pretended holiness (*OED* 3, from 1618): cf. 262, 'Vouch with me, heaven'. Or perhaps more general, pretended goodness.
356 **erring** wandering; straying; sinning. Cf. *extravagant*, 1.1.134n.
Barbarian native of Barbary, the Berber country (see p. 14); foreigner; a savage. Cf. *Barbary horse*, 1.1.110.

357 **super-subtle** super-crafty, referring to Desdemona as a typically depraved Venetian (see pp. 9–11) (unique in Shakespeare)
358 **tribe** i.e. population; 'and all the tribe of hell' may be an aside
360 **clean ... way** vaguely facetious (because a drowned body is clean and out of the way?) and colloquial. We would say 'that's barking up the wrong tree'. *Clean* = completely.
hanged (as a rapist?)
361 **compassing** obtaining; embracing
363–4 **fast ... issue** firmly fixed (to support) my hopes, if I await the outcome. Both *fast* and *depend* (*OED* 1: hang down, be suspended) imply tying.
365 **Thou ... me** Cf. 3.3.482, 'I am your own for ever.'
art sure can be sure

---

350 acerb as] acerbe as the *Q*; bitter as *F*   She ... youth] *F*; *not in Q*   352 error] *Q*; errors *F*   she must ... must] *Q*; *not in F*   357 a] *Q*; *not in F*   359 of] *F*; a *Q*   thyself] *F*; *not in Q*   359–60 it is] *F*; 'tis *Q*   363–4 if ... issue] *F*; *not in Q*   366 re-tell] *F*; tell *Q*

hate the Moor. My cause is hearted, thine hath no
less reason: let us be conjunctive in our revenge
against him. If thou canst cuckold him, thou dost
thyself a pleasure, me a sport. There are many events   370
in the womb of time, which will be delivered.
Traverse, go, provide thy money: we will have more
of this tomorrow. Adieu!

RODERIGO   Where shall we meet i'th' morning?

IAGO   At my lodging.   375

RODERIGO   I'll be with thee betimes.

IAGO   Go to, farewell. – Do you hear, Roderigo?

RODERIGO   What say you?

IAGO   No more of drowning, do you hear?

RODERIGO   I am changed. I'll sell all my land.   *Exit.*

IAGO   Go to, farewell, put money enough in your purse.   381
    Thus do I ever make my fool my purse:
    For I mine own gained knowledge should profane
    If I would time expend with such a snipe

367 **hearted** fixed in the heart, determined
368 **conjunctive** united. Occurs twice
in Shakespeare ('She is so conjunctive to my life and soul', *Ham* 4.7.14);
Q *communicatiue* (= in touch, in
communication) occurs nowhere else
in Shakespeare.
369 **cuckold** make (him) a cuckold (by
seducing his wife)
370 **sport** amusement
    events (from Lat. *evenire*, to come
    out or forth) consequences, outcomes
371 **delivered** i.e. brought forth (like a
new-born child); declared, made
known (in due time)
372 **Traverse** a military command (cf.
2H4 3.2.272) of uncertain meaning;
perhaps 'quick march!'
376 **betimes** early, in good time
377, 381 **Go to** a favourite phrase of his,
used to jolly others along, sometimes
almost meaningless (= come on; well

then). Also biblical (Genesis 11.4,
James 4.13, 5.1). 'The Folio compositor, one guesses, jumped from *Go too,
farewell*, opening 377, to the later line
which also opens with *Go to, farewell*,
and omitted the intervening words. A
conflation of Folio and Quarto is necessary to restore the original text'
(Sisson, *Readings*, 2.249).
378–81 **What ... purse** For the different readings of Q and F, see *Texts*,
47.
382 **ever** Iago is already a hardened
cheater.
383 **profane** treat (the sacred) irrever-
ently. He cynically misuses the word,
since his *knowledge* is evil, not sacred
as usually understood.
384 **expend** spend
    snipe fool (*OED*: a term of abuse,
    first recorded here); woodcock (a
    long-billed bird like a snipe) meant
    'gull' or 'dupe' before Shakespeare

367 hath] *F;* has *Q*   368 conjunctive] *F;* communicatiue *Q*   370 me] *F;* and me *Q*   378–
80 What . . . changed.] *Q; not in F*   380 I'll . . . land.] *F; not in Q;* Ile goe sell . . . land. *Q2*   381 Go
. . . purse.] *Q ; not in F*

But for my sport and profit. I hate the Moor   385
And it is thought abroad that 'twixt my sheets
He's done my office. I know not if't be true,
But I for mere suspicion in that kind
Will do as if for surety. He holds me well,
The better shall my purpose work on him.   390
Cassio's a proper man: let me see now,
To get his place, and to plume up my will
In double knavery. How? How? let's see:
After some time to abuse Othello's ear
That he is too familiar with his wife.   395
He hath a person and a smooth dispose
To be suspected, framed to make women false.
The Moor is of a free and open nature
That thinks men honest that but seem to be so,

385 **sport** Cf. 370, 2.3.374.
386 **And** 'Rarely is a conjunction used so effectively: the hate is prior, and a motive is then discovered' (Heilman, 31).
abroad i.e. generally, widely
387 **He's** *Has* (or, *h'as*, *ha's*) could = he has: cf. 2.1.67.
office service, duty, function. A curious word for marital intercourse. Cf. 4.3.86, 'Say that they slack their duties'.
388 **in that kind** of that nature
389 **do** proceed; perhaps picking up '*done* my office' (387), i.e. 'do *his* office' (cf. 2.1.293–7). Cf. *2H4* 2.1.41–2, 'do me your offices'.
for surety for certain (*OED* 4c), i.e. as if it's a certain fact
holds . . . well He is well-disposed towards me.
391 **proper** handsome; also admirable, perfect; appropriate (*OED* 6–9)
let me see . . . Cf. the free-wheeling improvisations of the 'clever slave' of classical comedy, and 402n.

392 **his place** Cf. 1.1.7ff.
plume up uncertain. Perhaps = ruffle the feathers, like a bird that 'displays', hence make a show of, exhibit. Cf. *Lust's Dominion* (printed 1657, dated *c*. 1600), 'Ambition plumes the *Moor* . . . to act deeds beyond astonishment' (Dekker, 4. 182).
will inclination; pleasure; determination
395 **he** Cassio
his Othello's
396 **person** bodily presence
smooth dispose insinuating disposition
397 **framed** made, formed
398 **free** spontaneous, frank, unreserved
open not given to concealing thoughts or feelings; without defence or protection (*OED* 16, 15). Curiously, Ben Jonson echoed these words in describing Shakespeare: see p. 105.
399 Cf. Dent, T221, 'They that think none ill are soonest beguiled.'

387 He's] Ha's *Q;* She ha's *F*   388 But] *F;* Yet *Q*   392 his] *F;* this *Q*   plume] *F;* make *Q*
393 In] *F;* A *Q*   knavery. How? How?] *F;* knauery – how, how, – *Q*   let's] *F;* let me *Q*   394
ear] *Q;* cares *F*   396 hath] *F;* has *Q*   398] *F;* The Moore a free and open nature too,
Q   399 seem] *F;* seemes *Q*

And will as tenderly be led by th' nose   400
As asses are.
I have't, it is engendered! Hell and night
Must bring this monstrous birth to the world's light.   *Exit.*

[2.1]   *Enter* MONTANO *and two* Gentlemen.

MONTANO
    What from the cape can you discern at sea?
1 GENTLEMAN
    Nothing at all, it is a high-wrought flood:
    I cannot 'twixt the haven and the main
    Descry a sail.
MONTANO
    Methinks the wind hath spoke aloud at land,   5
    A fuller blast ne'er shook our battlements:
    If it hath ruffianed so upon the sea
    What ribs of oak, when mountains melt on them,

---

400 **tenderly** easily, gently (sarcastic)
  led ... nose Cf. Dent, N233, 'To
  lead one by the nose (like a bear, ass)'.
402 **I have't** Cf. the clever slave's *habeo!*
  (= I've got it, I've solved the problem!) in Latin comedy: e.g. Terence,
  Andria, 344, 498, etc. Echoed by Elizabethan dramatists: cf. *TS* 1.1.189,
  Ham 4.7.154ff., 'Soft, let me see . . . I
  ha't!'
  engendered begotten, conceived
403 **birth** (*OED* 3b:) that which is borne
  in the womb. Cf. 371.
2.1.0.1 MONTANO probably the governor
  of Cyprus replaced by Othello: see
  t.n. and Honigmann, *Stability*, 44–6
1 **cape** projecting headland, land jut-
  ting into the sea. Presumably the
  Gentleman speaks from the side or
  back of the stage. In classical plays
  those on stage sometimes observe a
  ship at sea (Plautus, *Rudens*, 162ff.;

cf. *WT* 3.3.88ff.).
2 **high-wrought** agitated to a high
  degree (*OED*); or, flinging itself high
  into the air (cf. 12ff.) (unique in
  Shakespeare)
  flood (body of) water
3 **main** main sea, open ocean
4 **Descry** 'To catch sight of, esp. from a
  distance, as the scout or watchman
  who is ready to announce the enemy's
  approach' (*OED* 6)
5 **at land** on the land
6 **fuller** more complete (as in 'full
  flood', 'full tide': *OED* 8d)
7 **ruffianed** acted the ruffian (unique
  in Shakespeare as verb)
8 **ribs** curved frame-timbers of a ship
  mountains i.e. huge masses of
  water. Cf. 'hills of seas', 184. Adapted
  from Judges 5.5, 'The mountains
  melted from before the Lord'
  (Steevens).

---

400 led . . . nose] led bit'h nose *Q* ; lead by' th' Nose *F*   402 have't] *F;* ha't *Q*   403 SD] *Q ; not in
F*   2.1] *Actus* 2. / *Scoena* 1. *Q ; Actus Secundus. Scena Prima. F*   0.1] *F; Enter* Montanio, *Gouernor
of* Cypres, *with two other Gentlemen. Q*   3 haven] *Q ;* Heauen *F*   5 hath spoke] *F;* does speake
Q   7 hath] *F;* ha *Q*   8 when . . . them] *F;* when the huge mountaine meslt *Q*

Can hold the mortise? What shall we hear of this?

2 GENTLEMAN

A segregation of the Turkish fleet: 10
For do but stand upon the foaming shore,
The chidden billow seems to pelt the clouds,
The wind-shaked surge, with high and monstrous
      mane,
Seems to cast water on the burning bear
And quench the guards of th'ever-fired pole.   15
I never did like molestation view
On the enchafed flood.

MONTANO   If that the Turkish fleet
Be not ensheltered and embayed, they are drowned.
It is impossible to bear it out.

Enter a Third Gentleman.

---

9 ***hold the mortise** keep their joints
   intact (Sanders)
10 **segregation** dispersion, separation
   (unique in Shakespeare)
11 **foaming** Q *banning*, the 'harder reading', could mean cursing, chiding; an
   easy misreading, improbable here
12 **chidden** i.e. repelled by the shore
   pelt strike, beat (stronger than today:
   cf. *KL* 3.4.29, 'the pelting of this piti-
   less storm')
   clouds See LN.
13 **wind-shaked** unique in Shakespeare
   (but cf. *wind-shaken, Cor* 5.2.111)
   surge a high rolling swell of water
   mane with high-flying mane like a
   monstrous beast. Knight's spelling
   brings out the mane–main quibble.
   Furness compared *2H4* 3.1.20ff.,
   where *surge* and *winds* 'take the ruffian billows by the top, / Curling
   their monstrous heads'. According to
   Sisson, *Readings*, the 'sense of main is

as in "with might and main"' (=
power), and *monstrous* = portentous
(2.250). But *monstrous* could = huge,
gigantic (*OED* 4), and the line's im-
precision may be deliberate.
14 **bear** the constellation Ursa Minor
   (i.e. the Little Bear), 'since the *guards*
   are the two stars in that constellation
   next in brightness to the Pole Star'
   (Ridley)
15 See LN.
16 **molestation** unique in Shakespeare;
   from Cinthio (cf. p. 372). Lat. *molestia* = trouble, vexation; Shakespeare
   seems to mean turmoil.
17 **enchafed** (probably enchafèd, eliding
   the to *th'*): excited, furious
   If that if
18 **ensheltered** unique in Shakespeare
   embayed unique in Shakespeare (=
   sheltered in a bay)
19 **bear it out** hold out, survive it

---

9 mortise] morties *QF*   10 SP] 2 *Gent. Q;* 2 *F*   11 foaming] *F;* banning *Q*   12 chidden] *F;*
chiding *Q*   13 mane] *Knight;* mayne *Q;* Maine *F*   15 ever-fired] euer fired *Q;* euer-fixed *F*
19 to] *F;* they *Q*   19.1 Third] *Q; not in F*

3 GENTLEMAN

    News, lads: our wars are done!   20

    The desperate tempest hath so banged the Turks

    That their designment halts. A noble ship of Venice

    Hath seen a grievous wrack and sufferance

    On most part of their fleet.

MONTANO   How? Is this true?

3 GENTLEMAN

    The ship is here put in,   25

    A Veronessa; Michael Cassio,

    Lieutenant to the warlike Moor, Othello,

    Is come on shore; the Moor himself at sea,

    And is in full commission here for Cyprus.

MONTANO

    I am glad on't, 'tis a worthy governor.   30

3 GENTLEMAN

    But this same Cassio, though he speak of

        comfort

Enter CASSIO.

    Touching the Turkish loss, yet he looks sadly

    And prays the Moor be safe, for they were parted

---

20 **lads** With the QF variants, cf. *TC* 3.1.108, lad (Q), Lord (F); and *Texts*, 83, on *a:o* misreading.

21 **desperate** terrible

22 **designment** enterprise
halts (lit. 'is lame') is in doubt; stops
noble great, stately

23 **wrack** disaster, destruction (cf. 'wrack and ruin'); shipwreck
sufferance damage (inflicted on)

26 See LN.

29 **and is** (heading) for Cyprus with full delegated authority here (*OED* commission 5)

30 **governor** ungrudging praise from the man replaced as governor: see 2.1.0.1n.

31 **comfort** support, relief; a cause of satisfaction (*OED* 5)
*31.1 Cassio must enter earlier than QF direct, as he overhears Montano's speech. SDs were often placed in the margins of a text, not precisely where required (see Honigmann, 'Stage direction').

32 **sadly** gravely

---

20 SP] 3 *Gent. Q;* 3 *F (throughout)* lads] *F;* Lords *Q* our] *F;* your *Q* 21 Turks] *F; Turke Q* 22 A noble] *F;* Another *Q* 24 their] *F;* the *Q* 25–6] *as Q; one line F* 25 in,] in: *QF* 26 Veronessa] *Q; Verennessa F* 28 on shore] *F;* ashore *Q* himself] *QF;* himself's *Rowe* 30] *as Q; F lines* on't: / Gouernour. / 31.1] *this edn; after 42 QF* 33 prays] *Q;* praye *F*

With foul and violent tempest.

MONTANO   Pray heavens he be,
For I have served him, and the man commands   35
Like a full soldier. Let's to the seaside, ho!
As well to see the vessel that's come in
As to throw out our eyes for brave Othello,
Even till we make the main and th'aerial blue
An indistinct regard.

3 GENTLEMAN   Come, let's do so,   40
For every minute is expectancy
Of more arrivance.

CASSIO

Thanks, you the valiant of this warlike isle
That so approve the Moor. O, let the heavens
Give him defence against the elements,   45
For I have lost him on a dangerous sea.

MONTANO

Is he well shipped?

CASSIO

His bark is stoutly timbered, and his pilot
Of very expert and approved allowance,
Therefore my hopes, not surfeited to death,   50

---

34 **With** by
35 **served** served under
36 **full** perfect
39 **aerial** atmospheric: 'even till our eyes make the sea and atmospheric blue a single indistinguishable sight'
41 **expectancy** expectance (a new word *c.* 1600)
42 **arrivance** (a coinage, unique in Shakespeare) i.e. more arrivals
44 **approve** commend
48 **bark** a sailing vessel; 'in 17th century

sometimes applied to the *barca-longa* of the Mediterranean' (*OED* 3)
49 **approved** proved
allowance acknowledgement (*OED* 3), i.e. is acknowledged to be skilled and proved good by experience
50–1 **not ... cure** not indulged in excessively, persist in their optimism (*OED* stand 72; *bold* = confident, *cure* = care). 'A verbal bubble that disappears if one examines it too closely' (Ridley).

---

34 heavens] *F;* Heauen *Q*   38 throw out] *Q;* throw-out *F*   39–40 Even ... regard] *F; not in Q*   39 aerial] *Pope;* Eriall *F;* Ayre all *Q2*   40 SP] *as Q; Gent. F*   42 arrivance] *Q;* Arriuancie *F*   43 Thanks, you] Thankes you, *F;* Thankes to *Q*   this] *Q;* the *F*   warlike] *F;* worthy *Q*   44 O] *F;* and *Q*   45 the] *F;* their *Q*   48 pilot] *F (*Pylot*);* Pilate *Q*   50 hopes, not ... death] hope's not ... death *Q;* hope's (not ... death) *F*

Stand in bold cure.

A VOICE   (*within*)   A sail! a sail! a sail!

CASSIO

What noise?

2 GENTLEMAN

The town is empty: on the brow o'th' sea

Stand ranks of people, and they cry 'A sail!'

CASSIO

My hopes do shape him for the governor.   *A shot.*

2 GENTLEMAN

They do discharge their shot of courtesy,   56

Our friends at least.

CASSIO   I pray you sir, go forth

And give us truth who 'tis that is arrived.

2 GENTLEMAN

I shall.   *Exit.*

MONTANO

But, good lieutenant, is your general wived?   60

CASSIO

Most fortunately: he hath achieved a maid

That paragons description and wild fame;

One that excels the quirks of blazoning pens

And in th'essential vesture of creation

---

51 SD *within* i.e. off stage
53 **brow** projecting edge of a cliff (over-looking the sea)
54 **ranks** rows
55 **shape** shape him (in imagination) to be the governor; portray
56 **shot of courtesy** a cannon shot, in friendly salute (off stage)
60 **wived** not quite the same as 'married'. Cf. 3.4.195, 'womaned'.
61 **achieved** acquired

62 **paragons** surpasses (*OED* 3, first here)
   wild fame report at its wildest
63 **quirks** verbal subtleties
   blazoning describing; boasting; proclaiming
64 **And ... creation** = (?)in the essential clothing in which she was created. I suggest 'in her innermost nature' (*essential vesture* = soul, not body). Or, in the 'vesture that is her essence' (Capell).

---

51 *opp.* cure] *Enter a Messenger. Q*   SP] *Mess. Q ; Gent. F*   55 governor] *F; guernement Q*   SD] *Q (after* least *57); not in F*   56 SP] *Q ; Gent. F*   their] *F; the Q*   57 friends] *F; friend Q*   59 SP] *Q ; Gent. F*   SD] *Q ; not in F*   63 quirks of] *F; not in Q*   64 th'] *F; the Q*

Does tire the inginer.

Enter Second Gentleman.

How now? Who has put in?   65

2 GENTLEMAN

'Tis one Iago, ancient to the general.

CASSIO

He's had most favourable and happy speed.
Tempests themselves, high seas, and howling winds,
The guttered rocks and congregated sands,
Traitors ensteeped to clog the guiltless keel,   70
As having sense of beauty, do omit
Their mortal natures, letting go safely by
The divine Desdemona.

MONTANO   What is she?

CASSIO

She that I spake of, our great captain's captain,

---

65 **tire the inginer** = (?)exhaust the (powers of the) divine inventor (God); i.e. she is God's masterpiece. Inginer (= author, inventor) is modern 'engineer', but stressed on first syllable; could = a human artist (a painter, or one who describes verbally), i.e. exhausts the one who tries to do her justice. Muir notes that '"tyre" can mean "attire", as well as "weary". Possibly "tire" was suggested by "vesture" through an unconscious quibble.' Not too clear, hence Q's weak substitution.
put in landed

66 **ancient . . . general** i.e. Iago was attached to the general rather than to the army: see p. 335.

67 **happy** fortunate; successful
speed 'includes the idea of "fortune", as well as that of celerity' (Ridley)

68–73 The idea may come from the Orpheus legend: Orpheus' music

made wild animals *omit* their deadly natures.

69 **guttered** furrowed, grooved (by wind and water). Ovid mentioned the rocks that surround Cyprus (*Metamorphoses*, 10.6).
congregated sands sandbanks

70 **ensteeped** under water (a coinage). Q *enscerped* could = enscarped (= sloping, from *escarp*: Hulme, 282).
clog obstruct
guiltless having no familiarity with or experience of (these 'traitors') (*OED* 3, from 1667)

71 **omit** forbear to use

72 **mortal** deadly

73 **divine Desdemona** Cf. 'divine Zenocrate' in *1 Tamburlaine*, 5.1.135.

74 **captain's captain** So *AC* 3.1.22; cf. *Oth* 2.3.305, 'Our general's wife is now the general', *R3* 4.4.336, 'Caesar's Caesar', *TN* 3.1.102, 'Your servant's servant'.

---

65 tire the inginer] *F (*tyre the Ingeniuer*);* beare all excellency *Q*   SD] *Q (after 65); Enter Gentleman. F (after* Ingeniuer*)*   How] *F; not in Q*   66 SP] *as Q ;* Gent. *F*   67 SP] *as F; not in Q*   He's] He has *Q ;* Ha's *F*   68 high] *F;* by *Q*   69 guttered rocks] *Q ;* gutter'd-Rockes *F*   70 ensteeped] *F;* enscerped *Q*   clog] *Q ;* enclogge *F*   72 mortal] *F;* common *Q*   74] *F lines* of: / Captaine, /   spake] *F;* spoke *Q*

Left in the conduct of the bold Iago,   75
Whose footing here anticipates our thoughts
A se'nnight's speed. Great Jove, Othello guard,
And swell his sail with thine own powerful breath
That he may bless this bay with his tall ship,
Make love's quick pants in Desdemona's arms,   80
Give renewed fire to our extincted spirits
And bring all Cyprus comfort! –

Enter DESDEMONA, IAGO, RODERIGO *and* EMILIA.

                                        O, behold,
The riches of the ship is come on shore:
You men of Cyprus, let her have your knees!
Hail to thee, lady, and the grace of heaven,   85
Before, behind thee, and on every hand
Enwheel thee round!
DESDEMONA   I thank you, valiant Cassio.
What tidings can you tell me of my lord?
CASSIO
He is not yet arrived, nor know I aught
But that he's well, and will be shortly here.   90

75 **conduct** charge, conducting
76 **footing** setting foot upon land (*OED*
   1b, first here)
76–7 **Whose ... speed** occurs earlier
   than we expected by a week. She left
   after Cassio and Othello, who sailed
   together (91; 1.3.278).
77–8 In Renaissance maps and pictures
   supernatural beings blow ships, etc.,
   across the seas.
79 **tall** tall-masted
80 **love's quick pants** 'The quick
   breathing that accompanies and
   ensues upon the orgasm' (Partridge,
   162). Perhaps, but note that Cassio
   later resists sexual imagery applied to
   Desdemona (2.3.14ff.). The 'panting
   of loving hearts' was a commonplace

(Lyly, 2.373, and Lyly, *Sapho*,
   1.1.22), 'quick pants' less so.
81 **extincted** extinguished (unique in
   Shakespeare)
84 **let ... knees** kneel to her (out of
   courtesy)
85–7 Cassio uses (familiar) *thee* here, but
   you later (165). An echo of 'Hail
   Mary', reinforced by kneeling and
   'the grace of heaven'? See p. 107.
86 Could Shakespeare have known
   Donne's (unpublished) Elegy 19,
   'Going to Bed'? 'License my roving
   hands, and let them go / *Before*,
   behind, between, above, below'.
   on every hand on all sides
87 **Enwheel** encircle: a coinage

80 Make ... in] *F*; And swiftly come to *Q*   82 And ... comfort!] *Q*; *not in F*   SD] *as F; Enter
Desdemona, Iago, Emillia, and Roderigo. Q (after 80)*   83 on shore] *F*; ashore *Q*   84 You] *F*; Ye
Q   88 me] *Q*; *not in F*

DESDEMONA

O, but I fear . . . how lost you company?

CASSIO

The great contention of the sea and skies
Parted our fellowship.   (A VOICE *within:* 'A sail! a sail!')
                    But hark! a sail!

[A shot is heard.]

2 GENTLEMAN

They give their greeting to the citadel:
This likewise is a friend.

CASSIO   See for the news.

[Exit Gentleman.]

Good ancient, you are welcome. [*to Emilia*] Welcome,
    mistress.   96
Let it not gall your patience, good Iago,
That I extend my manners; 'tis my breeding
That gives me this bold show of courtesy.

[He kisses Emilia.]

IAGO

Sir, would she give you so much of her lips   100
As of her tongue she oft bestows on me
You'd have enough.

DESDEMONA   Alas! she has no speech.

---

93 **Parted our fellowship** separated
our ships
96, 97 **Good . . . good** Note the touch of
condescension in *good*: see p. 85.
97 **gall** vex. For Iago's delayed response,
cf. 167ff.
98–9 **That . . . courtesy** i.e. that I offer
a polite greeting to your wife; it is my
good manners (or upbringing) that
prompt me to this bold display of
elegant behaviour (kissing the ladies).
Such kissing was 'an English habit

rather than an Italian one' (Bullough,
219).
99.1 *Perhaps Emilia accepts the kiss
too willingly, irritating Iago. Does she
have to *give . ∴. her lips?*
101 **her tongue** Iago coarsely hints at
kissing, as well as scolding, with the
tongue.
bestows confers as a gift (sarcastic)
102 **Alas . . . speech** Poor thing! you
have put her out; or, alas, she's not a
talker.

91] *as Q; F lines* feare: / company? /   92 the sea] *Q;* Sea *F*   93 ¹SD] *[within.] A saile, a saile. Q
(after 91); Within.* A Saile, a Saile. *F (after 93)*   ²SD] *Guns / Capell; not in QF*   94 their] *Q;* this
F   95 See . . . news] *F;* So speakes this voyce: *Q*   SD] *Capell; not in QF*   96 SD] *Rowe; not in
QF*   99 SD] *as Johnson; not in QF*   100 Sir] *F;* For *Q*   101 oft bestows] *F;* has bestowed *Q*
102 You'd] *Q;* You would *F*

IAGO

In faith, too much!
I find it still when I have list to sleep.
Marry, before your ladyship, I grant,   105
She puts her tongue a little in her heart
And chides with thinking.

• EMILIA

You have little cause to say so.

IAGO

Come on, come on, you are pictures out of doors,
Bells in your parlours, wild-cats in your kitchens,   110
Saints in your injuries, devils being offended,
Players in your housewifery, and housewives in . . .
Your beds!

DESDEMONA   O, fie upon thee, slanderer!

IAGO

Nay, it is true, or else I am a Turk:

---

104 **still** always
   list inclination. F *leaue* is possible:
   when I have her permission to sleep
   (because she still goes on talking)
105 **before** in the presence of
106–7 'holds her tongue and thinks the
   more' (Ridley)
109–13 prose in F, verse in Q: could be
   either. Cf. Dent, W702, 'Women are
   in church saints, abroad angels, at
   home devils.' There were many variations before Shakespeare, e.g. 'a
   shrew in the kitchen . . . an ape in the
   bed'.
109 **you** He cheekily includes Desdemona!
   pictures 'silent appearances (of
   virtue)' (Sanders). Or, pretty as pictures, when you put on your best
   clothes to go out, 'with a suggestion
   that they owe their beauty to painting' (Kittredge).
110 **Bells** i.e. jangling bells
   parlours A parlour was originally a

room for conversation (Fr. *parler*).
   wild-cats Cf. *TS* 1.2.196, 'Will you
   woo this wild-cat?'
   kitchens i.e. in defending your
   territories
111 **Saints . . . injuries** 'When you have
   a mind to do injuries, you put on an
   air of sanctity' (Johnson); or, (you
   pretend to be) innocent when others
   have injured you.
112 **Players** i.e. you play at housekeep-
   ing; it is not what you give serious
   attention to
   ***housewives** After the antitheses of
   111, one expects 'workers in your
   beds'. Housewife = a woman who
   manages her household with skill, or
   a 'light' woman, now *hussy* (*OED* 1,
   2). Hence 'you are skilful managers
   in your beds' (notice the plural: he
   includes Desdemona).
114 **or . . . Turk** a variant of 'I am a
   Jew (rogue, villain) else' (Dent,
   J49.1)

---

103 In faith] *F;* I know *Q*   104 it . . . have] *F;* it, I; for when I ha *Q*   list] *Q ;* leaue *F*   108 have]
F; ha *Q*   109–13 Come . . . beds] *prose F; Q lines as verse* adores: / Kitchins: / offended: / beds. /
109 of doors] adores *Q ;* of doore *F*   112–13 in . . . / Your beds] *this edn*   113 SP] *F; not in Q*

You rise to play, and go to bed to work.   115

EMILIA

You shall not write my praise.

IAGO   No, let me not.

DESDEMONA

What wouldst thou write of me, if thou shouldst
    praise me?

IAGO

O, gentle lady, do not put me to't,
For I am nothing if not critical.

DESDEMONA

Come on, assay. There's one gone to the harbour?   120

IAGO

Ay, madam.

DESDEMONA

I am not merry, but I do beguile
The thing I am by seeming otherwise.
Come, how wouldst thou praise me?

IAGO

I am about it, but indeed my invention   125
Comes from my pate as birdlime does from frieze,

---

115 **You** He speaks even more directly to
Desdemona than at 109, attacking her
sense of sexual privacy. Cf. the voyeurism of 1.1.109ff., 3.3.413ff., 4.1.1ff.

117–64 'One of the most unsatisfactory
passages in Shakespeare' (Ridley).
Yet it shows how Iago wins an ascendancy over others, his improvising
skills (note how Cassio is overshadowed), and that Desdemona understands sexual innuendo.

117 **of me** She is not asking for compli-
ments, but wants to stop the marital
bickering and places herself in the
firing line (as later with Othello–
Cassio).

   shouldst were to; had to

118 **put me to't** challenge me to (do) it
(*OED* put 28)

119 **critical** censorious

120 **assay** try, put me to the test
   one someone

122–3 '**I . . . otherwise** perhaps an aside.
Cf. *AW* 2.2.60–1, 'I play the noble
housewife with the time, / To enter-
tain it so merrily with a fool.'

122 **beguile** disguise; divert attention
from. An ominous echo of Iago's 'I
am not what I am' (1.1.64)?

123 **The . . . am** i.e. the fact that I am
an anxious wife

125 **invention** inventiveness; the thing
invented. Slur as 'my 'nvention'. But
125–8 may be meant as prose.

126 **birdlime** a viscous preparation
spread on bushes to snare birds (Ridley)
   frieze coarse woollen cloth; i.e.
comes from my thick head just as
sticky birdlime comes (with difficulty) from frieze

---

117 wouldst thou] *Q ;* would'st *F*   120] *as Q ; F lines* assay. / Harbour? /   125–8] *as Q (verse);*
prose F

It plucks out brains and all; but my muse labours
And thus she is delivered:
If she be fair and wise, fairness and wit,
The one's for use, the other useth it.   130

DESDEMONA

Well praised. How if she be black and witty?

IAGO

If she be black, and thereto have a wit,
. She'll find a white that shall her blackness fit.

DESDEMONA

Worse and worse.

EMILIA

How if fair and foolish?   135

IAGO

She never yet was foolish that was fair,
For even her folly helped her to an heir.

127–8 **but … delivered** quibbles on being in labour and giving birth; *my muse* = my inspiring goddess (jocular: he compares himself with Homer and classical poets who invoke their Muse). Iago affects a gentlemanly facility as versifier: cf. Jonson's Stephano, who will 'write you your halfe score or your dozen of sonnets at a sitting' (*Jonson*, 3.228), and *LLL* 4.2.50ff.

129–30 **If … it** semi-proverbial. Cf. Dent, F28, 'Fair and foolish, black and proud, long and lazy, little and loud'; *fair* = beautiful, or fair-haired; *wit* = intellect, wisdom.

130 **The … it** Perhaps = each one is for use, and the other (beauty or brains) makes use of it, i.e. they both need each other.

131 **black** dark-haired. Traditionally, Desdemona is fair-haired, Emilia is dark.

witty endowed with good judgement

133 **find** Cf. 250, 'the woman hath found him already'.
white a quibble on *wight* (cf. 158) = person; man. Here *black* and *white* hint at a mixed union like Othello's and Desdemona's. Q *hit* is possible: cf. *The Wit of a Woman* (1604), B1b, 'when you haue your mistresse, hange your selfe, if you can not teach her a right hit it', and *LLL* 4.1.125–8.
blackness could = pudendum. 'To hit the white' = to hit the centre of the target (cf. *TS* 5.2.186), and 'shall her blackness hit' may quibble accordingly.

134 **said** admiringly in wit combats (Lyly, *Endimion*, 4.2.52; *Midas*, 1.2.101); i.e. 'progressively worse' (*OED* 1c)

137 **folly** foolishness; unchastity (cf. 5.2.130: 'She turned to folly, and she was a whore') (Sanders)
an heir to marry an heir; to have a bastard child

---

127 brains] *F*; braine *Q*   129–30, 132–3, 136–7, 141–2, 148–58, 160] *as Q; italics F*   130 useth] *F*; vsing *Q*   131] *as Q; F lines* prais'd: / Witty? /   133 fit] *F*; hit *Q*   137 an heir] *F*; a haire *Q*

DESDEMONA   These are old fond paradoxes to make
   fools laugh i'th' alehouse. What miserable praise hast
   thou for her that's foul and foolish?   140

IAGO

   There's none so foul, and foolish thereunto,
   But does foul pranks which fair and wise ones do.

DESDEMONA   O heavy ignorance, thou praisest the worst
   best. But what praise couldst thou bestow on a
   deserving woman indeed? One that in the authority   145
   of her merit did justly put on the vouch of very
   malice itself?

IAGO

   She that was ever fair and never proud,
   Had tongue at will, and yet was never loud,
   Never lacked gold, and yet went never gay,   150
   Fled from her wish, and yet said 'now I may',
   She that, being angered, her revenge being nigh,
   Bade her wrong stay, and her displeasure fly,

138 **fond** foolish
   paradoxes contradictory or absurd
   sayings
139 **miserable** miserly, stingy; wretched;
   despicable
140 **foul** ugly; dirty
142 **pranks** i.e. sexual pranks or acts (cf.
   3.3.205). Iago's rhymes have become
   more and more overtly sexual.
   do Cf. 3.3.435n.
143 **heavy** grievous; distressing
143–4 **thou ... best** (because he has
   said less in dispraise of the worst?)
145 **indeed** 'freq. placed after a word in
   order to emphasize it' (*OED* 1b), i.e.
   'a truly deserving woman'. Thinking
   of herself? Or pointing to Emilia?
146 **put on** encourage, urge on (*OED*
   46h), as in *KL* 1.4.208, 'That you
   protect this course and put it on / By
   your allowance.' Hence, 'one who, au-
   thorised by her merit, did reasonably
   encourage (others to give) the testimony of malice itself': i.e. one who,

sure of her own merit, did not fear
the worst that could be said against
her.
148–60 **She ... beer** Cf. the nonsense
verses in *KL* 3.2.81ff., spoken by the
Fool. Here Iago plays the fool to
mask his true character, as in 2.3.64ff.,
and to show off his cleverness.
149 **Had ... will** was never lost for
words. Hart compared Plutarch's
Lives (Cato), 'he became a perfect
pleader, and had tongue at will'.
150 **gay** finely dressed
151 i.e. modestly refrained from what
she wanted, and yet knew when she
might have it
153 i.e. did not seek to right her wrong
and commanded her anger to cease.
Cf. Plautus, *Stichus*, 119 ff., 'The best
proof of a woman's excellence of
character. Her ... having the chance
to do wrong and the self-restraint not
to.' Cf. *Son* 94.1, 'They that have
power to hurt and will do none'.

138 fond] *F; not in Q*   139 i'th'] *F;* i' the *Q*   142 wise ones] *Q ;* wise-ones *F*   143 thou praisest]
F; that praises *Q*   146 merit] *F;* merrits *Q*

She that in wisdom never was so frail
To change the cod's head for the salmon's tail,   155
She that could think, and ne'er disclose her mind,
See suitors following, and not look behind,
She was a wight, if ever such wights were –

DESDEMONA
To do what?

IAGO
To suckle fools, and chronicle small beer.   160

DESDEMONA O, most lame and impotent conclusion!
Do not learn of him, Emilia, though he be thy
husband. How say you, Cassio, is he not a most
profane and liberal counsellor?

CASSIO He speaks home, madam, you may relish him   165
more in the soldier than in the scholar.

IAGO [*aside*] He takes her by the palm; ay, well said,
whisper. With as little a web as this will I ensnare as
great a fly as Cassio. Ay, smile upon her, do: I will
gyve thee in thine own courtesies. You say true, 'tis   170

154 **frail** weak; morally weak, unable to resist temptation (cf. Mrs Frail in Congreve's *Love for Love*)
155 See LN.
156 Cf. *AYL* 3.2.249, 'Do you not know I am a woman? when I think, I must speak.'
158 **wight** creature, person. Iago now pretends to be stuck. Cf. 4.1.32n.
160 **chronicle** register, record; 'be concerned with trivialities' (Sanders)
    small beer trivialities (*OED*, first here, but likely to be earlier)
161 **lame** (crippled, hence) weak
    impotent ineffective, weak
164 **profane** brutal in expression (Johnson); irreverent
    liberal unrestrained, licentious; could = gentlemanly (as in 'liberal education'). Cassio picks up the second sense.
165 **home** directly, to the point

relish appreciate
166 **in** in the role of
    scholar an unfortunate remark, as Cassio's bookishness particularly irritates Iago (1.1.23ff.)
167 **palm** could = hand (*OED* 1); but cf. 257
    well said Cf. 4.1.116n.
168 **web** could = a subtly woven snare, something flimsy and unsubstantial (*OED* 4c). Iago stands aside, like a spider watching a fly. If Cassio still holds Desdemona's hand when Othello enters, this could be a poisonous image in Othello's mind later.
169 **fly** i.e. simpleton
170 *****gyve** fetter, shackle
    courtesies courtly or elegant gestures
    say true ironic: he does not hear what Cassio says, ridiculing his body language

157] *F; not in Q*   158 wights] *F;* wight *Q*   167 SD] *Rowe; not in QF*   168 With] *F; not in Q*   I] *F; not in Q*   169 fly] *F;* Flee *Q*   170 gyve . . . courtesies] giue thee in thine owne Court-ship *F;* catch you in your owne courtesies *Q*

so indeed. If such tricks as these strip you out of
your lieutenantry, it had been better you had not
kissed your three fingers so oft, which now again you
are most apt to play the sir in. Very good, well kissed,
and excellent courtesy: 'tis so indeed! Yet again, your   175
fingers to your lips? would they were clyster-pipes
for your sake! (*Trumpets within*)
The Moor! I know his trumpet!

CASSIO   'Tis truly so.

DESDEMONA
Let's meet him and receive him.

Enter OTHELLO *and Attendants.*

CASSIO   Lo, where he comes!

OTHELLO
O my fair warrior!

DESDEMONA   My dear Othello!   180

OTHELLO
It gives me wonder great as my content
To see you here before me! O my soul's joy,

171 **tricks** capricious or foolish acts; feats of dexterity (*OED* 2, 5). Could also refer to Iago's own tricks.
172 **lieutenantry** lieutenancy (*OED*, first here)
173 See LN.
174 **apt** ready, disposed
    sir gentleman. For Iago's 'class hatred', see pp. 35–7.
176 **clyster-pipes** 'a tube or pipe for administering clysters' (*OED*, first here). A clyster was a medicine injected into the rectum. Ridley glossed as 'syringe for a (vaginal) douche'. The imagery (fingers, lips, pipes) is partly sexual.
178 **trumpet** could = trumpeter; trumpet call; or, the instrument. 'Distinguished people had their own re-

cognizable calls . . . [cf.] *KL* 2.1.80 . . . [and] "Your husband is at hand; I hear his trumpet" (*MV* 5.1.121)' (Ridley).
179 **receive** i.e. welcome
    SD Notice the build-up for this entry.
180 **warrior** Cf. 1.3.249ff., 3.4.152. In love poetry the woman is sometimes addressed as a warrior (in love): cf. Spenser's *Amoretti*, 57.1, 'Sweet warriour! when shall I have peace with you?' Is it significant that Othello turns first to Desdemona, though he arrives on official duty as governor?
181 **content** pleasure, contentment; repeated (189, 194) the word acquires overtones of self-indulgent 'satisfaction'
182 **soul's joy** Notice how often he refers to his soul.

173 kissed] *F;* rist *Q*   174 Very] *F; not in Q*   175 and] *F;* an *Q*   176 to] *F;* at *Q*   clyster-pipes] *as Q;* Cluster-pipes *F*   177 SD] *Q (opp. 178); not in F*   178 The . . . trumpet!] *speech cont. Q; new line F*   179 SD] *after* trumpet *178 Q; after* comes *179 F*   182] *Q; F lines* me. / Ioy: /

If after every tempest come such calms
May the winds blow till they have wakened death,
And let the labouring bark climb hills of seas,   185
Olympus-high, and duck again as low
As hell's from heaven. If it were now to die
'Twere now to be most happy, for I fear
My soul hath her content so absolute
That not another comfort like to this   190
Succeeds in unknown fate.

DESDEMONA   The heavens forbid
But that our loves and comforts should increase
Even as our days do grow.

OTHELLO   Amen to that, sweet powers!
I cannot speak enough of this content,
It stops me here, it is too much of joy.   195
And this, and this the greatest discords be   *They kiss.*

183 Cf. Dent, S908, 'After a storm
comes calm'; *calms* = calms at sea;
inner tranquillity.
184 **wakened** aroused, summoned into
existence, i.e. till they threaten our
death
186 **Olympus-high** (a coinage) as high
as Mount Olympus, the fabled abode
of the gods in Greek mythology
187–91 **If . . . fate** a common sentiment
in classical writers. Cf. Virgil, *Aeneid*,
4.660, Terence, *The Eunuch*, 551–2,
'O heavens! this is a moment when I
could bear dissolution for fear life pol-
lute this exultation with some distress.'
187 **If it were** elliptical: if it were (my
fate) now . . .
189 **content** quibble on content = con-
taining capacity (*OED* 5)
190 **comfort** delight, gladness; relief
(after distress)
191 **Succeeds . . . fate** can follow in our
unknown, predetermined futures.
After *Olympus-high*, *unknown fate* has
Greek overtones.
191–2 **forbid / But that** double negative, i.e. ensure that

193 **grow** increase
Amen . . . powers *Amen* is biblical,
sweet powers suggests the pagan classical gods (esp. after 186, 191) (but cf.
Ham 3.1.141, 'Heavenly powers, restore him!'). Cf. 5.2.217, 'O heauenly
God' (Q), 'oh heauenly Powres' (F).
194 **speak enough of** perhaps 'speak
highly enough of' or 'my words
cannot express'. But Shakespeare
may have intended 'I cannot speak.
Enough of this content!' (referring
back to 181, 189).
195 **stops** chokes (*OED* 9). Preparing
for his later choking, esp. 4.1.36.
here pointing to his throat?
196 **this . . . this** two gestural kisses,
perhaps without physical contact, as
Othello's make-up might blacken
Desdemona's face (see 3.3.390n.)
discords absence of harmony
(music); disagreement, strife. From
Lat. *cor* = heart (cf. 197). Iago takes it
in the musical sense.
SD The usual formula is '[He] kisses
her'; Q '*they kisse*' may mean that she
gives as good as she gets.

183 calms] *F; calmenesse Q* 192] *as Q; F lines* Loues / encrease /   193 powers] *F;* power
Q   194 speak . . . content] *QF*   196 discords] *F;* discord *Q*   SD] *Q; not in F*

175

That e'er our hearts shall make.

IAGO [*aside*]

O, you are well tuned now: but I'll set down
The pegs that make this music, as honest
As I am.

OTHELLO   Come, let us to the castle.   200
News, friends, our wars are done, the Turks are
    drowned.
How does my old acquaintance of this isle?
Honey, you shall be well desired in Cyprus,
I have found great love amongst them. O my sweet,
I prattle out of fashion, and I dote   205
In mine own comforts. I prithee, good Iago,
Go to the bay and disembark my coffers.
Bring thou the master to the citadel,
He is a good one, and his worthiness
Does challenge much respect. Come, Desdemona;   210
Once more, well met at Cyprus.

                    [*Exeunt all but Iago and Roderigo.*]

198 **set down** slacken (the strings or
pegs of a musical instrument); perhaps also 'bring low, or take down the
(human) pegs (= Othello, Desdemona) that make this joyful music'
(*OED* set 143)

199–200 ***as . . . am** for all my supposed
honesty (Ridley). Why does Iago
suddenly bridle at the thought of his
honesty? I suspect that we need to
complete 197: 'That e'er our hearts
shall make. Honest Iago!' (Othello
greets Cassio warmly, and merely
nods to Iago saying 'Honest Iago!',
i.e. well met, then turns back to
Desdemona).

202 **old acquaintance** old friend(s). Cf.
1H4 5.4.102, 'What, old acquaintance! could not all this flesh / Keep
in a little life?' (Hal to Falstaff); *Auld
Lang Syne*, 'Should auld acquaint-

ance be forgot'.

203 **desired** sought after; with dramatic
irony, since Roderigo and Iago desire
her more literally

205 **out of fashion** improperly, contrary to what is expected (*OED* 11).
Cf. *Tem* 3.1.57, 'I prattle / Something too wildly'.

207 **coffers** trunks, baggage. In Latin
comedy a slave or servant sometimes
has to disembark his master's luggage
(e.g. Plautus, *Amphitruo*, 629; cf. *CE*
5.1.410). Othello treats Iago almost as
a personal servant.

208 **master** captain (of merchant vessel)
or navigating officer (of ship of war)
(*OED* 2)

210 **challenge** deserve

211 **at** As they are in Cyprus, *at* may be
an error, anticipating *at*, 212.

198 SD] *Rowe; not in QF*   198–200 O . . . am] *this edn; prose F; Q lines* now, / musique, / am.
/   201] *as Q; F lines* done: / drown'd. /   202 does my] *F;* doe our *Q* this] *F;* the
Q   211 SD] *Exit. Q; Exit Othello and Desdemona. F*

IAGO   Do thou meet me presently at the harbour. Come
hither: if thou be'st valiant – as, they say, base men
being in love have then a nobility in their natures,
more than is native to them – list me. The lieutenant   215
tonight watches on the court of guard. First I must
tell thee this: Desdemona is directly in love with him.
RODERIGO   With him? why, 'tis not possible.
IAGO   Lay thy finger thus, and let thy soul be instructed.
Mark me with what violence she first loved the Moor,   220
but for bragging and telling her fantastical lies – and
will she love him still for prating? let not thy discreet
heart think it. Her eye must be fed, and what delight
shall she have to look on the devil? When the blood is
made dull with the act of sport, there should be, again   225
to inflame it, and to give satiety a fresh appetite, loveliness in favour, sympathy in years, manners and

212 **Do . . . harbour** Perhaps addressed
to a soldier, as Iago tells Roderigo to
meet him at the citadel (281). *Exit*
does not have to mean that Iago and
Roderigo are left alone (211, QF).
presently in a little while
213–15 **as . . . them** This could be an
aside. Cf. Dent, D216, 'Despair (love)
makes cowards courageous.'
213 **base** worthless, ignoble
215 **native** natural
list listen to
216 **watches** is on duty or on guard
court of guard body of soldiers on
guard (*OED*, corps de garde); or, the
watchpost occupied by the soldiers
on guard
217 **directly** plainly; completely
219 **thus** 'On thy mouth, to stop it while
thou art listening to a wiser man'
(Johnson). Cf. *TC* 1.3.240, 'Peace,
Troyan, lay thy finger on thy lips!';
Judges 18.19, 'Hold thy peace: lay
thine hand upon thy mouth, and
come with us.'

let . . . instructed a mock catechism,
with Iago as priest!
221 **but . . . lies** Iago dislikes Othello's
high-flown speech (cf. 1.1.12–13); *but*
= only; *fantastical* = existing only in
imagination, fabulous.
222 **still** always, constantly
prating boasting; idle chatter
discreet discerning, judicious
223 **fed** *Feed* = gratify (the vanity or
passion of); *feed one's eyes* is pre-
Shakespearian (cf. *Faerie Queene*,
2.7.4).
224 **devil** Cf. 1.1.90n.
225 **dull** sluggish, listless
sport sexual intercourse: cf. 5.2.210,
'the act of shame'
226 **satiety** satiation
227 ***loveliness** loveableness; beauty.
For the QF 'common error' in punctuation, see *Texts*, 100.
favour attractiveness; appearance
(*OED* 8, 9)
sympathy affinity; likeness

213 hither] *Q*; thither *F*   215 list me] *Q*; list-me *F*   216 must] *F*; will *Q*   217 thee this:] *F*;
thee, this *Q*   221–2 ²and . . . love] *Q*; To loue *F*   222 thy] *F*; the *Q*   223 it] *F*; so
Q   225 again] *Q*; a game *F*   ²to] *F*; *not in Q*   226–7 appetite, loveliness] *Theobald*; appetite.
Loue lines *Q*; appetite. Louelinesse *F*

beauties, all which the Moor is defective in. Now for
want of these required conveniences, her delicate
tenderness will find itself abused, begin to heave the   230
gorge, disrelish and abhor the Moor – very nature
will instruct her in it and compel her to some second
choice. Now sir, this granted – as it is a most pregnant
and unforced position – who stands so eminent in
the degree of this fortune as Cassio does? a knave   235
very voluble, no farther conscionable than in putting
on the mere form of civil and humane seeming, for
the better compassing of his salt and most hidden
loose affection. Why none, why none: a slipper and
subtle knave, a finder out of occasions, that has an   240
eye, can stamp and counterfeit advantages, though
true advantage never present itself – a devilish knave;

229 **required** necessary
  conveniences correspondences; apti-
  tudes; advantages; comforts
230 **tenderness** youthfulness; sensitive-
  ness to impression (*OED* 1, 3)
  abused cheated; injured
230–1 **heave the gorge** vomit
231 **disrelish** *OED* dis- 6: *dis-* forms
  compound verbs which reverse the
  action of the simple verb. She rel-
  ished what went down as food but
  does not relish what comes up as vomit.
  very nature natural instincts themselves (Ridley)
233 **pregnant** obvious, cogent
234 **unforced position** natural proposition
  eminent high
235 **degree** (lit. step, one of a flight of
  steps) stairway leading to
  fortune good fortune
  knave crafty rogue
236 **voluble** inconstant, variable; fluent
  or glib of tongue (more true of Iago
  than Cassio!)

  conscionable governed by conscience
236–7 **putting on** feigning (*OED* put
  46e); putting on the mask of
237 **form** prescribed behaviour
  civil … seeming well-bred and
  courteous appearance
238 **compassing** attaining; embracing
  salt lecherous (cf. 3.3.407)
239 **loose** wanton, immoral
  affection emotion; lust
  slipper slippery
240 **subtle** skilful; crafty, cunning
  occasions opportunities
241 **eye** perhaps a roving eye. Cf. 2.3.21,
  'What an eye she has!'
  stamp make a coin; engender. Cf.
  Cym 2.5.4ff.: 'my father was I know
  not where / When I was stamped.
  Some coiner with his tools / Made
  me a counterfeit'.
  advantages opportunities
  *****though** Q *the* must be a misreading
  of *tho* (*Texts*, 44).
242 **true** honest, virtuous

232 in it] *F;* to it *Q*   234 eminent] *F;* eminently *Q*   236 farther] farder *Q;* further *F*   237
humane seeming] *F;* hand-seeming *Q*   238 compassing] *Q;* compasse *F*   238–9 most … affec-
tion] *F;* hidden affections *Q*   239 Why … ²none] *F; not in Q*   239–40 slipper and subtle] *F;*
subtle slippery *Q*   240 out of occasions] *Q;* of occasion *F*   has] *Q;* he's *F*   241–2 advantages …
advantage] *F;* the true aduantages *Q*   242 itself … knave] *as F;* themselues *Q*

178

besides, the knave is handsome, young, and hath all
those requisites in him that folly and green minds
look after. A pestilent complete knave, and the woman 245
hath found him already.

RODERIGO I cannot believe that in her, she's full of
most blest condition.

IAGO Blest fig's-end! The wine she drinks is made of
grapes. If she had been blest she would never have 250
loved the Moor. Blest pudding! Didst thou not see
her paddle with the palm of his hand? Didst not
mark that?

RODERIGO Yes, that I did, but that was but courtesy.

IAGO Lechery, by this hand: an index and obscure 255
prologue to the history of lust and foul thoughts.
They met so near with their lips that their breaths
embraced together. Villainous thoughts, Roderigo:
when these mutualities so marshal the way, hard at
hand comes the master and main exercise, th'in- 260

244 **folly** foolishness; wickedness; wantonness
green immature
245 **look after** search for
pestilent poisonous, confounded
(*OED* 4, often used humorously)
246 **found** unclear (deliberately?); 'seen
sympathetically what he is after'
(Sanders); or perhaps = had. Cf. 133,
KL 5.1.10–11, 'have you never found
my brother's way / To the forfended
place?'
247 **I . . . her** Like Sir Andrew (*TN*
1.3.67) he is comically overemphatic.
248 **condition** disposition; nature;
quality
249 **fig's-end** Cf. 1.3.320n.
249–50 **The . . . grapes** one of Iago's
vague general assertions, which we
have to interpret for ourselves. Cf.
Dent, W466, 'No wine made of
grapes but hath lees, no woman cre-

ated of flesh but hath faults' (1580).
251 **pudding** could = sausage (as in
black pudding). I suspect euphem-
isms for 'blest vagina' (249), 'blest
penis' (251).
252 **paddle** toy, fondle. So *Ham* 3.4.185,
'paddling in your neck with his
damned fingers', *WT* 1.2.115.
255 **index** table of contents prefixed to a
book; preface, prologue
obscure unclearly expressed, hidden
259 **mutualities** intimacies
hard close
260 **master** (adj.) principal
exercise action, exertion, (sexual)
'sport'
260–1 **incorporate** 'united in one
body', i.e. the 'beast with two backs'
(1.1.115). Cf. *VA* 539–40, 'Her arms
do lend his neck a sweet embrace; /
Incorporate then they seem, face
grows to face.'

246 hath] *F;* has *Q* 251 Blest pudding] *F; not in Q* 252–3 Didst . . . that?] *F; not in*
Q 254 that I did] *F; not in Q* 255 obscure] *F; not in Q* 258 Villainous . . . Roderigo] *F; not in*
Q 259 mutualities] *Q ;* mutabilities *F* hard] *F;* hand *Q* 260 master and] *F; not in Q* th'] *F;*
the *Q*

corporate conclusion. Pish! But, sir, be you ruled by me. I have brought you from Venice: watch you tonight. For the command, I'll lay't upon you. Cassio knows you not, I'll not be far from you, do you find some occasion to anger Cassio, either by speaking too 265 loud or tainting his discipline, or from what other cause you please which the time shall more favourably minister.

RODERIGO Well.

IAGO Sir, he's rash and very sudden in choler, and 270 haply with his truncheon may strike at you: provoke him that he may, for even out of that will I cause these of Cyprus to mutiny, whose qualification shall come into no true trust again but by the displanting of Cassio. So shall you have a shorter journey to your 275 desires, by the means I shall then have to prefer them, and the impediment most profitably removed, without the which there were no expectation of our prosperity.

RODERIGO I will do this, if you can bring it to any opportunity. 280

IAGO I warrant thee. Meet me by and by at the citadel:

---

261 **Pish!** Cf. 4.1.43: exclamation of disgust or vexation, it shows Iago reacting to his own voyeurism (or is he pretending?).

261–2 **But . . . me** Iago switches to *sir* and *you*: he is coming to the point.

261 **ruled** guided

263 **For . . . you** As for taking the lead (in our joint action), I'll leave it to you; 'I'll arrange for you to be appointed, given orders' (Bevington).

266 **tainting** disparaging
discipline military skill or professionalism

268 **minister** supply

270 **sudden** impetuous, abrupt, suddenly roused

choler (one of the four 'humours') in an irascible state

271 **haply** perhaps; by good luck
truncheon staff (carried by officers)

273 **mutiny** riot
qualification condition, nature; or, pacification: i.e. the Cypriots will not be trustworthy again except by the cashiering of Cassio

274 **displanting** removal

276 **prefer** advance

277 **profitably** advantageously

278 **prosperity** success. Note how Iago befogs with abstractions.

281 **warrant** assure, promise
thee Iago has won him over, and reverts to *thee*.

---

261 Pish] *F; not in Q* 263 the] *F;* your *Q* 267 cause] *Q;* course *F* 270 he's] *F;* he is *Q* 271 haply] *Q;* happely *F* with . . . truncheon] *Q (*Trunchen*); not in F* 274 trust] *Q;* taste *F* again] *F;* again't *Q* 278 the which] *F;* which *Q* 280 if you] *F;* if I *Q*

I must fetch his necessaries ashore. Farewell.

RODERIGO   Adieu.   *Exit.*

IAGO

That Cassio loves her, I do well believe it,

That she loves him, 'tis apt and of great credit.   285

The Moor, howbeit that I endure him not,

Is of a constant, loving, noble nature,

And I dare think he'll prove to Desdemona

A most dear husband. Now I do love her too,

Not out of absolute lust – though peradventure   290

I stand accountant for as great a sin –

But partly led to diet my revenge,

For that I do suspect the lusty Moor

Hath leaped into my seat, the thought whereof

Doth like a poisonous mineral gnaw my inwards . . .   295

And nothing can or shall content my soul

Till I am evened with him, wife for wife . . .

Or, failing so, yet that I put the Moor

At least into a jealousy so strong

---

282 **necessaries** i.e. coffers, 207.
  Farewell Iago dismisses him. *Adieu*, 283, is more 'upper-class'.
284 **loves** For Iago's curious reasoning, and the meaning of 'love', see Honigmann, *Seven Tragedies*, 87.
285 **apt** likely; fitting (in view of the theories he has expounded, 220ff.)
  credit credibility
286 **howbeit** however it may be
  endure him not cannot stand him
289 **dear** fond, loving
290 **absolute** mere, pure and simple
  peradventure as it happens
291 **accountant** responsible
  as . . . sin i.e. revenge
292 **diet** Why not 'feed'? Because revenge needs a special diet.
293 **For that** because

lusty lustful
294 **Hath . . . seat** Cf. *OED* leap 9: 'of certain beasts: to spring upon (the female) in copulation'; *1H4* 1.2.9, 'leaping-houses' (= brothels); *Son* 41.9, 'Ay me, but yet thou mightst *my seat* forbear'; *H5* 5.2.139, 'I should quickly leap into a wife'. *Seat* = sexual seat, his wife.
295 hinting at ulcers?
  mineral Cf. 1.2.74n.
296 echoing 189, 'My soul hath her content so absolute'
297 **evened** Cf. *womaned* (3.4.195), *weaponed* (5.2.264): made even or quits.
  wife for wife Cf. Exodus 21.1, 23–4, 'These are the laws . . . life for life, eye for eye, tooth for tooth'.

---

284 it] *Q*; 't *F*   286 howbeit] *F*; howbe't *Q*   287 loving, noble] *F*; noble, louing *Q*   291 accountant] *Q*; accomptant *F*   292 led] *F*; lead *Q*   293 lusty] *F*; lustfull *Q*   296 or] *F*; nor *Q*   297 evened] *F* (eeuen'd*); euen *Q*   ²wife] *Q*; wift *F*   299 jealousy] *as Q*; Ielouzie *F*

That judgement cannot cure; which thing to do,   300
If this poor trash of Venice, whom I trash
For his quick hunting, stand the putting on,
I'll have our Michael Cassio on the hip,
Abuse him to the Moor in the rank garb –
For I fear Cassio with my night-cap too –   305
Make the Moor thank me, love me, and reward me
For making him egregiously an ass,
And practising upon his peace and quiet
Even to madness. 'Tis here, but yet confused: 309
Knavery's plain face is never seen, till used.   *Exit.*

[2.2]   *Enter Othello's* Herald, *with a proclamation.*

HERALD   [*Reads.*] *It is Othello's pleasure, our noble and*
          valiant general, that, upon certain tidings now arrived,

300 **That ... cure** that no one's good
   sense can cure it
301 **poor trash** worthless person
   *****trash** See LN.
302 **For ... hunting** 'to prevent him
   from hunting too fast. Iago has had to
   restrain and pacify Roderigo many
   times, no doubt' (Kittredge). Cf. *for*
   = 'to prevent' in *2H6* 4.1.73–4, 'dam
   up this thy yawning mouth / For
   swallowing the treasure of the realm'.
   quick energetic (ironic)
   stand ... on goes along with my in-
   citement (*OED* put 46h)
303 **our** vaguely contemptuous: cf.
   2.3.56.
   on the hip at a disadvantage (a wres-
   tling term). Cf. *MV* 4.1.334, Dent,
   H474, 'To have one on the hip'.
304 **Abuse** slander
   rank lustful
   garb manner of doing anything, behaviour (*OED* 3); i.e. misrepresent
   him as lecherous

305 **night-cap** a head covering, worn in
   bed. Not likely to be worn by a lover:
   Iago's sense of humour runs away
   with him.
308 **practising upon** plotting against
309 **Even to** even till I bring him to
   here here in my head. Cf. the clever
   slave in classical comedy (Plautus,
   Pseudolus, 576).
   confused not yet clearly worked out
310 **plain** simple, honest (sarcastic). Cf.
   Luc 1532.
   seen i.e. seen clearly, until the
   moment comes when it has to be
   used
2.2.0.1 *****Herald** The Herald probably
   addresses the audience, as if it consists of Cypriots. It is not clear how
   much is read, how much spoken. QF
   print in roman throughout, I print 1–
   7 in italics (assuming that this is proclaimed, the rest spoken).
2 *upon* on the occasion of (*OED*
   7a)

301 ²trash] *Steevens;* crush *Q;* trace *F*   304 rank] *Q;* right *F*   305 night-cap] *Q;* Night-Cape
F   2.2] *Scena Secunda. F; not in Q*   0.1] *as F; Enter a Gentleman reading a Proclamation. Q*   1 SP]
F; not in Q   SD] *not in QF*   1–7] *italics this edn; roman QF*

importing the mere perdition of the Turkish fleet, every
man put himself into triumph: some to dance, some to
make bonfires, each man to what sport and revels his 5
addiction leads him. For besides these beneficial news, it
is the celebration of his nuptial. – So much was his
pleasure should be proclaimed. All offices are open,
and there is full liberty of feasting from this present
hour of five till the bell have told eleven. Heaven 10
bless the isle of Cyprus and our noble general
Othello! *Exit.*

[**2.3**] *Enter* OTHELLO, CASSIO *and* DESDEMONA.

OTHELLO
Good Michael, look you to the guard tonight.
Let's teach ourselves that honourable stop
Not to outsport discretion.

CASSIO
Iago hath direction what to do,
But notwithstanding with my personal eye 5
Will I look to't.

OTHELLO Iago is most honest.
Michael, good night. Tomorrow with your earliest
Let me have speech with you. Come, my dear love,

3 *importing* communicating, stating
  mere perdition total destruction
4 *triumph* public festivity, revelry (cf.
  the Venetian carnival)
6 **addiction* inclination; *addition*
  would = rank
  beneficial beneficent, good
8 **offices** kitchens, butteries, etc.
  (Ridley)
9 **liberty** freedom of behaviour, beyond

what is recognized as proper (*OED*
5), as in *MM* 1.3.29, 'liberty plucks
justice by the nose'
10 **told** counted; proclaimed; tolled
2.3.2 stop restraint
3 not to carry our revelling beyond the
  bounds of discretion; *outsport*: unique
  in Shakespeare
7 **with your earliest** at your earliest
  convenience

3 *every*] *as F; that* euery *Q* 4 *²to*] *F; not in Q* 6 *addiction*] *Q2;* minde *Q;* addition *F*
7 *nuptial*] *as F;* Nuptialls *Q* 9 of feasting] *F; not in Q* 10 have] *F;* hath *Q* 10–11 Heaven
bless] *Q;* Blesse *F* 12 SD] *F; not in Q* **2.3**] *new scene Theobald; scene cont. QF* 0.1] *as Q; Enter
Othello, Desdemona, Cassio, and Attendants. F* 2 that] *F;* the *Q* 4 direction] *F;* directed *Q* 6 't]
F; it *Q*

The purchase made, the fruits are to ensue:
That profit's yet to come 'tween me and you.   10
Good-night.   *Exeunt Othello and Desdemona*.

Enter IAGO.

CASSIO   Welcome, Iago, we must to the watch.

IAGO   Not this hour, lieutenant, 'tis not yet ten o'th'
clock. Our general cast us thus early for the love of
his Desdemona – whom let us not therefore blame;   15
he hath not yet made wanton the night with her, and
she is sport for Jove.

CASSIO   She's a most exquisite lady.

IAGO   And I'll warrant her full of game.

CASSIO   Indeed she's a most fresh and delicate creature.   20

IAGO   What an eye she has! methinks it sounds a parley
to provocation.

CASSIO   An inviting eye; and yet methinks right modest.

IAGO   And when she speaks is it not an alarum to love?

---

9 **purchase** (a richer word than now) acquisition; gain; bargain; prize; something bought
  fruits anything resulting from an action (*OED* 7), implying that the marriage has still to be consummated (see p. 42 n. 1). Cf. *Homilies*, 446 ('Of matrimony'): marriage was instituted by God 'to bring forth fruit', i.e. children.
10 **profit** benefit; but after *purchase* the commercial sense is also present
13–17 Iago switches to prose; Cassio (weakly?) follows suit.
13 **Not this hour** not for an hour yet
  ten Cf. 2.2.10, *five*.
14 **cast** got rid of
15 *****whom** Cf. 1.2.52n.
16 **hath … her** i.e. has not yet slept with her
17 **sport** Cf. 2.1.225.
  Jove Jupiter, a notorious womanizer

in classical legends
18 **exquisite** accomplished; consummately perfect or beautiful
19 **game** sport, spirit; 'expert in love-play' (Ridley)
20 Cassio comes halfway to Iago's view. He might speak thus of a prostitute (cf. *Per* 4.2.6–10, 'We were never so much out of creatures … let's have fresh ones'); *fresh* could = in prime condition; *delicate* could = pleasing to the palate. Is he weak – or innocent?
21 **What … has** Cf. Marlowe, *The Jew of Malta*, 4.2.127, 'What an eye she casts on me?' (Ithamore of the courtesan).
  parley makes a trumpet call to an opponent: the usual love–war metaphor
22 **provocation** challenge, defiance (military or sexual)
23 **right** properly; very
24 **alarum** call to arms; sudden attack

10 That] *F;* The *Q*   'tween] *F;* twixt *Q*   11 SD] *Q; Exit. F*   13–14 o'th' clock] *F;* aclock *Q*   15 whom] *F2;* who *QF*   18 She's] *F;* She is *Q*   20 she's] *F;* she is *Q*   21–2] *QF lines (as verse?)* has? / prouocation. /   22 to] *F;* of *Q*   23–4] *F lines* eye: / modest. / speakes, / Loue? /   24 alarum] *F;* alarme *Q*

CASSIO   She is indeed perfection.   25

IAGO   Well: happiness to their sheets! Come, lieutenant,
I have a stoup of wine, and here without are a brace
of Cyprus gallants that would fain have a measure to
the health of black Othello.

CASSIO   Not tonight, good Iago, I have very poor and   30
unhappy brains for drinking. I could well wish
courtesy would invent some other custom of
entertainment.

IAGO   O, they are our friends. But one cup, I'll drink for
you.   35

CASSIO   I have drunk but one cup tonight, and that was
craftily qualified too, and behold what innovation it
makes here! I am unfortunate in the infirmity, and
dare not task my weakness with any more.

IAGO   What, man, 'tis a night of revels, the gallants   40
desire it.

CASSIO   Where are they?

IAGO   Here, at the door, I pray you call them in.

CASSIO   I'll do't, but it dislikes me.   *Exit.*

IAGO
If I can fasten but one cup upon him,   45

---

25 **perfection** Cf. 1.3.101.

26 **sheets** Cf. *Pigmalions Image* (1598),
'Sweet sheetes ... Sweet happy
sheetes' (lover to loved one's bed-
sheets) (John Marston, *Poems*, ed. A.
Davenport [Liverpool, 1961], p. 58).

27 **stoup** flagon, tankard (of varying
sizes)
without outside
brace couple (Iago may understate,
to get Cassio to agree)

28 **fain** gladly
measure liquid measure, i.e. toast

31 **unhappy** troublesome; unfortunate
(*OED* 1, 3)

33 **entertainment** social behaviour; re-
ceiving guests (*OED* 4, 11)

34 **cup** wine cup (which could have a
foot and stem and lid); or, a cup with
the wine it contains, a cupful

37 **craftily** skilfully
qualified diluted
innovation revolution, change. What
is Iago to *behold*? Is Cassio unsteady
on his legs (= *here*, 38)?

39 **task** test

40 **man** (less polite, putting pressure on
Cassio)
gallants (military) followers; men of
pleasure

44 **it dislikes me** I'm not happy about it

45 **fasten ... upon** induce acceptance
of: 'if I can get him to drink just one
cupful'

---

25 She] *F;* It *Q*   29 black] *F;* the blacke *Q*   36 have] *F;* ha *Q*   38 unfortunate] *as Q;* infortunate *F*

With that which he hath drunk tonight already
He'll be as full of quarrel and offence
As my young mistress' dog. Now my sick fool,
    Roderigo,
Whom love hath turned almost the wrong side out,
To Desdemona hath tonight caroused   50
Potations pottle-deep, and he's to watch.
Three else of Cyprus, noble swelling spirits
That hold their honours in a wary distance,
The very elements of this warlike isle,
Have I tonight flustered with flowing cups,   55
And the watch too. Now 'mongst this flock of
    drunkards
Am I to put our Cassio in some action
That may offend the isle.

Enter CASSIO, MONTANO *and* Gentlemen.

But here they come.

47 **offence** aggressiveness, readiness to
give or take offence
48 **As ... dog** as any young lady's
lapdog (some small dogs are especially aggressive)
sick love-sick
Roderigo extra-metrical
49 perhaps 'whom love has made almost
the opposite of what he was'. Cf.
4.2.148, 'turned your wit the seamy
side without'.
50 **caroused** drunk (a health); drunk
repeatedly
51 **Potations** drinks, draughts
pottle-deep a coinage: to the bottom
of a half-gallon tankard
watch i.e. for Cassio: 2.1.260ff.
52 **else** others
swelling proud, haughty
53 that keep their honours cautiously at

a distance (from disgrace), i.e. that
are quick to take offence
54 **elements** essential constituents, i.e.
the life-blood. This word was sometimes spoken 'in inverted commas'
(cf. *TN* 3.1.58, 3.4.124).
this warlike isle Cf. 2.1.43.
55 **flustered** befuddled
flowing poured out without stint. So
H5 4.3.55.
56 **the** F *they* is possible. For final -*y* and
final twirls misread in Q and F, see
Texts, 85.
watch (military) watchmen or
sentinels
flock One thinks of sheep or geese.
57 **Am I to** I have to, the plan is to
our Cf. 2.1.301n.
58 **offend** vex; injure

48] *as Q ; F lines* dogge. / *Rodorigo,* /   49 hath] *F;* has *Q*   out] *F;* outward *Q*   51 watch.] *F;*
watch *Q*   52 else] *F;* lads *Q*   53 honours] *F;* honour *Q*   56] *as Q; F lines* too. / drunkards /
the] *Q;* they *F*   57 Am I] *F;* I am *Q*   to put] *Q;* put to *F*   58 SD] *F (after 58);* Enter Montanio,
Cassio, *and others. Q (opp. 58)*

186

If consequence do but approve my dream
My boat sails freely, both with wind and stream.   60
CASSIO   'Fore God, they have given me a rouse already.
MONTANO   Good faith, a little one, not past a pint, as
    I am a soldier.
IAGO   Some wine, ho!
    [*Sings.*]

> And let me the cannikin clink, clink,   65
> And let me the cannikin clink.
>   A soldier's a man,
>   O, man's life's but a span,
> Why then let a soldier drink!

Some wine, boys!   70
CASSIO   'Fore God, an excellent song!
IAGO   I learned it in England, where indeed they are
    most potent in potting. Your Dane, your German,
    and your swag-bellied Hollander – drink, ho! – are
    nothing to your English.   75

---

59 **if that which follows only confirms
    my daydream**, i.e. if the result bears
    out my hopes
60 Cf. Dent, W429, 'Sail with wind and
    tide'; *freely* = without hindrance, just
    as I want. For similar summing-up
    lines, cf. *TC* 2.3.266, 'Light boats sail
    swift, though greater hulks draw
    deep'; *JC* 5.1.67, 'Why now blow
    wind, swell billow, and swim bark!',
    Cym 4.3.46.
61 **rouse** carouse, a full bumper
65ff. For the song cf. p. 390.
65 **cannikin** small drinking can; *-kin* is
    diminutive (= German *-chen*), as
    probably in napkin (*OED* -kin, suffix)
    clink i.e. against someone else's
68 Cf. Dent, L251, 'Life is a span', from
    Psalms 39.6, 'thou hast made my days
    as it were a span long'; *span* = a short

distance or space of time.
72 **in England** This draws attention to
    the play as a play: cf. *Ham* 5.1.148ff.
73 **potent in potting** go in for drink-
    ing in a big way. Drinking songs
    before *Oth* praised the superior pot-
    ting of the English (Lyly, *Sapho*,
    3.2.76ff., 'O! thats a roring English-
    man, / Who in deepe healths do's so
    excell, / From Dutch and French he
    beares the bel') or of the singers
    themselves (Lyly, *Mother Bombie*,
    2.1.149ff.).
73–9 **Your** Note the force of Iago's re-
    peated *your* (not quite the same as the
    indefinite article or 'a typical Dane',
    etc.): Iago wants to generate cama-
    raderie.
74 **swag-bellied** with a belly that sags
    or wobbles

---

61 God] *Q*; heauen *F*   62–3] *prose F; verse Q* pint, /   Good faith] *Q*; Good-faith *F*   64.1]
Rowe; not in QF   65–9, 85–92] *italics QF (except 85 Q)*   65 cannikin] *Q*; Cannakin *F*
66 clink] *F*; clinke, clinke Q*   67–8] *one line QF*   68 O, man's] *F*; a Q*   71 God] *Q;*
Heauen *F*

187

CASSIO   Is your Englishman so exquisite in his drinking?

IAGO   Why, he drinks you with facility your Dane dead
    drunk; he sweats not to overthrow your Almain; he
    gives your Hollander a vomit ere the next pottle can
    be filled.   80

CASSIO   To the health of our general!

MONTANO   I am for it, lieutenant, and I'll do you
    justice.

IAGO   O sweet England!
    [*Sings.*]
        King Stephen was and-a worthy peer,   85
            His breeches cost him but a crown,
        He held them sixpence all too dear,
            With that he called the tailor lown.
        He was a wight of high renown
            And thou art but of low degree,   90
        'Tis pride that pulls the country down,
            Then take thine auld cloak about thee.
    Some wine, ho!

CASSIO   'Fore God, this is a more exquisite song than
    the other!   95

IAGO   Will you hear't again?

CASSIO   No, for I hold him to be unworthy of his place

---

76 **exquisite** accomplished. Cassio, drunk, gets 'stuck' on this word, which he had used before (2.3.18); slurred by some actors as 'ex-qust'.

78 **he … overthrow** he can easily outdrink
   Almain German

79 **pottle** a half-gallon tankard

82–3 **do you justice** drink level with you (Ridley)

85ff. See LN.

85 **and-a** Cf. *TN* 5.1.389, 'When that I was and a little tine boy'; *KL* 3.2.74. A metrical 'fill in' used in ballads (Furness).

86 **a crown** five shillings

88 **lown** loon, rogue; a man of low birth

89–91 Does Iago sing these lines at Cassio, thus provoking 105ff.?

91 perhaps 'it is extravagance in dress that causes hard times in our country' (Kittredge)

92 **auld** old, as in 'auld lang syne' (dialectal)

97 **unworthy** Vaguely aware of professional misconduct, he is too befuddled to pin down or complete his thought.

---

76 Englishman] *Q*; Englishmen *F*   exquisite] *F*; expert *Q*   82 I'll] *F*; I will *Q*   84 SD] *not in QF*   85 and-a] *F*; a *Q*   87 them] *F*; 'em *Q*   92 Then] *Q*; And *F*   thine] *Q*; thy *F*   auld] *owd Q*; awl'd *F*   94 'Fore God] *Q*; Why *F*   97 to be] *F*; not in Q*

that does . . . those things. Well, God's above all, and
there be souls must be saved, and there be souls must
not be saved.   100

IAGO   It's true, good lieutenant.

CASSIO   For mine own part, no offence to the general
nor any man of quality, I hope to be saved.

IAGO   And so do I too, lieutenant.

CASSIO   Ay, but, by your leave, not before me. The   105
lieutenant is to be saved before the ancient. Let's have
no more of this, let's to our affairs. God forgive us
our sins! Gentlemen, let's look to our business. Do
not think, gentlemen, I am drunk: this is my ancient,
this is my right hand, and this is my left. I am not   110
drunk now: I can stand well enough, and I speak well
enough.

GENTLEMAN   Excellent well.

CASSIO   Why, very well then; you must not think then
that I am drunk.   *Exit.*

MONTANO
To th' platform, masters, come, let's set the watch.   116

IAGO
You see this fellow that is gone before,

---

98 **God's above all** Cf. Dent, H348,
'Heaven (God) is above all.'
99 **be saved** find salvation, go to heaven.
Cf. Matthew 10.22, 'he that endureth
to the end shall be saved'.
102–3 Cf. Sir Andrew (*TN* 1.3.117–18)
who thinks himself as good as 'any
man in Illyria, whatsoever he be,
under the degree of my betters'.
103 **quality** high birth, good social position (i.e. excluding Iago)
105 **not . . . me** Cf. *MA* 4.2.19–20,
'write God first, for God defend but

God should go before such villains!'
107 **affairs** i.e. duties
107–8 **God . . . sins** Cf. the Lord's
Prayer.
110 **right . . . left** Cf. Dent, H74, 'He
knows not (knows) his right hand
from his left.'
116 **platform** gun-platform
masters gentlemen
set the watch mount the guard
117 **fellow** man; but could = worthless
person (*OED* 9, 10c), i.e. obliquely
contemptuous

---

98 does . . . those] *this edn;* does those *QF*   God's] *Q;* heau'ns *F*   99 ¹must] *F;* that must *Q*   99–
100 and . . . saved] *F; not in Q*   101 It's] *F;* It is *Q*   104 too] *F; not in Q*   106 have] *F;* ha
Q   107 God] *Q; not in F*   110 left] *F;* left hand *Q*   111 I speak] *F;* speake *Q*   113 SP] *Gent. F;*
All. Q   114 Why] *F; not in Q*   ²then] *F; not in Q*   116 To th' platform] *F;* To the plotforme *Q*

He is a soldier fit to stand by Caesar
And give direction. And do but see his vice,
'Tis to his virtue a just equinox,   120
The one as long as th'other. 'Tis pity of him:
I fear the trust Othello puts him in
On some odd time of his infirmity
Will shake this island.

MONTANO   But is he often thus?

IAGO

'Tis evermore the prologue to his sleep: 125
He'll watch the horologe a double set
If drink rock not his cradle.

MONTANO   It were well
The general were put in mind of it.
Perhaps he sees it not, or his good nature
Prizes the virtue that appears in Cassio   130
And looks not on his evils: is not this true?

Enter RODERIGO.

IAGO   [*aside*]
How now, Roderigo?

118 **stand by Caesar** i.e. as an equal; or, as his right-hand man
120 It counterbalances his virtue as exactly as day and night are equal at the equinox.
121 **pity of** a pity about
122 **trust** position of trust. But Capell's *in him* (for *him in*) may be right.
123 at some unusual (or, unexpected) time, when he suffers from his infirmity
124 **shake** (?)convulse (deliberately vague?)
125 **evermore** emphatic form of 'ever'
126 He'll stay awake twice round the clock or *horologe* ('while the clock strikes two rounds, or four-and-

twenty hours' [Johnson]).
127 **cradle** unexplained; perhaps 'if drink doesn't rock him asleep, like a baby in a cradle'. But this is suspiciously abrupt: cf. *2H4* 3.1.19–20, 'Seal up the ship-boy's eyes, and rock his brains / In cradle of the rude imperious surge', which is immediately intelligible. Perhaps a misreading (*cradle* for *nodle*)? Viz. 'if drink doesn't unsteady his brain'. Cf. *TS* 1.1.64, 'your noddle' (= your head).
128 **put in mind** made aware
130 **Prizes** esteems
    virtue unusual ability
131 **looks not on** disregards
    evils i.e. faults

118 He is] *Q*; He's *F*   122 puts] *F*; put *Q*   125 the] *Q*; his *F*   127–8 It were . . . it] *as F; one line Q*   127 It were] *F*; Twere *Q*   130 Prizes] *F*; Praises *Q*   virtue] *F*; vertues *Q* 131 looks] *F*; looke *Q*   132 SD] *Capell; not in QF*

I pray you, after the lieutenant, go!   *Exit Roderigo.*
MONTANO
　And 'tis great pity that the noble Moor
　Should hazard such a place as his own second   135
　With one of an ingraft infirmity.
　It were an honest action to say so
　To the Moor.
IAGO   Not I, for this fair island.
　I do love Cassio well, and would do much
                          A cry within: 'Help! help!'
　To cure him of this evil. But hark, what noise?   140

          Enter CASSIO *pursuing* RODERIGO.

CASSIO   Zounds, you rogue! you rascal!
MONTANO   What's the matter, lieutenant?
CASSIO   A knave teach me my duty? I'll beat the knave
　into a twiggen bottle!
RODERIGO   Beat me?   145
CASSIO   Dost thou prate, rogue?
MONTANO   Nay, good lieutenant! I pray you, sir, hold
　your hand.
CASSIO   Let me go, sir, or I'll knock you o'er the
　mazzard.   150

135–6 should risk such a place as that of his own deputy by entrusting it to one with an ingrained weakness (*ingraft* = engraffed, grafted on)
137 **action** three syllables. Perhaps 'so' should begin 138.
140.1 Q '*driuing in*' = *Tem* 5.1.255, '*Enter Ariell, driuing in Caliban*', i.e. chasing on to the stage, whereas usually *in* = off stage, like *within* (cf. 5.2.84ff.). See *Texts*, 161.
143 **beat** Social inferiors were beaten, equals had to be challenged. In classical comedy and its derivatives beat-

ings were a comic routine: cf. *TS* 4.1.165, etc., *CE* 2.2.23.
144 **twiggen** made of twigs or wickerwork (= Q *wicker*), 'like a Chianti flask' (Ridley); i.e. the criss-cross of weals on his body will look like wicker-work
146 **prate** chatter; could = speak boastfully or officiously
150 **mazzard** cup, bowl; (jocular) head. Cf. *Ham* 5.1.89. No doubt bottles and drinking cups were used in this scene.

---

133 SD] *Q*; *not in F*   137–8 It were . . . Moor] *as F; one line Q*   138 Not] *F*; Nor *Q*   139 SD] *Helpe, helpe, within Q; not in F*   140.1] *pursuing F; driuing in Q*   141 Zounds] *Q (*Zouns*); not in F*   143 duty? I'll] *as F*; duty: but I'le *Q*   144 twiggen bottle] Twiggen-Bottle *F*; wicker bottle *Q*   147–50] *as Q; F lines as verse* Lieutenant: / hand. / (Sir) / Mazard. /   147 Nay . . . I pray you] *F*; Good . . . pray *Q*

MONTANO   Come, come, you're drunk.
CASSIO   Drunk?   *They fight.*
IAGO   [*aside to Roderigo*]
   Away, I say, go out and cry a mutiny.   [*Exit Roderigo.*]
   Nay, good lieutenant! God's will, gentlemen –
   Help ho! Lieutenant! sir – Montano – sir –   155
   Help, masters, here's a goodly watch indeed.   *A bell rings.*
   Who's that which rings the bell? Diablo, ho!
   The town will rise, God's will, lieutenant, hold,
   You will be shamed for ever!

Enter OTHELLO *and Attendants.*

OTHELLO
   What is the matter here?
MONTANO   Zounds, I bleed still;   160
   I am hurt to th' death: he dies!   [*Lunges at Cassio.*]
OTHELLO   Hold, for your lives!
IAGO
   Hold, ho! Lieutenant! sir – Montano – gentlemen –
   Have you forgot all sense of place and duty?
   Hold, the general speaks to you: hold, for shame!
OTHELLO
   Why, how now, ho? From whence ariseth this?   165

153 **mutiny** riot
155 **ho!** could = *whoa*, a call to stop or
   cease what one is doing (*OED* int. 2)
156 **goodly** fine (ironical)
157 **the bell** the alarm bell
   Diablo devil. Only once in Shakespeare in this Spanish form (Iago is a
   Spanish name: see p. 334).
158 **rise** take up arms; revolt

159 **shamed** disgraced (*Texts*, 118, 141)
161 **he dies** I'll kill him (cf. 5.1.10).
   Some, following Q2, treat *he dies* as a
   SD, but (1) Montano does not die,
   (2) the metre requires *he dies*.
   for your lives if you value your lives
163 *Hanmer's transposition must be
   right.

151 you're] *F*; you are *Q*   152 SD] *Q*; *not in F*   153 ¹SD] Aside *Capell*; *not in QF*   ²SD] *not in QF*; Exit Rod. *Q2*   154 God's will] *Q*; Alas *F*   155 Montano – sir] *Montanio*, sir, *Q*; *Montano*: *F*   156 SD] *A bell rung: Q opp.* 153; *not in F*   157 which] *F*; that *Q*   158 God's will] *Q*; Fie, the *F*   hold] *Q*; *not in F*   159 You . . . shamed] *Q*; You'le be asham'd *F*   159.1] *F*; *Enter Othello, and Gentlemen with weapons. Q*   160 Zounds] *Q*; *not in F*   160–1 I bleed . . . dies] *one line F*   161 th'] *F*; the *Q*   he dies!] He dies. *F*; *not in Q*; he faints. *Q2 (SD)*   SD] *this edn*; *not in QF*; assailing Cassio again. *Capell*   162 ho] *F*; hold *Q*   sir – Montano –] *sir Montanio*, *Q*; Sir *Montano*, *F*   163 sense of place] *Hanmer*; place of sence *QF*   164 hold] *F*; hold, hold *Q*   165 ariseth] *F*; arises *Q*

Are we turned Turks? and to ourselves do that
Which heaven hath forbid the Ottomites?
For Christian shame, put by this barbarous brawl;
He that stirs next, to carve for his own rage,
Holds his soul light: he dies upon his motion.   170
Silence that dreadful bell, it frights the isle
From her propriety. What is the matter, masters?
Honest Iago, that look'st dead with grieving,
Speak: who began this? on thy love I charge thee.

IAGO

I do not know, friends all, but now, even now,   175
In quarter and in terms like bride and groom
Divesting them for bed; and then, but now,
As if some planet had unwitted men,
Swords out, and tilting one at other's breasts
In opposition bloody. I cannot speak   180
Any beginning to this peevish odds,
And would in action glorious I had lost
Those legs that brought me to a part of it.

166–7 See LN.
168 **put by** give up
  barbarous Cf. 1.3.356n.
169 **carve** cut, cleave. Cf. Dent, C110,
  'To be one's own carver'; *Faerie
  Queene*, 2.8.22, 'I can carve with this
  inchaunted brond [sword]'. Perhaps
  alluding to 'carving' meat at table.
170 **light** of small value
  upon his motion the instant he
  moves (Ridley)
171 **dreadful** (stronger than now)
  terrifying
172 **propriety** proper character, own
  nature (i.e. peacefulness)
  masters (He recognizes their social
  standing.)
174 **on ... thee** By your love (affection)
  for me, I order you (to speak).
175 **all,** Some editors drop F's comma.
  but only

176 **quarter** relations with, conduct towards, another (*OED* 17)
  terms language
  like ... groom Is this meant to be
  cheeky (glancing at Othello and
  Desdemona)?
177 **Divesting them** undressing themselves
178 **unwitted** deprived of wits (*OED*,
  first here). It was thought that plan-
  ets, if they came too near, could make
  men mad. Cf. Dent, P389, 'To be
  planet-struck', and 5.2.108–10.
179 **tilting** thrusting
180 **speak** reveal (*OED* 28)
181 **peevish** senseless; headstrong (*OED*
  1, 4)
  odds disagreement, quarrel (*OED*: in
  sixteenth century regularly construed
  as singular)
183 **a ... it** i.e. take part in it

167 hath] *F;* has *Q*   169 for] *F;* forth *Q*   172 What is] *F;* what's *Q*   173 look'st] *Hanmer;*
lookes *QF*   175 all,] *F;* all *Q*   177 for] *F;* to *Q*   179 breasts] *F;* breast *Q*   183 Those] *F;*
These *Q*

OTHELLO

How comes it, Michael, you are thus forgot?

CASSIO

I pray you pardon me, I cannot speak.   185

OTHELLO

Worthy Montano, you were wont to be civil:
The gravity and stillness of your youth
The world hath noted, and your name is great
In mouths of wisest censure. What's the matter
That you unlace your reputation thus   190
And spend your rich opinion for the name
Of a night-brawler? Give me answer to it.

MONTANO

Worthy Othello, I am hurt to danger:
Your officer Iago can inform you,
While I spare speech, which something now offends
          me,   195
Of all that I do know; nor know I aught
By me that's said or done amiss this night
Unless self-charity be sometimes a vice,
And to defend ourselves it be a sin
When violence assails us.

OTHELLO   Now, by heaven,   200
My blood begins my safer guides to rule
And passion, having my best judgement collied,

184 **are thus forgot** have thus forgotten
yourself
186 **civil** civilized (as befits a citizen)
187 **stillness** quietness of temper
188 **great** i.e. greatly praised
189 **In ... censure** in the mouths of
men of wisest judgement
190 **unlace** undo (the laces of a purse);
cut or carve (a boar or rabbit: a hunting term) (*OED* 1, 3)
191 **spend** waste, destroy
opinion reputation
192 **night-brawler** unique in Shakespeare

193 **to danger** to the point of danger
195 **something** somewhat
offends hurts (understatement)
198 **self-charity** regard for one's self
(unique in Shakespeare). Many new
compounds with 'self-' appeared in
the sixteenth and seventeenth centuries; Shakespeare coined several (cf.
3.3.203).
201 **blood** passion, anger
202 **collied** darkened: so *MND* 1.1.145,
'Brief as the lightning in the collied
night'

184 comes ... are] *F;* came ... were *Q* 186 Montano ... wont to] *F; Montanio ... wont
Q* 189 mouths] *F;* men *Q* 192 it] *F;* 't *Q* 198 sometimes] *F;* sometime *Q* 202 collied] *F;*
coold *Q;* quell'd *Capell*

Assays to lead the way. Zounds, if I once stir,
Or do but lift this arm, the best of you
Shall sink in my rebuke. Give me to know   205
How this foul rout began, who set it on,
And he that is approved in this offence,
Though he had twinned with me, both at a birth,
Shall lose me. What, in a town of war
Yet wild, the people's hearts brimful of fear,   210
To manage private and domestic quarrel?
In night, and on the court and guard of safety?
'Tis monstrous. Iago, who began't?

MONTANO
If partially affined or leagued in office
Thou dost deliver more or less than truth   215
Thou art no soldier.

IAGO   Touch me not so near.
I had rather have this tongue cut from my mouth
Than it should do offence to Michael Cassio,
Yet I persuade myself to speak the truth

203 **Assays** tries
   stir begin to act, bestir myself
205 **sink** fall; go down to hell (*OED* 2, obsolete)
   my rebuke the shameful check (or, disgrace; reprimand) that I shall give him
206 **foul rout** disgraceful brawl
207 **approved** confirmed (guilty)
208 **twinned ... birth** been my twin, both born at one birth. Twins can be born close together or with an interval between them.
209 **town of war** garrison town
210 **wild** unruly, uncontrolled
   the ... fear But cf. 2.1.200, 'our wars are done'.
211 **manage** conduct
   domestic internal
212 **In night** usually 'in th(e) night': in Shakespeare's hand *th* sometimes

looked like a meaningless squiggle (*Texts*, 84), so was dropped by a copyist
   and on ... safety and on the courtyard and (during) the guard duty meant to protect our general safety. But Theobald's transposition, 'of guard and', may be right (cf. 163).
213 **monstrous** a trisyllable (monsterous) (Malone)
214 ***If ... office** if bound (to Cassio) by partiality, or because he's a colleague
215 **more ... truth** Cf. Dent, T590, 'The truth, the whole truth, and nothing but the truth'.
216 **Touch** charge, take to task (*OED* 19)
   near closely
218 **offence** harm

203 Zounds] *as Q; not in F*   once] *F; not in Q*   210 brimful] *Q;* brim-full *F*   211 quarrel] *F;* quarrels *Q*   212 and guard of] *QF;* of Guard and *as Theobald*   213 began't] *F;* began *Q*   214 partially] *F;* partiality *Q*   leagued] *Pope;* league *QF*   217 have] *F;* ha *Q*   cut] *F;* out *Q*

Shall nothing wrong him. Thus it is, general: 220
Montano and myself being in speech,
There comes a fellow crying out for help
And Cassio following him with determined sword
To execute upon him. Sir, this gentleman
Steps in to Cassio and entreats his pause, 225
Myself the crying fellow did pursue
Lest by his clamour, as it so fell out,
The town might fall in fright. He, swift of foot,
Outran my purpose, and I returned the rather
For that I heard the clink and fall of swords 230
And Cassio high in oath, which till tonight
I ne'er might say before. When I came back,
For this was brief, I found them close together
At blow and thrust, even as again they were
When you yourself did part them. 235
More of this matter cannot I report.
But men are men, the best sometimes forget;
Though Cassio did some little wrong to him,
As men in rage strike those that wish them best,
Yet surely Cassio, I believe, received 240
From him that fled some strange indignity

220 **nothing** (adverb) not at all, in no way
Thus it is so *Cor* 1.3.96
223 **him** perhaps an error (anticipating *him*, 224) (Malone)
determined transferred epithet: Cassio was determined
sword At 2.1.269ff. Iago spoke of what might happen. At 2.3.143 Cassio said he would *beat* Roderigo, perhaps with the flat of his sword.
224 **execute upon** bring (a weapon) into operation against; but also implies 'put to death' (*OED* 1b, 6)
this gentleman Montano
225 **his pause** i.e. him to pause
229 **the rather** all the more quickly

230 **fall** downward stroke (of a sword): so *R3* 5.3.111
231 **high** loud (as in 'high words')
235 This short line may mark a pause (Iago wipes his brow?). It also marks a change of tactics: having described what happened, he 'defends' Cassio.
237 Cf. Dent, M541, 'Men are (but) men'; B316.1, 'The best go astray'; *forget* = forget themselves, or, forget their responsibilities.
238 **him** Montano
239 **those ... best** even those who are most favourably disposed towards them
241 **indignity** insult

220 Thus] *Q;* This *F*   229 the] *Q;* then *F*   231 oath] *F;* oaths *Q*   232 say] *F;* see *Q*
236 cannot I] *F;* can I not *Q*

Which patience could not pass.

OTHELLO   I know, Iago,
Thy honesty and love doth mince this matter,
Making it light to Cassio. Cassio, I love thee,

Enter DESDEMONA, *attended.*

But never more be officer of mine.   245
Look if my gentle love be not raised up!
I'll make thee an example.

DESDEMONA
What is the matter, dear?

OTHELLO   All's well now, sweeting,
Come away to bed. – Sir, for your hurts
Myself will be your surgeon. Lead him off.   250
                              [*Montano is led off.*]
Iago, look with care about the town
And silence those whom this vile brawl distracted.
Come, Desdemona: 'tis the soldier's life
To have their balmy slumbers waked with strife.
                    Exeunt [*all but Iago and Cassio.*]

IAGO   What, are you hurt, lieutenant?   255

242 **pass** let pass, agree to
243 **love** affection (for Cassio). The word is used three times in four lines, with different connotations.
mince this matter Cf. Dent, M755, 'To mince the matter'. Viz. make light of or extenuate this fault.
244 **Making . . . Cassio** making light of it for Cassio's benefit
245 Cf. LN, 1.1.8 and 1.1.16n. Othello personally appoints and dismisses his officers.
247 Cf. Dent, E212.1, 'To make one an example'.
248 **sweeting** sweetheart
250 I'll make it my business that your

wounds are properly treated, presumably by the general's surgeon (5.1.100). Some think that Othello himself dresses Montano's wounds (Bradshaw, 151, 164).
Lead him off. 'I am persuaded, these words were originally a marginal direction' (Malone), i.e. were accidentally printed as dialogue. Cf. *Texts*, 38.
252 **distracted** threw into confusion
254 **balmy slumbers** Having just heard that Othello and Desdemona are bride and groom (14, 171), are we really to believe in their balmy slumbers?

244.1] *F* (*after 245*); *Enter* Desdemona, *with others.* *Q* (*opp. 245, 246*)   248 dear] *F; not in Q*   now] *Q; not in F*   250 SD] *as Capell; not in QF*   252 vile] *Q;* vil'd *F*   254 SD] *Exit Moore,* Desdemona, *and attendants. Q (after 255); Exit. F*

CASSIO Ay, past all surgery.

IAGO Marry, God forbid!

CASSIO Reputation, reputation, reputation! O, I have
lost my reputation, I have lost the immortal part of
myself – and what remains is bestial. My reputation,   260
Iago, my reputation!

IAGO As I am an honest man I thought you had
received some bodily wound; there is more of sense
in that than in reputation. Reputation is an idle and
most false imposition, oft got without merit and lost   265
without deserving. You have lost no reputation at all,
unless you repute yourself such a loser. What, man,
there are ways to recover the general again. You are
but now cast in his mood, a punishment more in
policy than in malice, even so as one would beat his   270
offenceless dog to affright an imperious lion. Sue to
him again, and he's yours.

CASSIO I will rather sue to be despised, than to deceive
so good a commander with so slight, so drunken, and

---

257 **God forbid** common in the Bible
(Genesis 44.7, Joshua 22.29, Romans
3.4, 6, 31, etc.): usually a pious
person's phrase

259ff. Cf. *R2* 1.1.177–8, 'The purest
treasure mortal times afford / Is spot-
less reputation'; Dent, C817, 'He that
has lost his credit is dead to the
world.' Usually one's *soul* is 'the immortal part'.

263 **sense** capability of feeling

264 **idle** baseless, useless

265 **imposition** something imposed (by
others)

266–7 **You . . . loser** Cf. Dent, M254,
'A man is weal or woe as he thinks
himself so.'

267 **repute** consider

man Cf. 40.

268 **recover** regain (possession of), win
back

269 **cast . . . mood** cast off in his (passing) mood of anger

270 **malice** ill-will, enmity

270–1 **as . . . lion** Cf. Dent, D443, 'Beat
the dog (whelp) before the lion.' Also
proverbial in French: Cotgrave
glossed 'To punish a mean man in the
presence of and for an example to
the mighty'. Here the 'lion' is either
the Venetian army or the Cypriots
(Othello has to establish his authority
with both).

271 **offenceless** unoffending
Sue petition (him to pardon you)

274 **slight** worthless

---

257 God] *Q*; Heauen *F*   258–61] *as F*; *Q lines* my reputation: / selfe, / reputation, / reputation. /
258 Reputation] *twice Q*; *three times F*   O, I have] *F*; I ha *Q*   259 have] *F*; ha *Q*   part] *F*; part
sir *Q*   262 thought] *Q*; had thought *F*   263 of sense] *Cam 1892 (anon.)*; offence *Q*; sence *F*
268 ways] *Q*; more wayes *F*   274 slight] *F*; light *Q*

so indiscreet an officer. Drunk? and speak parrot? and   275
squabble? swagger? swear? and discourse fustian with
one's own shadow? O thou invisible spirit of wine, if
thou hast no name to be known by, let us call thee
devil!

IAGO   What was he that you followed with your sword?   280
What had he done to you?

CASSIO   I know not.

IAGO   Is't possible?

CASSIO   I remember a mass of things, but nothing distinctly; a quarrel, but nothing wherefore. O God, that   285
men should put an enemy in their mouths, to steal
away their brains! that we should with joy, pleasance,
revel and applause, transform ourselves into beasts!

IAGO   Why, but you are now well enough: how came you
thus recovered?   290

CASSIO   It hath pleased the devil drunkenness to give
place to the devil wrath; one unperfectness shows me
another, to make me frankly despise myself.

IAGO   Come, you are too severe a moraler. As the time,
the place and the condition of this country stands, I   295
could heartily wish this had not befallen; but since it
is as it is, mend it for your own good.

---

275 **indiscreet** lacking in sound judgement; inconsiderate
Drunk? F often uses ? where we
would put ! (as perhaps here).
speak parrot babble senselessly. Cf.
Dent, P60, 'To speak (prate) like a
parrot'.
276 **swagger** quarrel, squabble
fustian nonsense   .
287 **pleasance** pleasure, enjoyment
288 **transform . . . beasts** perhaps alluding to the Circe story
289–90 **how . . . recovered** How did it
come about that you have thus
recovered?
291–2 Cf. Ephesians 4.27, 'Neither give

place to the devil'. Drunkenness (=
gluttony?) and wrath could be two of
the seven deadly sins. 'The whole of
Cassio's apostrophe . . . finds a close
parallel in Ecclus. 31.25–31' (Noble,
217).
292 **wrath** could mean anger with himself (273ff.), and that he has not recovered, because still angry; or, anger
with Roderigo
unperfectness (unique in Shakespeare) imperfection
293 **frankly** undisguisedly; unreservedly
294 **moraler** moralizer (a coinage)
297 **mend** rectify

275 so] *F; not in Q*   275–7 Drunk? . . . shadow] *F; not in Q*   285 God] *Q; not in F*
287–8 pleasance, revel] *F; Reuell, pleasure Q*   289 Why,] *Q; Why? F*   295 and] *F; not in
Q*   296 not] *F; not so Q*

CASSIO   I will ask him for my place again, he shall tell
me I am a drunkard: had I as many mouths as Hydra,
such an answer would stop them all. To be now a   300
sensible man, by and by a fool, and presently a beast!
O strange! – Every inordinate cup is unblest, and the
ingredience is a devil.

IAGO   Come, come, good wine is a good familiar creature, if it be well used: exclaim no more against it.   305
And, good lieutenant, I think you think I love you.

CASSIO   I have well approved it, sir. I drunk?

IAGO   You, or any man living, may be drunk at some
time, man. I'll tell you what you shall do. Our
general's wife is now the general. I may say so in this   310
respect, for that he hath devoted and given up himself
to the contemplation, mark and denotement of her
parts and graces. Confess yourself freely to her,
importune her help to put you in your place again.

---

299 **Hydra** The many-headed monster
of Greek mythology, which it was one
of Hercules' tasks to destroy; 'as each
head was cut off, two more grew in
its place' (Ridley). Cf. Dent, H278,
'As many heads as Hydra'.
300 **stop** plug, close. Cf. Dent, M1264,
'To stop one's mouth'.
301 **by and by** soon afterwards
presently in a little while
beast Cf. Dent, B152.1, 'A drunken
man is a beast.'
302 **inordinate** immoderate. Only found
three times in Shakespeare: *Luc* 94,
1H4 3.2.12 both read *in-*, so F is
likely to be right here.
303 **ingredience** that which enters into
a mixture (*OED*); cf. *Mac* 1.7.11,
4.1.34.
304 **familiar** friendly; 'punning on the
sense of "familiar spirit", with an
emphasis on *good*; he half admits that

wine may be a devil, but good wine
well used is a *good* devil' (Ridley)
304–5 See LN.
305 **well** properly
307 **approved** proved by experience
sir Cassio senses that Iago puts pressure on him.
309–10 **Our ... general** Cf. 2.1.74;
Ovid, *Heroides*, 9.114, 'you are victor
over the beast, but she over you'.
311 **for that** that
312 **mark** marking, observation
***denotement** Cf. 3.3.126. Here =
noting(?); Q 'deuoted ... to the ...
deuotement' must be wrong. F followed Q; the corruption may involve
more than a turned letter (u/n).
313 **parts** personal qualities. Cf. *MA*
5.2.60, 'for which of my bad parts
didst thou first fall in love with me?'
graces pleasing qualities

---

300 them] *F;* em *Q*   302 O strange!] *F; not in Q*   inordinate] *F;* vnordinate *Q*   303 ingred-
ience] *Q;* Ingredient *F*   308 some] *Q;* a *F*   309 man] *F; not in Q*   I'll] *Q;* I *F*   311 hath]
F; has *Q*   312 mark] *Q;* marke: *F*   denotement] *Q2;* deuotement *QF*   314 help] *F;* shee'll
helpe *Q*

She is of so free, so kind, so apt, so blest a disposition   315
that she holds it a vice in her goodness not to do
more than she is requested. This broken joint between
you and her husband entreat her to splinter – and my
fortunes against any lay worth naming, this crack of
your love shall grow stronger than it was before.   320

CASSIO   You advise me well.

IAGO   I protest, in the sincerity of love and honest
kindness.

CASSIO   I think it freely, and betimes in the morning I
will beseech the virtuous Desdemona to undertake   325
for me. I am desperate of my fortunes if they check
me here.

IAGO   You are in the right. Good-night, lieutenant, I
must to the watch.   329

CASSIO   Good-night, honest Iago.   *Exit.*

IAGO

And what's he then that says I play the villain?
When this advice is free I give and honest,
Probal to thinking and indeed the course

---

315 **free** generous; ready, willing (to
grant) (*OED* 4, 20)
apt fit, ready
blest a disposition He appropriates
a thought he had previously ridiculed
(2.1.246–7).
317–18 **This ... splinter** Cf. Dent,
B515, 'A broken bone is the stronger
when it is well set'; *2H4* 4.1.220, 'like
a broken limb united, / Grow
stronger for the breaking'; *splinter* =
apply splints to.
319 **lay** wager
crack partial fracture (*OED* 7b)
323 **kindness** natural inclination;
affection
324 **freely** unreservedly
betimes early
325–6 **undertake for me** take my case

in hand
326 **I ... of** I have lost hope concerning
check stop
328 **You ... right** You are right; also
hinting 'you have justice on your
side', i.e. you have been badly treated.
331 He picks up where he left off at
2.1.308, but now *knavery* sees clearly
how to proceed. Note his alertness to
possible reactions.
332 **free** frank and open; honourable;
freely given
333 **Probal** probable; or, 'such as ap-
proves itself' (from Lat. *probo*, I
prove, make credible). A nonce word.
Cf. *admiral* = admirable (Dekker,
Patient Grissill, 2.2.91). Iago has a
habit of weighing probabilities:
2.1.282ff., 5.1.11ff.

---

315 of so] *F; so Q*   316 that] *Q; not in F*   317 broken joint] *F; braule Q*   320 it was] *F; twas Q*   324–5 I will] *F; will I Q*   327 here] *Q; not in F*   331] *as Q; F lines* then, / Villaine? /

201

To win the Moor again? For 'tis most easy
Th'inclining Desdemona to subdue   335
In any honest suit. She's framed as fruitful
As the free elements: and then for her
To win the Moor, were't to renounce his baptism,
All seals and symbols of redeemed sin,
His soul is so enfettered to her love   340
That she may make, unmake, do what she list,
Even as her appetite shall play the god
With his weak function. How am I then a villain
To counsel Cassio to this parallel course
Directly to his good? Divinity of hell!   345
When devils will the blackest sins put on
They do suggest at first with heavenly shows
As I do now. For whiles this honest fool
Plies Desdemona to repair his fortune,
And she for him pleads strongly to the Moor,   350
I'll pour this pestilence into his ear:

334 **win** regain the favour of
335 **inclining** mentally inclining (to be helpful); perhaps physically leaning (towards a suitor)
    subdue win
336 **framed** made, fashioned
    fruitful beneficial; generous
337 **As ... elements** It is her nature to be as beneficial (to others) as the unrestrained elements are there to be used.
338 **win** win over
339 **seals** tokens. Cf. Ephesians 4.30, 'the holy spirit of God, by whom ye are sealed unto the day of redemption' (i.e. the Anglican doctrine of baptism: Noble, 218).
    redeemed redeemèd (Christ as Redeemer delivers us from sin); paid for, ransomed
341 **list** likes
342 **her appetite** 'his desire for her'

(Ridley); or, her fancy, inclination
343 **weak** enslaved
    function natural instincts (Ridley); or perhaps 'functioning (of mental and moral powers)'
344 **parallel course** i.e. it seems to lead straight to his advantage but in fact takes him in the opposite direction, to his destruction.
345 **Divinity of hell!** 'O, the theology of hell!' Or, he addresses Satan, 'O god of hell!' Cf. 1.3.358.
346 **devils** (including himself!). Cf. Dent, D231, 'The devil can transform himself into an angel of light.'
    put on incite
347 **suggest** prompt, tempt
349 **Plies** solicits
351 **pestilence** that which is morally pernicious. Cf. *Ham* 1.5.63–4, 'in the porches of my ears did pour / The leprous distillment'.

334] *as Q; F lines* againe. / easie /   335 Th'] *F;* The *Q*   338 were't] *Q;* were *F*   346 the] *F;* their *Q*   348 whiles] *F;* while *Q*   349 fortune] *F;* fortunes *Q*

That she repeals him for her body's lust.
And by how much she strives to do him good
She shall undo her credit with the Moor –
So will I turn her virtue into pitch   355
And out of her own goodness make the net
That shall enmesh them all.

Enter RODERIGO.

How now, Roderigo?

RODERIGO   I do follow here in the chase not like a
hound that hunts, but one that fills up the cry. My
money is almost spent, I have been tonight   360
exceedingly well cudgelled, and I think the issue will
be I shall have so much experience for my pains: and
so, with no money at all, and a little more wit, return
again to Venice.

IAGO

How poor are they that have not patience!   365
What wound did ever heal but by degrees?
Thou know'st we work by wit and not by witchcraft,
And wit depends on dilatory time.
Does't not go well? Cassio hath beaten thee
And thou by that small hurt hast cashiered Cassio.   370

---

352 **repeals** tries to get him restored to his
former position (*OED* 3d); lit. recalls
354 **credit** reputation; trustworthiness
355 **pitch** suggests blackness and foul-
ness, and 'a snaring substance, like
birdlime … leading on to the *net*'
(Ridley)
357 **enmesh** catch or entangle, as in a
net (unique in Shakespeare). Cf.
2.1.168 *ensnare*; see p. 79 n. 5.
359 **cry** pack, 'the hounds who merely
give tongue as they follow those who
are really running the scent' (Ridley)

361 **cudgelled** Cf. 143n.
361–2 **I . . . pains** Cf. Dent, L1, 'He has
his labor for his pains'; i.e. so much
experience and nothing more.
363 **wit** sense
365 Cf. Dent, P103, 'He that has no
patience has nothing.'
367 **we** How much wit has Roderigo
contributed?
wit cleverness, good judgement
370 **cashiered** (succeeded in having Cassio) dismissed; cf p. 334 (to 'cass' = to
cashier).

357] *QF lines* all: / Roderigo? /   enmesh them] enmesh em *Q*; en-mash them *F*   SD] *opp.* all 357
Q; *after* 357 *Rodorigo F*   360 have] *F*; ha *Q*   361 and] *F*; not in *Q*   362–4 pains . . . Venice] *as F*;
paines, as that comes to, and no money at all, and with that wit returne to *Venice. Q*   365 have] *F*;
ha *Q*   367 know'st] *F*; knowest *Q*   369 Does't] Do'st *Q*; Dos't *F*   hath] *F*; has *Q*   370 hast] *Q*;
hath *F*

Though other things grow fair against the sun
Yet fruits that blossom first will first be ripe;
Content thyself a while. By the mass, 'tis morning:
Pleasure and action make the hours seem short.
Retire thee, go where thou art billeted,   375
Away, I say, thou shalt know more hereafter:
Nay, get thee gone.   *Exit Roderigo.*
               Two things are to be done:
My wife must move for Cassio to her mistress,
I'll set her on.
Myself the while to draw the Moor apart   380
And bring him jump when he may Cassio find
Soliciting his wife: ay, that's the way!
Dull not device by coldness and delay!   *Exit.*

[3.1]   *Enter* CASSIO *and some* Musicians.

CASSIO

Masters, play here, I will content your pains;

371–2 'Though other plants grow vigorously when exposed to (= *against*) the
sun, yet fruit trees that blossom first
will bear ripe fruit first' (NB this is
not always true); i.e. though others
thrive in Desdemona's favour, we'll
succeed in bringing our plots to frui-
tion. In this false analogy blossom =
Cassio's cudgelling!
373 **By the mass** a mild oath, hence
changed in F, found also in plays with
Protestant settings (*Ham* 2.1.50,
3.2.378, etc.). Cf. 3.3.74n.
374 Cf. Dent, H747, 'Hours of pleasure
are short.'
375 **billeted** assigned quarters (troops,
or others)
378 **My wife** Do husbands think of 'my
wife', or think of her by name? Here *my*

wife helps the audience. Cf. 5.2.95–6.
move solicit
379 Short lines in Iago's soliloquies suggest pauses, as he thinks of a new
stratagem (cf. 1.3.400, 3.3.323).
380 ***the while** in the meantime
381 **jump** precisely (at the moment
when)
383 **Dull** an imperative, addressed to
himself: 'don't let the plot lose its
momentum'
device plot, stratagem; pleasure,
desire (*OED* 3, 6)
coldness lack of enthusiasm
3.1.1–20 Cf. *RJ* 4.5.102ff., *AYL* 5.3.34ff.:
the Clown's baiting of the Musicians
was a 'comic turn'.
1 **content your pains** reward you for
taking the trouble

372 Yet] *F*; But *Q*   373 By the mass] *Q*; Introth *F*   377] *as Q*; *F lines* gone. / done: /   SD] *F*;
not in Q   Two] *F*; Some *Q*   379–80] *as Q*; *one line F*   380 Myself the while] *Theobald*; My selfe
awhile, *Q*; my selfe, a while, *F*   383 SD] *F*; *Exeunt. Q*   3.1] *Actus Tertius. Scena Prima. F*; *not in
Q*   0.1] *Enter Cassio, with Musitians and the Clowne. Q*; *Enter Cassio, Musitians, and Clowne. F*

Something that's brief, and bid 'Good morrow,
     general.'

They play. Enter CLOWN.

CLOWN   Why, masters, have your instruments been in
     Naples, that they speak i'th' nose thus?
1 MUSICIAN   How, sir? how?   5
CLOWN   Are these, I pray you, wind instruments?
1 MUSICIAN   Ay marry are they, sir.
CLOWN   O, thereby hangs a tail.
1 MUSICIAN   Whereby hangs a tail, sir?
CLOWN   Marry, sir, by many a wind instrument that I   10
     know. But, masters, here's money for you, and the
     general so likes your music that he desires you, for
     love's sake, to make no more noise with it.
1 MUSICIAN   Well, sir, we will not.
CLOWN   If you have any music that may not be heard,   15
     to't again. But, as they say, to hear music the general
     does not greatly care.
1 MUSICIAN   We have none such, sir.

2 **Good morrow** the traditional *aubade*
  to wake bride and groom after the
  wedding night. Cf. Donne's 'The
  Good-Morrow' (morrow = morning).
2.1 CLOWN   *Clown* could = peasant,
  countryman; ignorant or rude fellow;
  fool or jester (in a great house or in
  the theatre). Here the theatre clown
  plays a clown (a comic servant).
  Shakespeare gave names to most of
  his clowns and fools, but not in *Oth*
  and *KL*.
3–4 See LN.
8 **tail** i.e. a penis (or animal tail?). Cf.
  AYL 2.7.28; Dent, T48, 'Thereby

hangs a tale' (= there's a story about
that).
10 **wind instrument** 'Podex – or *ars
  musica*' (Partridge). A joke about
  flatulence.
12–13 **for love's sake** So Philemon, 1.9,
  'Yet for love's sake I rather beseech
  thee'; for Q's *of all loues*, cf. *MND*
  2.2.154.
13 **noise** could mean 'an agreeable or
  melodious sound' (*OED* 5): the clown
  specializes in ambiguous insults
18 **none such** perhaps a quibble: 'None-
  such' was the name of a popular tune
  (R. King, as in 3–4n.)

2.1] *as Q2 (They play, and enter the Clowne.); not in QF*   3 have] *F;* ha *Q*   in] *F;* at
Q   4 i'th'] *F;* i'the *Q*   5 SP] *Boy Q (throughout); Mus. F (throughout)*   6 pray you,] *F;* pray,
cald *Q*   12–13 for . . . sake] *F;* of all loues *Q*   18 have] *F;* ha *Q*

CLOWN   Then put up your pipes in your bag, for I'll
away. Go, vanish into air, away!   *Exeunt Musicians.*

CASSIO   Dost thou hear, mine honest friend?   21

CLOWN   No, I hear not your honest friend, I hear you.

CASSIO   Prithee keep up thy quillets; there's a poor piece
of gold for thee – if the gentlewoman that attends the
general's wife be stirring, tell her there's one Cassio   25
entreats her a little favour of speech. Wilt thou do
this?

CLOWN   She is stirring, sir; if she will stir hither, I shall
seem to notify unto her.

Enter IAGO.

CASSIO

Do, good my friend. (*Exit Clown.*) In happy time,
Iago.   30

IAGO

You have not been a-bed then?

CASSIO

Why no, the day had broke before we parted.
I have made bold, Iago, to send in
To your wife: my suit to her is that she will

19 **put … pipes** could = desist, 'shut
up' (*OED* pipe 1e), or pack up your
pipes
19–20 perhaps alluding to the practice of
carrying away a tedious Fool in a
cloak-bag (cf. Leslie Hotson, *Shakespeare's Motley*, 1952, ch. 4); i.e. put
your pipes, not me, in your bag, for
I'll go away on my own
22 To 'mistake the word' (*TGV* 3.1.284)
was a regular clown routine.
23 **keep up** refrain from
quillets quibbles
24 **gentlewoman** originally, a woman of
good birth; then, a female attendant
on a lady of rank
26 **entreats … speech** begs the favour

of briefly speaking with her (here
little looks like a transferred epithet)
28 **stirring** He understands it as 'sexually exciting' (cf. *OED* stirring 3,
quoting Dekker, 'Capon is a stirring
meate'; Partridge, stir).
28–9 **I … her** i.e. I shall have notified
her
29 The Clown makes fun of Cassio's
courtliness or accent (cf. Iago,
2.1.166ff.), and perhaps quibbles on
stir–steer.
30 **In happy time** well met; *happy* =
fortunate
31–9 These lines could be prose or verse
(see pp. 360).

19 up] *F; not in Q*   20 into air] *F; not in Q*   SD] *Exit Mu. F; not in Q*   21 hear, mine] heare my *Q ;*
heare me, mine *F*   22] *as Q ; F lines* Friend: / you. /   25 general's wife] *Q ;* Generall *F*   30 Do,…
friend] *Q ; not in F*   SD] *F (Exit Clo., after 29); not in Q*   31, 33 have] *F;* ha *Q*   32–6 Why …
access] *Q lines* parted: / her, / *Desdemona* / accesse. /; *F lines* parted. / wife: / *Desdemona* / accesse. /

To virtuous Desdemona procure me   35
Some access.

IAGO   I'll send her to you presently,
And I'll devise a mean to draw the Moor
Out of the way, that your converse and business
May be more free.

CASSIO
I humbly thank you for't.   *Exit [Iago.]*
                    I never knew   40
A Florentine more kind and honest.

Enter EMILIA.

EMILIA
Good morrow, good lieutenant. I am sorry
For your displeasure, but all will sure be well.
The general and his wife are talking of it,
And she speaks for you stoutly; the Moor replies   45
That he you hurt is of great fame in Cyprus
And great affinity,
And that in wholesome wisdom he might not but
Refuse you; but he protests he loves you
And needs no other suitor but his likings   50
To take the safest occasion by the front

---

37 **mean** opportunity
41 **Florentine** Did Shakespeare delete
1.1.19–20 (*Texts*, 36)? If he did,
Cassio is naively ignorant that Florence, the home of Machiavelli, was
not generally thought a centre of
honesty; if not, he praises Iago as if a
fellow countryman, and also misunderstands him.
43 **displeasure** loss of favour
all . . . well Cf. 3.4.19, 4.2.173, *RJ*
4.2.40: a common saying.
45 **stoutly** vigorously (stronger than
today)
47 **great** important, powerful
affinity kindred, family. This half-
line may have been deleted and print-

ed in error (*Texts*, 37). Cf. Ruth 2.20,
'The man is nigh unto us, and of our
affinity.'
48 **wholesome** beneficial; health-giving:
i.e. wisdom that restores the well-
being of Cyprus
he . . . but he could only; or, he was
forced to
49 **Refuse** dismiss; decline to reappoint;
i.e. he had (earlier or now) no choice
except to *refuse* you
loves is fond of
51 **front** forelock. The proverb (Dent,
T311, 'To take time (occasion) by the
forelock') refers to the classical *Oc-
casio*, long-haired in front, bald
behind.

---

40 for't] *F;* for it *Q* SD] *opp. 39 QF* 41.1] *Enter* Emilia. *Q; Enter Æmilia. F* 43 sure] *F;*
soone *Q* 46–9] *QF lines Cypres, /* wisedome, / loues you, / 51] *Q; not in F*

To bring you in again.

CASSIO   Yet I beseech you,
If you think fit, or that it may be done,
Give me advantage of some brief discourse
With Desdemon alone.

EMILIA   Pray you come in,   55
I will bestow you where you shall have time
To speak your bosom freely.

CASSIO   I am much bound to you.

Exeunt.

[3.2]   *Enter* OTHELLO, IAGO *and* Gentlemen.

OTHELLO

These letters give, Iago, to the pilot,
And by him do my duties to the Senate;
That done, I will be walking on the works,
Repair there to me.

IAGO   Well, my good lord, I'll do't.

OTHELLO

This fortification, gentlemen, shall we see't?   5

1 GENTLEMAN

We'll wait upon your lordship.

[3.3]   *Enter* DESDEMONA, CASSIO *and* EMILIA.   *Exeunt.*

52 **in** into favour
54 **advantage** opportunity
55 **Desdemon** This form of the name occurs seven times, but never in Q. The speaker is mostly Othello, which makes it sound more intimate than 'Desdemona'. Perhaps Shakespeare wrote the full name and wanted final and initial *a* to be slurred: 'Desdemona‿alone'.
56 **bestow** place
57 **bosom** bosom thoughts
3.2 This scene gives us a glimpse of Othello at work, undistracted by thoughts of Desdemona.

2 **do my duties** pay my respects
3 **works** defensive fortification
4 **Repair** come, make your way
   Well . . . do't an odd way of responding to an order?
6 **wait** attend
3.3 Location: Cassio has 'come in' (3.1.55), but the location is vague: 'yond marble heaven' (463) suggests that Shakespeare now thinks it an outdoor scene. On the 'unlocalized stage' such inconsistencies pass unnoticed.

55 Desdemon] *F; Desdemona Q*   57 I . . . you] *F; not in Q*   SD] *Q; not in F*   3.2] *Scoena Secunda. F; not in Q*   0.1] *F; . . . and other Gentlemen. Q*   1 pilot] *F;* Pilate *Q*   2 Senate] *F;* State *Q*   4 Well] *QF; om. Pope*   6 We'll] *F2 (*Weel*);* We *Q;* Well *F*   3.3] *Scoena Tertia. F; not in Q*

DESDEMONA

Be thou assured, good Cassio, I will do
All my abilities in thy behalf.

EMILIA

Good madam, do, I warrant it grieves my husband
As if the cause were his.

DESDEMONA

O, that's an honest fellow. Do not doubt, Cassio,   5
But I will have my lord and you again
As friendly as you were.

CASSIO   Bounteous madam,
Whatever shall become of Michael Cassio,
He's never anything but your true servant.

DESDEMONA

I know't, I thank you. You do love my lord,   10
You have known him long, and be you well assured
He shall in strangeness stand no farther off
Than in a politic distance.

CASSIO   Ay, but, lady,
That policy may either last so long,
Or feed upon such nice and waterish diet,   15
Or breed itself so out of circumstance,
That, I being absent and my place supplied,
My general will forget my love and service.

DESDEMONA

Do not doubt that: before Emilia here

---

3 **warrant** be bound (common asseveration); monosyllabic (warr'nt),
as in *Ham* 1.2.242, 'I warn't it will'
(Q2), *MND* 5.1.320.
7 **Bounteous** good, virtuous (Fr. *bonté*,
goodness, kindness)
9 **true** faithful, sincere
10 **You . . . lord** See p. 51 n. 2.
12 **strangeness** coldness, aloofness
13 **politic** sagacious, shrewd; i.e. than
the distance required by judicious-
ness

14 **policy** sagacity, diplomacy; an expe-
dient course of action
15 or feed on such a poor diet (i.e. as to
fade away); **nice** = delicate, thin
16 or engender itself to such an extent
from non-essential factors, i.e.
depend so much on chance
17–18 Cf. Dent, F596, 'Long absent
soon forgotten'.
17 **supplied** filled
19 **doubt** fear

3] *as Q ; F lines* do: / Husband, /   warrant] *F;* know *Q*   4 cause] *F;* case *Q*   10 I know't] *F;* O
sir *Q*   12 strangeness] *F;* strangest *Q*   14 That] *F;* The *Q*   16 circumstance] *Q ;* Circumstances *F*

I give thee warrant of thy place. Assure thee,   20
If I do vow a friendship I'll perform it
To the last article. My lord shall never rest,
I'll watch him tame and talk him out of patience,
His bed shall seem a school, his board a shrift,
I'll intermingle everything he does   25
With Cassio's suit: therefore be merry, Cassio,
For thy solicitor shall rather die
Than give thy cause away.

Enter OTHELLO *and* IAGO.

EMILIA

Madam, here comes my lord.

CASSIO

Madam, I'll take my leave.   30

DESDEMONA

Why, stay and hear me speak.

CASSIO

Madam, not now; I am very ill at ease,
Unfit for mine own purposes.

DESDEMONA

Well, do your discretion.   *Exit Cassio.*

IAGO   Ha, I like not that.

OTHELLO

What dost thou say?   35

IAGO

Nothing, my lord; or if – I know not what.

20 **warrant** assurance, pledge. This seems as impetuous as her elopement with Othello.
   Assure thee be certain
22 **article** item
23 **I'll ... tame** a metaphor from the training of hawks (*watch* = keep awake, to make obedient). Cf. *TC* 3.2.43, 'you must be watch'd ere you be made tame, must you?' (Ridley).
24 **bed ... board** Marriage was a 'bond

of board and bed' (*AYL* 5.4.142: cf. *3H6* 1.1.248); *board* = table, *shrift* = place of confession. Without realizing it, she puts her marriage at risk.
26 **merry** happy
27 **solicitor** advocate
28 **give ... away** abandon thy suit
34 **do your discretion** do as you think fit. Usually 'use your discretion' (*AYL* 1.1.146; Lyly, *Endymion*, 1.4.5).

28 thy cause away] *F;* thee cause: away *Q* 28.1] *F; Enter* Othello, Iago, *and Gentlemen. Q* 33 purposes] *F;* purpose *Q* 34 Ha,] *Q;* Hah? *F* 36 if –] *F;* if, *Q*

210

OTHELLO

    Was not that Cassio parted from my wife?

IAGO

    Cassio, my lord? no, sure, I cannot think it

    That he would steal away so guilty-like

    Seeing you coming.

OTHELLO   I do believe 'twas he.   40

DESDEMONA

    How now, my lord?

    I have been talking with a suitor here,

    A man that languishes in your displeasure.

OTHELLO

    Who is't you mean?

DESDEMONA

    Why, your lieutenant, Cassio. Good my lord,   45

    If I have any grace or power to move you

    His present reconciliation take:

    For if he be not one that truly loves you,

    That errs in ignorance and not in cunning,

    I have no judgement in an honest face.   50

    I prithee, call him back.

OTHELLO   Went he hence now?

DESDEMONA

    Yes, faith, so humbled

    That he hath left part of his grief with me

    To suffer with him. Good love, call him back.

OTHELLO

    Not now, sweet Desdemon, some other time.   55

DESDEMONA

    But shall't be shortly?

OTHELLO   The sooner, sweet, for you.

---

39 **steal away** Cf. *Cor* 1.1.252 SD, '*Citi-zens steale away*'.
    guilty-like unique in Shakespeare; his coinage
42 **suitor** petitioner
46 **grace** pleasing quality; privilege (*OED* 1, 8)

move influence
47 **present** immediate
    reconciliation restoration to favour (*OED* 1c)
    take accept, agree to
49 **in cunning** wittingly
50 **in** of

39 steal] *F;* sneake *Q*   40 you] *Q;* your *F*   52 Yes, faith] *Q;* I sooth *F*   53 hath] *F;* has *Q*   grief] *F;* griefes *Q*   54 To] *F;* I *Q*   55 Desdemon] *F; Desdemona Q*

DESDEMONA

    Shall't be tonight, at supper?

OTHELLO   No, not tonight.

DESDEMONA

    Tomorrow dinner then?

OTHELLO   I shall not dine at home.

    I meet the captains at the citadel.

DESDEMONA

    Why then, tomorrow night, or Tuesday morn;   60
    On Tuesday, noon or night; on Wednesday morn!
    I prithee name the time, but let it not
    Exceed three days: i'faith, he's penitent,
    And yet his trespass, in our common reason
    – Save that they say the wars must make examples   65
    Out of their best – is not, almost, a fault
    T'incur a private check. When shall he come?
    Tell me, Othello. I wonder in my soul
    What you would ask me that I should deny
    Or stand so mamm'ring on? What, Michael Cassio   70
    That came a-wooing with you? and so many a time
    When I have spoke of you dispraisingly
    Hath ta'en your part, to have so much to do
    To bring him in? By'r lady, I could do much! –

---

58 **dinner** a midday meal at this time

64 **common reason** general way of thinking

65 **wars** i.e. the military profession

66 **their best** their best men. If *wars* = war generally, singular *her* (as in QF) is possible. But *their* (or *ther*) could be misread as *her*.

    not, almost hardly. 'I have not breathed almost, since I did see it' (*CE* 5.1.181) (Ridley).

67 **check** rebuke

70 **mamm'ring** (1) hesitating, (2) stammering, muttering. Editors prefer (1), but (2) could be appropriate for

56ff. An unkind word, unique in Shakespeare, signalling her critical surprise. It echoes *Euphues*, 'neither stand in a mammering whether it be best to departe or not' (Lyly, 1.253) (Malone).

71 **That . . . you** Cf. 1.2.52n.

72 **dispraisingly** i.e. she has been critical of him before – 'of course, in order to hear Cassio praise him in reply' (Kittredge)

74 **bring him in** Cf. 3.1.52.

    By'r lady a mild oath, changed by F, found also in 'Protestant' plays (e.g. *Ham* 3.2.133). Cf. 2.3.373n.

---

60 or] *Q;* on *F*   61 Tuesday, noon] Tuesday morne, *Q;* Tuesday noone, *F*   on] *F;* or *Q*   63 i'faith] *Q;* Infaith *F*   65–6] (Saue . . . examples / . . . her best) *Q;* (Saue . . . example) / . . . her best) *F*   66 their best] *Rowe;* her best *QF*   67 T'] *F;* To *Q*   69 would] *F;* could *Q*   70 mamm'ring] *F* (mam'ring); muttering *Q*   What,] What *Q;* What? *F*   74 By'r lady] *Q;* Trust me *F*

OTHELLO

    Prithee, no more. Let him come when he will,   75

    I will deny thee nothing.

DESDEMONA   Why, this is not a boon,

    'Tis as I should entreat you wear your gloves,

    Or feed on nourishing dishes, or keep you warm,

    Or sue to you to do a peculiar profit

    To your own person. Nay, when I have a suit   80

    Wherein I mean to touch your love indeed

    It shall be full of poise and difficult weight

    And fearful to be granted.

OTHELLO   I will deny thee nothing.

    Whereon I do beseech thee, grant me this,

    To leave me but a little to myself.   85

DESDEMONA

    Shall I deny you? No, farewell, my lord.

OTHELLO

    Farewell, my Desdemona, I'll come to thee straight.

DESDEMONA

    Emilia, come. – Be as your fancies teach you:

    Whate'er you be, I am obedient.

                  Exeunt Desdemona and Emilia.

---

76 **I ... nothing** Cf. Plautus, *Trinummus*, 357, 'I cannot keep refusing you anything you wish': 'Non edepol tibi pernegare possum quicquam quod velis.'

    boon favour

77 **as** as if

    gloves worn by the well-off as a sign of their importance; i.e. to do what is normal and natural

79–80 **do ... person** i.e. do something that will be of special benefit to yourself

81 **touch** test

82 **poise** weight; balance

    difficult weight difficult to weigh;

i.e. it shall be so finely balanced (between the possible and impossible) that it will be a momentous thing for you to grant it. Cf. 2.3.120n. Or, more simply, it will be 'too heavy'.

83 **fearful** terrible (stronger than today)

84 **Whereon** almost = in return for which

87 **straight** immediately

88 **fancies** whims (another unkind word)

89 **obedient** Wives were expected to obey their husbands. She means, 'However good or bad you may be as a husband, I am a good wife.'

---

82 difficult weight] *F;* difficulty *Q*   87 to thee] *QF; om. Pope*   88 Be] *F;* be it *Q*   89 SD] *Exit Desd. and* Em. *Q ; Exit. F*

OTHELLO

    Excellent wretch! perdition catch my soul   90
    But I do love thee! and when I love thee not
    Chaos is come again.

IAGO

    My noble lord –

OTHELLO   What dost thou say, Iago?

IAGO

    Did Michael Cassio, when you wooed my lady,
    Know of your love?

OTHELLO   He did, from first to last.   95
    Why dost thou ask?

IAGO

    But for a satisfaction of my thought,
    No further harm.

OTHELLO   Why of thy thought, Iago?

IAGO

    I did not think he had been acquainted with her.

OTHELLO

    O yes, and went between us very oft.   100

IAGO

    Indeed?

OTHELLO

    Indeed? Ay, indeed. Discern'st thou aught in that?

---

90 **wretch** could be a term of endearment, or the opposite. Perhaps meant
to imply both, playfully. Cf. *RJ*
1.3.44, 'The pretty wretch left crying
and said, "Ay".'
perdition destruction, i.e. damnation
catch take

91 **But** could = 'if . . . not', i.e. 'may I be
damned if I don't love thee', almost
'may I be damned if I stop loving
thee'. Yet *but* could be a fairly meaningless part of an asseveration (*MV*
2.6.52, 'Beshrow me but I love her
heartily'). For *when* = if, see *OED* 8.

92 **Chaos** 'The allusion is to the classical legend that Love was the first of
the gods to spring out of original
chaos. Cf. Ben Jonson, *Love Freed
from Ignorance*, 26–7: "without me /
All again would Chaos be" ' (Sanders,
quoting a speech by Love).

97 **satisfaction** information that answers a person's demands, removal of
doubt; satisfying proof (*OED* 6b, first
in 1601)

99 **he had** probably one syllable

100 **went between** *OED* first records
go-between in *MW* 2.2.263.

102 **aught** i.e. anything strange

94–5 Did . . . love?] *Q ; F lines Cassio / loue? /* you] *Q ; he* F   95–6 He . . . ask?] *as F; one line*
Q 97 thought] *F;* thoughts *Q* 100 oft] *F;* often *Q* 102 Ay] *F (1); not in Q*

Is he not honest?

IAGO

Honest, my lord?

OTHELLO

Honest? Ay, honest.   105

IAGO

My lord, for aught I know.

OTHELLO

What dost thou think?

IAGO

Think, my lord?

OTHELLO

Think, my lord! By heaven, thou echo'st me
As if there were some monster in thy thought   110
Too hideous to be shown. Thou dost mean something,
I heard thee say even now thou lik'st not that
When Cassio left my wife: what didst not like?
And when I told thee he was of my counsel
In my whole course of wooing, thou criedst 'Indeed?' 115
And didst contract and purse thy brow together
As if thou then hadst shut up in thy brain
Some horrible conceit. If thou dost love me
Show me thy thought.

IAGO   My lord, you know I love you.

OTHELLO

I think thou dost.   120
And for I know thou'rt full of love and honesty
And weigh'st thy words before thou giv'st them breath,

---

110 **monster** prodigy; monstrosity; monstrous creature (cf. 168)

111 **hideous** ugly; repulsive; detestable

114 **of my counsel** i.e. in my confidence; or, he advised me

116 **purse** contract in wrinkles, 'suggesting the tightly drawn-in mouth of a purse' (*OED* 4, first here)

118 **conceit** idea, conception

119 **you ... you** 'a horrible reminiscence of Peter's "thou knowest that I love thee" (John 21.15–17)' (Ridley)

119–21 For the emphasis on knowing and thinking here, cf. *MM* 5.1.203–4, 'Who thinks he knows that he ne'er knew my body, / But knows he thinks that he knows Isabel's'.

121 **for** because

---

109 By . . . echo'st] By heauen he ecchoes *Q ;* Alas, thou ecchos't *F*   110 thy] *F;* his *Q*   111 dost] *F;* didst *Q*   112 even] *F;* but *Q*   115 In] *Q ;* Of *F*   118 conceit] *F;* counsell *Q*   121 thou'rt] *F;* thou art *Q*   122 weigh'st] *F;* weighest *Q*   giv'st them] *F;* giue em *Q*

Therefore these stops of thine fright me the more.
For such things in a false disloyal knave
Are tricks of custom, but in a man that's just   125
They're close delations, working from the heart,
That passion cannot rule.

IAGO   For Michael Cassio,
I dare be sworn, I think, that he is honest.

OTHELLO
I think so too.

IAGO   Men should be what they seem,
Or those that be not, would they might seem none.   130

OTHELLO
Certain, men should be what they seem.

IAGO
Why then I think Cassio's an honest man.

OTHELLO
Nay, yet there's more in this:
I prithee speak to me, as to thy thinkings,
As thou dost ruminate, and give thy worst of
    thoughts   135
The worst of words.

IAGO   Good my lord, pardon me;

---

123 **stops** pauses
125 **tricks** stratagems; characteristic
    practices (*OED* 1, 7)
    of custom customary
126 **close** secret
    *delations See LN.
127 **That ... rule** i.e. (self-accusations
    or self-betrayals) that passion cannot
    control
128 **be sworn** Q *presume* is attractive,
    creating uncertainty and confusion
    (Iago's aim in this scene).
    *think, The inserted comma makes
    Iago more doubtful.
129 **Men ... seem** Tilley, S214, 'Be

what thou would seem to be.'
130 'Or, those that be not (what they
    seem), would that they might not
    seem (honest) at all', taking *none* = by
    no means, not at all (*OED* adv. 3, first
    recorded 1651).
132 **then** (= in that case) hints at
    reservations
    I think Cf. 128.
134 **thinkings** spoken as if in inverted
    commas, *thy 'thinkings'*, picking up
    108, 128, 132
135 **ruminate** lit. chew the cud; hence,
    'just as thou dost turn them over in
    thy mind'

---

123 fright] *F*; affright *Q*   126 They're] *F*; They are *Q*   delations] *Steevens 1773*; dilations *F*;
denotements *Q*   128 be sworn] *F*; presume *Q*   think,] *this edn*; thinke *QF*   129 what] *F*; that
Q   133 this:] *F* (this?)   134 as to] *F*; to *Q*   135 thy] *F*; the *Q*   thoughts] *F*; thought
Q   136 words] *F*; word *Q*

216

Though I am bound to every act of duty
I am not bound to that all slaves are free to –
Utter my thoughts? Why, say they are vile and false?
As where's that palace whereinto foul things   140
Sometimes intrude not? Who has a breast so pure
But some uncleanly apprehensions
Keep leets and law-days and in session sit
With meditations lawful?

OTHELLO
    Thou dost conspire against thy friend, Iago,   145
If thou but think'st him wronged and mak'st his ear
A stranger to thy thoughts.

IAGO   I do beseech you,
Though I perchance am vicious in my guess
– As I confess it is my nature's plague
To spy into abuses, and oft my jealousy   150
Shapes faults that are not – that your wisdom
From one that so imperfectly conceits
Would take no notice, nor build yourself a trouble
Out of his scattering and unsure observance:

---

138 **that** what
  free to not bound to (do). Dent,
  T244, 'Thought is free.'
142 **uncleanly** filthy
  apprehensions ideas
143 **leets** special courts, held by some
  lords of the manor once or twice a year
  law-days days for the meeting of a
  court of law; the session of such a
  court
145 **friend** He speaks in general terms
  but clearly sees himself as the friend,
  redefining their relationship. Cf.
  5.2.150.
147ff. Two consecutive parentheses confuse Iago's thought, viz. 148 and 149–
  51 ('As . . . not'), interrupting 'I do
  beseech you that your wisdom'.

148 **Though** could = if (*OED* 4), but the
  sentence is deliberately serpentine
  vicious wicked; blameworthy; faulty,
  mistaken (*OED* 2, 3, 6). It suits Iago
  to use elastic words.
149 **plague** affliction
150 **spy into** look out for; pry into
  jealousy zeal (against abuses); devotion (to serve someone); vigilance
  (*OED* 1–3)
151 **Shapes** devises, imagines
152 **conceits** conceives, imagines; could
  be a misreading of Q *coniects* (= conjectures), the 'harder reading', preferred by some editors
154 **scattering** scattered, i.e. disordered
  observance observant care (*OED* 4);
  observation

---

138 that . . . to –] that all slaues are free to, *Q;* that: All Slaues are free: *F*   139 vile] *Q;* vild
F 141 a] *Q;* that *F* 142 But some] *Q;* Wherein *F* 143 session] *Q;* Sessions *F* 146 think'st]
F; thinkest *Q* mak'st] *F;* makest *Q* 150 oft] *Q;* of *F* 151 that your wisdom] *F;* I intreate you
then *Q* 152 conceits] *F;* coniects *Q* 153 Would] *F;* You'd *Q* 154 his] *F;* my *Q*

It were not for your quiet nor your good   155
Nor for my manhood, honesty and wisdom
To let you know my thoughts.

OTHELLO   Zounds! What dost thou mean?

IAGO

Good name in man and woman, dear my lord,
Is the immediate jewel of their souls:
Who steals my purse steals trash – 'tis something-
    nothing,   160
'Twas mine, 'tis his, and has been slave to thousands –
But he that filches from me my good name
Robs me of that which not enriches him
And makes me poor indeed.

OTHELLO   By heaven, I'll know thy thoughts!

IAGO

You cannot, if my heart were in your hand,   165
Nor shall not whilst 'tis in my custody.

OTHELLO

Ha!

IAGO   O beware, my lord, of jealousy!
It is the green-eyed monster, which doth mock

---

155 **were not for** would not be condu-
cive to
quiet peace of mind
159 See LN.
160 **purse** (= money, 161). Cf. his advice
to Roderigo, 1.3.340ff.
trash could = slang for money (*OED*
3d), as in *JC* 4.3.72ff., 'wring / From
the hands of peasants their vile trash'
***something-nothing** (?)something
trivial. Cf. Dent, S620.1, 'Something
nothing', quoting Porter, *Two Angry
Women* (1599), 'let me heare that
something nothing then' (MSR 698),
T. Powell, *Welch Bayte* (1603, C2b),
'newes of a something nothing'.

165 Cf. Dent, H331.2, 'To have someone's heart (leaping, panting) in one's
hand', and 1.1.63. The hearts of traitors were ripped out and held up
immediately after their execution.
Here *if* = even if.
168 **green-eyed**   Cf.   *MV*   3.2.110,
'green-eyed jealousy'; *OED* green 3,
'of bilious hue, indicative of fear or
jealousy', hence 'green with envy'.
monster Cf. *KL* 1.1.122, 'Come not
between the dragon and his wrath':
an emotion is externalized.
doth mock makes sport of, teases
(*OED* 2b, 3) (perhaps as a cat with a
mouse)

---

156 and] *F; or Q*   157 Zounds . . . mean?] Zouns. *Q;* What dost thou meane? *F*   158 woman, . . .
lord,] woman's deere my Lord; *Q;* woman (deere my Lord) *F*   159 their] *F;* our *Q*   160] *as Q; F
lines* trash: / nothing; /   something-nothing] *this edn;* something, nothing *QF*   164 By heaven]
Q; not in F   thoughts] *F;* thought *Q*   167 OTHELLO Ha!] *Oth.* Ha? *F; not in Q*   my lord, of] *F;
not in Q*   168 mock] *as QF;* make *Hanmer (Theobald)*

The meat it feeds on. That cuckold lives in bliss
Who, certain of his fate, loves not his wronger,   170
But O, what damned minutes tells he o'er
Who dotes yet doubts, suspects yet strongly loves!

OTHELLO

O misery!

IAGO

Poor and content is rich, and rich enough,
But riches fineless is as poor as winter   175
To him that ever fears he shall be poor.
Good God, the souls of all my tribe defend
From jealousy.

OTHELLO

Why – why is this?
Think'st thou I'd make a life of jealousy   180
To follow still the changes of the moon
With fresh suspicions? No: to be once in doubt
Is once to be resolved. Exchange me for a goat
When I shall turn the business of my soul

169 **meat** food; i.e. suspicions. But the image of a self-devourer is also present, as in *Cor* 4.2.50, 'Anger's my meat; I sup upon myself.'
cuckold (refers to Othello indirectly, but still an explosive word)
170 **Who . . . fate** who, though sure that his wife is unfaithful
wronger = wife, or wife's lover. Othello probably spoke of his love for Cassio in Iago's presence (2.3.244).
171 'what accursed minutes does he suffer (count)'; *minutes* = dragging minutes, slow time
172 **dotes** is infatuated; hinting 'is weak-minded from age' (*OED* 2, 3), which points at Othello
strongly intensely
174 **Poor and content** Cf. 1.1.40ff. (Iago is not content to be poor), 2.1.129ff.; Dent, C629, 'Contentment is great riches.'
175 **fineless** boundless
177 **Good God** not the modern (devalued) exclamation but an appeal to God's goodness. Cf. Dent, J38.1, 'From jealousy the good Lord deliver us' (not recorded before Shakespeare).
tribe Cf. 1.1.180n.
180 **make** suffer (*OED* 64); i.e. that I would let jealousy take over my life
181 wax and wane (in suspicion) like the moon (Ridley), i.e. to act like a lunatic; *still* = always
183 **once** once for all. But F could be right: 'Is – to be resolved.'
resolved determined (on a course of action); freed from doubt
goat because a horned animal? Or because goats, highly sexed, spend too much time in lustful activity?

169 The] *F;* That *Q*   172 strongly] *Q;* soundly *F;* fondly *Knight*   177 God] *Q;* Heauen *F*   183 Is once] *Q;* Is *F*

To such exsufflicate and blown surmises,   185
Matching thy inference. 'Tis not to make me jealous
To say my wife is fair, feeds well, loves company,
Is free of speech, sings, plays and dances well:
Where virtue is, these are more virtuous.
Nor from mine own weak merits will I draw   190
The smallest fear or doubt of her revolt,
For she had eyes and chose me. No, Iago,
I'll see before I doubt, when I doubt, prove,
And on the proof there is no more but this:
Away at once with love or jealousy!   195

IAGO

I am glad of this, for now I shall have reason
To show the love and duty that I bear you
With franker spirit: therefore, as I am bound,
Receive it from me. I speak not yet of proof:

185 ***exsufflicate** = (?)inflated, i.e. improbable. *OED* records no other
example, but cites exsufflation (sixteenth century) from Lat. *exsufflare* =
blow up.
blown Editors suggest (1) fly-blown,
(2) inflated, (3) rumoured.
surmises allegations (esp. if un-
founded or unproved); suspicions;
conjectures (*OED* 2–4).
186 **inference** 'It looks as though the
unhappy confusion of "infer" and
"imply" was as old as the Elizabethans' (Ridley, citing *2H4* 5.5.14,
R3 3.7.12, *Tim* 3.5.72); or, conclusion, i.e. the conclusion you have
drawn from the evidence (*OED* 2,
first in 1612).
jealous F always has *iealious*, an alternative spelling.
187 **feeds well** could be an 'irrelevant
interpolation', making this a long
line. So Walker, citing Cinthio on
women who 'with beauty of body and
under a semblance of virtue, for instance in *singing, playing, dancing*

lightly and *speaking* sweetly, hide an
ugly and abominable soul' (Bullough,
7.240). But Othello's point is that a
woman given over to sociable and
physical pleasures need not have an
'ugly soul', so *feeds well* fits in. Cf.
343n.
188 **free** unreserved
190 **weak** deficient
    draw deduce
191 **revolt** 'any "falling off" from al-
legiance or obedience'; can = revul-
sion, as in *TN* 2.4.99, 'their love
may be called appetite . . . That suffer surfeit, cloyment, and revolt'
(Ridley)
193 **prove** prove it one way or the other
194 **on the proof** when I have proof
195 i.e. either love or jealousy will be
ruled out. *Away*: a gesture is needed.
Cf. 266.
197 **love and duty** Cf. 1.1.58, 'not I for
love and duty'!
198 **franker** more open, unreserved
199 **proof** proof of guilt. Othello spoke
of proof of guilt *or innocence*.

185 exsufflicate] *Malone;* exufflicate *QF*   blown] *Q;* blow'd *F*   188 well] *Q; not in F*   196 this]
F; it *Q*

Look to your wife, observe her well with Cassio.   200
Wear your eyes thus, not jealous nor secure;
I would not have your free and noble nature
Out of self-bounty be abused: look to't.
I know our country disposition well –
In Venice they do let God see the pranks   205
They dare not show their husbands; their best
    conscience
Is not to leave't undone, but keep't unknown.

OTHELLO

Dost thou say so?

IAGO

She did deceive her father, marrying you,
And when she seemed to shake, and fear your looks,   210
She loved them most.

OTHELLO   And so she did.

IAGO   Why, go to then:

She that so young could give out such a seeming
To seel her father's eyes up, close as oak –

200 **Look to** echoing 1.3.293, 'Look to
her, Moor'
  Cassio a dangerous moment: he
names Cassio (prepared for in 94ff.)
201 **Wear** present (the look of) (*OED* 7)
  thus A gesture is needed.
  secure free from apprehension
202 **free** generous
203 **self-bounty** Shakespeare's coinage.
Many new 'self-'compounds appeared in the sixteenth and seventeenth centuries (see 2.3.198; *OED*).
Here *self* = your own, as in *TC*
2.3.171–2, 'pride / That quarrels at
self-breath'. For *bounty* (= kindness,
goodness), cf. 7n.
  abused abuse = take advantage of;
cheat, deceive; injure, wrong
204 **our country** our country's. Implies
that Iago, despite his Spanish name,
is a Venetian. Cf. 5.1.89. He means 'I
know, *but you cannot know* . . .'.
205 **In Venice** See pp. 9–11. He means

'they prefer to defy God rather than
their husbands', a variant of a commonplace: cf. *R3* 1.4.197–8, 'Will you
then / Spurn at his [God's] edict,
and fulfill a man's?'; Acts 5.4.
  pranks Cf. 2.1.142n.
206–7 i.e. the best their conscience as-
pires to is not to leave it (wickedness)
undone, but to keep it unknown. Cf.
The Book of Common Prayer, 'We
have left undone those things which
we ought to have done' (Noble, 219).
209 again echoing 1.3.293–4
211 **go to** there you are
212 **give out** give it out to be believed
(that such a 'seeming' was the truth).
Cf. 129–31.
213 **seel** Cf. 1.3.270n.
  close as oak Cf. Dent, O1, 'As close
as oak' (not recorded before Shakespeare). 'Usually explained by reference to the close grain of oak'
(Ridley).

201 eyes] *F;* eie *Q*   205 God] *Q;* Heauen *F*   206] *as Q; F lines* Husbands. / Conscience, /
207 leave't] *F;* leaue *Q*   keep't] *F (*kept*);* keepe *Q*

221

He thought 'twas witchcraft. But I am much to
   blame,
I humbly do beseech you of your pardon   215
For too much loving you.

OTHELLO
I am bound to thee for ever.

IAGO
I see this hath a little dashed your spirits.

OTHELLO
Not a jot, not a jot.

IAGO   I'faith, I fear it has.
I hope you will consider what is spoke   220
Comes from my love. But I do see you're moved;
I am to pray you not to strain my speech
To grosser issues nor to larger reach
Than to suspicion.

OTHELLO
I will not.

IAGO   Should you do so, my lord,   225
My speech should fall into such vile success
As my thoughts aimed not at: Cassio's my worthy
   friend.

---

214 **to** QF *too* may be a reading taken by F from Q (see *Texts*, 94ff.), but 'too blame' is found elsewhere.

215 **of** for

217 **bound** indebted; tied (cf. 482n.)

218 Iago's delight in Othello's alleged misfortune expresses itself in faked solicitude.

219 **Not a jot** a common phrase (e.g. *Ham* 5.1.113, 207)

221 F *your* could = my love of you

222 **am** have (*OED* be 16a)

223 'There is a suggestive undertone of our sense of "gross" and of the Elizabethan sense of "large" = "licen-

tious", as in "some large jests he will make" (*Ado* 2.3.198)' (Ridley); *issues* = conclusions; *reach* = scope, extent of application (*OED* 9); *gross* could = flagrant.

225 **Should ... lord** completes a pentameter with 224: 'I will not' is probably an interruption (cf. 1.1.101n.)

226 **fall ... success** come to such a vile result; *success* = outcome (good or bad)

227 **aimed** F *aym'd* (without *at*) is probably correct (*OED* 3: to guess, conjecture).

214] *as Q ; F lines* Witchcraft. / blame: /   to] too *QF*   219 I'faith] *Q ;* Trust me *F*   221] *as Q ; F lines* Loue. / moou'd: /   my] *Q ;* your *F*   you're] *F (y*'arc*) ;* you are *Q*   226 vile] *Q ;* vilde *F*   227] As my thoughts aime not at: *Cassio's* my trusty friend: *Q ;* Which my Thoughts aym'd not. / *Cassio's* worthy Friend: / *F*

My lord, I see you're moved.

OTHELLO   No, not much moved.

I do not think but Desdemona's honest.

IAGO

Long live she so; and long live you to think so.   230

OTHELLO

And yet how nature, erring from itself –

IAGO

Ay, there's the point: as, to be bold with you,
Not to affect many proposed matches
Of her own clime, complexion and degree,
Whereto we see, in all things, nature tends –   235
Foh! one may smell in such a will most rank,
Foul disproportion, thoughts unnatural.
But pardon me, I do not in position
Distinctly speak of her, though I may fear
Her will, recoiling to her better judgement,   240
May fall to match you with her country forms,
And happily repent.

OTHELLO   Farewell, farewell.

---

229 **but** but that: 'I do not think Desdemona is anything other than *honest*' (= chaste, honourable)
230 **and ... so** 'and long may you live thinking so'. *Think* is meant to ring alarm bells, after 107ff., 132ff.
233–5 He follows up Othello's recollection of 1.3.63 by echoing Brabantio again (1.2.67–71).
233 **affect** like
proposed proposèd
234 **of her own** *clime* (= region, country), *temperament* (the combination of qualities that determines the nature of a person; or, *skin colour*), and *rank*
235 Cf. Tilley, L286, 'Like will to like.'
236 **smell** could = suspect. Cf. *KL* 1.1.16, 'Do you smell a fault?'

will wilfulness; carnal desire. Cf. 240, and *Texts*, 16–18 (Shakespeare's wish to protect Desdemona from the charge of wilfulness).
rank rebellious; excessive; lustful; (after smell) rancid, foul-smelling
237 **disproportion** lack of a sense of proportion
238–9 **in position / Distinctly** in (making this) proposition speak specifically of her
240 **recoiling to** i.e. giving way to
241 may come to compare you with the *forms* of her own country; *form* = body (in its outward appearance); example; behaviour. *Fall to* = come to, or sink (so low as) to.
242 **happily** perchance (with a hint of 'fortunately'?)

---

228 you're] *F* (y'are*); you are *Q*   230] *as Q ; F lines* so; / . . . so. /   232] *as Q ; F lines* point: / you) /   236 Foh! one] *F;* Fie we *Q*   237 disproportion] *Q;* disproportions *F*   242–4] *Q lines* if more / set on / *Iago.* /; *F lines* farewell: / know more: / obscrue. / *Iago.* /

If more thou dost perceive, let me know more:
Set on thy wife to observe. Leave me, Iago.

IAGO

My lord, I take my leave.

OTHELLO   Why did I marry?   245
This honest creature doubtless
Sees and knows more – much more – than he unfolds.

IAGO

My lord, I would I might entreat your honour
To scan this thing no farther. Leave it to time;
Although 'tis fit that Cassio have his place,   250
For sure he fills it up with great ability,
Yet if you please to hold him off a while
You shall by that perceive him, and his means:
Note if your lady strain his entertainment
With any strong or vehement importunity,   255
Much will be seen in that. In the meantime
Let me be thought too busy in my fears
– As worthy cause I have to fear I am –
And hold her free, I do beseech your honour.

OTHELLO

Fear not my government.   260

IAGO

I once more take my leave.   *Exit.*

---

245 **Why ... marry?** Cf. Thorello, the
jealous husband, in *Every Man in His
Humour* (1601), 3.3.15, 'what meant I
to marrie?'

246 **creature** could = fellow, person
(without contemptuousness) but here
sounds unflattering. Othello speaks to
himself.

247 **unfolds** reveals

249 Cf. Dent, T324, 'Time brings the
truth to light.'

251 Cf. *JC* 3.2.99, 'And sure he is an
honourable man' (Antony, like Iago,
means the opposite of what he says).

253 **means** intermediaries; methods
(*OED* 9, 10)

254 **strain his entertainment** press
(insist on) his reinstatement

257 **busy** officious, meddlesome

258 **worthy** good

259 **hold her free** consider her innocent; or, let her have her freedom
(to betray herself)

260 **government** self-government, man-
agement: 'don't be uneasy about the
way I'll handle it (or, about my self-
control)'

245–6 Why ... doubtless] *as F; one line Q*   248 SP] *Qc, F; not in Qu*   249 farther] *F; further
Q*   250 Although 'tis] *F; Tho it be Q*   252 hold] *Q; not in F; put F2*   254 his] *F; her
Q*   261 SD] *Qc, F; not in Qu*

OTHELLO
   This fellow's of exceeding honesty
   And knows all qualities, with a learned spirit,
   Of human dealings. If I do prove her haggard,
   Though that her jesses were my dear heart-strings,   265
   I'd whistle her off and let her down the wind
   To prey at fortune. Haply for I am black
   And have not those soft parts of conversation
   That chamberers have, or for I am declined
   Into the vale of years – yet that's not much –   270
   She's gone, I am abused, and my relief
   Must be to loathe her. O curse of marriage
   That we can call these delicate creatures ours
   And not their appetites! I had rather be a toad
   And live upon the vapour of a dungeon   275

263 **qualities** characters, natures
264 **dealings** intercourse
   haggard wild, untamed (lit. a wild female hawk caught in her adult plumage)
265 **Though that** even if
   jesses straps, fastened round the legs of a hawk, attached to the falconer's wrist
   heart-strings tendons or nerves supposed to brace and sustain the heart (in early anatomy)
266 Hawks were sent off with a whistle, against the wind in pursuit of prey, with the wind when turned loose; i.e. Desdemona is too wild to tame. Cf. Dent, W432, 'To go down the wind' = to go to ruin. N.B. He does not intend to kill Desdemona at this stage.
267 **To ... fortune** to fend for herself; to prey as fortune wills
   Haply for perhaps because
268–9 **soft ... have** pleasing qualities in my social behaviour that drawing-room gallants have (*chamberers* here first in this sense). Cf. Romans 13.13,

'Let us walk honestly ... not in rioting and drunkenness, neither in chambering and wantonness.'
270 **vale of years** Alluding to 'the valley of the shadow of death' (Psalms 23.4)?
271 **gone** ruined, undone (*OED* gone 1)
   abused wronged
   relief assistance in time of need; alleviation of a pain; 'deliverance (esp. in *Law*) from some ... burden, or grievance' (*OED* 6, from 1616)
272 **O ... marriage** *either* 'it is the curse of marriage that', *or* 'O, the curse of marriage! – that'
273 **ours** Upper-class English wives were, in effect, the property of their husbands and addressed them as 'my lord' (= my master): 1.3.184n.
274–7 Cf. 4.2.58ff. Kean spoke these lines 'with a peculiar, snarling, sardonic laugh, but yet extremely quiet in manner' (Rosenberg, 64).
274 **toad** a type of anything hateful or loathsome; pre-Shakespeare (*OED* 1b)

263 qualities] *Q*; Quantities *F*   learned] *Q*; learn'd *F*   264 dealings] *F*; dealing *Q*   267 Haply]
F; Happily *Q*   270 vale] *F*; valt *Q*   275 of] *F*; in *Q*

Than keep a corner in the thing I love
For others' uses. Yet 'tis the plague of great ones,
Prerogatived are they less than the base;
'Tis destiny unshunnable, like death –
Even then this forked plague is fated to us   280
When we do quicken.

Enter DESDEMONA *and* EMILIA.

                      Look where she comes:
If she be false, O then heaven mocks itself,
I'll not believe't.

DESDEMONA   How now, my dear Othello?
Your dinner, and the generous islanders
By you invited, do attend your presence.   285

OTHELLO
I am to blame.

DESDEMONA   Why do you speak so faintly?
Are you not well?

---

276 **corner** *keep a corner* = reserve a small place (*OED* 6c), here with secondary sexual sense. Cf. *Cambises* (1st edn, n.d., *c.* 1570), B1a–b: 'Wheresoeuer I goe, in eche corner I will grope. *Ambidexter*. What and ye run in the corner of some prittie maide? *Snuf.* To grope there good fellow I will not be afraid.'
    thing Cf. 306n.
277 **uses** Cf. 5.2.69n.
277–81 Ridley thought this nonsense: 'There is no question of the great being either less or more liable to be cuckolded than the base; every one is equal.' But Shakespeare may mean that great ones are in greater danger because their duties keep them from home.

277 **plague** affliction
278 **Prerogatived** privileged
    base lower orders
279 **unshunnable** inescapable. A coinage (cf. *MM* 3.2.60, 'an unshunned consequence'; Dent, C889, 'Cuckolds come by destiny').
280 **forked** forkèd: horned
281 **do quicken** are conceived
282 **mocks** makes a mockery of; counterfeits, makes a false pretence of (*OED* 4b)
284 **generous** noble. We hear no more of the dinner, but perhaps should now hear laughter from a nearby room, voices, music?
285 **attend** await; give attendance to
286 **to blame** blameworthy, i.e. I'm wrong (*OED* blame 6)

---

276 the] *F*; a *Q*   277 of great ones] *Q*; to Great-ones *F*   281 SD] *after* beleeue it *283 Q*; *after 281 F*   Look . . . she] *F*; *Desdemona Q*   282 O . . . mocks] *Q*; Heauen mock'd *F*   283 't] *F*; it *Q*   284 islanders] *F*; Ilander *Q*   286 do . . . faintly] *F*; is your speech so faint *Q*   286–7 Why . . . well?] *as F; one line Q*

OTHELLO

I have a pain upon my forehead, here.

DESDEMONA

Faith, that's with watching, 'twill away again.
Let me but bind it hard, within this hour   290
It will be well.

OTHELLO   Your napkin is too little.

[*She drops her handkerchief.*]

Let it alone. Come, I'll go in with you.

DESDEMONA

I am very sorry that you are not well.

Exeunt Othello and Desdemona.

EMILIA

I am glad I have found this napkin,
This was her first remembrance from the Moor.   295
My wayward husband hath a hundred times
Wooed me to steal it, but she so loves the token
– For he conjured her she should ever keep it –
That she reserves it evermore about her
To kiss and talk to. I'll have the work ta'en out   300
And give't Iago: what he will do with it
Heaven knows, not I,

288 Cf. Thorello (as in 245n.), 1.4.191, 'Troth my head akes extreamely on a suddaine': he fears horns. Othello *may* have a headache, but 287 gives him an excuse for claiming one.
289 **watching** i.e. not sleeping enough
291 **napkin** handkerchief
  *SD See LN.
292 **in** i.e. to join the others. Or are they out of doors (cf. 3.3n)?
293 SD The F SD may mean that Othello sweeps out without listening to Desdemona's last line, or it may be misplaced.
295 **remembrance** keepsake
296 **wayward** self-willed; wrong-headed;

perverse. Might be confused with *weird*, which could be spelt *weyward* (as in *Mac* 1.3.33).
297 **token** love token
298 **conjured** conjùred: earnestly entreated
299 **reserves** preserves
300 **To . . . to** Desdemona is scarcely older than a child (see pp. 41–2).
  work pattern; embroidery
  ta'en out copied (*OED* 85e). From Cinthio: see pp. 378, 381; cf. 3.4.180, 4.1.153.
302 Cf. Dent, G189.1, 'God he knows, not I' (cf. *R3* 3.1.26). She implies 'I don't want to know.' See p. 47.

289 Faith] *Q;* Why *F*   290 it hard] *F;* your head *Q*   291 well] *F;* well againe *Q*   SD] *Rowe; not in QF*   293 SD] *Ex.* Oth. *and* Desd. *(opp. 294) Q; Exit. (opp. 292) F*   300 have] *F;* ha *Q*   301 he will] *F;* hee'll *Q*

I nothing, but to please his fantasy.

Enter IAGO.

IAGO

How now! What do you here alone?

EMILIA

Do not you chide, I have a thing for you –   305

IAGO

You have a thing for me? it is a common thing –

EMILIA   Ha?

IAGO

To have a foolish wife.

EMILIA

O, is that all? What will you give me now

For that same handkerchief?

IAGO   What handkerchief?   310

EMILIA

What handkerchief?

Why, that the Moor first gave to Desdemona,

That which so often you did bid me steal.

IAGO

Hast stolen it from her?

EMILIA

No, faith, she let it drop by negligence   315

And, to th'advantage, I being here, took't up.

---

303 **I nothing** 'I am nothing (in his eyes;
he thinks I'm here) only to please his
whims'; or, 'I know nothing, except
to please . . .'. The clearest sign yet
that they don't get on (see p. 38).
   fantasy could = habit of deluding
oneself (*OED* 3)

305 **a thing** could = something (*Ham*
5.2.90)

306 **thing** Iago pretends to misunderstand *thing* as pudendum: cf. *TGV*

3.1.351, *1H4* 3.3.115ff.
   common free to be used by everyone; undistinguished, ordinary (*OED*
6, 11)

310 **handkerchief** This is F's form
throughout; Q always reads *handkercher*, and this may be what Shakespeare wrote (*Texts*, 70).

312 **that** that which

316 **to th'advantage** i.e. seizing the
opportunity

---

303 but to please] *F;* know, but for *Q*   303.1] *as F; opp. 302 Q*   306] *as Q ; F lines* me? / thing – /
You have] *F; not in Q*   308 wife] *F;* thing *Q*   310 handkerchief] *F (throughout);* handkercher
Q (throughout)   314 stolen] *F (*stolne*);* stole *Q*   315 No, faith,] *as Q ;* No: but *F*   316 th'] *F;*
the *Q*

Look, here it is.

IAGO   A good wench, give it me.

EMILIA

What will you do with't, that you have been so
    earnest
To have me filch it?

IAGO   [*Snatching it*]   Why, what's that to you?

EMILIA

If it be not for some purpose of import   320
Give't me again. Poor lady, she'll run mad
When she shall lack it.

IAGO   Be not acknown on't,
I have use for it. Go, leave me.   *Exit Emilia.*
I will in Cassio's lodging lose this napkin
And let him find it. Trifles light as air   325
Are to the jealous confirmations strong
As proofs of holy writ. This may do something.
The Moor already changes with my poison:
Dangerous conceits are in their natures poisons
Which at the first are scarce found to distaste   330
But with a little art upon the blood

317 **A good wench** good girl. *Wench*
(girl, young woman) could be 'an en-
dearing form of address' (*OED* 1c).
318 **you have** elide: *you've*
319 **filch** pilfer (something of small
value)
*SD Some Iagos snatch the handker-
chief, others get it by coaxing
(Sprague, 197).
Why . . . you Dent, W280.4, 'What
is that to you?'
320 **import** weighty significance
321 **run mad** Cf. *1H4* 3.1.209, 'Nay, if
you melt, then will she run mad.' We
would say 'go frantic'.
322 **lack** miss; need
acknown unique in Shakespeare;
usually acknown *of* (*OED* 4d). Seems
to mean 'acknowledged'; in effect,

don't acknowledge that you have a
part in it, keep out of it.
323 **leave me** Cf. 85, Othello's request
to *his* wife to leave: the two marriages
are brought into focus.
325 **Trifles . . . air** Cf. Dent, A90, 'As
light as air'. Perhaps he toys with the
handkerchief (blows it into the air? Cf.
448).
327 **As . . . writ** alluding to the Bible as
Holy Writ, i.e. holy writing
329 **conceits** thoughts
330 **distaste** cause disgust, offend the
taste (*OED*, first here)
331 **art** skill. Iago prides himself on his
'art' elsewhere: cf. 'double knavery'
(1.3.393 and 400), 'we work by wit'
(2.3.367–8).
upon the blood to arouse passion

317 it is] *Q;* 'tis *F*   318–9] *verse Q (bin/); prose F*   318 't] *F;* it *Q*   319 SD] *Rowe; not in QF*
what's] *Q;* what is *F*   321 Give't me] *F;* Giue mee't *Q*   322–3 Be . . . me] *as F;* one line *Q*
322 acknown] *F;* you knowne *Q*   328] *F; not in Q*   329 natures] *QF;* nature *Pope*   331 art] *Q;* acte *F*

Burn like the mines of sulphur.

Enter OTHELLO.

                          I did say so:
Look where he comes. Not poppy nor mandragora
Nor all the drowsy syrups of the world
Shall ever medicine thee to that sweet sleep   335
Which thou owedst yesterday.

OTHELLO   Ha! Ha! false to me?

IAGO

    Why, how now, general? No more of that.

OTHELLO

    Avaunt, be gone, thou hast set me on the rack!
    I swear 'tis better to be much abused
    Than but to know't a little.

IAGO   How now, my lord?   340

OTHELLO

    What sense had I of her stolen hours of lust?
    I saw't not, thought it not, it harmed not me,
    I slept the next night well, fed well, was free and
       merry;

---

332 Cf. Pliny, quoted Hart: 'Sulphur . . . is engendered within the Islands of Aeolia, which lie between Italy and Sicily . . . [which] do always burn by reason thereof' (i.e. are difficult to put out).

333 **poppy** opium
    mandragora (the juice of the) mandrake plant, a soporific. Cf. *AC* 1.5.4–5, 'Give me to drink mandragora . . . That I might sleep out this great gap of time', and Marlowe, *Jew of Malta*, 5.1.80–1.

334 **drowsy** inducing sleepiness

335 **medicine** bring by medicine (nonce use)

336 **owedst** didst own or possess
    Ha! Ha! *Ha*, like *O*, was a signal to the actor to make the appropriate noise: cf. *OED* 1, 4.2.56n.

337 **how now** what's this

338 **Avaunt** away!
    rack Cf. *KL* 4.7.45–6, 'I am bound / Upon a wheel of fire'.

339 **abused** wronged, deceived

340 **Than . . . little** than only to know a little of what has happened

341 Othello's imagination has persuaded him of Desdemona's guilt (in Iago's absence!).
    sense feeling, consciousness
    stolen secret

342 Cf. Dent, K179.1, 'What one does not know does not hurt.'

343 **fed well** Cf. *feeds well*, 187.
    free unreserved in behaviour; (?)carefree

---

332 mines] *F*; mindes *Q*   SD] *opp. 331 Q*; *after 332 F*   336 owedst] *Q*; owd'st *F*   to me?] *F*; to me, to me? *Q*   340 know't] *F*; know *Q*   341 'of] *Q*; in *F*   343 fed well] *F*; *not in Q*

I found not Cassio's kisses on her lips;
He that is robbed, not wanting what is stolen,   345
Let him not know't, and he's not robbed at all.

IAGO

I am sorry to hear this.

OTHELLO

I had been happy if the general camp,
Pioneers and all, had tasted her sweet body,
So I had nothing known. O now for ever   350
Farewell the tranquil mind, farewell content!
Farewell the plumed troops and the big wars
That makes ambition virtue! O farewell,
Farewell the neighing steed and the shrill trump,
The spirit-stirring drum, th'ear-piercing fife,   355
The royal banner, and all quality,
Pride, pomp and circumstance of glorious war!

345–6 Cf. Ovid, *Amores*, 3.14, 'That you should not err, since you are fair, is not my plea, but that I be not compelled, poor wretch, to know it . . . let me think you honest though you are not'; *Son* 138; Dent, L461, 'He that is not sensible of his loss has lost nothing.'
345 **wanting** missing
348 **camp** i.e. army
349 **Pioneers** the lowest kind of soldier; carried spades, pickaxes, etc., to dig trenches – perhaps relevant, in view of Othello's inflamed imagination
and all Cf. *KL* 3.6.62, 'The little dogs and all'.
tasted handled, explored by touch; had carnal knowledge of (*OED* 1, 3b, citing *Cym* 2.4.57–8, 'make't apparent / That you have tasted her in bed', as first example). See p. 22.
350 **So** so long as
350–60 The 'farewell' speech was a commonplace (e.g. Ovid, *Heroides*, 9.165ff.). Shakespeare's version was much echoed by other dramatists, esp. Beaumont and Fletcher (in *Bonduca*; *The Loyal Subject*; *The Prophetess*, 'farewell Pride and Pomp / And circumstance of glorious Majestie, /

Farewell for ever' (4.6.72–4, quoted Malone).
351 **tranquil** serene, peaceful (*OED*, from Lat. *tranquillus*, first here)
352 **plumed** plumèd: decked with feathers
big mighty; violent
353 **makes** Cf. 1.1.148–9n.
354–5 perhaps an echo of Lyly's *Campaspe*, 2.2.35; Alexander the Great, in love, neglects 'the warlike sound of *drumme* and *trumpe* . . . the *neighing* of barbed *steeds*'. *Trump* = trumpet.
356 **royal** magnificent (*OED* 8–10): Othello did not proclaim his own royal descent (1.2.19ff.).
quality essential nature
357 **Pride, pomp** usually deplored, not admired (as here). Cf. L. Wright, *Summons for Sleepers* (1589), A4a: 'pomp, pride, and superfluity'; Plutarch, *Lives* (1579), '[he] brought all the pride and pomp of those Courts into GRÆCE' ('Agis and Cleomenes', p. 850); *Homilies*, 280, 282.
circumstance formality, ceremony. See Parker (as in 126n.).
glorious possessing glory; eager for glory; ostentatious, boastful (*OED* 1–5)

347 this.] *Q* ; this? *F*   352 troops] *F*; troope *Q*   355 th'] *F*; the *Q*

And, O you mortal engines whose rude throats
Th'immortal Jove's dread clamours counterfeit,
Farewell: Othello's occupation's gone.   360

IAGO

Is't possible? my lord?

OTHELLO

Villain, be sure thou prove my love a whore,
Be sure of it, give me the ocular proof,

                                   [Catching hold of him]

Or by the worth of man's eternal soul
Thou hadst been better have been born a dog   365
Than answer my waked wrath!

IAGO   Is't come to this?

OTHELLO

Make me to see't, or at the least so prove it
That the probation bear no hinge nor loop
To hang a doubt on, or woe upon thy life!

IAGO

My noble lord –   370

---

358 **mortal** deadly
   engines machines, i.e. cannons
   rude rough, rugged
359 **clamours** (Lat. *clamor*, a shout), i.e.
   thunder
360 **occupation** employment, hence
   life, because life has lost all meaning
   for him. Hulme (124) thinks Othello
   refers to his military role but 'must
   refer also to his loss of Desdemona'
   (since *occupy* could = cohabit with).
   Iago spoke of the *trade* of war (1.2.1).
361 'Is it possible that you should feel
   like this?'
362ff. close to Cinthio: cf. p. 377. Brabantio flared up more quickly (1.1.116).
   Barton Booth took Iago by the throat
   during this speech; other actors did
   so later (371) – an action authenti-
   cated by 5.2.353.

362 **my love** Does he still love her?
363 **ocular proof** Cf. *Cynthia's Revels*
   (1600), 2.3.11ff., 'You shall now, as
   well be the ocular, as the eare-
   witnesse'; *Poetaster* (1601), 4.5.75,
   'wilt thou suffer this ocular
   temptation?'
364 See LN.
366 **answer** have to answer to, or defend
   yourself against
368–9 **That . . . on** 'that the proof per-
   mits of no support to attach a doubt
   to'. *Hinge* = pivot (*OED* 4, first
   here); *loop* = looped string or cord.
   Cf. *OED* hang 9b, 'to be supported
   or suspended at the side, as on a
   hinge or pivot, so as to be free to turn
   or swing horizontally': i.e. the proof
   must be so secure that doubts will not
   move it.

---

358 you] *F*; ye *Q*   rude] *F*; wide *Q*   359 Th'] *F*; The *Q*   dread clamours] *F*; great clamor
Q   361 possible? my] *Capell subst.*; possible my *QF*   362 thou] *Qc, F*; you *Qu*   363 SD] *Rowe*;
not in QF   364 man's] *Q*; mine *F*

OTHELLO

If thou dost slander her and torture me
Never pray more, abandon all remorse;
On horror's head horrors accumulate,
Do deeds to make heaven weep, all earth amazed,
For nothing canst thou to damnation add   375
Greater than that!

IAGO   O grace! O heaven forgive me!
Are you a man? have you a soul, or sense?
God buy you, take mine office. O wretched fool
That lov'st to make thine honesty a vice!
O monstrous world! Take note, take note, O world,   380
To be direct and honest is not safe.
I thank you for this profit, and from hence
I'll love no friend, sith love breeds such offence.

OTHELLO

Nay, stay, thou shouldst be honest.

IAGO

I should be wise, for honesty's a fool   385

371ff. Cf. *KJ* 4.3.117–34, 'Beyond the infinite and boundless reach / Of mercy, if thou didst this deed of death, / Art thou damn'd'.

372 **remorse** repentance (because you cannot win forgiveness for what you have done); compassion

373 **head** perhaps = summit (*OED* 12)
accumulate heap up. Cf. a similar image in *Ham* 5.1.280ff., 'let them throw / Millions of acres on us'.

374 **heaven weep** Cf. *MM* 2.2.122: man 'makes the angels weep'.
amazed stronger than today: 'paralyzed with horror' (Kittredge)

376 **forgive** i.e. for daring to be 'honest': more subtle than Q *defend*

377 **sense** consciousness; intelligence

378 **God buy you** here = (God be with you, i.e.) God help you, I wash my hands of you
office his position of trust, *either* as

ensign, *or* as Othello's 'friend' and informer

378–9 **O . . . vice** He addresses himself; vice = defect, fault.

380 could be punctuated 'O monstrous! world, take note . . .' Cf. *KL* 4.1.10, 'World, world, O world!'; *TC* 5.10.36.

381 **direct** straightforward
honest honourable

382 **profit** profitable lesson (Sanders). Cf. Montaigne, bk 3, ch. 1, 'Of profit and honesty'.
from hence henceforth

383 **sith** since (archaic)
breeds begets
offence hurt; pain; disgrace

384 **stay** *Either* Iago is about to slip away, *or* Othello asks him not to proceed in that way of thinking.
shouldst be appear to be, or, ought to be

385 **should be** ought to be

376 forgive] *F*; defend *Q*   378 buy you] *F*; buy, you *Q*   mine] *Qc, F*; thine *Qu*   379 lov'st] *F*; liuest *Q*   thine] *Qc, F*; mine *Qu*   383 sith] *F*; since *Q*

And loses that it works for.

OTHELLO   By the world,
I think my wife be honest, and think she is not,
I think that thou art just, and think thou art not.
I'll have some proof. Her name, that was as fresh
As Dian's visage, is now begrimed and black   390
As mine own face. If there be cords or knives,
Poison, or fire, or suffocating streams,
I'll not endure it. Would I were satisfied!

IAGO

I see, sir, you are eaten up with passion.
I do repent me that I put it to you.   395
You would be satisfied?

OTHELLO   Would? nay, and I will!

IAGO

And may – but how? how satisfied, my lord?
Would you, the supervisor, grossly gape on?
Behold her topped?

OTHELLO   Death and damnation! O!

386 **By the world** common asseveration, as in *LLL* 4.3.17, 5.1.102, 105;
R3 4.4.375; but more meaningful
here, after 380 (cf. also 90–2,
4.3.63–9)
387–8 elide: 'she's', 'thou'rt not' (*Texts*,
119)
388 **just** honourable (in what you say)
389 **I'll have** I must have
*Her name** Ridley defends F:
'Othello is maddened by the be-
foulment of his own honour.' But the
comparison with Diana (the moon
goddess, patron of chastity) points
to a woman and *her* chastity, not to
a man.
390 **begrimed** *grime* = soot, smut, coal
dust. The actor's face was *begrimed*:
he had to be careful to keep his
makeup off Desdemona's clothes
(Lois Potter in *The Arts of Performance*,

ed. Murray Biggs [1991], 118). A
curious way to speak of his own face?
391–3 Is he thinking of suicide (Sanders)? In *Faerie Queene*, 1.9.50, Despair offers 'swords, ropes, poison,
fire, / And all that might him to perdition [i.e. suicide] draw'. But Othello may have in mind murder, not
suicide: cf. 445, 4.1.175.
393 **satisfied** set free from doubt, satisfied one way or the other. Iago plays
with the word to suggest a voyeur's
satisfaction. Cf. *WT* 1.2.232ff.
394 **eaten up** devastated. Cf. *gnaw my
inwards* (2.1.295).
395 **put** suggested
398 **supervisor** onlooker, spectator
(*OED* 2, first here; previously 'one
who directs the work of others')
grossly indelicately, brutally
399 **topped** Cf. 1.1.88n., 5.2.134.

386–93 By . . . satisfied!] *F; not in Q*   389 Her] *Q2*; My *F*   394 sir] *Q; not in F*   396 Would? . . .
and] *as F*; Would, nay *Q*   398 supervisor] *Q*; super-vision *F*   399 topped] topt *Q*; top'd *F*;
tupp'd *Theobald*

IAGO

It were a tedious difficulty, I think,   400
To bring them to that prospect. Damn them then
If ever mortal eyes do see them bolster
More than their own. What then? how then?
What shall I say? where's satisfaction?
It is impossible you should see this   405
Were they as prime as goats, as hot as monkeys,
As salt as wolves in pride, and fools as gross
As ignorance made drunk. But yet, I say,
If imputation and strong circumstances
Which lead directly to the door of truth   410
Will give you satisfaction, you may have't.

OTHELLO

Give me a living reason she's disloyal.

IAGO

I do not like the office.
But sith I am entered in this cause so far,
Pricked to't by foolish honesty and love,   415

---

400 **tedious** tiresome; disagreeable
401 **prospect** view; spectacle
　　Damn them then He appears to
　　pick up 399 ('Yes, their death and
　　damnation is right'), but changes
　　construction ('May they be damned
　　if ever . . .').
402 **bolster** must mean 'have sexual in-
　　tercourse'. *OED* guesses 'to lie on the
　　same bolster'! Perhaps a misreading
　　of *balter* = tumble about, dance
　　clumsily; to form tangled knots, stick
　　together (by coagulation) (*OED* 1, 5).
403 **More** other
404 **satisfaction** (?)satisfying proof
　　(*OED* 6b, first in 1601). He edges to-
　　wards the thought that to behold her
　　'topped' can give pleasure.
406–7 See LN.
407 **gross** stupid

409 **imputation** attribution (Lat. *impu-
　　tare*, to bring into the reckoning)
　　circumstances circumstantial evi-
　　dence
410 **door** 'I think the slightest of pauses
　　after *door*; Othello is led in imagina-
　　tion to stand outside the closed bed-
　　room door' (Ridley).
411 **may** I prefer Q *may*, repeating 397
　　may.
412 **living** valid. Perhaps on the analogy
　　of 'the living God' (Hebrews 10.31).
413 **office** task, duty. Iago manoeuvres
　　to a position of pretended reluctance
　　to speak: cf. 2.3.216, 3.3.196, 4.1.277,
　　etc.
414 **cause** matter
415 **Pricked** urged or spurred on, like a
　　horse or beast: pretending that he is
　　helpless

---

401 them] *F*; em *Q (twice)*　402 do] *F*; did *Q*　411 may have't] may ha't *Q*; might haue't *F*　412 she's] *F*; that shee's *Q*　414 in] *F*; into *Q*

235

I will go on. I lay with Cassio lately
And being troubled with a raging tooth
I could not sleep. There are a kind of men
So loose of soul that in their sleeps will mutter
Their affairs – one of this kind is Cassio.   420
In sleep I heard him say 'Sweet Desdemona,
Let us be wary, let us hide our loves,'
And then, sir, would he gripe and wring my hand,
Cry 'O sweet creature!' and then kiss me hard
As if he plucked up kisses by the roots   425
That grew upon my lips, lay his leg o'er my thigh,
And sigh, and kiss, and then cry 'Cursed fate
That gave thee to the Moor!'

OTHELLO   O monstrous! monstrous!

IAGO

Nay, this was but his dream.

OTHELLO

But this denoted a foregone conclusion.   430

---

416 **I lay** i.e. shared a bed with (bed-sharing was not uncommon: cf. the great bed of Ware, *TN* 3.2.48). Erotic dreams are already found in classical literature (e.g. Ovid, *Heroides*, 15, 123ff.), but Cassio's dream is Iago's fabrication: see p. 51.

417 **raging** aching furiously. Before modern dentistry, toothache was more of a problem: cf. the 'hellish torment of the teeth' (Epigram 36 in *Epigrammes and Elegies* [*c.* 1599] of Sir John Davies and Marlowe).

419 **loose** dissolute
sleeps The plural was idiomatic when referring to more than one person (*OED* 2b).

420 **affairs** could be three syllables (Abbott, 477)

421–8 See p. 74 (*Arden of Faversham*), and *Doctor Dodypoll* (1600), B3a,

where lovers cry out and betray themselves in their sleep (both plays prior to *Oth*).

423ff. **then** Notice the force of repeated *then*: it seems to authenticate several actions by placing them in sequence.
gripe clutch, grasp
would he governs *gripe, wring, Cry, kiss, lay, sigh, kiss, cry* (which all become repeated actions)

424 **hard** passionately (cf. *WT* 2.1.5)

426 ***lay** I guess that Q misread *laye* as *layd*, then misread or changed the following verbs, and that F *laid* followed Q; *lay his* probably slurred as *lay's*.

427 **Cursed** cursèd
fate See pp. 72–3.

430 **foregone conclusion** a coinage (not in modern sense); *conclusion* = experiment, trial (Malone); *foregone* = previous

---

417–20] *as F; Q lines* sleep. / soule, / affaires, / *Cassio:* /   422 wary] *F;* merry *Q*   424 Cry 'O] Cry, oh *F;* Cry out, *Q*   and] *Q; not in F*   426–8 That … Moor!] *as F; Q lines* leg / then / Moore. /   426 lay] *Rowe;* then layed *Q;* laid *F*   o'er] *F;* Ouer *Q*   427 sigh … kiss … cry] *F;* sigh'd … kissed … Cried *Q*

IAGO

'Tis a shrewd doubt, though it be but a dream,
And this may help to thicken other proofs
That do demonstrate thinly.

OTHELLO

I'll tear her all to pieces!

IAGO

Nay, yet be wise, yet we see nothing done,   435
She may be honest yet. Tell me but this,
Have you not sometimes seen a handkerchief
Spotted with strawberries, in your wife's hand?

OTHELLO

I gave her such a one, 'twas my first gift.

IAGO

I know not that, but such a handkerchief,   440
I am sure it was your wife's, did I today
See Cassio wipe his beard with.

OTHELLO   If it be that —

---

431 This line could be Othello's, as in F.
Alexander and Sisson prefer Q. Othello 'does not entangle himself; he is
entangled [by Iago]' (Sisson).
shrewd strongly indicative; vexatious; sharp
doubt suspicion; fear
432 **thicken** i.e. confirm
433 **demonstrate** establish the truth
(*OED* 4, first intransitive use); accent
on second syllable
thinly weakly. Cf. 1.3.109, *thin*
evidence.
434 Is the urge to *tear her* a sign of his
'primitiveness'? Not necessarily: cf.
RJ 5.3.35, 'I will tear thee joint by
joint', *Cym* 2.4.147, 'tear her limb-
meal', and also Psalms 50.22.
435 ¹*yet* If we retain F *yet*, the third *yet*
(436) in two lines receives a special
emphasis: 'She may be honest – yet'
(i.e. even if not for long).
²*yet* up to now

wise Cf. 4.1.233.
done Perhaps a quibble on *do* = copulate: cf. *Tit* 4.2.76, 'I have done thy
mother'; *MM* 1.2.87–8, 'what has he
done? *Pompey*. A woman.'
436 **yet** still; nevertheless; after all
Tell ... this The same words occur,
in a scribe's hand, in *Sir Thomas
More*, Addition II, 237 (usually assigned to Shakespeare).
438 **Spotted** decorated
strawberries might suggest a hidden
evil, or the purity of the Virgin (L. J.
Ross, in *Studies in the Renaissance*, 7
[1960], 225–40). Or drops of blood?
439 **first gift** Cf. 295.
440 **I ... that** He validates his lies by
refusing to say more than he knows.
441 **today** As Iago has only just received
it (319), he takes a risk in saying this.
Othello could have seen it if it was
Desdemona who dropped it: cf. 291
SD n.

---

431 SP] *Q ; not in F*   432 And] *Q ; Iago. And F*   435 ¹yet] *F ; but Q*   442 it] *F ; 't Q*

IAGO

If it be that, or any that was hers,
It speaks against her with the other proofs.

OTHELLO

O that the slave had forty thousand lives!   445
One is too poor, too weak for my revenge.
Now do I see 'tis true. Look here, Iago,
All my fond love thus do I blow to heaven:
'Tis gone!
Arise, black vengeance, from the hollow hell,   450
Yield up, O love, thy crown and hearted throne
To tyrannous hate! Swell, bosom, with thy fraught,
For 'tis of aspics' tongues!

IAGO   Yet be content!

OTHELLO

O blood, blood, blood!   *Othello kneels.*

IAGO

Patience, I say, your mind perhaps may change.   455

OTHELLO

Never, Iago. Like to the Pontic sea

---

443 *²that** could be written 'y" and misread as *yt* (it), hence Malone's
emendation
444 **proofs** What proofs?
445 Cf. 4.1.175. The *slave* = Cassio.
447–8 Some action is required ('Look
here', '*thus*'), but what? He blows
something upwards, then looks down
and addresses 'vengeance' in hell.
448 **fond** foolish; affectionate
450 **black vengeance** Cf. *A Larum for
London* (1602; SR: 27 May 1600),
A4b, 'send blacke vengeance to that
hated towne'.
   hollow hell See LN.
451 **hearted** fixed in the heart (*OED* 5,
first here; but cf. 1.3.367)
452 **fraught** burden
453 **aspics'** (*aspic* = asp, a small venom-

ous serpent, found in Egypt and
Libya): cf. 3.4.58
content calm; satisfied in mind (a
harmless word, yet calculated to infuriate him). Cf. *satisfied*, 396–9.
454 SD SDs placed in the margin (as in
Q) are not always placed precisely
in manuscripts: the kneel could be
intended for 457 or 463. For re-
vengers who kneel, cf. *Tit* 4.1.87ff.;
Arden of Faversham (Revels), 9.37,
'Then he kneels down and holds up
his hands to heaven'; Marlowe,
Edward II, 3.1.127, *Jew of Malta*,
1.2.165.
456–9 Cf. Pliny (quoted p. 5). The
Pontic Sea, Propontic and Hellespont
= Black Sea, Sea of Marmora and the
Dardanelles.

---

443 ²that] *Malone;* it *QF*   447 true] *F;* time *Q*   448–9] *one line QF*   450 the . . . hell] *F;* thy . . .
Cell *Q*   453 Yet] *F;* Pray *Q*   454] *F;* O blood, Iago, blood. *Q*   SD] *Q (he kneeles. opp. 453); not
in F*   455 perhaps] *Q; not in F*   456–63 Iago . . . heaven] *F; not in Q*

Whose icy current and compulsive course
Ne'er keeps retiring ebb but keeps due on
To the Propontic and the Hellespont:
Even so my bloody thoughts with violent pace   460
Shall ne'er look back, ne'er ebb to humble love
Till that a capable and wide revenge
Swallow them up. Now by yond marble heaven
In the due reverence of a sacred vow
I here engage my words.

IAGO   Do not rise yet.   *Iago kneels.*
Witness, you ever-burning lights above,   466
You elements that clip us round about,
Witness that here Iago doth give up
The execution of his wit, hands, heart,
To wronged Othello's service. Let him command   470
And to obey shall be in me remorse

---

457 **compulsive** caused by compulsion, compelled; or, compelling
458 See LN.
461 **humble** The lover is usually humble; appropriate here because Lat. *humilis* (from *humus*, earth) could = low-lying. Olivier paused after *humble* and then 'forced himself to say the word "love"' (J. R. Brown, quoted Hankey, 253).
462 **capable** able to receive, contain; capacious (*OED* 1, 2)
wide vast, spacious
463 **marble** indifferent to the sufferings of others. Malone compared *Antonio and Mellida* (printed 1602, acted 1599 or 1600), 'pleased the marble heavens' (Revels, 2.1.230). Cf. *Tim* 4.3.191, 'the marbled mansion all above', *Cym* 5.4.87, 'Peep through thy marble mansion' (both = heaven).
464 **due** proper; necessary
465 **engage** pledge
466 **Witness** Such formal invocations were more often addressed to God

or heaven: cf. *TGV* 2.6.25, *2H6* 4.8.62.
ever-burning Cf. 2.1.15, *ever-fired*. Implies 'ever-watchful' and 'never-ending'.
467 **elements** heavenly bodies (*OED* 10); or, powers of nature (Ridley)
clip clasp; encompass
469 **execution** performance; implying the 'execution' of Cassio
wit mind
470 **Othello's** Speaking of 'Othello' to his face, Iago takes a liberty acknowledged by 472, *thy love*. Cf. 4.1.48n.
service At 1.1.41ff. he saw himself as Othello's servant; now, despite his assurances, Othello is almost the ventriloquist's dummy.
471 **remorse** glossed as 'a solemn obligation' by *OED* (4c, first here, citing no other instance). But the usual sense (= pity, compassion) is possible: 'to obey shall be an act of pity (for "wronged Othello") whatever bloody task I have to undertake'.

---

458 ¹keeps] *F;* feels *Q2;* Never retiring ebbs, but keeps due on *Sisson*   465 SD] *Q (*Iago kneeles.*)*
opp. 467; not in F   469 execution] *F;* excellency *Q*   hands] *F;* hand *Q*   471 in me] *F; not in Q*

What bloody business ever.

OTHELLO   I greet thy love
Not with vain thanks but with acceptance bounteous,
And will upon the instant put thee to't.
Within these three days let me hear thee say   475
That Cassio's not alive.

IAGO   My friend is dead,
'Tis done – at your request. But let her live.

OTHELLO
Damn her, lewd minx: O damn her, damn her!
Come, go with me apart; I will withdraw
To furnish me with some swift means of death   480
For the fair devil. Now art thou my lieutenant.

IAGO   I am your own for ever.   *Exeunt.*

[3.4]   *Enter* DESDEMONA, EMILIA *and* CLOWN.

DESDEMONA   Do you know, sirrah, where lieutenant
Cassio lies?

---

472 **ever** soever
greet welcome; salute
473 **vain** empty
bounteous 'normally used of the giver rather than the receiver' (Ridley). Cf. 203n. Implies 'whole-hearted', or perhaps a bounteous reward?
474 **to't** to the test
476 **My . . . dead** Cf. 2.3.161, *he dies!*
477 **But . . . live** He means the opposite, noticing that Othello seems preoccupied with Cassio.
478 **lewd** (a richer word than now) base, worthless; wicked; lascivious
minx wanton (woman), trull: cf. 4.1.152
479 **apart** aside, away from here
480 **some . . . death** He has not decided on the *means.*
481 **Now . . . lieutenant** The first sign that he knows of Iago's wish for promotion. See pp. 34–5.
482 **for ever** Cf. 1.3.365, 3.3.217: a

special emphasis on *for ever*. Cf. LN, 1.1.8. Othello welcomes Iago as '*my* lieutenant'; Iago acknowledges this, 'I am your own – for ever' (also implying the opposite: '*you* belong to *me* through all eternity'. So Faustus belongs to his servant–master Mephistopheles).
3.4.1–22 This clown episode was once regularly omitted in performance (Sprague, 202). The Clown, like the Porter in *Macbeth* (2.3), arrests the play as it gathers tragic momentum, and is equally self-absorbed.
1 **sirrah** term of address used for servants or social inferiors
lieutenant Othello dismissed him, but she gives him his title.
2ff. **lies** Cf. the quibbles on *hear* (3.1.22), and on *lives* in *TN* 3.1.1ff. The clowns in *TN* and *Oth* were probably played by the same actor, Robert Armin.

---

472 business] *F;* worke so *Q*   477] *as Q; F lines* Request. / liue. / at your request.] *F; as you* request, *Q*   478] *one line Q; F lines* Minx: / her. / ³damn her] *F; not in Q*   481] *as Q; F lines* Diuell. / Lieutenant. /   3.4] *Scoena Quarta. F; not in Q*   1 lieutenant] *F;* the Leiutenant *Q*

CLOWN   I dare not say he lies anywhere.

DESDEMONA   Why, man?

CLOWN   He's a soldier, and for me to say a soldier lies,   5
'tis stabbing.

DESDEMONA   Go to, where lodges he?

CLOWN   To tell you where he lodges is to tell you
where I lie.

DESDEMONA   Can anything be made of this?   10

CLOWN   I know not where he lodges, and for me to
devise a lodging and say he lies here, or he lies there,
were to lie in mine own throat.

DESDEMONA   Can you enquire him out and be edified by
report?   15

CLOWN   I will catechize the world for him, that is, make
questions and by them answer.

DESDEMONA   Seek him, bid him come hither, tell him I
have moved my lord on his behalf, and hope all will
be well.   20

CLOWN   To do this is within the compass of man's wit,
and therefore I will attempt the doing it.   *Exit.*

---

6 **stabbing** i.e. to run the risk of being stabbed. Cf. Raleigh, *The Lie*: 'Because, to give the lie, / Deserves no less than stabbing'.

9 **I lie** *Lie* could = dwell, as in *MW* 2.1.179–80, 'Does he lie at the Garter?' The Clown quibbles 'To tell you where *he* lies is to tell you where *I* lie (because I don't know)'.

12 **devise** invent; guess (*OED* 5, 10)

13 **lie ... throat** to lie foully or infamously (*OED* throat 3c). In the finely graded art of giving the lie (for which see *AYL* 5.4.68ff.), to say that someone lied in his throat was a stronger reproof than simply to say he lied: cf. *R3* 1.2.93, *TN* 3.4.156, Dent, T268.

14 **edified** informed, instructed, often in religious sense. Cf. *TN* 5.1.290, 'Look then to be well edified when the fool delivers the madman.'

16 **catechize** Cf. *TN* 1.5.62ff., '*Clown*. I must catechize you for it, madonna': perhaps joking at a 'clown routine' (cf. 2n., 14n.).

17 **questions ... answer** (as in the Catechism)
by them 'i.e. and by them, when answered, form my own answer to you' (Malone)

19 **moved** urged

21 **compass** due limits: so *RJ* 4.1.47, 'It strains me past the compass of my wits.'

---

5 SP] *F; not in Q*   He's] *F;* He is *Q*   me] *F;* one *Q*   6 'tis] *F;* is *Q*   8–10] *F; not in Q*   12 here ... there] *F;* there *Q*   13 mine own] *F;* my *Q*   17 by] *QF;* bid *Theobald*   19 on] *F;* in *Q*   21 man's wit] *F;* a man *Q*   22 I will] *F;* I'le *Q*   it] *F;* of it *Q*

DESDEMONA

Where should I lose that handkerchief, Emilia?

EMILIA

I know not, madam.

DESDEMONA

Believe me, I had rather have lost my purse   25
Full of crusadoes; and but my noble Moor
Is true of mind, and made of no such baseness
As jealous creatures are, it were enough
To put him to ill-thinking.

EMILIA   Is he not jealous?

DESDEMONA

Who, he? I think the sun where he was born   30
Drew all such humours from him.

EMILIA   Look where he comes.

Enter OTHELLO.

DESDEMONA

I will not leave him now till Cassio
Be called to him. How is't with you, my lord?

OTHELLO

Well, my good lady. [*aside*] O hardness to dissemble! –
How do you, Desdemona?

DESDEMONA   Well, my good lord.   35

23 **should I lose** could I have lost
24 This is a turning point in the play,
   and should be felt as such: see p. 44
   and 3.3.302.
25 **my purse** Cf. 3.3.160, 'Who steals
   my purse steals trash'.
26 **crusadoes** Portuguese coins, bearing
   the figure of the cross. Mentioned
   nowhere else by Shakespeare – why
   here? Perhaps to remind us that
   Christian Venice was threatened by
   Muslim states. A *crusado* was also a
   crusader.

but except that
27 **baseness** inferior quality
29 **Is . . . jealous** probably meant as a
   warning: see 100 and p. 44.
31 **humours** the four chief fluids of the
   body, which were thought to determine a person's mental and physical
   qualities; moods, whims
34 **O . . . dissemble** The stock formula
   was 'I must dissemble!' (as in *2H6*
   5.1.13, *Per* 2.5.23); here = O how
   hard it is to dissemble!

23 that] *Q*; the *F*   25 have lost] *F*; loose *Q*   31.1] *F*; *opp.* 31 *Q*   32–3] *as Steevens 1793; Q lines*
now, / Lord? /; *F lines* be / Lord? /   32 till] *F*; 'Tis *Qu*; Let *Qc*   33 is't] *F*; is it *Q*   34 SD]
Hanmer; not in QF

OTHELLO

Give me your hand. This hand is moist, my lady.

DESDEMONA

It yet hath felt no age, nor known no sorrow.

OTHELLO

This argues fruitfulness and liberal heart:
Hot, hot, and moist. This hand of yours requires
A sequester from liberty, fasting and prayer,   40
Much castigation, exercise devout,
For here's a young and sweating devil, here,
That commonly rebels. 'Tis a good hand,
A frank one.

DESDEMONA   You may indeed say so,
For 'twas that hand that gave away my heart.   45

OTHELLO

A liberal hand. The hearts of old gave hands
But our new heraldry is hands, not hearts.

DESDEMONA

I cannot speak of this. Come, now, your promise.

OTHELLO

What promise, chuck?

---

36 **moist** Cf. Tilley, H86, 'A moist hand argues an amorous nature'; *AC* 1.2.52–3, 'if an oily hand be not a fruitful prognostication'.

38 **argues** gives grounds for inferring
fruitfulness fertility in offspring
liberal bountiful; unrestrained, licentious. Here ambiguous near-synonyms (fruitful, liberal) can be taken favourably or unfavourably (Elliott, 30): so *frank*, 44.

39 **Hot** could = passionate; lustful, sexually excited

40 **sequester** sequestration, isolation; probably séquester, lib'rty

41 **castigation** corrective discipline
exercise devout exercises of devotion, religious discipline

42 **sweating** i.e. hot and moist; toiling (for Satan)

44 **frank** free (from restraint); generous, lavish

45 (in the troth-plighting or marriage ceremony)

46 **gave** perhaps with a quibble on *give* = display as armorial bearing (*OED* 24)

47 See LN.
heraldry heraldic practice

48 **I . . . this** Cf. 3.3.440, 'I know not that'.

49 **chuck** term of endearment (perhaps = chick). So Macbeth to Lady Macbeth (3.2.45), Antony to Cleopatra (4.4.2).

36] *as Q ; F lines* your hand. / Lady. /   37 yet hath] yet has *Q ;* hath *F*   39 Hot, hot] *F;* Not hot *Q*   40 prayer] *F;* praying *Q*   46 hearts . . . hands] *QF;* hands . . . hearts *Hanmer*   48] *as Q ; F lines* this: / promise. /   Come, now] *F;* come, come *Q*

DESDEMONA

I have sent to bid Cassio come speak with you.   50

OTHELLO

I have a salt and sullen rheum offends me,
Lend me thy handkerchief.

DESDEMONA

Here, my lord.

OTHELLO

That which I gave you.

DESDEMONA

I have it not about me.   55

OTHELLO

Not?

DESDEMONA

No, faith, my lord.

OTHELLO   That's a fault. That handkerchief
Did an Egyptian to my mother give,
She was a charmer and could almost read
The thoughts of people. She told her, while she kept
    it   60
'Twould make her amiable and subdue my father
Entirely to her love; but if she lost it
Or made a gift of it, my father's eye
Should hold her loathed and his spirits should hunt
After new fancies. She, dying, gave it me   65
And bid me, when my fate would have me wive,

51 **salt** vexatious
   sullen unyielding; F *sorry* would =
   painful, grievous
   rheum offends running cold that
   troubles
57–8 Cf. 5.2.215n.
58 **Egyptian** probably a true Egyptian
   (see p. 4), not a Gipsy
59 **charmer** one who uses spells and
   enchantments
59–60 **and . . . people** N.B. the importance of reading 'the thoughts of
   people' in *Othello*!
61 **amiable** lovable
62–5 This sounds like superstition but
   (if not fabricated by Othello) the prediction later comes true, in so far as
   Othello and Desdemona are
   concerned.
64 **loathed** perhaps loathèd
   spirits perhaps an error for *spirit*
65 **fancies** amorous inclinations, loves

51 sullen] *Q*; sorry *F*   56 Not?] *F*; Not. *Q*   57 faith] *Q*; indeed *F*   62] *line repeated Q from foot
of H4ᵛ to top of I1*   64 loathed] *F*; lothely *Q*   66 wive] *Q*; Wiu'd *F*

To give it her. I did so, and – take heed on't!
Make it a darling, like your precious eye! –
To lose't or give't away were such perdition
As nothing else could match.

DESDEMONA   Is't possible?   70

OTHELLO

'Tis true, there's magic in the web of it.
A sibyl that had numbered in the world
The sun to course two hundred compasses,
In her prophetic fury sewed the work;
The worms were hallowed that did breed the silk,   75
And it was dyed in mummy, which the skilful
Conserved of maidens' hearts.

DESDEMONA   I'faith, is't true?

OTHELLO

Most veritable, therefore look to't well.

DESDEMONA

Then would to God that I had never seen't!

OTHELLO

Ha! wherefore?   80

DESDEMONA

Why do you speak so startingly and rash?

---

67 **her** i.e. my wife
take heed on't pay attention; or, look after it
68 Cf. Dent, E249.1, 'To love as one's own eye'.
69 **perdition** loss; ruin; echoing 3.3.90
71 **web** woven fabric
72–3 See LN.
74 **prophetic fury** Perhaps Ariosto's 'furor profetico' (*Orlando Furioso*, c. 46, st. 80); if so, Shakespeare knew Ariosto in the original, as the English translation had no 'prophetic fury'. But he may have found the phrase in the writings of Joshua Sylvester (Muir, *Sources*, 183, 305n.).
fury inspired frenzy

sewed The fabric was woven but the embroidered *work* (3.3.300n.) was sewn.
75 **worms** T. Moffett's *The Silkewormes* was published in 1599. A matter of topical interest?
hallowed consecrated
breed produce
76 **mummy** medicinal liquid, supposedly made from embalmed bodies
77 **Conserved of** made or preserved from
maidens' virgins'
78 **veritable** unique in Shakespeare
81 **startingly** (?)disconnectedly (Ridley); or, jumpily (*OED* start 5); startlingly
rash hastily, urgently

67 so,] *Q;* so; *F*   68 eye!] eye, *Q;* eye: *F*   69 lose't] *F;* loose *Q*   73 course] *F;* make *Q*   76 which] *F;* with *Q*   77 Conserved] *F;* Conserues *Q*   I'faith] *Q;* Indeed? *F*   79 God] *Q;* Heauen *F*   seen't] *F;* seene it *Q*   80 Ha!] Ha, *Q,* Ha? *F*   81 rash] *F;* rashly *Q*

OTHELLO

    Is't lost? Is't gone? Speak, is't out o'the way?

DESDEMONA

    Heaven bless us!

OTHELLO

    Say you?

DESDEMONA

    It is not lost, but what an if it were?   85

OTHELLO

    How?

DESDEMONA

    I say it is not lost.

OTHELLO   Fetch't, let me see't.

DESDEMONA

    Why, so I can, sir; but I will not now.

    This is a trick to put me from my suit.

    Pray you, let Cassio be received again.   90

OTHELLO

    Fetch me the handkerchief, my mind misgives.

DESDEMONA

    Come, come,

    You'll never meet a more sufficient man.

OTHELLO

    The handkerchief!

DESDEMONA   I pray, talk me of Cassio.

---

82 **out ... way** lost, missing. Cf. 1.3.359–60.

83 **Heaven bless us** expresses surprise, but could be ironical = what's all the fuss about (*OED* bless 9)

84 **Say you?** 'do you say so!' or 'what do you say?' Cf. *Ham* 4.5.28, *MM* 5.1.274, *Cym* 4.2.379.

85 This sounds like a lie, because *we* know that she has lost it (cf. 23); but *she* may believe that, though missing, it will turn up again. See p. 58; *an if* = if.

88 **sir** This word creates distance between them.

90 **received** readmitted to his post as lieutenant; received as guest

91–9 See p. 77.
    misgives has misgivings. Cf. *RJ* 1.4.106, 'my mind misgives / Some consequence yet hanging in the stars'.

93 **sufficient** capable

94 F's omission could be caused by eye-skip. Equally, the Q compositor might have 'cast off' badly and invented these words to fill a gap: *talk me* is unusual (*Texts*, 47).

82 is't] *F*; is it *Q* o'the] *Q*; o'th' *F* 83 Heaven bless] *Q*; Blesse *F* 86 How?] *F*; Ha. *Q* 87 see't] *F*; see it *Q* 88 sir] *Q*; *not in F* 90 Pray you] *F*; I pray *Q* 91] *as Q*; *F lines* Handkerchiefe, / mis-giues. / the] *F*; that *Q* 92–3] *one line QF* 94] *Q*; *not in F*

OTHELLO
  The handkerchief!
DESDEMONA   A man that all his time   95
  Hath founded his good fortunes on your love,
  Shared dangers with you –
OTHELLO
  The handkerchief!
DESDEMONA   I'faith, you are to blame.
OTHELLO
  Zounds!   *Exit.*
EMILIA
  Is not this man jealous?   100
DESDEMONA
  I ne'er saw this before,
  Sure there's some wonder in this handkerchief;
  I am most unhappy in the loss of it.
EMILIA
  'Tis not a year or two shows us a man.
  They are all but stomachs, and we all but food: 105
  They eat us hungerly, and when they are full
  They belch us.

Enter IAGO *and* CASSIO.

  Look you, Cassio and my husband.

IAGO
  There is no other way, 'tis she must do't,

96 i.e. has relied on your affection for his
   advancement in the world
98 **to blame** at fault, in the wrong (to
   treat me like this)
99 **Zounds** F *Away* looks like a substitution for Q's profanity.
100 **Is . . . jealous** Cf. 29.
102 **wonder** marvellous quality (because
   the Egyptian's prediction is coming
   true?)

103 **unhappy** unfortunate; miserable
104 i.e. a year or two does not fully reveal to us (women) what (a monster)
   a man is
105 **but** nothing but
   stomachs i.e. appetites
106 **hungerly** greedily. So *TS* 3.2.175,
   Tim 1.1.253. Variant of *hungrily*,
   which is not found in Shakespeare.
107 **belch** vomit

98 I'faith] *Q ;* Insooth *F*   99 Zounds] *Q (*Zouns*);* Away. *F*   103 the] *Qc, F;* this *Qu*   of it] *F;*
not in Q   107 SD] *as F; after 103 Q*   108 do't] *F;* doe it *Q*

And lo, the happiness! go and importune her.
DESDEMONA
How now, good Cassio, what's the news with you?   110
CASSIO
Madam, my former suit. I do beseech you
That by your virtuous means I may again
Exist, and be a member of his love
Whom I, with all the office of my heart
Entirely honour. I would not be delayed: 115
If my offence be of such mortal kind
That nor my service past nor present sorrows
Nor purposed merit in futurity
Can ransom me into his love again,
But to know so must be my benefit;   120
So shall I clothe me in a forced content
And shut myself up in some other course
To fortune's alms.
DESDEMONA   Alas, thrice-gentle Cassio,
My advocation is not now in tune;
My lord is not my lord, nor should I know him   125
Were he in favour as in humour altered.
So help me every spirit sanctified

109 **happiness** lucky chance (happy =
lucky). Cf. Lyly, *Sapho*, 5.3.2, 'And
loe how happilye shee sitteth in her
caue.'
  importune sue to; probably impòr-
tune
112 **by . . . means** by your good (or
efficacious) help; or, 'by means of
you, virtuous madam' (Kittredge)
113 **Exist** be myself (as Lieutenant
Cassio)
  member of one who participates in
114 **office** duty (Lat. *officium*)
115 **I . . . be** I don't want to be
116 **mortal** fatal
117 that neither my (military) service in
the past nor my regrets now (for
misbehaving)
119 **ransom** elliptical: set me free (from
his displeasure, and bring me back)

into his love
120 merely to know that must be my
gain (because I'll know the worst)
121 so I shall invest myself with en-
forced contentment (*OED* clothe 7b,
citing Job 39.19)
122–3 and commit myself to some other
course (leading) to fortune's charit-
able relief. Cf. *Mac* 2.1.16, 'shut up /
In measureless content'; *KL* 1.1.277–
8, 'receiv'd you / At fortune's alms'.
123 **thrice-gentle** unique in Shakespeare
124 **advocation** (unique in Shakespeare)
advocacy
125 **My . . . lord** Cf. 1.1.64, 'I am not
what I am.'
126 **favour** appearance
  humour mood
127 Cf. 'so help me God'.

114 office] *F;* duty *Q*   117 nor my] *F;* neither *Q*   122 shut] *F;* shoote *Q*

248

As I have spoken for you all my best
And stood within the blank of his displeasure
For my free speech. You must awhile be patient: 130
What I can do I will, and more I will
Than for myself I dare. Let that suffice you.

IAGO

   Is my lord angry?

EMILIA   He went hence but now,
And certainly in strange unquietness.

IAGO

   Can he be angry? I have seen the cannon   135
And when it hath blown his ranks into the air
And like the devil, from his very arm,
Puffed his own brother – and can he be angry?
Something of moment then. I will go meet him,
There's matter in't indeed, if he be angry.   140

DESDEMONA

   I prithee do so. (*Exit* [*Iago.*]) Something sure of state
Either from Venice, or some unhatched practice
Made demonstrable here in Cyprus to him,
Hath puddled his clear spirit, and in such cases
Men's natures wrangle with inferior things   145

---

128 **all my best** to the best of my ability

129 **blank** once explained as 'the white spot in the centre of a target' (so *OED*). But J. R. Hale shows that *blank* here = 'point-blank range' ('The true Shakespearian blank', *SQ*, 19 [1968], 33–40).

130 **free** frank, unreserved

134 **unquietness** disquiet, perturbation

135 **Can . . . angry?** Iago knows that he can be angry (3.3.434ff.). Elliptical: 'I have seen his ranks blown into the air . . . *and meanwhile have seen him cool and unruffled*. And can he now be angry?' (Malone).

138 **brother** In this scene we hear of Othello's father, mother, brother, the Egyptian, the sibyl – i.e. his background.

139 **moment** importance

140 **There's . . . indeed** some importance attaches to it (*OED* matter 11c)

141 **Something . . . state** surely some affair of state

142 **unhatched practice** plot that is still hatching

143 **demonstrable** known, 'capable of being proved' (unique in Shakespeare)

144 **puddled . . . spirit** muddied or confused his (usually) clear mind

145–6 **wrangle . . . object** dispute angrily about (or with) less important things though important ones are their real concern. She appears to class herself with the less important things, taking for granted that Othello's business comes first.

138 can . . . be] *Q* ; is he *F*   141 SD] *F (opp. 140); not in Q*

Though great ones are their object. 'Tis even so,
For let our finger ache and it indues
Our other healthful members even to that sense
Of pain. Nay, we must think men are not gods
Nor of them look for such observancy   150
As fits the bridal. Beshrew me much, Emilia,
I was, unhandsome warrior as I am,
Arraigning his unkindness with my soul,
But now I find I had suborned the witness
And he's indicted falsely.

EMILIA   Pray heaven it be   155
State matters, as you think, and no conception
Nor no jealous toy, concerning you.

DESDEMONA
Alas the day, I never gave him cause.

EMILIA
But jealous souls will not be answered so:
They are not ever jealous for the cause,   160

147 **indues** (?)brings to a certain state (*OED* 4b, first here, no other instance cited). At this time *indue* and *endue* were interchangeable, and included 'all the senses of *endow*' (*OED*).
148 **members** limbs or parts of the body
to i.e. with
149 **think** keep in mind
men . . . gods Cf. Dent, M593, 'We are but men, not gods.'
150 **observancy** respectful attention; observance of forms (unique in Shakespeare)
151 **As . . . bridal** as befits the wedding
Beshrew me evil befall me (mild oath)
152 **unhandsome** unskilful (*OED* 3, first here, no other instance cited); could = unseemly, discourteous (*OED* 4, from 1645; handsome = seemly, recorded 1597); or, unsol-

dierly (handsome = soldierly, first in 1665)
warrior Cf. 2.1.180, 'O my fair warrior!'
153 **Arraigning** accusing, calling to account
unkindness (a richer word than now) unnatural conduct; lack of natural affection; unkind action
with my soul i.e. from my heart and soul
154 **suborned** corrupted
witness i.e. herself
156 **conception** mere fancy
157 **jealous** F *Iealious* could be two syllables (as in 159) or three
toy fantastic notion; unreasoning dislike; trifle (*OED* 4, 5)
158 **Alas the day** Cf. 4.2.43.
159–62 an indirect comment on Iago's 'motivelesss malignity' (see pp. 33–4), not really true of Othello?

146–9] *as F; Q lines* obiect, / ake, / members, / thinke, / gods, /   146 their] *F;* the *Q*   148 that] *Q;* a *F*   150 observancy] *F;* obseruances *Q*   155–7] *as F; Q lines* thinke, / toy / you.

But jealous for they're jealous. It is a monster
Begot upon itself, born on itself.

DESDEMONA

Heaven keep that monster from Othello's mind!

EMILIA

Lady, amen.

DESDEMONA

I will go seek him. Cassio, walk here about,   165
If I do find him fit I'll move your suit
And seek to effect it to my uttermost.

CASSIO

I humbly thank your ladyship.

Exeunt Desdemona and Emilia.

Enter BIANCA.

BIANCA

Save you, friend Cassio!

CASSIO   What make you from home?
How is't with you, my most fair Bianca?   170
I'faith, sweet love, I was coming to your house.

BIANCA

And I was going to your lodging, Cassio.
What, keep a week away? seven days and nights?
Eight score eight hours? and lovers' absent hours
More tedious than the dial, eight score times!   175

---

161 **monster** Cf. 3.3.168n.; *Cor* 5.3.36, 'As if a man were author of himself'. For a similar monster, cf. *Faerie Queene*, 4.10.41, 'She syre and mother is her selfe alone, / Begets and eke conceives, ne needeth other none.'

165 **here about** Othello and Desdemona talked in a private place (a garden?): Cassio now walks to a more public place, where Bianca finds him.

166 **fit** i.e. in a suitable mood

168.1 SD BIANCA Elizabethan prostitutes apparently wore red petticoats: cf. *1H4* 1.2.10, 'a fair hot wench in a flame-coloured taffeta' (Ard², n.).

169 **Save** God save, i.e. protect, as in 'God save the King'
make you are you doing

173–5 For the play's 'double time', see pp. 68–72. Bianca counts correctly (168 hours): has she been brooding about her wrongs?

175 **dial** clock

161 they're ... It is] *F;* they are ... tis *Q*   163 that] *Q;* the *F*   165 here about] *QF;* hereabout *F3*   168 SD] *as Q (opp. 166); Exit F (opp. 167)*   168.2] *F; opp. Cassio* 169 *Q*   169 Save] *Q;* 'Saue *F*   170 is't] *F;* is it *Q*   171 I'faith] *Q;* Indeed *F*

O weary reckoning!

CASSIO   Pardon me, Bianca,
I have this while with leaden thoughts been pressed,
But I shall in a more continuate time
Strike off this score of absence. Sweet Bianca,
                    [*Giving her Desdemona's handkerchief*]
Take me this work out.

BIANCA   O Cassio, whence came this?   180
This is some token from a newer friend!
To the felt absence now I feel a cause:
Is't come to this? Well, well.

CASSIO   Go to, woman,
Throw your vile guesses in the devil's teeth
From whence you have them! You are jealous now   185
That this is from some mistress, some remembrance:
No, by my faith, Bianca.

BIANCA   Why, whose is it?

CASSIO
I know not neither, I found it in my chamber.
I like the work well: ere it be demanded,
As like enough it will, I'd have it copied.   190
Take it, and do't, and leave me for this time.

---

176 **O weary reckoning** Cf. Ovid,
Heroides, 2.7, 'Should you count the
days, which we count well who love'.

177 **leaden** oppressive (cf. *R3* 5.3.105,
'leaden slumber')
pressed oppressed; harassed

178 **continuate** uninterrupted; long-
continued. Cf. *Tim* 1.1.11, 'an untir-
able and continuate goodness'.

179 **Strike ... score** i.e. pay my account, so that it can be struck out
(cancelled); *score* = reckoning (quibbling on 174, 176).

180 **Take ... out** the very words of
Emilia (3.3.300)!

181 **friend** mistress

183 **Well, well** Cf. Dent, W269, 'Well,
well is a word of malice.'
Go to get away with you!
woman Cf. 5.2.146n.

184 i.e. and not in *my* teeth. Cf. Dent,
T429, 'To cast (hit) in the teeth'.

186 **remembrance** keepsake

188 **I know not** And yet Desdemona
kept it 'evermore about her / To kiss
and talk to' (3.3.299–300)! See p. 71
n. 1.
neither used to strengthen a preceding negative (*OED* 3)

191 **leave me** Cf. 3.3.323n.

---

176 O] *F* (Oh); No *Q*   reckoning] *Q*; reck'ning *F*   177 leaden] *F*; laden *Q*   178 continuate] *F*;
conuenient *Q*   179 SD] *Rowe*; *not in QF*   182 felt absence now] *as Q*; felt-Absence: now
F   183 Well, well.] *F*; *not in Q*   Go to, woman] *QF*; Woman, go to! *Capell*   184 vile] *Q*; vilde
F   187 by ... faith] *Q*; in good troth *F*   whose] *Q2*; who's *QF*   188] *as Q*; *F lines* neither: /
Chamber, /   neither] *F*; sweete *Q*   190 I'd] *Q*; I would *F*

BIANCA

Leave you? Wherefore?

CASSIO

I do attend here on the general
And think it no addition, nor my wish,
To have him see me womaned.

BIANCA   Why, I pray you?   195

CASSIO

Not that I love you not.

BIANCA

But that you do not love me.
I pray you, bring me on the way a little,
And say if I shall see you soon at night.

CASSIO

'Tis but a little way that I can bring you   200
For I attend here, but I'll see you soon.

BIANCA

'Tis very good: I must be circumstanced.   *Exeunt.*

[**4.1**]   *Enter* OTHELLO *and* IAGO.

IAGO

Will you think so?

OTHELLO   Think so, Iago?

IAGO   What,

---

193 **attend . . . on** wait for
194 **addition** usually = title, or ad-
    ditional title, as at 4.1.105, but here
    'seems to be "credit"' (Ridley). Or
    perhaps 'no (good) addition to have
    him see me with a woman (added)',
    quibbling on two kinds of addition.
195 **womaned** (encumbered) with a
    woman (unique in Shakespeare)
197 Bianca interrupts?
199 **soon at night** Cf. Dent, S639.1,
    'Soon at night (i.e., tonight)'.
202 **circumstanced** unique in Shake-
    speare; 'subject to or governed by cir-

cumstance' or 'surrounded with conditions' (*OED*). Or, adapting the
noun (*OED* circumstance III, 'That
which is non-essential . . . or subor-
dinate'), 'I must be treated as
insignificant.'
4.1.0.1 Q may be right in making Iago
    lead, Othello follow.
  1 As at 1.1.1, the opening words imply
    that the speakers have talked for a
    while. Othello now echoes Iago, re-
    versing their roles (cf. 3.3.103ff.);
    Iago continues to work on Othello's
    visual imagination.

195–6] *F; not in Q*   202 SD] *Q; Exeunt omnes. F*   **4.1**] *Actus. 4. Q; Actus Quartus. Scena Prima.
F*   0.1] *F; Enter* Iago *and* Othello. *Q*

To kiss in private?

OTHELLO   An unauthorized kiss!

IAGO

Or to be naked with her friend in bed
An hour or more, not meaning any harm?

OTHELLO

Naked in bed, Iago, and not mean harm?   5
It is hypocrisy against the devil:
They that mean virtuously, and yet do so,
The devil their virtue tempts, and they tempt heaven.

IAGO

So they do nothing, 'tis a venial slip;
But if I give my wife a handkerchief –   10

OTHELLO

What then?

IAGO

Why, then 'tis hers, my lord, and being hers
She may, I think, bestow't on any man.

OTHELLO

She is protectress of her honour too:
May she give that?   15

IAGO

Her honour is an essence that's not seen,

---

2 **unauthorized** i.e. not authorized by the conventions of polite society, which permitted some kissing (2.1.97ff.)

3–4 Early romances sometimes manoeuvred lovers into bed, 'not meaning any harm' (Chaucer's *Troilus*, bk 3, st. 157; Sidney's *Arcadia*, 1593 edn, fo. 190b), but not usually naked. See also A. S. Cairncross, 'Shakespeare and Ariosto', *RQ*, 29 (1976), 178–82.

6 **against** in front of, in full view of (*OED* 1; cf. 2.3.365). Or, towards (if they really mean no harm, they try to dissimulate with the devil); 'to cheat the devil' (Johnson).

8 **tempts** puts to the test; incites to

evil. Cf. Matthew 4.1, 7: Jesus went into the wilderness 'to be tempted of the devil', and said to him 'Thou shalt not tempt the Lord thy God' (Henley, in Malone).

9 **So as long as**
do nothing Cf. 2.1.142, and *R3* 1.1.99–100, 'He that doth naught with her (excepting one) / Were best to do it secretly alone.'
venial slip A venial sin is a pardonable sin, admitting of remission; a *venial slip* would be less serious (*slip* = fault).

16 **essence** something that *is*, an entity; that by which anything subsists; foundation of being (*OED* 2, 5)

3, 5 in bed] *F*; abed *Q*   9 So] *Q*; If *F*

They have it very oft that have it not.
But for the handkerchief –

OTHELLO
By heaven, I would most gladly have forgot it!
Thou said'st – O, it comes o'er my memory   20
As doth the raven o'er the infectious house
Boding to all – he had my handkerchief.

IAGO
Ay, what of that?

OTHELLO   That's not so good now.

IAGO
What if I had said I had seen him do you wrong?
Or heard him say – as knaves be such abroad   25
Who, having by their own importunate suit
Or voluntary dotage of some mistress
Convinced or supplied them, cannot choose
But they must blab –

OTHELLO   Hath he said anything?

IAGO
He hath, my lord, but be you well assured   30
No more than he'll unswear.

OTHELLO   What hath he said?

IAGO
Faith, that he did – I know not what. He did –

17 'One of Iago's cryptic remarks, meaning . . . that many people are erroneously credited with the possession of
this invisible essence' (Ridley).
21–2 **As . . . all** Cf. Dent, R33, 'The
croaking raven bodes misfortune.'
21 **infectious** presumably infected with
the plague
22 **Boding** predicting (ominously)
23 **That's . . . now** Cf. Dent, G324.1,
'That's not so good (now).' A
characteristic understatement. A
nine-syllable line: perhaps *That's*
should be *That is* (see *Texts*, ch. 12), a
more ruminative line.
24 **I had** = I'd (twice)
25 **abroad** at large

27 **voluntary dotage** self-induced in-
fatuation
28 **Convinced** (convincèd) overcome
supplied satisfied a need or want
(*OED* 5). '*Supplied* relates to the
words *voluntary dotage*, as *convinced*
does to *their own importunate suit*.
"Having by their importunacy *con-
quered* the resistance of a mistress, or,
in compliance with her own request
. . . *gratified her desires*"' (Malone).
29 **blab** chatter; tell (what should be
concealed)
32 ***He did** – I repunctuate, and assume
that Iago pauses tantalizingly (*Texts*,
132). Cf. 2.1.158n.

21 infectious] *F;* infected *Q*   27 Or] *F;* Or by the *Q*   28 Convinced] *Qc, F;* Coniured
Qu   32 Faith] *Q;* Why *F*   what. He did –] *this edn;* what he did. *QF*

OTHELLO
What? what?

IAGO
Lie.

OTHELLO   With her?

IAGO   With her, on her, what you will.

OTHELLO   Lie with her? lie on her? We say lie on her   35
when they belie her! Lie with her, zounds, that's
fulsome! – Handkerchief! confessions! handkerchief!
– To confess, and be hanged for his labour! First to be
hanged, and then to confess: I tremble at it. Nature
would not invest herself in such shadowing passion   40
without some instruction. It is not words that shakes
me thus. Pish! Noses, ears, and lips. Is't possible?
Confess! handkerchief! O devil!

[He] falls in a trance.

---

34 **what you will** Cf. Dent, W280.5, 'What you will'. A poisonous phrase: it implies 'anything you like to think (or do with her)'.

35–43 Othello's fit in some ways resembles the 'pill' episode in *Poetaster*, 5.3.465ff. (performed 1601: see p. 77), and the raging of the hero in Greene's *Orlando Furioso* (printed 1594). With his loss of control, cf. also Cassio's drunkenness (2.3.60ff.).

35–6 He worries at the meaning of lying *with* and *on* her (cf. 34). *Lie on* could = tell lies about (*OED* 2), therefore 'We say lie *on* her when they (i.e. people) tell lies about (belie) her.' But he cannot reason away lie *with* her (= copulate with her).

37 **fulsome** nauseating; obscene

38–9 **First . . . confess** Cf. Dent, C587, 'Confess and be hanged' (a proverbial phrase meaning, roughly, 'You lie' [*OED* confess 10]), L.590, 'First hang and draw, then hear the cause.' Cf.

also 2.3.105ff. (Cassio on the correct sequence of things): tragedy teetering on the edge of comedy.

39–42 He tries to rationalize his trembling before he falls. 'Nature would not clothe (or endue) herself in such an all-enfolding passion without some special information (i.e. instinctive knowledge of the truth of what Iago has said, expressed in my trembling).' (*OED* invest 3; shadow 6b; instruction 3.)

41 **words** mere words

42 **Noses . . . lips** surrogate genital images. The thought is filled out later ('I see that nose of yours . . .'); or, as Steevens proposed, Othello imagines 'the familiarities which he supposes to have passed between Cassio and his wife' (as in *WT* 1.2.285–6).

43 SD *trance* J. P. Emery has shown that Othello suffers from several specific epileptic symptoms (in *Psychoanalysis and the Psychoanalytic Review*, 46 (1959), 30–2).

---

33 What? what?] *F;* But what? *Q*   36 zounds] *Q; not in F*   37 Handkerchief . . . handkerchief!] *as F;* handkerchers, Confession, hankerchers. *Q*   38–43 To . . . devil!] *as F; not in Q*   43 SD] *F subst.; not in Qu; He fals downe. Qc (after 37)*

IAGO

Work on,
My medicine, work! Thus credulous fools are caught,   45
And many worthy and chaste dames even thus,
All guiltless, meet reproach. – What ho! my lord!
My lord, I say! Othello!

Enter CASSIO.

How now, Cassio?

CASSIO

What's the matter?

IAGO

My lord is fallen into an epilepsy;   50
This is his second fit, he had one yesterday.

CASSIO

Rub him about the temples.

IAGO   No, forbear:
The lethargy must have his quiet course,
If not, he foams at mouth, and by and by
Breaks out to savage madness. Look, he stirs;   55
Do you withdraw yourself a little while,
He will recover straight. When he is gone
I would on great occasion speak with you.

[*Exit Cassio.*]

45 **medicine** i.e. poison. Cf. 2.1.292ff.
work F *workes* is possible.
47 **reproach** disgrace; censure. 'Almost
always in Shakespeare stronger than
our sense, e.g. "black scandal or
foul-faced reproach" (*R3* 3.7.231)'
(Ridley).
What ... lord He calls when he
hears someone approaching.
48 **Othello** He addresses Othello by
name, perhaps because Othello is still
unconscious.
50 **epilepsy** also known as 'the falling
sickness' (*JC* 1.2.254). Here it is *petit
mal*, a milder form of the illness (cf.

43n.), but still a most difficult, exhausting episode for the actor. In
Look About You (1600, acted by the
Admiral's Men) a pursuivant has a
similar fit (F1b): this could have
given Shakespeare the idea to stage a
seizure.
53 **lethargy** morbid drowsiness (here,
coma)
his its
54 **by and by** immediately; or, soon
afterwards
55 **savage** enraged
58 **on great occasion** about an important matter

44–8] *as F; prose Q*   45 work] *Q; workes F*   48 SD] *as F; opp. Cassio 48 Q*   52 No, forbear] *Q;
not in F*   58 SD] *Q2 (after* mocke me? *60); not in QF*

How is it, general? have you not hurt your head?

OTHELLO

Dost thou mock me?

IAGO   I mock you? no, by heaven!   60

Would you would bear your fortune like a man!

OTHELLO

A horned man's a monster, and a beast.

IAGO

There's many a beast then in a populous city,

And many a civil monster.

OTHELLO

Did he confess it?

IAGO   Good sir, be a man,   65

Think every bearded fellow that's but yoked

May draw with you. There's millions now alive

That nightly lie in those unproper beds

Which they dare swear peculiar: your case is better.

O, 'tis the spite of hell, the fiend's arch-mock,   70

---

59 **hurt your head** i.e. in falling. Othello thinks by sprouting horns.

60 **Dost ... me?** so Lyly, *Mother Bombie*, 2.1.24, 'Doest thou mocke me, *Dromio?*'
no For final *-t* variants (*no:not*), see *Texts*, 85.

61 **Would** I wish
fortune bad fortune (but Iago, being Iago, also hints gleefully at 'good fortune'; cf. 'satisfaction', 3.3.404n.)

62 Cf. Dent, C876.2, 'A cuckold is a beast (monster)'; *beast* = horned beast.

64 **civil** civilized, courteous; city-dwelling (from Lat. *civis*, a citizen). Monsters were not usually *civil*: for the same pleasantry, cf. *Tem* 2.2.89, 'a most delicate monster'.

65 **be a man** Cf. 1.3.336: Iago has gained an ascendancy very like his

hold on Roderigo. The phrase helps to *unman* Othello.

66 **bearded fellow** Cassio has a beard (3.3.442). This could mean that Othello is bearded as well.
yoked yoked in marriage; suggesting, yoked like an ox (a horned beast)

67 **draw** pull (like an ox)

68 **unproper** 'not (solely) his own; *proper* often means little more than *own*' (Ridley). Also = improper, not in accordance with decorum. Unique in Shakespeare.

69 **peculiar** restricted to themselves. Cf. 3.3.79n.
your ... better i.e. because you know the truth

70 **spite** envious malice
arch-mock a coinage. Note how the fiend Iago mocks throughout this scene (4.1.2ff., 61, 67–8, 102n.).

---

60 you? no, by heaven] *Q*; you not, by Heauen *F*   61 fortune] *F*; fortunes *Q*   65 confess it] *F*; confesse *Q*   Good] *Qc*, *F*; God *Qu*   68 lie] *F*; lyes *Q*

To lip a wanton in a secure couch
And to suppose her chaste. No, let me know,
And, knowing what I am, I know what she shall be.

OTHELLO

O, thou art wise, 'tis certain.

IAGO

Stand you a while apart,   75
Confine yourself but in a patient list.
Whilst you were here o'erwhelmed with your grief
– A passion most unsuiting such a man –
Cassio came hither. I shifted him away
And laid good 'scuse upon your ecstasy,   80
Bade him anon return and here speak with me,
The which he promised. Do but encave yourself
And mark the fleers, the gibes and notable scorns
That dwell in every region of his face;

71 *To ... couch roughly = to kiss an
unchaste woman in a bed free from
anxiety (transferred epithet). But the
words are more suggestive, esp. *lip*,
which could = kiss obscenely (cf. *WT*
1.2.286); also, because the *wanton*
points to Desdemona.

72–3 a slippery comparison of one who
supposes with one who *knows*, for
'knowing what I am' (viz. an imperfect creature) only leads to another
supposition, 'I know what she shall
be' (i.e. she's bound to be unchaste).
Cf. 1.3.350ff., and *Ham* 4.5.43–4, 'we
know what we are, but know not what
we may be'.

74 'tis certain *Either* it is certain that
Iago is wise, *or* that Desdemona is
unchaste.

75 Stand ... apart A comedy routine: a
victim is tricked into overhearing
what others want him to hear. Cf.
Plautus, *Miles Gloriosus*, 1175ff., *MA*
2.3.40ff., 3.1, 3.3.144ff.

76 i.e. only keep yourself within the

boundary of patience. Cf. *TN* 1.3.8,
'confine yourself within the modest
limits of order'.

77 o'erwhelmed o'erwhelmèd; *ere while,
mad* is one of Q's clearest instances of
misreading: *Texts*, 41–2, 89.

78 unsuiting unique in Shakespeare.
The Q press-corrector probably consulted the manuscript, otherwise he
would not have changed *vnfitting*.

79 I ... away I got him out of the way
(*OED* shift 16, first here).

80 'scuse i.e. explanation (implying that
Othello's fit was somehow shameful)
ecstasy state of unconsciousness
(swoon, trance, etc.)

81 anon soon; or, immediately

82 encave a coinage = conceal. Cf. *Cym*
4.2.138, 'Cave here, hunt here' (= to
lurk, as in a cave).

83 fleers sneers
notable striking, noticeable

84 dwell abide; persist
region part or division of the body
(*OED* 6)

71 couch] *F* (Cowch); Coach *Q*   73 she shall] *QF*; shall *Steevens conj.*   74 wise,] *Q*; wise:
F   77 o'erwhelmed] *F*; ere while, mad *Q*   78 unsuiting] vnsuting *Qc*; vnfitting *Qu*;
resulting *F*   80 'scuse] *Q* (scuse); scuses *F*   81 Bade] *F*; Bid *Q*   return] *F*; retire *Q*   82 Do]
F; *not in Q*   83 fleers] *F*; Ieeres *Q*

For I will make him tell the tale anew   85
Where, how, how oft, how long ago, and when
He hath and is again to cope your wife.
I say, but mark his gesture; marry, patience,
Or I shall say you're all in all in spleen
And nothing of a man.
OTHELLO   Dost thou hear, Iago?   90
I will be found most cunning in my patience
But – dost thou hear? – most bloody.
IAGO   That's not amiss,
But yet keep time in all. Will you withdraw?
                              [*Othello withdraws.*]
Now will I question Cassio of Bianca,
A housewife that by selling her desires   95
Buys herself bread and clothes: it is a creature
That dotes on Cassio – as 'tis the strumpet's plague
To beguile many and be beguiled by one.
He, when he hears of her, cannot refrain
From the excess of laughter. Here he comes.   100

Enter CASSIO.

87 **hath** A teasing pause is effective (cf. 32n.), and helps to explain the change of construction.
cope encounter, come into contact with, i.e. copulate with. A *cope(s)mate* is a paramour (*OED* 3).
88 **gesture** bearing, deportment; expression
89 ¹**all . . . spleen** altogether turned into spleen (the seat of melancholy and sudden or violent passion)
91 Cf. *TC* 5.2.46, the comedy routine of the impatient man swearing patience.
92 **not amiss** quite in keeping with the object in view (*OED* 2). A strangely detached remark.
93 **keep time** Cf. Dent, T308.1, 'Keep time in all'; = maintain control

(Ridley); or, everything in good time.
SD In fact he *hides* (becoming more like Iago, who habitually 'hides').
94 **of** about
95 **housewife** Perhaps we should read hussy (a woman of light character, or prostitute: cf. 1.3.273n.).
97–8 Cf. Dent, D179, 'He that deceives (beguiles) another is oft deceived himself', and 'Wily beguiled' (Tilley, W406). *Plague* = affliction; *beguile* = deceive; charm.
99 **refrain** F *restraine* is possible (*OED* 7 = refrain). Q or F misreads.
100 **Here he comes** Cassio's opportune arrival suggests that everything plays into Iago's hands: see p. 72.

87 hath] *F;* has *Q*   89 you're] *F (y'are);* you are *Q*   93 SD] *Rowe; not in QF*   96 clothes] *Q;* Cloath *F*   99 refrain] *Q;* restraine *F*   100.1] *as F; opp. 98 Q*

As he shall smile, Othello shall go mad.
And his unbookish jealousy must construe
Poor Cassio's smiles, gestures and light behaviour
Quite in the wrong. How do you now, lieutenant?

CASSIO

The worser, that you give me the addition   105
Whose want even kills me.

IAGO

Ply Desdemona well, and you are sure on't.
[*Speaking lower*] Now if this suit lay in Bianca's
        power
How quickly should you speed!

CASSIO   Alas, poor caitiff!

OTHELLO

Look how he laughs already!   110

IAGO

I never knew a woman love man so.

CASSIO

Alas, poor rogue, I think i'faith she loves me.

OTHELLO

Now he denies it faintly, and laughs it out.

IAGO

Do you hear, Cassio?

OTHELLO   Now he importunes him

---

102 **unbookish** a coinage. Cf. 1.1.23:
    Iago is equally scornful about the
    bookish and unbookish!
    *construe interpret. See *Texts*, 83.
103 **light** frivolous
104 **in the wrong** erroneously
105 **addition** title
106 **want** lack
107 **Ply** handle; keep working on
    sure on't i.e. sure to get what you
    want

108 **power** Sisson thinks Iago has
    Bianca's 'marriage to Cassio in mind'
    and reads *dower* (= F). A turned
    letter (*p:d*)?
109 **speed** succeed
    caitiff wretch
112 **rogue** could be a term of
    endearment
113 **faintly** i.e. without expecting to
    carry conviction
    out away

102 construe] *Rowe;* conster *Q;* conserue *F*   103 behaviour] *Q;* behauiours *F*   104 now] *Q; not in F*   108 SD] *Rowe; not in QF*   power] *Q;* dowre *F*   110–57] *all Othello's speeches marked 'Aside', Theobald; not in QF*   111 a] *Q; not in F*   112 i'faith] *Q;* indeed *F*   114–15 him . . . o'er] *as F;* him to tell it on, *Q*

To tell it o'er; go to, well said, well said.   115

IAGO

She gives it out that you shall marry her;
Do you intend it?

CASSIO

Ha, ha, ha!

OTHELLO

Do ye triumph, Roman, do you triumph?

CASSIO   I marry! What, a customer! prithee bear some   120
charity to my wit, do not think it so unwholesome.
Ha, ha, ha!

OTHELLO   So, so, so, so: they laugh that win.

IAGO   Faith, the cry goes that you shall marry her.

CASSIO   Prithee say true!   125

IAGO   I am a very villain else.

OTHELLO   Have you stored me? Well.

CASSIO   This is the monkey's own giving out. She is

---

115 **o'er** i.e. over again
well said = well done (sarcastic). Often said when no words have been spoken (e.g. 5.1.98; *Poetaster*, 3.4.345).
118 **Ha, ha, ha** a signal for the actor to laugh, for as long as he sees fit: cf. 5.1.62n.
119 **triumph** prevail (over an enemy); exult; celebrate a triumph (a ceremonial entry by a victorious general). 'Othello calls him *Roman* ironically. *Triumph*, which was a Roman ceremony, brought Roman into his thoughts' (Johnson).
120 **customer** one who purchases (sexual services) (= Cassio); or, a prostitute (= Bianca) (*OED* 3, 4)
120–1 **bear ... wit** think more kindly of my judgement
121 **unwholesome** unhealthy, defective

123 **they ... win** Cf. Dent, L93, 'He laughs that wins', i.e. they that laugh last laugh best.
124 **cry goes** rumour is current
126 I am a true villain if it's not so. Cf. 2.1.114n.
127 **stored** could mean to provide for the continuance of a stock or breed, or to produce offspring (cf. Heywood, *Golden Age* [1611], H2, 'from your own blood you may store a prince / To do those sacred rights', quoted *OED* 2): i.e. 'Have you begotten children for me?' F's *scoar'd* (= wounded) is less likely.
128 **monkey's** 'Used as a term of playful contempt, chiefly of young people' (*OED* 2b), more usually of boys than girls. Cf. *Mac* 4.2.59, 'God help thee, poor monkey!'; *Tem* 3.2.45.

---

115 ²well said] *F; not in Q*   119 ye] *F;* you *Q*   120–2] *QF line as verse* wit / ha. / *Q ;* beare / it / ha. *F*   120 marry!] *as F;* marry her? *Q*   What ... customer!] *F; not in Q*   prithee] *F;* I prethee *Q*   123 they] *F; not in Q*   win] *F4;* wins *QF*   124 Faith] *Q ;* Why *F*   that you shall] you shall *Q ;* that you *F*   127 Have] *F;* Ha *Q*   stored] *Q* (stor'd)*;* scoar'd *F*   me?] *F;* me well. *Q*   128–30] *prose Q ; F lines* out: / marry her / promise. /

persuaded I will marry her, out of her own love and
flattery, not out of my promise. 130

OTHELLO Iago beckons me: now he begins the story.

CASSIO She was here even now, she haunts me in every
place. I was the other day talking on the sea-bank
with certain Venetians, and thither comes the bauble
and, by this hand, falls me thus about my neck – 135

OTHELLO Crying 'O dear Cassio!' as it were: his gesture
imports it.

CASSIO So hangs and lolls and weeps upon me, so
shakes and pulls me! Ha, ha, ha!

OTHELLO Now he tells how she plucked him to my 140
chamber. O, I see that nose of yours, but not that
dog I shall throw it to.

CASSIO Well, I must leave her company.

IAGO Before me! look where she comes!

Enter BIANCA.

---

130 **flattery** in the sense of 'she flatters
herself that' (Ridley)

131 **beckons** makes a signal to. Could be
spelled *becon* (*OED*); F probably misread *becon(e)s*.

133 **sea-bank** sea coast or shore

134 **bauble** a childish or foolish person
(*OED* 5b, first here): originally a
child's toy or childish foolery

135 **by this hand** probably omitted
from F by Crane (*Texts*, 166)
me ethic dative

137 **imports** implies

138 **lolls** hangs down, dangles

139 **shakes** Q *hales* = hauls, drags

141 **chamber** private room; bedroom
nose Cf. Martial: 'Husband, you
have disfigured the wretched gallant,

and his countenance, deprived of
nose and ears, regrets the loss of its
original form' (2.83; cf. 3.85); also
42 above: 'Noses, ears, and lips.'
Hulme, 135, thinks *nose* suggests
penis.

141–2 **but ... to** Cf. Exodus 22.30,
'neither shall ye eat any flesh that is
torn of beasts in the field, but shall
cast it to a dog'.

143 **company** could mean 'sexual connection', as in Caxton, 'Thamar, that
had company with her husbondes
fader' (*OED* 2)

144 **Before me** perhaps formed on the
analogy of 'before God' (= by God).
So *TN* 2.3.178, 'Before me, she's a
good wench'; *Cor* 1.1.120.

---

131 beckons] *Q ;* becomes *F*   133 the other] *F ;* tother *Q*   134 the] *F ;* this *Q*   135 and ... me]
by this hand she fals *Q ;* and falls me *F*   138–9] *prose Q ; F lines* vpon me: / ha. /   139 shakes] *F ;*
hales *Q*   140–2] *prose F ; Q lines* Chamber, / to. /   141 O] *F ; not in Q*   142 it] *F ;* 't *Q*   144.1]
as F ; opp. 143 Q

CASSIO 'Tis such another fitchew; marry, a perfumed 145
one. What do you mean by this haunting of me?

BIANCA Let the devil and his dam haunt you! What
did you mean by that same handkerchief you gave
me even now? I was a fine fool to take it – I must
take out the work! A likely piece of work, that you 150
should find it in your chamber and know not who
left it there! This is some minx's token, and I must
take out the work? There, give it your hobby-horse;
wheresoever you had it, I'll take out no work on't!

CASSIO How now, my sweet Bianca, how now, how now? 155

OTHELLO By heaven, that should be my handkerchief!

BIANCA If you'll come to supper tonight, you may; if
you will not, come when you are next prepared for. *Exit.*

IAGO After her, after her!

CASSIO Faith, I must, she'll rail in the streets else. 160

IAGO Will you sup there?

CASSIO Faith, I intend so.

IAGO Well, I may chance to see you, for I would very
fain speak with you.

CASSIO Prithee come, will you? 165

IAGO Go to, say no more. *Exit Cassio.*

---

145 **such another** another of the same
sort (*OED* 1c); like all the rest of
them (Ridley)
  fitchew polecat, notoriously mal-
odorous and lecherous. Cf. *OED*
polecat 2: a vile person; prostitute.
145–6 **marry ... one** F's punctuation
could imply 'Do they think that I'll
marry a perfumed fitchew?!'
147 Cf. Dent, D225, 'The devil and his
dam'; *dam* = mother (dame).
149 **even** just
149–50 **I must ... work** Cf. 3.4.180n.
150 **A ... work** i.e. a likely story! A *piece*

of work was a set phrase, as in *Ham*
2.2.303, 'What a piece of work is a
man'.
152 **minx's** Cf. 3.3.478n.
  token pledge, present
153 **hobby-horse** loose woman, prostitute
154 **on't** from it
155 **How now** (meant to soothe or
restrain)
156 **should** i.e. must
158 **when ... for** when next I make
preparations for you, i.e. never
164 **fain** gladly

---

145 SP] *F; not in Q* 145–6 fitchew; marry, . . . one.] ficho; marry a perfum'd one, *Q ;* Fitchew:
marry a perfum'd one? *F* 150 the] *F;* the whole *Q* 151 know not] *F;* not know *Q* 153 your]
F; the *Q* 155] *as Q; F lines Bianca? / now? /* 157 If] *F;* An *Q* if] *F; an Q* 160 Faith] *Q ; not
in F* in . . . streets] *F;* i'the streete *Q* 162 Faith] *Q ;* Yes *F* 166 SD] *Q ; not in F*

OTHELLO   How shall I murder him, Iago?

IAGO   Did you perceive how he laughed at his vice?

OTHELLO   O Iago!

IAGO   And did you see the handkerchief?   170

OTHELLO   Was that mine?

IAGO   Yours, by this hand: and to see how he prizes the
foolish woman your wife! She gave it him, and he
hath given it his whore.

OTHELLO   I would have him nine years a-killing. A fine   175
woman, a fair woman, a sweet woman!

IAGO   Nay, you must forget that.

OTHELLO   Ay, let her rot and perish and be damned
tonight, for she shall not live. No, my heart is turned
to stone: I strike it, and it hurts my hand. O, the   180
world hath not a sweeter creature: she might lie by
an emperor's side and command him tasks.

IAGO   Nay, that's not your way.

OTHELLO   Hang her, I do but say what she is: so
delicate with her needle, an admirable musician. O,   185
she will sing the savageness out of a bear! of so high
and plenteous wit and invention!

IAGO   She's the worse for all this.

167ff. For the first time Iago and Othello
converse in prose.

172–4 **Yours ... whore** Q's omission
comes at the end of a page (K1a), an
error in 'casting off' (*Texts*, 46–7).

172 **prizes** esteems

175 **a-killing** in the killing, i.e. I'd have
him die a very slow death (unique in
Shakespeare)

175–6 **A ... ³woman** Here, and in the
next speeches, with their sudden flip-
over from hate to love, tragedy comes
close to farce: cf. *MV* 3.1.97ff.

179–80 **my ... stone** Dent, H311, 'A
heart of (as hard as a) stone'. Cf. Job
41.15, 'His heart is as hard as a stone,

and as fast as the stithy that the smith
smiteth upon.'

181 **creature** any created being; person

181–2 **she ... tasks** i.e. (if she had been
chaste) her sweetness would have had
an irresistible power over an emperor.
An image inspired by folk tale or romance? Normally the lady commanded tasks *before* marriage.

183 **your way** 'like you' or 'the best
course'

185–6 **O ... bear** like Orpheus?

186 **high** superior

187 **wit and invention** even if taken as
'understanding and imagination', unexpected attributes

---

167 murder] *Q*; murther *F*   172–4] *F*; *not in Q*   175–6] *prose Q*; *F lines* killing: / woman? /
177 that] *F*; *not in Q*   178 Ay] *F (I)*; And *Q*   181 hath] *F*; has *Q*

OTHELLO   O, a thousand, a thousand times: and then
of so gentle a condition.   190
IAGO   Ay, too gentle.
OTHELLO   Nay, that's certain. But yet the pity of it, Iago
– O, Iago, the pity of it, Iago!
IAGO   If you are so fond over her iniquity, give her
patent to offend, for if it touch not you it comes near   195
nobody.
OTHELLO   I will chop her into messes! Cuckold me!
IAGO   O, 'tis foul in her.
OTHELLO   With mine officer!
IAGO   That's fouler.   200
OTHELLO   Get me some poison, Iago, this night. I'll
not expostulate with her, lest her body and beauty
unprovide my mind again. This night, Iago.
IAGO   Do it not with poison, strangle her in her bed –
even the bed she hath contaminated.   205

190 **so ... condition** probably 'so
sweet-natured a disposition', but
could = so well bred in social background. Cf. 2.1.247–8.
191 **gentle** mild; yielding, pliant
192 **the ... it** Cf. *MM* 2.3.42, ''Tis pity
of him' (*of* = in respect of: *OED* pity
3b). Othello appeals as the weaker to
the stronger.
  pity Cf. 1.3 162, ''Twas pitiful,
'twas wondrous pitiful', 169: pity
plays a significant part in their
relationship.
193 **O ... Iago!** Cf. 2.3.260–1, 'My reputation, Iago'.
194–5 If you be so doting as regards her
wickedness, give her a licence to sin
(*OED* over *prep.* 4c: concerning).
195 **patent** licence; a papal licence or
indulgence. Malone compared *E3*
2.1.422 (1596 edn, D1b), 'Why then
giue sinne a pasport to offend'
(meaning a sexual offence, in both
plays).
195–6 **if ... nobody** if it doesn't hurt
you it hurts nobody. See p. 377; Holland's *Livy* (1600): 'In this last speech
he came neere unto the LL. of the
Senat, and touched them to the
quick' (quoted *OED*, near, 12b).
197 **messes** (servings of) meat; we
might say 'chop her into mince-
meat'. The 'Barbarian' has many
European cousins: cf. Plautus, *Trucu-
lentus*, 613, 'I'll take this blade and
here hew thee into gobbets!'
199 **officer** an act of whoredom and
insubordination!
202 **expostulate** set forth my grievances, argue
203 **unprovide** i.e. disarm

189–90] *as Q* ; *F lines* times: / condition? 189 O ... ²thousand] *F;* A thousand thousand *Q* 192–
3] *as Q ; F lines* certaine: / 192 Nay] *F;* I *Q* 193 O, Iago ... Iago!] *F;* the pitty. *Q* 194 are] *F;*
be *Q* 195 touch] *F;* touches *Q* 199 officer!] Officer? *F* 201 night. I'll] *F;* night I'le *Q* 204–
9] *prose Q ; F lines* bed, / contaminated. / good: / very good. / vndertaker: / midnight. /

OTHELLO   Good, good, the justice of it pleases; very good!

IAGO   And for Cassio, let me be his undertaker. You shall hear more by midnight.

OTHELLO   Excellent good. *A trumpet within.* What 210 trumpet is that same?

IAGO   I warrant something from Venice.

Enter LODOVICO, DESDEMONA *and Attendants.*

'Tis Lodovico, this, comes from the duke.
See, your wife's with him.

LODOVICO   God save you, worthy general.   215

OTHELLO   With all my heart, sir.

LODOVICO

The duke and senators of Venice greet you.

[*Gives him a letter.*]

OTHELLO

I kiss the instrument of their pleasures.

[*Opens the letter and reads.*]

DESDEMONA

And what's the news, good cousin Lodovico?

206–7 **Good . . . good** Some repetitions in this scene suggest that Othello's mind is half tranced (see p. 80). Cf. Marston, *Antonio and Mellida* (Revels), 3.2.30, 'Good, very good, very passing, passing good'. There are comic overtones, as in *AYL* 5.1.27, ' "So, so" is good, very good, very excellent good'.

206 **justice of it** Cf. 193, 'the pity *of it*'.

208 **undertaker** one who (1) carries out work for another; (2) takes up a challenge; (3) 'takes on' something. *OED* first records 'one who makes arrangements for funerals' in 1698, but this sense may be glanced at.

212.1 Though not named, Gratiano probably enters here.

213 Iago several times identifies others near at hand for Othello, who ought to know them: see pp. 17–19.

216 **With . . . heart** (I thank you) with all my heart, or, (I wish it) with all my heart. One expects Othello to return the wish. He merely accepts it.

218 **instrument** formal document in which they express their commands (*OED* pleasure 2)

219 **cousin** could = kinsman. Gratiano is Desdemona's uncle (5.2.252): Shakespeare reminds us that she is well connected in Venice.

210 SD] A Trumpet. *Q (opp. 209); not in F*   212–14] *F;* Something from *Venice* sure, tis *Lodouico,* / Come from the Duke, and see your wife is with him. *Q;* 'Tis Lodovico – this comes from the Duke. *Sisson*   212.1] *QF (after 209)*   215 God save] *Q;* Saue *F*   you] *F;* the *Q*   217 and] *Q;* and the *F*   SD] *Rowe; not in QF*   218 SD] *Capell subst.; not in QF*

IAGO

I am very glad to see you, signior. 220
Welcome to Cyprus.

LODOVICO

I thank you. How does Lieutenant Cassio?

IAGO

Lives, sir.

DESDEMONA

Cousin, there's fallen between him and my lord
An unkind breach, but you shall make all well – 225

OTHELLO

Are you sure of that?

DESDEMONA

My lord?

OTHELLO [*Reads.*]

This fail you not to do, as you will –

LODOVICO

He did not call, he's busy in the paper.
Is there division 'twixt my lord and Cassio? 230

DESDEMONA

A most unhappy one: I would do much
T'atone them, for the love I bear to Cassio.

OTHELLO

Fire and brimstone!

DESDEMONA   My lord?

OTHELLO   Are you wise?

220 Iago butts in, as often elsewhere.
223 Cf. Plautus, *Curculio*, 235, '*quid agis?*
   – *Vivo* (How are you? – Living [lit. I
   live])'; *Persa*, 17; also *2H4* 3.2.200.
225 **unkind** unnatural; strange
   breach disagreement, quarrel; a
   breaking of relations (*OED* 5, first
   recorded 1605)
229 **in** in reading
230 **division** disagreement
231 **unhappy** unfortunate
232 **atone** reconcile

love affection, goodwill (Othello
thinks sexual love)
233 **Fire and brimstone** first recorded
by *OED* as ejaculation in *TN* 2.5.50,
but biblical in origin (Genesis 19.24,
Revelation 19.20). *Fire* is disyllabic
here (Abbott, 480). Traditionally associated with hell (*Faerie Queene*,
1.9.49).
wise in your right mind, sane
(*OED* 4)

220–1] *as F; prose Q*   226] (Aside) *Theobald*   228 SD] *Theobald; not in QF*   230 'twixt my] *F;*
betweene thy *Q*   232 T'] *F;* To *Q*

DESDEMONA

What, is he angry?

LODOVICO   Maybe the letter moved him.

For, as I think, they do command him home,   235

Deputing Cassio in his government.

DESDEMONA

By my troth, I am glad on't.

OTHELLO   Indeed!

DESDEMONA   My lord?

OTHELLO

I am glad . . . to see you mad.

DESDEMONA   Why, sweet Othello?

OTHELLO

Devil!   [*Striking her*]

DESDEMONA

I have not deserved this.   240

LODOVICO

My lord, this would not be believed in Venice

Though I should swear I saw't. 'Tis very much;

Make her amends, she weeps.

OTHELLO   O devil, devil!

If that the earth could teem with woman's tears

Each drop she falls would prove a crocodile: 245

236 **Deputing** appointing (not neces-
     sarily as deputy)
     government appointment as gover-
     nor (*OED* 3b, first in 1617); tenure of
     office (*OED* 4b, first in 1603)
237 **on't** of it
     Indeed as at 3.3.101, but with differ-
     ent implications
238 He echoes or mimics Desdemona's
     'I am glad', i.e. to see you so foolish
     (mad) (as to admit your love for
     Cassio). But *mad* may be corrupt.
     Why, sweet Othello? This could be
     an exclamation of surprise or remon-
     strance, rather than a question. Cf.
     AYL 4.3.157, 'Why, how now,

     Ganymed, sweet Ganymed'.
239 *SD Some actors strike her with the
     letter (see p. 92), but 272 suggests
     that he strikes her with his hand.
     Calderwood thinks that the letter
     'arouses his passion' (p. 88), but
     Desdemona's innocent remarks are
     surely the cause.
241–2 Cf. Dent, E264.1, 'To believe
     one's (own) eyes'.
242 **'Tis very much** it goes too far
244 **teem** give birth, bring forth (as a
     result of women's tears)
245 **falls** lets fall. Cf. Dent, C831, 'Croc-
     odile tears'.
     prove turn out to be

234 the letter] *Q*; thLetter *F*   237 By . . . troth] *Q*; Trust me *F*   Indeed!] Indeed. *Q*; Indeed?
F   238 glad . . .] *this edn*; glad *QF*   Why] *F*; How *Q*   239 SD] *Theobald*; *not in QF*   244
woman's] *F*; womens *Q*

Out of my sight!

DESDEMONA   I will not stay to offend you.

LODOVICO

Truly, an obedient lady.

I do beseech your lordship, call her back.

OTHELLO

Mistress!

DESDEMONA

My lord?   250

OTHELLO

What would you with her, sir?

LODOVICO   Who, I, my lord?

OTHELLO

Ay, you did wish that I would make her turn.

Sir, she can turn, and turn, and yet go on

And turn again. And she can weep, sir, weep.

And she's obedient: as you say, obedient,   255

Very obedient. – Proceed you in your tears. –

Concerning this, sir – O well-painted passion! –

I am commanded home. – Get you away.

I'll send for you anon. – Sir, I obey the mandate

And will return to Venice. – Hence, avaunt! –   260

                              [*Exit Desdemona.*]

---

249 **Mistress** not the normal way of addressing one's wife. Cf. 1.3.178, 5.2.181.

250 **My lord?** her fourth 'My lord?' since 227, part of the crescendo effect here

252–3 **turn turn** back; be fickle (turn = change); also implying 'the best turn i'th' bed' (*AC* 2.5.59). A. Shickman compared 'turning pictures', which could show different images of a person at the same time (weeping, a devil, etc.) (*N&Q*, 223 [1978], 145–6).

255 **obedient** yielding to desires or

wishes; compliant (*OED* 3): he means sexually compliant.

256 **Proceed ... tears** This could be a question (Warner, in Malone, 1821).

257 **this** i.e. the letter from Venice
well-painted well-pretended

258 **home** might = Venice or Mauretania (4.2.226), but 260 proves that he understands it as Venice. Q *here* looks like misreading but is possible (giving an unfinished sentence).

259 **mandate** command

260 **avaunt** (usually expresses loathing or horror) away! be off!

247 an] *Q; not in F*   258 home] *F;* here *Q*   260 SD] *Rowe; not in QF*

Cassio shall have my place. And, sir, tonight
I do entreat that we may sup together.
You are welcome, sir, to Cyprus. Goats and monkeys! *Exit.*

LODOVICO

Is this the noble Moor whom our full senate
Call all in all sufficient? This the nature   265
Whom passion could not shake? whose solid virtue
The shot of accident nor dart of chance
Could neither graze nor pierce?

IAGO   He is much changed.

LODOVICO

Are his wits safe? Is he not light of brain?

IAGO

He's that he is: I may not breathe my censure   270
What he might be; if what he might, he is not,
I would to heaven he were!

LODOVICO   What! strike his wife!

IAGO

Faith, that was not so well; yet would I knew

---

261 **Cassio ... place** This may be
shouted at Desdemona as or after she
leaves; *place* = his place as commander; perhaps, his place as lover
(cf. *KL* 5.1.10–11, 'have you never
found my brother's way / To the forfended place?').
263 **Goats and monkeys** Cf. 'as prime
as goats, as hot as monkeys' (3.3.406–
7n.). 'These words, we may suppose,
still ring in the ears of Othello'
(Malone).
264 **full** complete
265 **sufficient** competent, capable
   *This the nature Q *noble* and F *Is*
look like unconscious repetitions.
266 **shake** upset. (Has Othello been
shaking with passion? Cf. 39ff.,
5.2.44.)
   solid substantial (*OED* 13, first in
1601)
   virtue (moral) excellence; manliness

267 (neither) accidental shot nor a
chance spear (thrust), i.e. no unforeseen misfortune
269 **safe** in sound health
270–2 Cf. 2.3.117–24, where Iago also
draws attention to a change (in
Cassio) that he has brought about.
270 **breathe** whisper
   censure opinion; criticism
271–2 'Perhaps the most cryptic of all
Iago's similar remarks' (Ridley).
Might seems to change its meaning:
first, Othello might be at fault (therefore to be censured); second, he
might be unchanged (hence 'would to
heaven he were'). Or, 'if he isn't of
unsound mind, then it might be
better to wish he were in fact insane,
since only that could excuse his wild
behaviour' (Bevington).
273 **that ... well** Cf. 23, 'That's not so
good now.'

263] *as Q; F lines* Cyprus. / Monkeys. / SD] *Qc, F; not in Qu*   265 This the nature] *as Pope;*
This the noble nature *Q ;* Is this the Nature *F*   270 is:] *F; is, Q*   censure] *(see Furness);* censure,
Q ; censure. *F*   271 be: if what] *F;* be, if as *Q*

That stroke would prove the worst.

LODOVICO   Is it his use?
   Or did the letters work upon his blood   275
   And new-create this fault?

IAGO   Alas, alas!
   It is not honesty in me to speak
   What I have seen and known. You shall observe him,
   And his own courses will denote him so
   That I may save my speech. Do but go after   280
   And mark how he continues.

LODOVICO
   I am sorry that I am deceived in him.   *Exeunt.*

[4.2]   *Enter* OTHELLO *and* EMILIA.

OTHELLO
   You have seen nothing, then?

EMILIA
   Nor ever heard, nor ever did suspect.

OTHELLO
   Yes, you have seen Cassio and . . . she together.

EMILIA
   But then I saw no harm, and then I heard
   Each syllable that breath made up between them.   5

OTHELLO
   What, did they never whisper?

---

274 **stroke** blow; (?)masterstroke (first recorded in later seventeenth century)
   use custom
275 **blood** passion
279 **courses** habitual actions
   denote be the outward visible mark of (*OED* 3), reveal
282 **I am . . . I am** read 'I'm . . . I am'; or 'I am sorry that I'm'
   deceived mistaken
4.2 Location: this scene starts indoors (cf. 28), and in some productions in Desdemona's bedroom. Later Roderigo wanders in (174n.), and it

seems to be outdoors: one of the advantages of unlocalized staging.
1–11 Note the abrupt opening. And the tug between prose and verse rhythms, coming to rest in 'That's strange'.
2 **suspect** Othello may interrupt before she can finish.
3 ***seen . . . she** While *she* was sometimes used as object, I assume that Othello hesitates to use Desdemona's name. Cf. *AC* 3.13.98 (repunctuated), 'So saucy with the hand of – she here, what's her name'.

276 this] *Q;* his *F*   4.2.1 then?] *F;* then. *Q*   3 you] *F;* and you *Q*   and . . . she] *this edn;* and she *QF*   5 them] *F;* 'em *Q*

EMILIA   Never, my lord.

OTHELLO

Nor send you out o'th' way?

EMILIA

Never.

OTHELLO

To fetch her fan, her gloves, her mask, nor nothing?

EMILIA

Never, my lord.   10

OTHELLO

That's strange.

EMILIA

I durst, my lord, to wager she is honest,
Lay down my soul at stake: if you think other
Remove your thought, it doth abuse your bosom.
If any wretch have put this in your head   15
Let heaven requite it with the serpent's curse,
For if she be not honest, chaste and true
There's no man happy: the purest of their wives
Is foul as slander.

OTHELLO   Bid her come hither; go.   *Exit Emilia.*
She says enough; yet she's a simple bawd   20
That cannot say as much. This is a subtle whore,
A closet, lock and key, of villainous secrets;

---

9 **mask** Venetian ladies wore masks during the Carnival.

12 **honest** chaste

13 **at stake** at hazard (after *wager*); at the stake (like a martyr dying for his faith)

14 **abuse** deceive; wrong
bosom breast (considered as the seat of secret thoughts and feelings: *OED* 6a). Cf. 3.1.57.

15 She contradicts her earlier view that jealousy is self-begotten (3.4.159–62). This prepares for 132ff.

16 **serpent's curse** Cf. Genesis 3.14,

where God curses the serpent.

20 **enough** elliptical: enough to sound plausible
simple naive, artless, feeble
bawd procuress

21 **This** seems to refer to Emilia, but *kneel and pray* to Desdemona

22 **closet** private room; safe, cabinet (as in *Mac* 5.1.6)
lock and key with lock and key. But cf. *Homilies*, 385, 'this article . . . is even the very lock and key of all our Christian religion'.

---

7 o'th'] *F;* o'the *Q*   9 gloves, her mask] *F;* mask, her gloues *Q*   15 have] *F;* ha *Q*   16 heaven] *F;* heauens *Q;* requite] *Q;* requit *F*   18 their wives] *F;* her Sex *Q*   19 SD] *F; opp.* slander *Q*   21 subtle] *Q;* subtile *F*   22 closet, . . . key,] *Q;* Closset Locke and Key *F;* closset-lock and key *Rowe*

And yet she'll kneel and pray, I have seen her do't.

Enter DESDEMONA *and* EMILIA.

DESDEMONA
  My lord, what is your will?
OTHELLO   Pray, chuck, come hither.
DESDEMONA
  What is your pleasure?
OTHELLO   Let me see your eyes.   25
  Look in my face.
DESDEMONA   What horrible fancy's this?
OTHELLO [*to Emilia*]
  Some of your function, mistress,
  Leave procreants alone and shut the door;
  Cough, or cry hem, if anybody come.   29
  Your mystery, your mystery: nay, dispatch!   *Exit Emilia.*
DESDEMONA
  Upon my knees, what doth your speech import?
  I understand a fury in your words
  But not the words.
OTHELLO
  Why, what art thou?
DESDEMONA
  Your wife, my lord: your true and loyal wife.   35
OTHELLO
  Come, swear it, damn thyself,

---

23 **she'll** (special emphasis: he avoids naming Desdemona as at 3, but may mean Emilia here)
24 **chuck** Cf. 3.4.49.
25 **pleasure** wish, will
27 **function** the action proper to a person who is the holder of an office. He treats Emilia as if she has a function in a brothel: 'behave as a bawd should, leave us alone'.
28 **procreants** procreators (usually an adjective, as in *Mac* 1.6.8)
29 **cry hem** give a warning cough
30 **mystery** trade; here, facetiously, your trade as bawd
   dispatch hurry
31 **Upon my knees** Kneeling in submission was not unusual.

23 have] *F;* ha *Q* 24 Pray] *Q;* Pray you *F* 27 SD] *Hanmer; not in QF* 30 nay] *Q;* May *F* 31 knees] *Q;* knee *F* doth] *F;* does *Q* 33 But . . . words] *Q; not in F* 36–9 Come . . . honest!] *as Q; prose F*

Lest, being like one of heaven, the devils themselves
Should fear to seize thee: therefore be double-
    damned,
Swear thou art honest!

DESDEMONA   Heaven doth truly know it.

OTHELLO
Heaven truly knows that thou art false as hell.   40

DESDEMONA
To whom, my lord? with whom? how am I false?

OTHELLO
Ah, Desdemon, away, away, away!

DESDEMONA
Alas the heavy day, why do you weep?
Am I the motive of these tears, my lord?
If haply you my father do suspect   45
An instrument of this your calling back,
Lay not your blame on me: if you have lost him
Why, I have lost him too.

OTHELLO   Had it pleased heaven
To try me with affliction, had they rained
All kinds of sores and shames on my bare head,   50

37–8 **Lest ... thee** Devils may only carry off to hell those who spiritually belong to them. *Lest* = for fear that.

38 **double-damned** (1) for adultery, (2) for perjury

40 **false as hell** Cf. Dent, H398, 'As false as hell' (not recorded before Shakespeare).

42 **away** *Either* she clings to him and he pushes her away, *or* he wants to get away, *or* he means 'let's get away from this pointless talk': cf. *TC* 5.3.88, *KL* 1.4.89–91, *Cor* 1.1.12.

43 **heavy** sorrowful. Cf. 3.4.158.

44 **motive** cause

45 **haply** by chance

46 **instrument** usually 'a person made use of by another person for the accomplishment of a purpose' (*OED* 1b); here 'as instrumental in'
calling back recall (to Venice)

47 **lost him** lost him as a friend

48–54 Referring to the *afflictions* of Job: God *rained* these (sores, poverty, etc.) upon him: Job 2.7, 20.23.

48–9 **heaven ... they** Should we read *he* for *they* (cf. *Texts*, 83), *God* for *heaven*?

49 **rained** Note the 'water' imagery: *rained, Steeped, drop, fountain, current, dries up, cistern*.

41] *as Q; F lines* Lord? /false? /   42 Ah, Desdemon] *F;* O *Desdemona Q*   44 motive ... these] *F;* occasion ... those *Q*   45 haply] *Q;* happely *F*   47, 48 lost] *F;* left *Q*   48 Why] *Q; not in F*   49 they rained] *F;* he ram'd *Q*   50 kinds] *Q;* kind *F*   bare head] *Q;* bare-head *F*

Steeped me in poverty to the very lips,
Given to captivity me and my utmost hopes,
I should have found in some place of my soul
A drop of patience; but, alas, to make me
The fixed figure for the time of scorn   55
To point his slow and moving finger at!
Yet could I bear that too, well, very well:
But there where I have garnered up my heart,
Where either I must live or bear no life,
The fountain from the which my current runs   60
Or else dries up – to be discarded thence!
Or keep it as a cistern for foul toads
To knot and gender in! Turn thy complexion there,

51 perhaps alluding to Tantalus, who was punished in hell with intense thirst and placed in water up to the chin, but unable to drink

52 **utmost** lit. 'farthest from the centre'; greatest; latest. Perhaps referring to his *utmost* descendants.

55 Perhaps we should read 'The fixed figure, for the time, of scorn', i.e. the fixed target of scorn for the whole age (*OED* time 4) to point its (his) slow and (relentlessly) moving finger at. Or does 'the time of scorn' merely = the scornful time?
  fixed fixèd
  figure Cf. Hebrews 10.33, 'ye were made a gazing stock both by reproaches and afflictions'.

56 Cf. Dent, D321, 'To move as does the dial hand, which is not seen to move'. Perhaps referring to 'the finger of God' (Exodus 8.19 and Luke 11.20). 'The finger of the scornful world is slowly raised to the position of pointing; and then . . . it becomes *unmoving*' (Kittredge, defending Q). No: Othello sees himself as unmoving (the 'fixed figure'), so Q seems unlikely here. *Finger* (if F is correct) may be a collective noun.

*For Q *oh, oh*, cf. 5.1.62n.

58ff. The sequence *there where, where, from the which, thence, there, here*, 'helps the passage to cohere' (Elliott, 180).
  garnered up stored (the products of the earth) as in a garner. Perhaps *heart* = all my emotions, or hopes.

60 See LN.

62 **cistern** an artificial reservoir for water; a pond (*OED* 3, first in *AC* 2.5.94–5, 'So half my Egypt were submerged and made / A cestern for scaled snakes').
  toads Cf. 3.3.274n.

63 **knot . . . gender** i.e. copulate. A 'Marstonian' image: cf. *Antonio's Revenge* (1602), 'Clipping the strumpet with luxurious twines . . . clinged in sensuality' (Revels, 1.4.18, 31); also *TC* 2.3.158–9, 'I do hate a proud man, as I do the engend'ring of toads.'
  complexion countenance, face (*OED* 4c, only this instance cited). The gloss 'Grow pale when that happens' (Sanders) is unlikely: after *there*, 58, *Turn* must mean 'switch', not 'change colour'. A corrupt line?

52 utmost] *F; not in Q*   53 place] *F;* part *Q*   55 The] *F;* A *Q*   time] *QF;* hand *Rowe*   56 and moving] *F;* vnmouing *Q*   finger at] *F;* fingers at – oh, oh *Q*

Patience, thou young and rose-lipped cherubin,
Ay, here look, grim as hell!   65

DESDEMONA

I hope my noble lord esteems me honest.

OTHELLO

O, ay, as summer flies are in the shambles,
That quicken even with blowing. O thou weed
Who art so lovely fair and smell'st so sweet
That the sense aches at thee, would thou hadst ne'er
    been born!   70

DESDEMONA

Alas, what ignorant sin have I committed?

OTHELLO

Was this fair paper, this most goodly book
Made to write 'whore' upon? What committed!

---

64 **Patience** 'Even Patience, that rose-
lipped cherub, will look grim and pale
at this spectacle' (Bevington). Cf. a
near-contemporary personification,
'She sate like Patience on a monument,
/ Smiling at grief' (*TN* 2.4.114–15).
   rose-lipped a coinage (with sexual
overtones?)
   cherubin survived in popular usage
as a singular to the eighteenth century (*OED*)
65 ***here look,** First he speaks obliquely
of Desdemona (58–64), now he turns
on her: it is not some remote place he
means, it is *here*, it is Desdemona!
The difference between *here, look* and
here look, is not huge. Both are possible, as is *there* (for *here*): *Texts*, 90.
   grim unrelenting; cruel, savage
66 **honest** chaste, virtuous
67 **shambles** slaughter-house; meat
market
68 **quicken** receive life, are inseminated,
i.e. with the blowing of the wind
68–9 Weeds are neither lovely nor sweet-
smelling: he means, 'thou weed, pre-

tending to be a beautiful flower'. But
weed could = any herb or small plant
(*OED* 2: 'chiefly poetical'). He perhaps savours the sweet smell, anticipating 5.2.15ff. (see p. 21).
70 a regular verse line if we read 'would
thou'dst ne'er been born!' (*Texts*,
119)
   aches 'the keenness and intensity of
the pleasure becomes even painful'
(Kittredge)
71 **ignorant** unknowing (transferred
epithet: she, not the sin, is ignorant);
or, unknown (*OED* 4). Cf. Middleton,
The Witch (MSR 752), 'What secreat
syn haue I committed'.
72 For the loved one as a book, cf. *RJ*
1.3.87, 'This precious book of love,
this unbound lover', *KJ* 2.1.485.
73 **committed** 'Othello's furious iteration of Desdemona's unhappily
chosen word depends on its Elizabethan use absolutely as = "commit
adultery"; "commit not with man's
sworn spouse" (*KL* 3.4.81)' (Ridley).
Cf. *OED* 6c.

---

64 thou] *F;* thy *Q*   65 here look,] *this edn;* here looke *QF;* there look *Theobald;* there, look *Capell*
67 as] *Q, Fc;* as a *Fu*   summer] *F (Sommer);* summers *Q*   68–70] O . . . faire? / at thee, / borne.
Q; weed: / sweete, / at thee, / borne. *F*   68–9 thou weed / Who] *F;* thou blacke weede, why
Q   69 and] *F;* Thou *Q*   70 thou hadst] *QF;* thou'dst *F4*   ne'er] *Q;* neuer *F*   73 upon] *F;* on *Q*

Committed? O thou public commoner!
I should make very forges of my cheeks   75
That would to cinders burn up modesty
Did I but speak thy deeds. What committed!
Heaven stops the nose at it, and the moon winks,
The bawdy wind that kisses all it meets
Is hushed within the hollow mine of earth   80
And will not hear't. What committed!
Impudent strumpet!

DESDEMONA   By heaven, you do me wrong.

OTHELLO
Are not you a strumpet?

DESDEMONA
No, as I am a Christian.
If to preserve this vessel for my lord   85
From any hated foul unlawful touch
Be not to be a strumpet, I am none.

OTHELLO
What, not a whore?

DESDEMONA   No, as I shall be saved.

74 **public commoner** common whore
75 **forges** A forge consisted of an open hearth with bellows attached, used for heating iron: here the *cheeks* are the bellows, her *modesty* is tough as iron.
78 **Heaven ... it** Cf. Ezechiel 39.11, 'those that travel thereby, shall stop their noses'.
   moon (symbol of chastity)
   winks shuts its eye(s)
79 Cf. Dent, A88, 'As free as the air (wind)'; John 3.8, 'The wind bloweth where it listeth'; *MV* 2.6.16, 'the strumpet wind'.
80 **mine** cave. In Virgil (*Aeneid*, 1.52), Aeolus, controller of the winds, keeps the winds in a vast cavern. Cf. *2H6* 3.2.89, 'he that loos'd them [winds] forth their brazen caves'.
81 **will not** refuses to

82 **Impudent** (shockingly) shameless: stronger than now
85 **vessel** body. Cf. 1 Thessalonians 4.3ff., 'abstain from fornication: That every one of you should know how to possess his vessel in holiness and honour'; 1 Peter 3.7, let the husband give honour to his wife, 'as unto the weaker vessel'. Cf. jokes in other plays about woman as 'the weaker vessel' (*AYL* 2.4.6), 'the emptier vessel' (*2H4* 2.4.60).
86 **hated** F *other* might imply that Othello's touch is foul and unlawful.
   touch Cf. Plautus, *Amphitruo*, 831ff. (a wife to her suspicious husband), 'I swear ... no mortal man, save you only, has taken me to him as a wife' (*corpus corpore contigit* = has touched my body with his).

74–7 Committed? ... committed!] *F; not in Q*   80 hollow] *F;* hallow *Q*   81 hear't] *QF;* hear it *Steevens*   82 Impudent strumpet] *Q ; not in F*   86 hated] *Q ;* other *F*

OTHELLO

   Is't possible?

DESDEMONA

   O heaven, forgive us!

OTHELLO   I cry you mercy then,   90

   I took you for that cunning whore of Venice

   That married with Othello. You! Mistress!

Enter EMILIA.

   That have the office opposite to Saint Peter

   And keep the gates of hell – you, you, ay you!

   We have done our course, there's money for your

      pains,   95

   I pray you turn the key and keep our counsel.   *Exit*.

EMILIA

   Alas, what does this gentleman conceive?

   How do you, madam? how do you, my good lady?

DESDEMONA

   Faith, half asleep.

EMILIA

   Good madam, what's the matter with my lord?   100

---

89 **Is't possible?** Note how this question echoes through the play: 2.3.283, 3.3.361, 3.4.70, 4.1.42.

90 **O ... us** With Q, compare *R2* 5.5.90, 'Forgiveness, horse!' But as Desdemona has done no wrong, *forgive us* (i.e. for misunderstanding and hurting each other?) seems more appropriate. Perhaps she now collapses, and Othello rants as she lies insensible, coming out of a state of shock at 99 (hence Emilia's concern). This would then be her equivalent to Othello's fit.

90–1 **I ... for** 'I beg your pardon, I mistook you for' (sarcastic). Cf. *KL*

3.6.52, 'Cry you mercy, I took you for a join-stool' (the same pretence of misunderstanding).

93–4 Cf. Matthew 16.18–19, 'the gates of hell shall not prevail . . . I will give unto thee the keys of the kingdom of heaven' (Noble, 276).

95 **course** the rush together of two combatants, bout, i.e. sexual encounter

96 **keep our counsel** i.e. don't give us away

97 **this gentleman** Cf. 3.4.100, 'this man'.

   conceive imagine

99 **asleep** stunned, numb (*OED* 4)

---

90 forgive us] *F;* forgiuenesse *Q*   then] *F; not in Q*   92.1] *as F; opp.* saued *88 Q*   94 keep] *Rowe;* keepes *QF*   gates] *Q;* gate *F*   of] *F;* in *Q*   ¹you . . . ³you] *F;* I, you, you, you *Q*   95 have] *F;* ha *Q*   100] *as Q; F lines* Madam, / Lord? /

DESDEMONA
  With whom?

EMILIA
  Why, with my lord, madam.

DESDEMONA
  Who is thy lord?

EMILIA   He that is yours, sweet lady.

DESDEMONA
  I have none. Do not talk to me, Emilia;
  I cannot weep, nor answers have I none   105
  But what should go by water. Prithee, tonight
  Lay on my bed my wedding sheets; remember,
  And call thy husband hither.

EMILIA   Here's a change indeed!

                                                    Exit.

DESDEMONA
  'Tis meet I should be used so, very meet.
  How have I been behaved that he might stick   110
  The small'st opinion on my greatest misuse?

                Enter IAGO *and* EMILIA.

IAGO
  What is your pleasure, madam? How is't with you?

DESDEMONA
  I cannot tell. Those that do teach young babes

---

101 *whom For omitted *m*, see *Texts*, 89.
106 go by water be conveyed by tears. There was much traffic 'by water' on the River Thames.
107 wedding sheets to remind Othello of their former love (but, according to 'short time', their wedding sheets were used the previous night: see pp. 68ff.). Also ominous, as wives were sometimes buried in their wedding sheets.

109 meet fitting
    used treated
110–11 i.e. 'how have I misbehaved myself that he thinks it right to attach the smallest (adverse) judgement to my greatest fault?' Walker paraphrased F, 'how enormous my smallest fault must have been that the least significance could be attached to it'.
112 How . . . you? so *Ham* 3.4.116

---

101 whom] *F2*; who *QF*   103] *F*; *not in Q*   104 have] *F*; ha *Q*   105 answers] *F*; answer *Q*   107 ²my] *F*; our *Q*   108 Here's] *F*; Here is *Q*   109 ²meet] *F*; well *Q*   111 small'st] *F*; smallest *Q*   greatest] *Q*; least *F*   misuse] *F*; abuse *Q*   112] *as QF; Q lines* Madam, / you? /

Do it with gentle means and easy tasks.
He might have chid me so, for, in good faith,   115
I am a child to chiding.

IAGO   What is the matter, lady?

EMILIA

Alas, Iago, my lord hath so bewhored her,
Thrown such despite and heavy terms upon her
That true hearts cannot bear it.

DESDEMONA

Am I that name, Iago?

IAGO   What name, fair lady?   120

DESDEMONA

Such as she said my lord did say I was.

EMILIA

He called her whore. A beggar in his drink
Could not have laid such terms upon his callat.

IAGO

Why did he so?

DESDEMONA

I do not know; I am sure I am none such.   125

IAGO

Do not weep, do not weep: alas the day!

EMILIA

Hath she forsook so many noble matches,
Her father, and her country, and her friends,

---

114 **tasks** perhaps = reproofs, from *task*
(*OED vb* 5) = chide, censure. Cf. *KL*
1.4.343, 'much more at task for want
of wisedome, / Then prai'sd for
harmefull mildnesse' (F).

117 **bewhored** i.e. berated her as if she
were a whore; a coinage, from the
verb 'to whore' (as in *Ham* 5.2.64,
'whor'd my mother'), to make a
whore of, with prefix *be-* (=
thoroughly)

118 **despite** outrage; anger; abuse
heavy angry; violent; distressing
terms words

122 **whore** She feels Desdemona's pain,
yet adds to it by repeating the word.
in ... drink when drinking or drunk

123 **laid ... upon** applied to
callat slut

127 **forsook** declined, given up
matches marriages; husbands

---

115 have] *F;* ha *Q*   116 to] *F;* at *Q*   119 That ... bear it] *Fc (*heart *Fu);* As true hearts cannot
beare *Q*   121 said] *F;* sayes *Q*   127–8] *punctuated as Q; F punctuates* Matches? ... Father? ...
Country? ... Friends?   127 Hath] *F;* Has *Q*   128 ²and] *F;* all *Q*

To be called whore? would it not make one weep?

DESDEMONA

It is my wretched fortune.

IAGO   Beshrew him for't,   130

How comes this trick upon him?

DESDEMONA   Nay, heaven doth know.

EMILIA

I will be hanged if some eternal villain
Some busy and insinuating rogue,
Some cogging, cozening slave, to get some office,
Have not devised this slander, I'll be hanged else!   135

IAGO

Fie, there is no such man, it is impossible.

DESDEMONA

If any such there be, heaven pardon him.

EMILIA

A halter pardon him, and hell gnaw his bones!
Why should he call her whore? who keeps her
    company?
What place, what time, what form, what likelihood?   140
The Moor's abused by some most villainous knave,

130 **Beshrew** evil befall (a refined oath)
131 **trick** a freakish or stupid act
   heaven doth know (only) heaven
   knows
132 **I will** let me
   eternal 'Used to express extreme
   abhorrence' (*OED* 7, citing *JC*
   1.2.159–60, 'There was a Brutus once
   that would have brooked / Th'eternal devil to keep his state in Rome');
   or, used as an intensive (Hart). Cf.
   15–16. An *eternal villain* almost =
   a devil.
133 **busy** meddlesome
   insinuating wriggling into favour,
   subtly penetrating (as in *1H6* 2.4.35,
   'base insinuating flattery')
134 some cheating, deceiving scoundrel,

to obtain some position. Emilia
senses that someone like Iago is responsible, and may suspect him: cf.
147–9 and pp. 44–6.
138 **A halter** the hangman's noose. Cf.
   T. Harman, *Groundworke of Conny-
   catching* (?1592), C1b, 'a halter
   blesse him for mee'.
   hell ... bones Cf. Middleton, *Your
   Five Gallants* (?1608), D4a, 'Hel
   gnawe these dice'.
140 **form** manner, way. Presumably
   Shakespeare knew that his 'short
   time' allowed no *time* or *likelihood* for
   adultery (see p. 68 ff.), and trusted his
   audience not to notice.
141 **abused** deceived

130 for't] *F;* for it *Q;* 135 I'll] *Q;* I will *F*   138–40] *as Q; F lines* him: / bones. / Whore? /
companie? / Time? / liklyhood? /   141 most villainous] *F;* outragious *Q*

Some base notorious knave, some scurvy fellow.
O heaven, that such companions thou'dst unfold
And put in every honest hand a whip
To lash the rascals naked through the world   145
Even from the east to th' west.

IAGO   Speak within doors.

EMILIA

O fie upon them! some such squire he was
That turned your wit the seamy side without
And made you to suspect me with the Moor.

IAGO

You are a fool, go to.

DESDEMONA   O God, Iago,   150
What shall I do to win my lord again?
Good friend, go to him, for, by this light of heaven,
I know not how I lost him. Here I kneel:
If e'er my will did trespass 'gainst his love
Either in discourse of thought or actual deed,   155

---

142 **notorious** gross (Johnson: but *OED* 6 first records in 1666)
  scurvy contemptible, worthless
143 **companions** fellows (contemptuous)
  unfold expose
145 Cf. 4.3.37–8, her other geographical fantasy: the guilty have to travel huge distances in some discomfort.
  lash Sexual and minor offenders were lashed in public. Cf. *KL* 4.6.160–1, 'Thou rascal beadle, hold thy bloody hand! / Why dost thou lash that whore?'
146 Cf. Dent, E43.1, 'as far as (from) the east from (to) the west'.
  within doors less loudly (*OED* door 5: speak so as not to be heard outside the door). Or perhaps 'keep your thoughts to yourself'.

147 **squire** used contemptuously (*OED* 1d)
148 **the ... without** inside out. The *seamy side* of a garment = the worst or roughest side. Cf. 2.3.49, 1.3.385–7, 2.1.289ff.
150 **go to** Cf. 194n.
  ***God** F *Alas* looks like expurgated profanity: cf. 2.3.147, 5.2.116, where F *alas* is clearly expurgated. Q *Good* could be an error for *God* (cf. 4.1.65 t.n.; *good* was not normally capitalized). Cf. *Ham* 5.2.344, 'O *god* Horatio, what a wounded name' (Q2; *good* F).
151 **win** regain the affection of
154 **trespass** sin (noun or verb)
155 **discourse** process. Noble (34–5) notes that here Q2 has independent support from the Liturgy: 'sins (committed) by thought, word, and deed' (taking discourse = word).

143 heaven] *Q ;* Heauens *F* thou'dst] thoudst *Q ;* thou'd'st *F*   145 rascals] *F;* rascall *Q*   146 to th'] *F;* to the *Q* doors] *Q ;* doore *F*   147 them] *F;* him *Q*   150 O God] *this edn;* O Good *Q ;* Alas *F*   153–66 Here . . . me.] *F; not in Q*   155 of] *F;* or *Q2*

Or that mine eyes, mine ears or any sense
Delighted them in any other form,
Or that I do not yet, and ever did,
And ever will – though he do shake me off
To beggarly divorcement – love him dearly,   160
Comfort forswear me! Unkindness may do much,
And his unkindness may defeat my life
But never taint my love. I cannot say whore:
It does abhor me now I speak the word;
To do the act that might the addition earn   165
Not the world's mass of vanity could make me.

IAGO

I pray you, be content, 'tis but his humour;
The business of the state does him offence
And he does chide with you.

DESDEMONA

If 'twere no other –

IAGO   'Tis but so, I warrant.   170

[*Trumpets.*]

Hark how these instruments summon to supper:
The messengers of Venice stay the meat,

156 **that if** (= 158)
157 **form** (human) body; person
158 **Or ... yet** or if I do not still
159 **shake me off** Cf. 3.3.266, 'I'd whistle her off'.
161 **Comfort** may relief or aid (in want or distress)
   forswear abandon
   Unkindness absence of affection; unnatural conduct; hostility
162 **defeat** destroy
163 **taint** corrupt
164 **It ... me** I feel abhorrence. A quibble, as in 'Abhorson' (*MM* 4.2.19), though *abhor* comes from Lat. *abhorreo* and *whore* from OE. *hore*. Cf. *Homilies*, 109 ('against Whoredom'), 'whoredom ... ought to be abhorred'.
165 **addition** title

166 **mass** greater part (*OED* 6)
   vanity vain or worthless things (treasure? fine clothes?). Cf. Ecclesiastes 1.2, 'Vanity of vanities ... all is vanity.'
167 **be content** don't worry
   humour temporary state of mind (*OED* 5)
168 **does him offence** displeases him, gives him pain
169 **And** and therefore
   chide quarrel (*OED* 2b)
170–1 Q has *you* in 170 and 171, both omitted by F. Perhaps *you* was a later addition for 170 (where *warrant* could be a monosyllable), marked unclearly, and so wrongly inserted in 171.
172 **stay** stay for, await
   meat food

157 them in] *Q2*; them: or *F*   169] *Q; not in F*   170 'Tis] Tis *Q*; It is *F*   warrant] *F;* warrant you *Q*   SD] *Rowe (after 171); not in QF*   171 summon] *F;* summon you *Q*   172 The ... meat] *as F (staies the meate); And the great Messengers of Venice stay Q*

Go in, and weep not; all things shall be well.

Exeunt Desdemona and Emilia.

Enter RODERIGO.

How now, Roderigo?

RODERIGO   I do not find that thou deal'st justly with me.   175

IAGO   What in the contrary?

RODERIGO   Every day thou doff'st me with some device,
Iago, and rather, as it seems to me now, keep'st from
me all conveniency than suppliest me with the least
advantage of hope. I will indeed no longer endure it;   180
nor am I yet persuaded to put up in peace what
already I have foolishly suffered.

IAGO   Will you hear me, Roderigo?

RODERIGO   Faith, I have heard too much; and your
words and performances are no kin together.   185

IAGO   You charge me most unjustly.

RODERIGO   With nought but truth. I have wasted myself
out of my means. The jewels you have had from me to
deliver to Desdemona would half have corrupted a
votarist. You have told me she hath received them,   190

---

173 **all ... well** a common saying (cf.
  3.1.43, 3.4.19–20)
175 a verse line (it follows a verse passage) or prose (it begins a passage of
  prose)?
177 **doff'st** dost put me off, get rid of
  me
  device trick
179 **conveniency** opportunity (*OED* 4c,
  first in 1645)
180 **advantage** opportunity, favourable

occasion
181 **put up** put up with
184–5 ***Faith ... together** For the
  misplaced 'And hell gnaw his bones'
  (t.n.), see Walton, 215–27.
  your ... together Cf. Dent, P602,
  'Great promise small performance'.
190 **votarist** one bound by vows to a religious life (and to renounce
  fornication)

173 SD] *as F; Exit women. Q*   173.1] *F; opp. 174 Q*   175] *as Q; F lines* finde / me. /   177–82]
prose F; Q lines Iago; / from me, / least / indure it, / already / sufferd. /   177 doff'st] dofftst *Q;*
dafts *F*   178 now, keep'st] *F;* thou keepest *Q*   184–5 RODERIGO ... words and] *as Q, Fc;* And
hell gnaw his bones, *Fu*   184 Faith] *Q; not in F*   185 performances] *F;* performance
Q   187 With ... truth.] *F; not in Q*   188 my means] *F;* meanes *Q*   189 deliver to] *Q;* deliuer
F   190 hath] *F;* has *Q*   them] *F;* em *Q*

and returned me expectations and comforts of sudden
respect and acquittance, but I find none.

IAGO   Well, go to; very well.

RODERIGO   'Very well,' 'go to'! I cannot go to, man,
nor 'tis not very well. By this hand, I think it is   195
scurvy, and begin to find myself fopped in it.

IAGO   Very well.

RODERIGO   I tell you, 'tis not very well! I will make
myself known to Desdemona: if she will return me
my jewels I will give over my suit and repent my   200
unlawful solicitation; if not, assure yourself I will
seek satisfaction of you.

IAGO   You have said now.

RODERIGO   Ay, and said nothing but what I protest
intendment of doing.   205

IAGO   Why, now I see there's mettle in thee, and even
from this instant do build on thee a better opinion
than ever before. Give me thy hand, Roderigo. Thou
hast taken against me a most just exception – but yet

191–2 **returned ... acquittance** sent
back favourable promises and en-
couragements (implying) imminent
consideration and repayment. F *acquaintance* is possible.

194 **²go to** Roderigo takes Iago's all-
purpose phrase (= be quiet; come,
come; yes, yes; or, leave me alone) as
'copulate'. Cf. Montaigne, 1.97,
'Married men, because ... they may
go to it when they list, ought never to
press'; *AC* 1.2.63–4, 'O, let him
marry a woman that cannot go, sweet
Isis'; *Per* 4.6.74.

196 **scurvy** shabby
fopped fobbed, cheated; made a fool

198–9 **²I ... known** I will introduce
myself (to Desdemona and ask for an

explanation).

200 **repent** a curious repentance, standing on conditions!

201 **solicitation** petition; sexual soliciting

202 **satisfaction** repayment; atonement
for an offence; the opportunity of satisfying one's honour by a duel (*OED*
4, first in 1602)

203 **said** said your say (statement or
question)

204–5 **protest intendment** solemnly
declare my intention

206 **mettle** spirit, courage; quibbling on
metal, after *satisfaction*, with its hint
of a duel

209 **taken ... exception** made objec-
tion, found fault

---

191 expectations] *F*; expectation *Q*;   192 acquittance] *Q*; acquaintance *F*   193 well] *F*; good
Q   194–5 nor 'tis] *F*; it is *Q*   By this hand] *Q*; Nay *F*   think it is] *F*; say tis very *Q*   196 fopped]
fopt *QF*; fob'd *Rowe*   198 I ... 'tis] *F*; I say it is *Q*   201 I will] *F*; I'le *Q*   204 and said] *F*; and I
haue said *Q*   207 instant] *F*; time *Q*   209 exception] *F*; conception *Q*

I protest I have dealt most directly in thy affair.   210

RODERIGO   It hath not appeared.

IAGO   I grant indeed it hath not appeared, and your
suspicion is not without wit and judgement. But,
Roderigo, if thou hast that in thee indeed which I
have greater reason to believe now than ever – I mean   215
purpose, courage, and valour – this night show it. If
thou the next night following enjoy not Desdemona,
take me from this world with treachery and devise
engines for my life.

RODERIGO   Well – what is it? Is it within reason and   220
compass?

IAGO   Sir, there is especial commission come from
Venice to depute Cassio in Othello's place.

RODERIGO   Is that true? Why, then Othello and
Desdemona return again to Venice.   225

IAGO   O no, he goes into Mauretania and taketh away
with him the fair Desdemona, unless his abode be
lingered here by some accident – wherein none can
be so determinate as the removing of Cassio.

RODERIGO   How do you mean, removing of him?   230

IAGO   Why, by making him uncapable of Othello's place:
knocking out his brains.

RODERIGO   And that you would have me to do!

IAGO   Ay, if you dare do yourself a profit and a right.

---

210 **directly** straightforwardly; correctly
  affair business
216 **purpose** determination
219 **engines** plots, snares; engines of
  torture (*OED* 5b)
221 **compass** the bounds of possibility
223 **depute** appoint
226 **Mauretania** the homeland of the
  north African Moors. If this is a lie
  (cf. 4.1.235), what does Iago gain by
  it? In Mauretania Desdemona will be

out of Roderigo's reach, so he must
act now.
227 **abode** abiding, stay
228 **lingered** prolonged
229 **determinate** decisive
  removing See 2.1.274–5, 'the *displanting* of Cassio'; and *KL* 5.1.64–5,
  'Let her who would be rid of him
  devise / His speedy taking off'.
234 **profit** benefit

---

210 affair] *F;* affaires *Q*   214 in] *F;* within *Q*   217 enjoy] *F;* enioyest *Q*   220 what is it?] *F; not
in Q*   222 especial] *QF;* a special *(Malone)*   commission] *F;* command *Q*   222–8] *prose F; Q
lines as if verse Venice,* / *place.* / *Desdemona* / *Venice.* / him / linger'd   226 taketh] *F;* takes
Q   230 removing of] *Q;* remouing *F*   231–2] *prose F; Q lines as if verse* place, / braines. /
234 if] *F;* and if *Q*   a right] *F;* right *Q*

He sups tonight with a harlotry, and thither will I go   235
to him. He knows not yet of his honourable fortune:
if you will watch his going thence – which I will
fashion to fall out between twelve and one – you may
take him at your pleasure. I will be near to second
your attempt, and he shall fall between us. Come,   240
stand not amazed at it, but go along with me: I will
show you such a necessity in his death that you shall
think yourself bound to put it on him. It is now high
supper time, and the night grows to waste: about it.

RODERIGO   I will hear further reason for this.   245

IAGO   And you shall be satisfied.   *Exeunt.*

[**4.3**]   *Enter* OTHELLO, LODOVICO, DESDEMONA, EMILIA
and Attendants.

LODOVICO
I do beseech you, sir, trouble yourself no further.

---

235 **harlotry** harlot (so *RJ* 4.2.14, *1H4* 2.4.395).

236 **He ... fortune** Iago cannot know this for certain. It implies that Cassio will not be attended, as the new governor might be, and can be struck down more easily.

238 **fashion** arrange, contrive
fall out happen

239 **take** strike; come upon suddenly (*OED* 5, 8b); i.e. kill
second support

240 **fall between us** fall down (or, be wounded; or, die) by our joint action. Deliberately vague.

241 **go along** walk; join in

241–3 **I ... him** Iago (or Shakespeare) sometimes shrugs off explanations (3.3.322–3, 5.2.301–2, 320); in this instance the explanations follow off stage (5.1.8–10).

243 **put** *Put*, like *removing* (229) and *take*

(239), is vague, screening the suggestion of murder. Cf. *Ham* 5.2.383, 'deaths put on by cunning and forced cause', *WT* 3.3.34–5.
high well advanced (as in high noon, high time)

244 **grows to waste** approaches its end (*OED* waste 10c); implies 'we're wasting our time (talking)'
about it i.e. bestir yourself, make a move!

246 **satisfied** content (with satisfactory reasons); convinced

4.3.0.1–2 Q's entry, two lines before the end of 4.2, looks like another misplaced or misinterpreted marginal SD. The scene seems to be a public room or place, but later becomes a more private place where Desdemona unpins.

1–8 prose or verse? The short lines confuse the issue. See p. 360.

---

235 harlotry] *F*; harlot *Q*   246 SD] *Ex. Iag. and* Rod. *Q* ; *Exeunt. F*   4.3] *Scena Tertia. F*; *not in Q*   0.1–2 SD] *as F*; Enter *Othello, Desdemona, Lodouico, Emillia,* and Attendants. *Q (after 4.2.244)*

OTHELLO

O, pardon me, 'twill do me good to walk.

LODOVICO

Madam, good night: I humbly thank your ladyship.

DESDEMONA

Your honour is most welcome.

OTHELLO   Will you walk, sir?

O, Desdemona –

DESDEMONA   My lord?

OTHELLO   Get you to bed   5

On th'instant, I will be returned forthwith.

Dismiss your attendant there: look't be done.

DESDEMONA

I will, my lord.

Exeunt Othello, Lodovico and Attendants.

EMILIA

How goes it now? He looks gentler than he did.

DESDEMONA

He says he will return incontinent,   10

And hath commanded me to go to bed

And bid me to dismiss you.

EMILIA   Dismiss me?

DESDEMONA

It was his bidding; therefore, good Emilia,

Give me my nightly wearing, and adieu.

We must not now displease him.   15

EMILIA

Ay. – Would you had never seen him!

---

6 **returned** back
10 **incontinent** at once. Could also
mean 'wanting in self-restraint: chiefly with reference to sexual appetite'
(*OED* 1), therefore an odd word here.
Cf. *AYL* 5.2.38–9.
14 **wearing** apparel
15 **We** Associating Emilia with herself,

Desdemona unconsciously indicates
that she needs help.
16 ***Ay** 'I' was a normal spelling for
'Ay', and F's comma suggests a stop
after *Ay*. Heard in the theatre, 'I' and
'Ay' would be indistinguishable, hence
Desdemona's reply (*Texts*, 132–3).

2 'twill] *F;* it shall *Q*   4–7] *prose QF*   6 On th'] *F;* o'the *Q*   7 Dismiss] *F;* dispatch *Q*   't] *F;* it
Q   8.1] *Exeunt. Q; Exit. F (opp. 7 QF)*   11 And] *F;* He *Q*   12 bid] *F;* bad *Q*   16 Ay. – Would]
this edn; I would *Q ;* I, would *F;* Would *Q2*

289

DESDEMONA

So would not I: my love doth so approve him
That even his stubbornness, his checks, his frowns
– Prithee unpin me – have grace and favour.

EMILIA

I have laid those sheets you bade me on the bed.   20

DESDEMONA

All's one. Good faith, how foolish are our minds!
If I do die before thee, prithee shroud me
In one of these same sheets.

EMILIA   Come, come, you talk.

DESDEMONA

My mother had a maid called Barbary,
She was in love, and he she loved proved mad   25
And did forsake her. She had a song of 'willow',
An old thing 'twas, but it expressed her fortune
And she died singing it. That song tonight

---

17 **approve** commend
18 **stubbornness** roughness: cf. 1.3.228.
   checks reprimands
19, 33 **unpin** The word occurs nowhere
   else in Shakespeare. It refers to the
   unpinning of Desdemona's dress or
   hair. Ellen Terry wrote 'Hair' in her
   text (Hankey, 297), but editors and
   stage histories give little help. Either
   way, the unpinning brings the two
   women intimately together (see pp.
   54–5).
19 **grace and favour** So *Homilies*, 469,
   R3 3.4.91, *KL* 1.1.229; *favour* =
   charm, attractiveness.
20 **those sheets** Perhaps the bed is already visible (see p. 86 n. 2), and she
   points to those sheets. But beds were
   less easy to bring on stage than
   chairs: *those* probably means 'those
   sheets you asked for' (4.2.107).
21 **All's one** It's all the same, it doesn't
   matter.
   ***faith** F's misreading, *Father*, is also

found in *RJ* 4.4.21 (Q2), 'good father
(= faith) tis day'. See *Texts*, 169.
   foolish i.e. in thinking about death (a
   half-apology)
23 **you talk** i.e. how you talk! She
   speaks almost as if to a child; Desdemona's reference to her mother continues this redefinition of their roles.
24 **Barbary** Cf. 1.1.110. The name suggests the Barbary coast, home of the
   Moors. Did her mother have a maid
   who was a Moor? Not necessarily: the
   name was in use in England. Shakespeare's lawyer, Francis Collins, had a
   daughter called 'Barbery', named in
   his will, 1617.
25 **proved** turned out to be
   mad lunatic; or 'wild' (Johnson)
26 **willow** F's *Willough* was probably
   Crane's spelling (*Texts*, 66).
27 **fortune** fate
28 **And . . . it** Desdemona's attendant,
   Emilia, also dies singing the Willow
   Song (5.2.245ff.).

---

18 ³his] *F;* and *Q*   19 favour] *F;* fauour in them *Q*   20 those] *F;* these *Q*   21 one. Good faith,]
one good faith: *Q;* one: good Father, *F*   22 before thee] *Q;* before *F*   23 these] *F;* those
Q   26 had] *F;* has *Q*   willow] *Q;* Willough *F (throughout)*

Will not go from my mind. I have much to do
But to go hang my head all at one side   30
And sing it like poor Barbary. Prithee dispatch.

EMILIA   Shall I go fetch your night-gown?

DESDEMONA   No, unpin me here.

EMILIA   This Lodovico is a proper man. A very handsome man.   35

DESDEMONA   He speaks well.

EMILIA   I know a lady in Venice would have walked
barefoot to Palestine for a touch of his nether lip.

DESDEMONA   [*Sings.*]

The poor soul sat sighing by a sycamore tree,
Sing all a green willow: 40
Her hand on her bosom, her head on her knee,
Sing willow, willow, willow.
The fresh streams ran by her and murmured her
moans,
Sing willow, willow, willow:

29–30 **I ... But** it is all I can do not to
(Ridley)

30 **hang my head** let my head droop (in
despondency)

31 **dispatch** hurry

32 **night-gown** dressing-gown

34–5 ***This ... man** F prints 'This ...
proper man' as one line, as if it is
verse (which it may be). I follow
Ridley's conjecture in moving the SP.
For Desdemona to praise Lodovico at
this point seems out of character.
Shakespeare sometimes omitted SPs
or added them later (cf. his pages in
STM), so misplaced SPs are under-
standable: but see S. N. Garner,
'Shakespeare's Desdemona' (*SSt*, 9
[1976], 233ff.).

34 **proper** good-looking; admirable;
complete

37–8 This suggests a penitential pilgrimage: the chastest kiss would have

required a considerable mortification
of the flesh! But pilgrims normally
went from Venice to Palestine by sea
(as in *The Book of Margery Kempe*,
ch. 28).

38 **nether lip** Cf. 5.2.43, 'Alas, why
gnaw you so your nether lip?'

39ff. For the song, see LN.

39 **sycamore** a species of fig tree. 'It
was not traditionally associated with
the forsaken in love (except perhaps
by the punning "sick-amour"); but
it is in a grove of sycamore that
the love-sick Romeo is found wandering by Benvolio (*RJ* 1.1.121)'
(Sanders).

40 **a** of. Steevens quoted a ballad printed
in 1578 with the refrain 'Willow,
willow, willow, sing all of green
willow'.
willow symbol of grief for unre-
quited love or the loss of a mate

29–52 I have ... next.] *F; not in Q*   34 SP] *Ard²; before* A very *F*   39 SD] *as Q2; not in F*   39ff.]
song in italics F 39 sighing] *Q2; singing Fc; sining Fu*

Her salt tears fell from her and softened the
　　stones,　　　　　　　　　　　　　　　　45
　　　　Sing willow, willow, willow.
[*Speaks.*] Lay by these.
　　　　Willow, willow –
[*Speaks.*] Prithee hie thee: he'll come anon.
　　Sing all a green willow must be my garland.　　50
　　Let nobody blame him, his scorn I approve –
[*Speaks.*] Nay, that's not next. Hark, who is't that
　　knocks?

EMILIA

It's the wind.

DESDEMONA　　[*Sings.*]

I called my love false love; but what said he then?
　　　　Sing willow, willow, willow:　　　　　　55
　　If I court moe women, you'll couch with moe men.
[*Speaks.*] So, get thee gone; good night. Mine eyes do
　　itch,
Doth that bode weeping?

EMILIA　　　　　　　　　　　'Tis neither here nor there.

DESDEMONA

I have heard it said so. O, these men, these men!
Dost thou in conscience think – tell me, Emilia –　60
That there be women do abuse their husbands
In such gross kind?

EMILIA　　　　　　　There be some such, no question.

---

45 Cf. Dent, D618, 'Constant dropping will wear the stone.'
47 **Lay by these** put these things aside
49 **hie** haste
51–2 **Let ... next** a Freudian slip (unconsciously she wants to shield Othello from blame)?
56 **moe** more
　　couch lie. See pp. 52, 86.

57–8 **Mine ... weeping** 'I find in MacGregor's *Folklore of North-East Scotland* that "An itching in the eyes indicated tears and sorrow"' (Hart).
58 Cf. Dent, H438, 'It is neither here nor there.'
60 **in conscience** truly
62 **gross kind** disgusting manner

47, 49, 52, 57 SD] *this edn*　49 hie] high *F*　52 who is't] *F;* who's *Q*　53 It's] *F;* It is *Q*
54–6] *F; not in Q*　57–8] *F; Q lines* night; / weeping? /　57 So] *F;* Now *Q*　58 Doth] *F;* does
Q　59–62 DESDEMONA . . . question.] *F; not in Q*

DESDEMONA
Wouldst thou do such a deed for all the world?

EMILIA
Why, would not you?

DESDEMONA   No, by this heavenly light!

EMILIA
Nor I neither, by this heavenly light: 65
I might do't as well i'th' dark.

DESDEMONA
Wouldst thou do such a deed for all the world?

EMILIA
The world's a huge thing: it is a great price
For a small vice.

DESDEMONA   Good troth, I think thou wouldst not.

EMILIA   By my troth, I think I should, and undo't when I   70
had done. Marry, I would not do such a thing for
a joint-ring, nor for measures of lawn, nor for gowns,
petticoats, nor caps, nor any petty exhibition. But for
all the whole world? ud's pity, who would not make

63–6 *Why … dark See *Texts*, 34–5. I
think that these lines were cancelled
by Shakespeare, who reused 63 as 67.
Emilia knows, after 4.2, that Desdemona's chastity is not a joking matter.
63 Cf. Matthew 16.26, 'For what doth it
profit a man if he win all the whole
world and lose his own soul?'
   do … deed = have sexual intercourse (Partridge, citing *LLL*
3.1.198–9, 'one that will do the deed /
Though Argus were her eunuch and
her guard')
   for … world resumes 4.2.165–6 (as
'by this heavenly light' picks up 'by
this light of heaven', 4.2.152). She
and Othello both think each other,
and 'honesty', worth the whole
world.
64 **by … light** an oath not used else-

where by Shakespeare (but cf.
4.2.152, 'by this light of heaven');
adapted from 'by this light' or
'[God]'s light'
68 **price** price to be paid; or, prize (variant spelling)
72 **joint-ring** a finger-ring formed of
two separable halves to make one, like
husband and wife. Often given by
lovers. She perhaps implies 'for a
mere promise of marriage'.
   measures of lawn quantities of fine
linen
73 **petty** trivial; inferior
   exhibition gift, present
74 **ud's** God's. Cf. 5.2.69.
74–5 **who … monarch** Her 'easy
virtue' is in character, but her willingness to do anything for Iago less
so. Is she joking?

66 do't] *F*; doe it *Q*   i'th'] *F*; in the *Q*   67 Wouldst] *F*; Would *Q*   deed] *F*; thing *Q*   68–9] *as*
Q; *F lines* thing: / vice. /   68 world's] *F*; world is *Q*   69 Good troth] *Q*; Introth *F*   70 By my
troth] *Q*; Introth *F*   71 done] *F*; done it *Q*   72 'nor] *F*; or *Q*   73 petticoats] *F*; or Petticotes
Q   petty] *F*; such *Q*   74 all] *F*; *not in Q*   ud's pity] *Q*; why *F*

her husband a cuckold to make him a monarch? I   75
should venture purgatory for't.

DESDEMONA
Beshrew me, if I would do such a wrong
For the whole world!

EMILIA   Why, the wrong is but a wrong i'th' world; and
having the world for your labour, 'tis a wrong in your   80
own world, and you might quickly make it right.

DESDEMONA   I do not think there is any such woman.

EMILIA   Yes, a dozen, and as many to th' vantage as would
store the world they played for.
But I do think it is their husbands' faults   85
If wives do fall. Say that they slack their duties
And pour our treasures into foreign laps;
Or else break out in peevish jealousies,
Throwing restraint upon us; or say they strike us,

76 **venture** risk
   purgatory a reminder that the play
   is set in a Catholic world
77 **Beshrew me** Cf. 3.4.151n.
82 Cf. 4.2.136.
83–4 A prose beginning for a verse
   speech is unusual, but 85–102 are
   more likely to be a cut in Q than an
   afterthought in F: see *Texts*, 12.
83 **a dozen** a facetious understatement,
   cancelled out by what follows. Cf.
   Falstaff, who 'went to a bawdy-house
   not above once in a quarter – of an
   hour' (*1H4* 3.3.16–17).
   to th' vantage over and above
84 **store** stock
   played gambled; sported amorously
85–102 She resumes 3.4.104–7. Though
   she begins by thinking of Othello, it
   is soon clear that she refers to her
   own marriage. Such protests against
   'double standards' were not uncommon: cf. *CE* 2.1.10ff.
86 **fall** fall from virtue
   slack neglect; cease to prosecute in a
   vigorous manner (*OED* 1, 2)
   duties The *Book of Common Prayer*

('Of matrimony') explained 'the duty
of husbands toward their wives, and
wives toward their husbands', but
sexual duties were treated less explicitly than in some bibles. Cf. 1 Corinthians 7.2–3, 'But because of fornication let every man have his own wife
... Let the husband render his debt
to the wife'. (This is the Catholic
'Rheims' bible of 1582; for *debt* Protestant bibles read 'due benevolence'.)
87 perhaps alluding to the myth of
   Danaë, who was impregnated by Zeus
   disguised as a shower of gold. But
   treasure = seed was not uncommon:
   cf. *1H4* 2.3.45, 'my treasures and my
   rights of thee' (Lady Hotspur to Hotspur); *Son* 20, 'Mine be thy love, and
   thy love's use their treasure'.
   foreign another woman's
   laps lap could = pudendum (*OED*
   2b)
88 **peevish** foolish; mad; spiteful; perverse; irritable (a word that has nar-
   rowed in meaning)
89 **Throwing ... us** i.e. restricting our
   freedom

76 for't] *F; for it Q*   79 i'th'] *F; i'the Q*   83 to th'] *F; to the Q*   85–102 But ... so.] *F; not in
Q*   89 upon] *F; on Rowe³*

Or scant our former having in despite,   90
Why, we have galls: and though we have some grace
Yet have we some revenge. Let husbands know
Their wives have sense like them: they see, and smell,
And have their palates both for sweet and sour
As husbands have. What is it that they do   95
When they change us for others? Is it sport?
I think it is. And doth affection breed it?
I think it doth. Is't frailty that thus errs?
It is so too. And have not we affections?
Desires for sport? and frailty, as men have?   100
Then let them use us well: else let them know,
The ills we do, their ills instruct us so.

DESDEMONA

Good night, good night. God me such usage send
Not to pick bad from bad, but by bad mend!   *Exeunt.*

[5.1]   *Enter* IAGO *and* RODERIGO.

IAGO

Here, stand behind this bulk, straight will he come.
Wear thy good rapier bare, and put it home;

---

90 or reduce what we had before (our 'treasures') out of spite
91 **we have galls** i.e. we can feel resentment
   grace mercy
93 **sense** sensation, or sensual appetite (Malone); or, emotional consciousness (*OED* 16)
96 **change** exchange
   sport recreation, fun
97 **affection breed** passion (or lust) produce
98 **frailty** moral weakness
101 **use us well** Cf. 1.3.292, 'use Desdemona well', and 5.2.69n.
102 **ills** wicked or sinful acts
   so i.e. so to do (Malone). Cf. *MV* 3.1.71–2, 'The villainy you teach me,

I will execute'. This speech (Shylock's 'Hath not a Jew eyes?') is close to Emilia's here.
103 **usage** treatment; behaviour
104 not to select (and copy) bad from what is bad, but to improve by (knowing what is) bad
5.1 another 'dark' scene (see p. 87)
1 ***Here, stand** So F (no comma Q). Or, 'Here stand,'. In *Arden of Faversham* killers also wait for their victim outside a shop when it is 'very late' ('stand close, and take your fittest standing', Revels, 3.39): see pp. 73–5.
   bulk stall, a framework projecting from the front of a shop
2 **bare** ready, drawn
   home i.e. as far as it will go

103] *as Q; F lines* good night: / send, / God] *Q;* Heauen *F*   usage] *Q;* vses *F*   5.1] *Actus.* 5. *Q;*
Actus Quintus. Scena Prima. F   1] *as Q; F lines* Barke, / come: /   bulk] *Q;* Barke *F*

295

Quick, quick, fear nothing, I'll be at thy elbow.
It makes us or it mars us, think on that
And fix most firm thy resolution.   5
RODERIGO
Be near at hand, I may miscarry in't.
IAGO
Here, at thy hand: be bold, and take thy stand.

                                                        [*Retires.*]

RODERIGO
I have no great devotion to the deed
And yet he hath given me satisfying reasons:
'Tis but a man gone. Forth, my sword: he dies.   10
IAGO
I have rubbed this young quat almost to the sense
And he grows angry. Now, whether he kill Cassio
Or Cassio him, or each do kill the other,
Every way makes my gain. Live Roderigo,
He calls me to a restitution large   15
Of gold and jewels that I bobbed from him
As gifts to Desdemona:
It must not be. If Cassio do remain

---

3 **at thy elbow** Cf. Dent, EE5, 'To be at one's elbow'; D243.1, 'The devil is at one's elbow.'

4 **It . . . ²us** Dent, M48, 'To make or mar'.

5 **resolution** five syllables

7 **stand** position. Cf. *JC* 2.4.25, 'I go to take my stand, / To see him pass.'

8 **devotion** enthusiasm for; incongruous, suggesting religious devotion (to commit murder)

9 **reasons** Cf. 4.2.245–6, 5.2.305–9. We do not hear the reasons: Shakespeare sometimes states that there are reasons without giving them (*KL* 4.3.51 ff., *Tem* 1.2.266). Scan 'he'th giv'n'.

10 **Forth** Only now does he manage to draw his sword!

11 **quat** pimple, small boil, 'which rubbing irritates' (Ridley). Note that Iago, aged 28, thinks Roderigo *young*: he may be a boy in his teens (cf. 1.3.341n.).
to the sense to the quick

12 **angry** could = inflamed (*OED* 8: 'sores with often touching waxe angry')

14 **gain** profit. Q *game* = 'gives me the game' (Ridley; so Kittredge).
Live should Roderigo live

16 **bobbed** diddled (more playful than 'cheated')

18 **It . . . be** metrically 'amphibious', because these words could also complete 17 (*Texts*, 105–6)

---

4 on] *F; of Q*   7 stand] *F; sword Q*   SD] *as Capell; not in QF*   8 deed] *F; dead Q*   9 hath] *F; has Q*   11 quat] *F; gnat Q*   12 angry. Now,] *F; angry now: Q*   14 gain] *F; game Q*   16 Of] *F; For Q*

He hath a daily beauty in his life
That makes me ugly; and besides, the Moor   20
May unfold me to him – there stand I in much peril.
No, he must die. Be't so! I hear him coming.

Enter CASSIO.

RODERIGO
I know his gait, 'tis he. Villain, thou diest!
                        [Makes a thrust at Cassio.]

CASSIO
That thrust had been mine enemy indeed
But that my coat is better than thou know'st: 25
I will make proof of thine.
                    [Draws, and wounds Roderigo.]

RODERIGO   O, I am slain!
    [Iago from behind wounds Cassio in the leg, and exit.]

CASSIO
I am maimed for ever! Help, ho! murder! murder!

Enter OTHELLO.

OTHELLO
The voice of Cassio. Iago keeps his word.

---

19 **daily beauty** i.e. an ever-present attractiveness. Does this suggest sear-
ing self-contempt (so Rosenberg, 174)
on the part of Iago? Or is he describing the conventional view of Cassio's
beautiful manners (cf. 2.1.98ff.)
compared with his own bluntness
(2.1.164ff.)?
21 **unfold** expose. Scan 'May 'nfold me
to'm' (*Texts*, 121).

25 **coat** undercoat (of proof armour)
26 **make proof** test (the proof of)
   ²SD Iago wounds him in the leg,
having heard that his *coat* protects his
upper body (Malone).
27 **maimed** For Q *maind*, cf. 1.3.100n.
27.1 Othello usually enters 'above'. Does
he arrive by chance, or did Iago tell
him that Cassio would be killed
here?

---

19 hath] *F;* has *Q* 21 much] *F; not in Q* 22 Be't] *Q;* But *F* hear] *Q;* heard *F* 23 SD]
Rowe subst. (He runs at Cassio, *and wounds him.); not in QF* 24 mine] *F;* my *Q* 25 know'st]
F; think'st *Q* 26 ¹SD] *this edn; not in QF* ²SD] *Theobald subst. (Fight. Iago cuts Cassio behind
in the Leg, and* Exit.*); not in QF* 27ff. murder] *Q;* murther *F throughout scene* 27] *as Q; F lines
euer: / murther. /* maimed] *F;* maind *Q* Help] *F;* light *Q* 27.1] *QF; Enter* Othello, *above at a
Window / Rowe*

RODERIGO

O, villain that I am!

OTHELLO   It is even so.

CASSIO

O, help ho! light! a surgeon!   30

OTHELLO

'Tis he. O brave Iago, honest and just,

That hast such noble sense of thy friend's wrong!

Thou teachest me. Minion, your dear lies dead,

And your unblest fate hies; strumpet, I come.

Forth of my heart those charms, thine eyes, are
   blotted,   35

Thy bed, lust-stained, shall with lust's blood be
   spotted.   *Exit.*

Enter LODOVICO *and* GRATIANO.

CASSIO

What ho, no watch, no passage? murder, murder!

GRATIANO

'Tis some mischance, the voice is very direful.

CASSIO

O help!

LODOVICO

Hark!   40

---

29 **O ... am** Cf. Romans 7.24, 'O
wretched man that I am'.
   It ... so Q *Harke* implies that Othello can hear but not see. He does not
know about Roderigo, cannot see
him, and thinks Cassio speaks. *Even*
= just.

31 **brave** worthy, good; courageous

32 **sense** Cf. 4.3.94n.
   friend's Having called himself 'thy
friend' (3.3.145) to get information
from Iago, while thinking of him as
'This . . . creature' (3.3.246), he now
thinks Iago a friend.

33 **Minion** hussy (contemptuously, ad-

dressing the absent Desdemona);
more usually 'darling' (endearingly)

34 **unblest** unholy (i.e. she is damned)
   hies makes haste, hurries nearer

35 **Forth** out
   blotted obliterated

36 **blood** Cf. 3.3.454 ('O blood, blood,
blood!'), 4.1.201ff., 5.2.3. Is it Shakespeare or Othello who cannot decide
how she should be killed?
   spotted stained

37 **passage** i.e. people passing

38 **mischance** mishap
   direful dreadful, terrible

---

29 It is] *F*; Harke tis *Q*   34 unblest fate hies] *F* (highes); fate hies apace *Q*   35 Forth] *Q*; For
F   37] *as Q*; *F lines* passage ?/Murther. /   38 voice] *F*; cry *Q*

RODERIGO

O wretched villain!

LODOVICO

Two or three groan. It is a heavy night;
These may be counterfeits, let's think't unsafe
To come in to the cry without more help.

RODERIGO

Nobody come? then shall I bleed to death.   45

Enter IAGO, *with a light.*

LODOVICO

Hark!

GRATIANO

Here's one comes in his shirt, with light and weapons.

IAGO

Who's there? Whose noise is this that cries on
     murder?

LODOVICO

We do not know.

IAGO   Did not you hear a cry?

CASSIO

Here, here! for heaven's sake help me!

IAGO   What's the matter?   50

GRATIANO

This is Othello's ancient, as I take it.

---

42 **heavy** overcast, dark
44 **come in to** approach(?); or, Cassio
     and Roderigo staggered into the *bulk*
     (1) and he fears to follow. Cf. 59.
45 This could be two questions.
47 **in his shirt** in his night attire; with-
     out his outer garments (*OED* 2b)
48 **noise** Q *noise* could be a misreading
     of *voice*, leading to a 'common error'
     in F: 'whose noise is this, that cries'

sounds odd. Cf. 5.2.85 t.n.
     cries on exclaims against
50 **heaven's** F *heauen* could be the old
     genitive, as in *KJ* 4.1.77, 'For heauen
     sake', or Chaucer, *Wife of Bath's
     Tale*, 325, 'Jesus, hevene king', or *-s*
     dropped before *s*, as in *MV* 4.1.379,
     Q, 'for Godsake'. Cf. *Barnavelt* (a
     Crane manuscript; MSR 1383), 'for
     heaven-sake'.

---

42 groan. It is a] grones, it is a *Q;* groane. 'Tis *F*   44 in to] *Capell;* into *QF*   45.1] *as Q; Enter
Iago. F*   47 light] *F;* lights *Q*   49 We] *F;* I *Q*   Did] *Q;* Do *F*   50 heaven's] *Q;* heauen *F*

LODOVICO

The same indeed, a very valiant fellow.

IAGO

What are you here that cry so grievously?

CASSIO

Iago? O, I am spoiled, undone by villains!

Give me some help.   55

IAGO

O me, lieutenant! What villains have done this?

CASSIO

I think that one of them is hereabout

And cannot make away.

IAGO   O treacherous villains!

What are you there? Come in, and give some help.

RODERIGO

O, help me here!   60

CASSIO

That's one of them.

IAGO   O murderous slave! O villain!

[*Stabs Roderigo.*]

RODERIGO

O damned Iago! O inhuman dog!

IAGO

Kill men i'th' dark? Where be these bloody thieves?

How silent is this town! Ho, murder, murder!

52 **fellow** They do not remember his name (he is a social inferior), but he remembers theirs (67, 93).

53 **grievously** piteously, wretchedly

54 **spoiled** destroyed. Cf. *CE* 5.1.37.

56 **O me** A 'genteel' exclamation: cf. *RJ* 1.1.173.

58 **make** i.e. get

59 **What . . . there?** What kind of men are you there? This seems to anticipate 65, but might also be printed 'What, are you there?' (addressing supposed villains).

Come in Iago has entered the *bulk* (1) to help Cassio.

62 [1]**O . . . dog!** Q's 'o, o, o' is a signal to the actor to groan or make whatever noise is appropriate; more common in F than in Q texts. See Honigmann, 'Stage direction'.

64 Iago enjoys uproar: cf. 1.1.66ff., 2.3.153.

56] *as Q; F lines* Lieutenant! / this? /   me,] *F (*mee,*); my Q*   57 that] *F; the Q*   60 here] *Q; there F*   61 them] *F; 'em Q*   murderous] *Q; mur'd'rous F*   SD] *as Q2, Rowe; not in QF*   62 dog!] *as F; dog, – o, o, o. Q*   63] *as Q; F lines* darke? / Theeues? /   men i'th'] *F; him i' the Q*   these] *F; those Q*

300

What may you be? Are you of good or evil? 65
LODOVICO
As you shall prove us, praise us.
IAGO
Signior Lodovico?
LODOVICO
He, sir.
IAGO
I cry you mercy: here's Cassio hurt by villains.
GRATIANO
Cassio? 70
IAGO
How is't, brother?
CASSIO   My leg is cut in two.
IAGO
Marry, heaven forbid!
Light, gentlemen, I'll bind it with my shirt.

Enter BIANCA.

BIANCA
What is the matter, ho? who is't that cried?
IAGO
Who is't that cried?
BIANCA   O my dear Cassio! 75
My sweet Cassio! O Cassio, Cassio, Cassio!

---

65 Lodovico and Gratiano have kept their distance, and now step forward. **of** on the side of. The idea is familiar (Joshua 5.13, 'Art thou on our side, or on our adversaries'?') but the phrasing is odd.
66 **prove** find or prove (us to be) **praise** appraise, value. Cf. Dent, P614.2, 'Prove (assay, try) ere you purpose (... praise)'; i.e. as you prove our value, so esteem us.
69 **I ... mercy** I beg your pardon (*you* is indirect object): a 'genteel' phrase.
71 **brother** From Cinthio: discovering

the wounded Cassio, Iago grieved 'as if he had been his own brother' (cf. p. 382), the words of the narrator. Shakespeare gives the word to Iago, who wants to impress the Venetians.
72 **heaven forbid** Cf. 2.3.257n.
73 **Light** Iago has put down his own light, to bind Cassio's wounds.
75 **Who ... cried** Iago has a dangerous tendency to mock others by echoing them: cf. 1.1.116, 2.1.249, 3.3.104ff., 306, 443.
Cassio three syllables, for emphasis. Two in 76.

---

71 is't] *F*; is it *Q* 76 My] *F*; O my *Q* O] *F*; *not in Q*

IAGO

O notable strumpet! Cassio, may you suspect
Who they should be that have thus mangled you?

CASSIO

No.

GRATIANO

I am sorry to find you thus;   80
I have been to seek you.

IAGO

Lend me a garter. So. – O for a chair
To bear him easily hence!

BIANCA

Alas, he faints! O Cassio, Cassio, Cassio!

IAGO

Gentlemen all, I do suspect this trash   85
To be a party in this injury.
Patience awhile, good Cassio. Come, come,
Lend me a light. Know we this face, or no?
Alas, my friend and my dear countryman,
Roderigo? No – yes sure! – O heaven, Roderigo!   90

GRATIANO

What, of Venice?

IAGO   Even he, sir. Did you know him?

GRATIANO

Know him? Ay.

IAGO

Signior Gratiano? I cry you gentle pardon:
These bloody accidents must excuse my manners

---

77 **notable** known, conspicuous
strumpet Cf. *R3* 3.4.71, 74, where
another murderer's moral outrage at a
strumpet is equally hypocritical.
77–8 **may . . . be** have you any idea who
they are
78 **mangled** hacked; wounded
80–1 Even with elision (I'm, I've) this
would be an irregular verse line.

82 **garter** a band, worn as a sash or belt
85 **trash** Cf. 2.1.301, 3.3.160.
87 **Cassio** three syllables
89 **countryman** fellow countryman
93 **I . . . pardon** a 'genteel' turn of
phrase, again! A variant of 'I cry you
mercy' (69n., 4.2.90).
94 **accidents** unforeseen happenings

78 have thus] *F;* thus haue *Q*   80–3] *divided as F*   82–3] *F; not in Q*   86 be] *F;* beare *Q*   party
. . . injury] *F;* part in this *Q*   87 Come, come] *F; not in Q*   90 O heaven] *Q ;* Yes, 'tis *F*   93 you]
Q ; your *F*

That so neglected you.

GRATIANO   I am glad to see you.   95

IAGO

How do you, Cassio? O, a chair, a chair!

GRATIANO

Roderigo?

IAGO

He, he, 'tis he. [*A chair is brought in.*] O, that's well
    said, the chair.

Some good man bear him carefully from hence,

I'll fetch the general's surgeon. [*To Bianca.*] For you,
    mistress,   100

Save you your labour. – He that lies slain here,
    Cassio,

Was my dear friend. What malice was between you?

CASSIO

None in the world, nor do I know the man.

IAGO   [*to Bianca*]

What, look you pale? – O, bear him out o'th' air.

 – Stay you, good gentlemen. – Look you pale,
    mistress?   105

 – Do you perceive the gastness of her eye?

 – Nay, if you stare we shall hear more anon.

 – Behold her well, I pray you, look upon her:

---

95 **neglected** ignored, paid no attention
  to
96 **chair** i.e. a seat (or litter?) to carry
  Cassio to the surgeon
98 **well said** Cf. 4.1.115n.
  the chair F *the* presupposes 82–3, Q
  a doesn't (Q omits 82–3). Revision?
99 **man** Emend to *men*?
100 **For** as for
101 **Save . . . labour** don't trouble yourself, i.e leave him alone

102 **malice** ill-will
104 **O . . . air** Cf. Tilley, A93, 'Fresh air
  is ill for the diseased or wounded
  man.'
106 **gastness** dread, terror; ghastliness
107 **Nay . . . anon** i.e. if you stare (it is
  a sign of guilt and) we'll soon hear
  more (we'll make you confess). Q
  stirre (= try to get away) would imply
  much the same. Cf. 5.2.184, 'Nay,
  stare not'.

98] *as Q; F lines* 'tis he / Chaire. / He, he] *F;* He Q   SD] *Capell subst.; not in QF*   the] *F;*
a Q   100 SD] *Johnson; not in QF*   102 between] *F;* betwixt Q   104 out] Q; *not in F*   105
gentlemen] *F;* Gentlewoman Q   106 gastness] *F;* icastures Q   107 if] *F;* an Q   stare] *F;*
stirre Q   hear] *F;* haue Q

Do you see, gentlemen? nay, guiltiness will speak
Though tongues were out of use.

Enter EMILIA.

EMILIA   'Las, what's the matter?   110
What's the matter, husband?
IAGO
Cassio hath here been set on in the dark
By Roderigo and fellows that are 'scaped:
He's almost slain, and Roderigo dead.
EMILIA
Alas, good gentleman! alas, good Cassio!   115
IAGO
This is the fruits of whoring. Prithee, Emilia,
Go know of Cassio where he supped tonight.
What, do you shake at that?
BIANCA
He supped at my house, but I therefore shake not.
IAGO
O, did he so? I charge you, go with me.   120
EMILIA
O fie upon thee, strumpet!
BIANCA   I am no strumpet
But of life as honest as you, that thus
Abuse me.
EMILIA   As I? Foh, fie upon thee!

109–10 **nay . . . use** i.e. guilt will betray
  itself, even if we were all struck dumb
  (*out of use* = not used). Dent, M1315,
  'Murder will out.'
114 **dead** Cf. 5.2.326.
115 She seems to think the two men
  equally 'good'. This brings out her
  failure to look below the surface.
116 **This . . . whoring** Cf. *R3* 2.1.135,
  'This is the fruits of rashness', and 77n.
117 **know** learn

120 **charge** order
121–3 *sometimes printed as irregular
  verse lines, but can be spoken as verse
  if *I am* is slurred as *I'm*, and heavy
  stress on *you*: see *Texts*, 123
122 **honest** i.e. sexually honest. In a
  more general sense she is indeed
  more honest than Emilia, who lied
  about the handkerchief (3.4.24).
123 **Foh** signifies disgust, *fie* disapproval.
  Cf. *Ham* 2.2.587, 'Fie upon't, foh!'

109–10] *as F; Q lines* guiltinesse / vse. /   110 SD] *Q (Enter* Em.) *opp.* vse; *not in F* 'Las,
what's] *Q*; Alas, what is *F*   111 What's] *Q*; What is *F*   112 hath] *F;* has *Q*   114 dead] *Q;* quite
dead *F*   116 fruits] *F;* fruite *Q*   Prithee] *F;* pray *Q*   121 O fie] *F;* Fic, fie *Q*   121–3] *this edn;
QF lines* honest, / me. / thee. /   123 Foh, fie] *Q (*fough*);* Fie *F*

304

IAGO

Kind gentlemen, let's go see poor Cassio dressed.
Come, mistress, you must tell's another tale.   125
Emilia, run you to the citadel
And tell my lord and lady what hath happed.
– Will you go on afore? – This is the night
That either makes me or fordoes me quite.

Exeunt.

[5.2] *Enter* OTHELLO, *with a light.* DESDEMONA *in her bed*
[*asleep*].

OTHELLO

It is the cause, it is the cause, my soul!
Let me not name it to you, you chaste stars,
It is the cause. Yet I'll not shed her blood
Nor scar that whiter skin of hers than snow

124 **Kind** almost = good (but more ingratiating)
dressed bandaged
125 Cf. Dent, T49, 'To tell another tale'; *tell's* = tell us.
127 **and lady** Should Iago register that he thinks the lady already dead, perhaps by the slightest hesitation after *lord*?
128–9 **This ... quite** He fails to realize that the night may make *and* 'fordo' him.
129 **makes me** i.e. brings me success
fordoes me quite ruins, undoes me completely (*quite* = completely, *OED* 1). He repeats 5.1.4.
5.2 For the staging, see LN. For 5.2.1–20 see also pp. 363–6.
1 **cause** could = ground for action; the case of one party in a law suit; a matter before a court for decision. How characteristic of Othello that he does not define the cause (= chastity? purity? the good of the world in gen-

eral?)! See pp. 83–4, and also J. Money, in *SS*, 6 (1953), 94–105.
my soul Addressing one's soul is common in the Bible (Genesis 49.6, Psalms 16.2, etc.) and in classical literature. For the biblical imagery of this speech, see J. E. Hankins, *Shakespeare's Derived Imagery* (1953); also J. Tobin, in *N&Q*, NS 24 (1977), 112; and in *SS*, 31 (1978), 33–43.
2 **stars** any celestial bodies, including the chaste moon (*MND* 2.1.162). In classical myth reluctant ladies pursued by Zeus were changed into stars.
4 Cf. Dent, S591, 'As white as (the driven) snow'. Snow, though, was connected with chastity (Money, as in 1n., citing *Cym* 2.5.13, 'As chaste as unsunn'd snow'), so contradicts the charge of Desdemona's unchastity. Shakespeare also reanimates the cliché by *not* writing 'that skin of hers whiter than snow'.

124] *as Q ;* F *lines* Gentlemen: / drest. /   127 hath] *F;* has *Q*   128 aforc] *F;* I pray *Q*   129 makes] *F;* markes *Q*   quite] *Q ; F (*quight*)*   5.2] *Scœna Secunda. F; not in Q*   0.1–2] *Enter* Othello *with a light. Q ; Enter* Othello, *and* Desdemona *in her bed. F*

And smooth as monumental alabaster: 5
Yet she must die, else she'll betray more men.
Put out the light, and then put out the light!
If I quench thee, thou flaming minister,
I can again thy former light restore
Should I repent me. But once put out thy light,   10
Thou cunning'st pattern of excelling nature,
I know not where is that Promethean heat
That can thy light relume: when I have plucked the
    rose
I cannot give it vital growth again,
It needs must wither. I'll smell thee on the tree;   15
O balmy breath, that dost almost persuade

5 **monumental** i.e. as used for monu-
ments; here referring to funeral mon-
uments (where effigies often lie on their
backs, heads resting on a stone 'pillow',
hands pressed together in prayer, as if
awaiting the resurrection. A hint for
staging? The 'church' tableau is also
suggested by Othello's candle).
alabaster often spelt alablaster *c.*
1600 (= QF). Cf. *Luc* 419, 'her alablaster skin', Dent, A95.2, 'As white
as alabaster'.
6 **betray** prove false to; cheat (*OED* 2, 3)
more men His motives are as confused as Iago's. Does he really care
what happens to *more men?*
7 **and . . . light** i.e. extinguish her life.
Cf. Sidney's *Arcadia* (1593 edn, fos
231b, 237, of killing a princess), 'so
soone may the fayrest light in the
world be put out', 'become not the
putters out of the worlds light' (from
Steevens); C. A., *A Fig for Fortune*
(1596), B3b, 'Out with thy candle [=
life], let it burne no more', *Mac*
5.5.23, 'Out, out, brief candle!' A
commonplace.
8 **flaming minister** Cf. Psalms 104.4,
'God maketh his angels spirits: and

his ministers a flaming fire', Hebrews
1.7; *minister* = servant.
10 **repent me** (reflexive verb) regret it,
change my mind
But once but if I once
11 **thou** most skilful instance (or speci-
men, image, design, model) of nature
excelling herself. Cf. 2.1.63–5, 'One
that excels . . .'.
12 **Promethean** 'Shakespeare seems to
be combining two separate Greek
myths about Prometheus, one in
which Prometheus gave fire to
human-kind and one in which he was
the creator of human-kind' (Folger).
13 **relume** relight (*OED*, first here,
from late Lat. *reluminare*)
14 **vital** living
15 **needs** necessarily, inevitably
16 **O** Q*A* could = Ah.
balmy deliciously fragrant; cf. 20,
'So sweet', and p. 21. Q's SD, '*He
kisses her*', may refer to three kisses
but, as the sense of smell is so important to him, I think he smells at 17,
again at 19, here finishing with a kiss,
as is also suggested by the placing of
Q's SD. Q2 and later editors moved
the SD, without authority.

5 alabaster] *QF (*Alablaster*)* 7 then put] *QF;* then – put *Hanmer* 10 thy light] *F;* thine
Q 11 cunning'st] *F;* cunning *Q* 13] *as Q; F lines* re-Lume. / Rose, / relume] *F;* returne
Q the] *Q;* thy *F* 15 needs must] *F;* must needes *Q* thee] *F;* it *Q* 16 O] *F;* A *Q* dost] *F;*
doth *Q*

Justice to break her sword! Once more, once more:
Be thus when thou art dead and I will kill thee
And love thee after. Once more, and that's the last.

> *He [smells, then] kisses her.*

So sweet was ne'er so fatal. I must weep,   20
But they are cruel tears. This sorrow's heavenly,
It strikes where it doth love. She wakes.

DESDEMONA
Who's there? Othello?

OTHELLO   Ay, Desdemona.

DESDEMONA
Will you come to bed, my lord?

OTHELLO
Have you prayed tonight, Desdemon?

DESDEMONA   Ay, my lord.   25

OTHELLO
If you bethink yourself of any crime
Unreconciled as yet to heaven and grace,
Solicit for it straight.

DESDEMONA
Alack, my lord, what may you mean by that?

---

17 **Justice ... sword** The sword and
scales were emblems of Justice (traditionally female). The scales weighed
the evidence (not here!), the sword
punished.

17, 19 **Once** Either *one* or *once* looks like
a minim error, common in Shake-
speare generally (*Texts*, 82). Each is
possible; I prefer *once more* since he
refers, initially, to smelling, not kissing. But Shakespeare could have revised this speech (see p. 365).

20 **fatal** destructive; fateful

21 **cruel tears** 'meaning, I think, that
the tears are no sign of faltering pur-

pose' (Ridley)

21–2 **This ... love** Cf. Proverbs 3.12,
'For whom the Lord loveth, him he
chasteneth', Hebrews 12.6.

23 **Ay** Note this word in this scene: at
first quietly menacing (here, 33, 41,
70), then still resolute (139, 143), finally exhausted (295). Here it could
be the pronoun: '(Yes, it is indeed) I,
Desdemona.'

26 **bethink yourself** call to mind
crime sin

27 **grace** (the source of grace, i.e.) God.
So *AW* 1.3.220.

28 **Solicit** pray for pardon

17] Iustice her selfe to breake her sword once more, *Q*; Iustice to breake her Sword. One more, one
more: *F*   19 Once] *Q*; One *F*   that's] *F*; this *Q*   SD] *Q* (*opp. 19, 20*); not in *F*   SD smells, then]
this edn; not in QF   22 where it doth] *F*; when it does *Q*   She wakes] *QF*; as SD (*Cam
anon.*)   23 Ay] *QF* (*I*)   25 Desdemon] *F*; *Desdemona Q*   29] as *Q*; *F lines* Lord, / that? /
Alack] *F*; Alas *Q*

307

OTHELLO

    Well, do it, and be brief; I will walk by.   30

    I would not kill thy unprepared spirit,

    No, heaven forfend, I would not kill thy soul.

DESDEMONA

    Talk you of killing?

OTHELLO   Ay, I do.

DESDEMONA   Then, heaven,

    Have mercy on me!

OTHELLO   Amen, with all my heart.

DESDEMONA

    If you say so, I hope you will not kill me.   35

OTHELLO   Hum!

DESDEMONA

    And yet I fear you, for you're fatal then

    When your eyes roll so. Why I should fear I know

        not,

    Since guiltiness I know not. But yet I feel I fear.

OTHELLO

    Think on thy sins.

DESDEMONA   They are loves I bear to you.   40

OTHELLO

    Ay, and for that thou diest.

DESDEMONA

    That death's unnatural that kills for loving.

---

30 **by** i.e. aside

31–2 If he killed her *unprepared spirit* he would 'kill' her soul by sending it to hell (cf. *Ham* 3.3.73–95). Cf. Matthew 10.28, 'fear ye not them which kill the body, but are not able to kill the soul . . . fear him which is able to destroy both body and soul in hell'.

32 **heaven forfend** Cf. 182. Already a set phrase (as in *1H6* 5.4.65); *forfend* = forbid.

33–4 **Then . . . me!** Cf. 'Lord have mercy upon us!', a frequent response in the *Book of Common Prayer*. Cf. 57.

34 **Amen** a liturgical response, as at 57

36 **Hum!** probably our 'hmm!', a threatening sound

38 **Why . . . not** Cf. Ovid, *Heroides*, 1.71 'quid timeam, ignoro' (what – or how, why – I am to fear I know not).

40 **They . . . you** 'An allusion to the sin of loving a human being more than God' (Sanders). Yet she does not say she loves him more than God. Did Shakespeare write *bore*, misread *bere*? Then Othello would mean 'you die because you have stopped loving me'.

42 **That death's** i.e. that killing is

---

32 heaven] *Q*; Heauens *F* 33–4 Then . . . me] *as Cam³; one line QF* 35 so] *Q*; *not in F* 36 Hum] *Q*; *F (*Humh*)* 37 you're] *F*; you are *Q* 38] *as Q*; *F lines* so. / not, / 41 Ay] *F (*I*)*; *not in Q*

Alas, why gnaw you so your nether lip?
Some bloody passion shakes your very frame,
These are portents: but yet I hope, I hope   45
They do not point on me.

OTHELLO   Peace, and be still.

DESDEMONA
I will. So: what's the matter?

OTHELLO   That handkerchief
Which I so loved and gave thee, thou gavest
To Cassio.

DESDEMONA   No, by my life and soul:
Send for the man and ask him.

OTHELLO   Sweet soul, take heed,   50
Take heed of perjury. Thou art on thy death-bed.

DESDEMONA
I? – but not yet to die!

OTHELLO   Yes, presently.
Therefore confess thee freely of thy sin,
For to deny each article with oath
Cannot remove nor choke the strong conception   55

43 Cf. *R3* 4.2.27, 'The King is angry,
   see, he gnaws his lip.' Burbage played
   both Richard and Othello.
44 **bloody** portending bloodshed
   frame body
45 **portents** omens
46 **They ... me** i.e. they are not portents for me.
   Peace ... still Cf. Mark 4.39, 'he
   arose, and rebuked the wind, and said
   unto the sea, Peace, and be still'.
47 ***I will. So:** 'I will so' (as in most
   editions) is odd. 'Be still' implies that
   she is agitated: she becomes still ('I
   will'), then adds 'So' = So, I have
   done as you asked. Cf. 5.1.82, 'Lend
   me a garter. So.'
48 strong accusing stress on *thou*
50 **Sweet soul** usually an expression of
   tenderness (*MV* 5.1.49, *H5* 4.6.17)

51 **Thou art** scan 'Thou'rt'
52 ***I?** could be 'Ay,', but a strange reply
   either way; *but not yet to die* is a cry,
   an appeal, not a statement
   presently immediately
53 confess your sin unreservedly, without holding anything back. He seems
   to mean 'confess to heaven *and to
   me*'.
54 **article** item (in the accusation)
55 **choke** smother, silence
   strong grievous; irresistible (*OED*
   11, 16)
   conception notion. But could =
   embryo, offspring: this submerged
   image makes Othello the mother who
   groans and wants to *remove* an un-
   wanted child (the notion of her adultery). For similar images, cf. 1.3.402–
   3, 2.1.127–8.

45 ²I hope] *F; not in Q*   47 will. So:] *this edn*; will, so, *Q*; will so: *F*   47–52] *Q lines* gaue thee, /
Cassio. / soule, / him. / periury, / death-bed. / die. / presently: /; *F lines* Handkerchiefe / *Cassio. /*
man, / him. / Periury, /   48 gavest] *Q;* gau'st *F*   52 I? – but] *this edn;* I, but *QF*   die!] *this edn;*
die. *QF*   Yes] *Q; not in F*   55 conception] *F;* conceit *Q*

That I do groan withal. Thou art to die.

DESDEMONA

Then Lord have mercy on me.

OTHELLO   I say amen.

DESDEMONA

And have you mercy too. I never did
Offend you in my life, never loved Cassio
But with such general warranty of heaven   60
As I might love: I never gave him token.

OTHELLO

By heaven, I saw my handkerchief in's hand!
O perjured woman, thou dost stone my heart
And makest me call what I intend to do
A murder, which I thought a sacrifice!   65
I saw the handkerchief.

DESDEMONA   He found it then,
I never gave it him. Send for him hither,
Let him confess the truth.

OTHELLO   He hath confessed.

DESDEMONA

What, my lord?

OTHELLO   That he hath – ud's death! – used thee.

57 Cf. 33–4n., and Psalms 6.2, 9.13, 27.7.
59 **Offend** wrong, sin against
60 **warranty** authorization
61 **might** am allowed to
   token i.e. love token
63 **stone** turn to stone, make hard like stone (*OED* 2, first here). Repeating 4.1.179–80.
   my Johnson defended Q *thy*: thou dost harden thy heart, leaving this life 'in the state of the *murdered* without preparation for death, when *I intended* that thy punishment should have been *a sacrifice* atoning for thy crime'.
65 Cf. *JC* 2.1.166; see p. 33n.2.
68 **confess** declare, testify to

*the truth a 'common error' (*Texts*, 95)? That is, F followed Q. At 126 Q again misprints *a* (for *the*) *truth*.
69 **That ... thee** As F normally softens or omits profanity, and Q has lost something leading up to 'How, vnlawfully?', I retain both Q *vds death* and F *vs'd thee*, even though *vds* and *vsd* consist of the same three letters (which suggests transposition in Q or F). To retain Q profanity and eke out obvious Q omissions from F is normal procedure, and here yields regular metre.
   used had sexual intercourse with (*OED* 10b). Cf. 3.3.277; *Tim* 4.3.84, 'Be a whore still. They love thee not that use thee', *Son* 20.14.

57 Then Lord] *Q;* O Heauen *F* 58–9] *as F; Q* lines too: / *Cassio,* / 62 in's] *F;* in his *Q* 63 my] *F;* thy *Q* 64 makest] *Q;* makes *F* 65ff. murder] *Q;* Murther *F throughout scene* 68 Let] *F;* And let *Q* the] *this edn; a QF* 69 hath] *F;* has *Q* ud's death! – used thee] *Alexander;* vds death. *Q;* vs'd thee. *F*

310

DESDEMONA
How? unlawfully?
OTHELLO   Ay.
DESDEMONA   He will not say so.   70
OTHELLO
No, his mouth is stopped. Honest Iago
Hath ta'en order for't.
DESDEMONA   O, my fear interprets!
What, is he dead?
OTHELLO   Had all his hairs been lives
My great revenge had stomach for them all.
DESDEMONA
Alas, he is betrayed, and I undone.   75
OTHELLO
Out, strumpet, weep'st thou for him to my face?
DESDEMONA
O, banish me, my lord, but kill me not!
OTHELLO
Down, strumpet!
DESDEMONA
Kill me tomorrow, let me live tonight!
OTHELLO
Nay, if you strive –   80

70 **He will not** i.e. surely he will not.
71 **mouth is stopped** Cf. 2.3.300.
72 **ta'en order** taken measures
   interprets i.e. guesses the worst
73 **Had ... lives** Cf. Dent, H30, 'As many as there are hairs on the head'; Psalms 40.15, 'my sins . . . are more in number than the hairs of my head'.
74 **had stomach** would have had appetite (to consume them all). Cf. 3.3.462–3.
75 **betrayed** treacherously destroyed by his enemies; Othello thinks 'revealed (as her lover)' (*OED* 6)
76 **Out** exclamation of abhorrence or reproach
   weep'st ... him He misinterprets again.
77 **banish** send or drive away
78 **Down** The stage image (a man forcing a woman down on a bed) is suggestive: see p. 52. Note that his three speeches in Q make up a pentameter: 'Downe strumpet. – Nay, an you striue. – It is too late.'
80 **strive** struggle, resist

71–2] *this edn; QF lines* stop'd, / for't. /   72–4] *this edn; Q lines* dead? / liues, / all. /; *F lines* dead? / Reuenge / all. /   72 O . . . interprets] *F;* My feare interprets then *Q*   74 them] *F;* 'em *Q*   76 Out] *F;* O *Q*   weep'st] *F;* weepest *Q*   80 if] *F;* an *Q*

DESDEMONA
  But half an hour!
OTHELLO   Being done, there is no pause –
DESDEMONA
  But while I say one prayer!
OTHELLO   It is too late.
DESDEMONA
  O Lord! Lord! Lord! [*He*] *smothers her.*
EMILIA   (*within*)
  My lord, my lord! what ho, my lord, my lord!
OTHELLO
  What noise is this? Not dead? not yet quite dead?   85
  I that am cruel am yet merciful,
  I would not have thee linger in thy pain.
  So, so.
EMILIA   (*within*) What ho! my lord! my lord!
OTHELLO   Who's there?
EMILIA   [*within*]
  O good my lord, I'd speak a word with you.
OTHELLO
  Yes. 'Tis Emilia. – [*to Emilia.*] By and by. – She's
  dead.   90

81 **But** only
  Being . . . pause perhaps = (while it
  is) being done, there must be (room
  for) no pause (stopping or hesitation)
82 **But . . . prayer** a common request:
  cf. Marlowe, *Massacre*, 301, 'O let me
  pray before I dye'. Othello's disre-
  gard of it reflects on his Christianity.
  I assume that she cries 'O Lord . . .'
  before he begins to smother her: it is
  more a prayer than a shriek.
83 **O . . . ³Lord!** Granville-Barker defended Q's line, omitted by some editors.
  'Imagine it: Desdemona's agonised
  cry to God, and as the sharp sound
  of it is slowly stifled, Emilia's voice

  at the door rising through it, using
  the same words in another sense. A
  macabre duet' (*Othello* [1945], p.
  122).
  SD See LN.
85 In some productions Emilia knocks
  on the door, with an effect like that of
  the 'knocking at the gate in *Macbeth*'
  (see De Quincey's famous essay).
88 **So, so** Cf. 4.1.123. Some actors and
  critics think Othello now stabs
  Desdemona (see M. Ware, in *ES*, 45
  [1964], 177–80; Furness, 302ff.;
  Hankey, 319): I think it unlikely.
90 **By and by** soon. Common in Shakespeare and the Bible.

81 OTHELLO Being . . . pause] *F; not in Q* 82 It is] *F;* 'Tis *Q* 83 O . . . ³Lord] *Q; not in F* SD]
he stifles her. Q ; Smothers her. F (QF place SD after too late *82)* 84 SD] Emillia *calls within. Q ;*
Aemilia at the doore. F 84] as *Q ; F lines* hoa? / Lord. / 85 noise] *F;* voyce *Q* 86 that am] *Q,*
Fc; am that *Fu* 88 SD] *F; not in Q* 89 SD] *Malone; not in F* I'd] *Q ;* I would *F* 90] *this*
edn; Yes, tis *Emillia,* by and by: shee's dead: *Q ;* Yes: 'Tis *Aemilia:* by and by. Shee's dead. *F*

'Tis like she comes to speak of Cassio's death,
The noise was high. Ha, no more moving?
Still as the grave. Shall she come in? were't good?
I think she stirs again. No – what's best to do?
If she come in, she'll sure speak to my wife.   95
My wife, my wife! what wife? I have no wife.
O insupportable, O heavy hour!
Methinks it should be now a huge eclipse
Of sun and moon, and that th'affrighted globe
Should yawn at alteration.

EMILIA   [*within*]   I do beseech you   100
That I may speak with you! O good my lord!

OTHELLO

I had forgot thee: O come in, Emilia.
Soft, by and by. Let me the curtains draw.
Where art thou? What's the matter with thee now?
                                    [*He unlocks the door.*]

Enter EMILIA.

EMILIA

O my good lord, yonder's foul murders done!   105

---

91 **like** likely
92 **high** loud. The brawl outside was
   audible indoors (which explains the
   arrival of Lodovico and Gratiano in
   5.1).
93 **Still ... grave** Dent, D133.1, 'As
   dumb (silent, still) as death (the
   grave)'.
93, 95 **she** Emilia
94 **she** Desdemona
95 **my wife** Cf. 2.3.378n., 4.2.104.
97 **insupportable** unendurable. Could
   be an exclamation on its own (= O
   insupportable loss!) or an adjective
   qualifying *hour*. Cf. 1.3.259n. and *JC*
   4.3.151, 'O insupportable and touching loss!'

heavy sorrowful
98–100 See LN.
99 **globe** earth
100 **yawn** gape (i.e. chasms should open
   in response to the changed appearance of sun and moon). Hart quoted
   Pliny, 2.80, 'Of the Gaping Chinks of
   the Earth': 'They [earthquakes] fortune also to be when the Sun and
   Moon are eclipsed.'
   alteration this change (brought
   about by Desdemona's death). A limp
   last word: could it be an error?
103 **curtains** bed curtains
104 **What's ... now?** What do you want
   now?

---

92 high] *F;* here *Q*   moving?] *F;* mouing, *Q*   94 best to do?] *F;* the best *Q*   96 what ... have] *F;*
my wife; I ha *Q*   97 insupportable,] *this edn;* insupportable: *Q;* insupportable! *F*   99 th'] *F;* the
Q   100] Should *Q;* Did *F*   SD] *not in QF*   101 That] *F; not in Q*   O] *F; not in Q*   104.1] *as
Theobald; not in QF*   104.2] *as F; opp. 103 Q*

OTHELLO

What? now?

EMILIA

But now, my lord.

OTHELLO

It is the very error of the moon,
She comes more nearer earth than she was wont
And makes men mad.

EMILIA   Cassio, my lord, hath killed   110
A young Venetian, called Roderigo.

OTHELLO

Roderigo killed? and Cassio killed?

EMILIA

No, Cassio is not killed.

OTHELLO   Not Cassio killed?
Then murder's out of tune, and sweet revenge
Grows harsh.

DESDEMONA   O falsely, falsely murdered!   115

EMILIA

O lord, what cry is that?

OTHELLO

That? what?

---

106 **What? now?** I prefer F to Q: it
better conveys his sense of shock.
107 **But now** just now, only this
moment (*OED* but 6b)
108 **very** *either* 'solely' (adverb), *or*
'indeed' (intensive) (Elliott, 104)
error mistake; wandering off course
(Lat. *erro*, I wander)
109 **She** *Luna*, the moon, is feminine in
Latin. Cf. 17n.
more nearer double comparative,
common in Shakespeare
110 **makes men mad** The word lunacy
shows how long and firmly men have
believed in a connection between the
moon and madness (Ridley).
111 **Venetian** (four syllables)
113 **Not ... killed?** more disorientated

than 'Cassio not killed!'
114–15 **and ... harsh** and (the sweet
music of) revenge grows harsh
115 **falsely** wrongly, mistakenly. She
seems to reply to 114. See also 325–
6n., and *Warning for Fair Women*
(1599), F1a, 'What sound was that?
it was not he that spake' (a 'dead'
person speaks).
murdered disyllabic, which gives a
nine-syllable line. The verse can be
divided differently but, however we re-
arrange it, always breaks down. The
broken lines highlight the speakers'
tension.
116 **cry** utterance (not necessarily loud).
Desdemona is concealed behind the
bed curtains.

---

106 What? now?] *F;* What, now? *Q*   109 nearer] *F;* neere the *Q*   110 hath] *F;* has *Q*   113–15]
this edn; QF lines tune, / harsh. / murdered. /   116 O lord] *Q ;* Alas *F*

EMILIA

Out and alas, that was my lady's voice:

[*She draws the bed-curtains.*]

Help, help, ho, help! O lady, speak again,

Sweet Desdemona, O sweet mistress, speak!   120

DESDEMONA

A guiltless death I die.

EMILIA   O, who hath done

This deed?

DESDEMONA   Nobody. I myself. Farewell.

Commend me to my kind lord – O, farewell!   *She dies.*

OTHELLO

Why, how should she be murdered?

EMILIA   Alas, who knows?

OTHELLO

You heard her say herself it was not I.   125

EMILIA

She said so; I must needs report the truth.

OTHELLO

She's like a liar gone to burning hell:

'Twas I that killed her.

EMILIA   O, the more angel she,

And you the blacker devil!

OTHELLO

She turned to folly, and she was a whore.   130

EMILIA

Thou dost belie her, and thou art a devil.

118 **Out and alas** Cf. 76n. Usually 'out alas' (*Tit* 2.3.258, *MW* 4.5.63, *WT* 4.4.110); 'Out and' may be for emphasis.

121–2 Dividing as here, 'done / This deed', is unusual, but gives two consecutive pentameters instead of short lines. A slight pause after *done* mirrors Emilia's consternation. See *Texts*, 108.

124 **how . . . be** how should she come to be

127–8 Perhaps he thinks also of 58ff., though primarily of 122–3.

130 **folly** wickedness; unchastity (*OED* 2, 3). Cf. Deuteronomy 22.21, 'She hath wrought folly in Israel, to play the whore in her father's house.'

131 **Thou** Cf. *you* 129. Her indignation carries her away. *Belie* = slander.

118   that was] *F;* it is *Q*   SD] *Cam² subst.; not in QF*   121 hath] *F;* has *Q*   121–2 O . . . deed?] *as Capell; one line QF*   123 SD] *Q; not in F*   125 heard] *Q;* heare *F*   126 the truth] *F;* a truth *Q*   127 burning] *QF;* burne in *Q3*   128–9 O . . . devil] *as Q; prose F*

OTHELLO
  She was false as water.

EMILIA   Thou art rash as fire to say
  That she was false. O, she was heavenly true!

OTHELLO
  Cassio did top her: ask thy husband else.
  O, I were damned beneath all depth in hell   135
  But that I did proceed upon just grounds
  To this extremity. Thy husband knew it all.

EMILIA
  My husband?

OTHELLO   Thy husband.

EMILIA   That she was false?
  To wedlock?

OTHELLO   Ay, with Cassio. Had she been true,
  If heaven would make me such another world   140
  Of one entire and perfect chrysolite,
  I'd not have sold her for it.

EMILIA   My husband?

---

132 **false as water** Cf. Dent, W86.1, 'As unstable (false) as water' (from Genesis 49.4).
  rash as fire Cf. Dent, F246.1, 'As hasty as fire'. Scan 'wat'r / Thou'rt' (Abbott, 464, 465).

133 **heavenly true** Cf. Dent, G173, 'As false as God is true'. True = true to you; virtuous.

134 **top** Cf. 1.1.88n.
  else i.e. if you don't believe me (*OED* 4c)

135 Cf. Psalms 86.13, 'thou hast delivered my soul from the nethermost hell'.

137 **extremity** utmost penalty; extreme rigour or measure (*OED* 3b, 6, 9)

138, 142, 145 **My husband?** 'Emilia's repeated astonishment at Iago's complicity is the argument in favour of her not having suspected him to be

the "eternal villain" [of 4.2.132]' (Hart). Hart, however, interpreted QF '?' as '!' in all three lines. If we retain '?', she could speak quietly at first, adjusting to an explanation that she had already suspected (a different kind of surprise): see pp. 44–6.

138–9 Cf. 121–2: an unusual line division again gives 'regular' metre (*Texts*, 120).

140 **such another** (*OED* 1c) another of the same sort (but made of chrysolite)

141 Cf. *Faerie Queene*, 1.7.33 (Arthur's shield), 'But *all of Diamond perfect* pure and cleene / It framed was, one massy *entire* mould.'
  entire complete, perfect, pure
  chrysolite See LN.

142 **sold** exchanged. Cf. *2H6* 3.1.92, 'Or sell my title for a glorious grave'.

132–3 Thou ... true] *as* F; *Q lines* fire, / true. / 132 art] *F; as Q* 134 top] *QF;* tup *Pope²* 138–9 That ... wedlock] *this edn; one line QF* 139 Had] *as F;* nay, had *Q*

OTHELLO

    Ay, 'twas he that told me on her first;

    An honest man he is, and hates the slime

    That sticks on filthy deeds.

EMILIA   My husband!

OTHELLO   What needs   145

    This iterance, woman? I say thy husband.

EMILIA

    O mistress, villainy hath made mocks with love!

    My husband say she was false?

OTHELLO   He, woman;

    I say thy husband: dost understand the word?

    My friend thy husband, honest, honest Iago.   150

EMILIA

    If he say so, may his pernicious soul

    Rot half a grain a day! he lies to th' heart:

    She was too fond of her most filthy bargain!

OTHELLO

    Ha!

EMILIA

    Do thy worst: .   155

    This deed of thine is no more worthy heaven

    Than thou wast worthy her.

OTHELLO   Peace, you were best!

143 **on** of; *tell on* = play the informer (*OED* 16)

144 **slime** suggests sexual slime: *filthy* (= obscene) *deeds* are sexual here (cf. 4.2.72ff., 4.3.63ff.)

146 **iterance** repetition. Shakespeare's coinage; Q *iteration* was common.

146 **woman** deliberately discourteous, as often in the Bible (John 2.4, 'Jesus sayth unto her, Woman, what have I to do with thee?')

147 **made mocks with** usually *at* or *of*: 'made a mock(ery) of'

150 **friend** Cf. 3.3.145, 5.1.32n.

151 **pernicious** destructive; evil

152 **grain** particle. A slow death is the worst: cf. 4.1.176, 'nine years a-killing'.
lies . . . heart lies down to his very heart, i.e. he's an out-and-out liar. More emphatic than the proverbial 'To lie in one's throat' (Dent, T268).

153 **filthy** a 'racist' jibe, provoked by his *filthy* 145

156 **worthy** worthy of. She returns to 127ff., their dispute about the *angel* and *devil*.

157 **you were best** it would be best for you

143 on her] *F; not in Q*   145–6 What . . . husband] *one line Q; F lines* Woman? / Husband. /
146 iterance, woman?] *F subst.;* iteration? woman, *Q*   147–50] *F; not in Q*   147] *F lines* Mistris, /
loue: /; *one line Q2*   154 Ha!] *QF (*Ha?*)*

EMILIA

 Thou hast not half that power to do me harm
 As I have to be hurt. O gull, O dolt,
 As ignorant as dirt! Thou hast done a deed   160
       [*He threatens her with his sword.*]
 – I care not for thy sword, I'll make thee known
 Though I lost twenty lives. Help, help, ho, help!
 The Moor hath killed my mistress! Murder, murder!

   Enter MONTANO, GRATIANO *and* IAGO.

MONTANO

 What is the matter? How now, general?

EMILIA

 O, are you come, Iago? you have done well   165
 That men must lay their murders on your neck.

GRATIANO

 What is the matter?

EMILIA

 Disprove this villain, if thou be'st a man;
 He says thou told'st him that his wife was false,
 I know thou didst not, thou'rt not such a villain. 170
 Speak, for my heart is full.

IAGO

 I told him what I thought, and told no more
 Than what he found himself was apt and true.

EMILIA

 But did you ever tell him she was false?

158–9 **Thou ... hurt** i.e. she can endure more than he can inflict (*harm* = hurt). Cf. *H8* 3.2.387ff., 'able ... To endure more miseries ... Than my weak-hearted enemies dare offer'.
159 **gull** dupe
 dolt block-head, i.e. slow thinker
160 **dirt** resuming *filthy* (153), a jibe that went home. *OED* 1 glosses dirt as 'ordure = excrement', so this is another racist jibe at Othello's colour.
161 **care not for** don't fear
 make thee known expose you
164 **How now** could be a question or interjection (*OED* how 4: modern equivalent 'What?' or 'What!')
166 **on your neck** to your charge
173 **apt** likely

158 that] *F;* the *Q* 160 SD] *not in QF* 161 known] *F;* know *Q* 162 ho] *F (*hoa*);* O *Q* 163 hath] *F;* has *Q* 163.1] *F; Enter* Montano, Gratiano, Iago, *and others. Q* 166 murders] *F (*Murthers*);* murder *Q* 167 SP] *as F; All Q* 170 thou'rt] *F;* thou art *Q* 172] *as Q; F lines* thought, / more / 174] *as Q; F lines* him, / false? /

IAGO

    I did.   175

EMILIA

    You told a lie, an odious, damned lie!

    Upon my soul, a lie, a wicked lie!

    She false with Cassio? Did you say with Cassio?

IAGO

    With Cassio, mistress. Go to, charm your tongue.

EMILIA

    I will not charm my tongue, I am bound to speak: 180

    My mistress here lies murdered in her bed.

ALL

    O heavens forfend!

EMILIA

    And your reports have set the murder on.

OTHELLO

    Nay, stare not, masters, it is true indeed.

GRATIANO

    'Tis a strange truth.   185

MONTANO

    O monstrous act!

EMILIA

    Villainy, villainy, villainy!

    I think upon't, I think I smell't, O villainy!

    I thought so then: I'll kill myself for grief!

    O villainy, villainy!   190

---

176 **odious, damned** *either* 'o-di-ous damn'd', *or* 'od-yus dam-nèd'
177 **Upon my soul** by the salvation of my soul (more deeply felt than the later ''pon my soul')
    wicked evil, depraved, malicious (a richer word than today)
179 **charm** control. Cf. *TS* 4.2.58, *2H6* 4.1.64.
180 **bound** duty-bound; compelled, obliged (*OED* 7)

183 **set . . . on** incited
184 **masters** Cf. 2.3.116n.
185 **a strange truth** Cf. *MND* 5.1.2, *MM* 5.1.44.
187 **Villainy** a richer word than now, ranging from boorishness to discourtesy to extreme wickedness (*OED* 1, 6)
188 **think upon** remember, call to mind (*OED* 5c): see p. 46.
    smell suspect, detect
189 **then** See p. 46.

178] *as Q ; F lines* Cassio? / Cassio? /   179] *as Q ; F lines* Mistris? / tongue. /   180] *as Q ; F lines* Tongue; / speake, /   181–90] *F; not in Q*   181 murdered] *F (*murthered*)*   182 heavens] *F (*Heauens,*)*   184] *Q2; F lines* Masters, / indeede. /   188 think I smell't, O] *this edn;* thinke: I smel't: O *F*

IAGO

    What, are you mad? I charge you, get you home.

EMILIA

    Good gentlemen, let me have leave to speak.

    'Tis proper I obey him – but not now.

    Perchance, Iago, I will ne'er go home.   194

OTHELLO

    O! O! O!   *Othello falls on the bed.*

EMILIA

    Nay, lay thee down and roar

    For thou hast killed the sweetest innocent

    That e'er did lift up eye.

OTHELLO   O, she was foul.

    I scarce did know you, uncle: there lies your niece

    Whose breath, indeed, these hands have newly

       stopped;   200

    I know this act shows horrible and grim.

GRATIANO

    Poor Desdemon, I am glad thy father's dead;

    Thy match was mortal to him, and pure grief

    Shore his old thread in twain. Did he live now

    This sight would make him do a desperate turn,   205

---

193 Cf. Ephesians 5.24, 'as the Church is subject unto Christ, likewise the wives to their own husbands in all things'.

195 a prolonged *roar*, not three separate sounds. Cf. 5.1.62n. A 'Herculean' feature: 'so did he with his roarings smite the stars' (Seneca, *Hercules Oetaeus*, 801ff.).

196 **Nay** used as an introductory word, without any negation (*OED* 1d); almost = yes

198 **lift up eye** Cf. Luke 6.20 and Psalms 121.1, 'I will lift up mine eyes unto the hills'; perhaps implying that she usually kept her eyes modestly down.

199 **uncle** i.e. Desdemona's uncle, pre-

sumably Brabantio's brother: cf. 1.1.173; see p. 23.

200 **these hands** He speaks as if his hands, not he, killed Desdemona. Cf. Macbeth's 'detached' hands, 2.2.56, 'What hands are here? Hah! they pluck out mine eyes.'

201 **shows** appears
    grim merciless, cruel

203 **mortal** fatal
    pure (intensive: *OED* 3b) utter

204 **Shore** sheared. Cf. *MND* 5.1.340, 'you have shore / With shears his thread'.
    thread i.e. thread of life, 'which it was the prerogative of the Fate Atropos to sever with her shears' (Ridley)

205 **turn** act

191] *as Q ; F lines* mad? / home. /   195 SD] *Q ; not in F*   201 horrible] *F;* terrible *Q*   202] *as Q ; F lines Desdemon*: / dead, /   Desdemon] *F; Desdemona Q*   204 in twain] *F;* atwane *Q*

Yea, curse his better angel from his side
And fall to reprobance.

OTHELLO

'Tis pitiful; but yet Iago knows
That she with Cassio hath the act of shame
A thousand times committed. Cassio confessed it,   210
And she did gratify his amorous works
With that recognizance and pledge of love
Which I first gave her: I saw it in his hand,
It was a handkerchief, an antique token
My father gave my mother.   215

EMILIA

O God, O heavenly God!

IAGO   Zounds, hold your peace!

EMILIA

'Twill out, 'twill out! I peace?
No, I will speak as liberal as the north.
Let heaven and men and devils, let them all,
All, all cry shame against me, yet I'll speak.   220

---

206 **better angel** Cf. the Good and Bad Angel in Marlowe, *Doctor Faustus*, and *Son* 144, 'Tempteth my better angel from his side'.
207 **reprobance** a coinage: the state of being a reprobate, a sinner rejected by God. With QF *reprobation–Reprobance*, cf. QF *iteration–itterance* (146) and *Texts*, 86.
208 **pitiful** Cf. 4.1.192–3.
209 **act of shame** Cf. 2.1.225, 'the act of sport'.
210 **A thousand** See p. 70 ('long time').
211 **gratify** reward
   works acts, deeds (*OED* 1), i.e. caresses
212 **recognizance** token
214 **antique** olden, belonging to former times; or, old-fashioned (*OED* 3, first in 1647). Perhaps stressed on first syllable.
215 This contradicts 3.4.57ff. Some think that he wanted to frighten Desdemona in 3.4, but the contradiction may be an oversight.
217–18 These lines may be revised in F: see *Texts*, 18.
217 **'Twill out** i.e. the facts will come out. But is there a hint that Emilia has bottled up a guilty secret (see pp. 44–6), which now bursts forth? Cf. *Look About You* (1600), D4a, 'Twill out, twill out, my selfe my selfe can ease'.
218 **¹as . . . north** as freely as the north wind speaks (or blows). Cf. 2.1.5, 'the wind hath spoke aloud', *TC* 1.3.253, 'Speak frankly as the wind'.
220 **shame** because she defies her husband?

---

207 reprobance] *F;* reprobation *Q*   212 that] *F;* the *Q*   216 ¹God] *Q;* Heauen *F*   ²God] *Q;* Powres *F*   Zounds] *Q;* Come *F*   217–18] *F;* 'Twill out, 'twill: I hold my peace sir, no, / I'le be in speaking, liberall as the ayre, *Q*   219 them] *F;* em *Q*

IAGO

Be wise, and get you home.

EMILIA

I will not.   [*Iago tries to stab Emilia.*]

GRATIANO   Fie! Your sword upon a woman?

EMILIA

O thou dull Moor, that handkerchief thou speak'st of
I found by fortune and did give my husband,
For often, with a solemn earnestness   225
– More than indeed belonged to such a trifle –
He begged of me to steal't.

IAGO   Villainous whore!

EMILIA

She give it Cassio? No, alas, I found it
And I did give't my husband.

IAGO   Filth, thou liest!

EMILIA

By heaven I do not, I do not, gentlemen!   230
O murderous coxcomb, what should such a fool
Do with so good a wife?

                    [*Othello runs at Iago. Iago stabs his wife.*]

OTHELLO   Are there no stones in heaven
But what serves for the thunder? Precious villain!

GRATIANO

The woman falls, sure he hath killed his wife.   234

222 **Your sword upon** use your sword against
223 **dull** obtuse, stupid
224 **fortune** chance
225 **solemn** imposing
226 **belonged** was appropriate
231 **coxcomb** (a cap worn by a professional fool, hence) fool, simpleton
232 **Do** have to do (*OED* 40), i.e. what business has he to have so good a wife?
  SD ***runs at*** either 'rushes at', or 'runs his sword at, strikes at' (*OED* 5, 14,

48). Apart from entrances and exits, this is the only centred SD in Q, and it is unusually specific. Note the sequence: Othello attacks, Iago dodges away and, doing so, stabs Emilia.
stones thunderbolts or 'thunderstones' (*JC* 1.3.49), to punish offenders; cf. *Cym* 5.5.240. 'Has not heaven one supernumerary bolt, to hurl directly at . . . this atrocious villain? Must all . . . of its arsenal be reserved for . . . ordinary thunder?' (Malone).
233 **Precious** (intensive) egregious

222 SD] *as Rowe (*Iago *offers to stab his wife); not in QF*   223] *as Q; F lines* Moore, / of /   of] *F;* on *Q*   227 't] *F;* it *Q*   228 give] *F;* gaue *Q*   232 wife] *F;* woman *Q*   SD] *The Moore runnes at* Iago. Iago *kils his wife. Q; not in F*   233] *as Q; F lines* Thunder? / Villaine. /   Precious] *QF;* pernitious *Q2*   234] *as Q; F lines* falles: / Wife. /   hath] *F;* has *Q*

EMILIA

Ay, ay; O lay me by my mistress' side.   *Exit Iago.*

GRATIANO

He's gone, but his wife's killed.

MONTANO

'Tis a notorious villain. Take you this weapon
Which I have here recovered from the Moor;
Come, guard the door without, let him not pass
But kill him rather. I'll after that same villain,   240
For 'tis a damned slave.   *Exeunt Montano and Gratiano.*

OTHELLO   I am not valiant neither,
But every puny whipster gets my sword.
But why should honour outlive honesty?
Let it go all.

EMILIA   What did thy song bode, lady?
Hark, canst thou hear me? I will play the swan   245
And die in music. [*Sings.*] Willow, willow, willow.
– Moor, she was chaste, she loved thee, cruel Moor,
So come my soul to bliss as I speak true!

---

237 **notorious** obvious, evident (*OED* 3, first in 1608)
238 **recovered** obtained, got hold of (*OED* 6); not 'taken back from'
239 **without** from the outside
241 **damned** damnable, accursed. Probably 'damnèd', although 'damn'd' and 'I'm' would give a pentameter.
neither 'used to strengthen a preceding negative: = either' (*OED* 3). He seems to voice an unspoken train of thought: I am a 'dull Moor', I have failed to kill Iago, I am a failure – and 'I am not valiant either'. He is no longer the 'valiant Othello' of 1.3.48–9. A process of self-assessment has begun.
242 **whipster** an insignificant person; one who wields a whip. This is not to disparage Montano: he means 'every whip can defeat my sword'.
gets = takes
sword The Moors in other plays carry a scimitar (see p. 17): not Othello.
243 **honour** esteem (from others), an honourable reputation
honesty integrity
244 **Let . . . all** more emphatic than 'Let it all go.' But *all* may be an adverb = entirely.
bode forebode; mean
245 **Hark . . . me** alluding to the belief that the souls of the dead linger near the body for a while
swan Cf. Dent, S1028, 'Like a swan, he sings before his death', *MV* 3.2.44, *KJ* 5.7.21.

---

235 SD] *Q ; not in F*   237 you this] *F;* your *Q*   238 here] *Q ; not in F*   241 SD] *Exit* Mont. *and* Gratiano. *Q ; Exit. F*   244–6 What . . . ³willow] *F; not in Q*   246 SD] *as Dyce; not in QF*   Willow] *F (Willough)*

323

So speaking as I think, alas, I die.   *She dies.*

OTHELLO

I have another weapon in this chamber,   250
It is a sword of Spain, the ice-brook's temper;
O, here it is. Uncle, I must come forth.

GRATIANO   [*within*]

If thou attempt it it will cost thee dear;
Thou hast no weapon, and perforce must suffer.

OTHELLO

Look in upon me then, and speak with me,   255
Or, naked as I am, I will assault thee.

[*Enter* GRATIANO.]

GRATIANO

What is the matter?

OTHELLO   Behold, I have a weapon,
A better never did itself sustain
Upon a soldier's thigh. I have seen the day
That with this little arm and this good sword   260
I have made my way through more impediments
Than twenty times your stop: but, O vain boast,
Who can control his fate? 'Tis not so now.
Be not afraid, though you do see me weaponed:
Here is my journey's end, here is my butt   265

---

249 Cf. Dent, S725, 'To speak as one thinks'.
  alas, I die sometimes substituted for profanity in F (e.g. 2.3.154, 5.2.116) so Q *I die* may be corrupt. *I die, I die* sounds uncomfortably like *MND* 5.1.306, 'Now die, die, die, die, die'.
251 See LN.
252 **Uncle** Cf. 199n.
254 **suffer** i.e. be injured or killed
256 **naked** without weapon (or armour) (*OED* 4)
258 **sustain** maintain its position (*OED* 11c)
259 **I . . . day** Cf. Dent, D81.1, 'I have

seen the day'; *RJ* 1.5.21, *KL* 5.3.277.
262 **your stop** the obstruction you offer
  vain empty; vainglorious
263 **control** command, exercise control over
  fate Cf. Dent, F83, 'It is impossible to avoid fate'; see p. 72. He blames fate, the stars, luck, etc. (270, 339) to minimize his own guilt.
264 **weaponed** armed. Cf. *wived*, *womaned* (2.1.60, 3.4.195).
265 **Here** Desdemona? Or, here in this place?
  butt terminal point; that towards which his efforts are directed, end

---

249 alas, I die] F; I die, I die Q   SD] Q; *not in* F   251 is] Q; was F   ice-brook's] F *(Ice brookes)*; Isebrookes Q   253 SD] Q *(Gra. within.) opp. 252*   255 with] F; to Q   256.1] *as Theobald; not in* QF   262 your] F; you Q   264–70] F; *not in* Q

And very sea-mark of my utmost sail.
Do you go back dismayed? 'tis a lost fear:
Man but a rush against Othello's breast
And he retires. Where should Othello go?
Now: how dost thou look now? O ill-starred wench,   270
Pale as thy smock. When we shall meet at compt
This look of thine will hurl my soul from heaven
And fiends will snatch at it. Cold, cold, my girl,
Even like thy chastity. O cursed, cursed slave!
Whip me, ye devils,   275
From the possession of this heavenly sight!
Blow me about in winds, roast me in sulphur,
Wash me in steep-down gulfs of liquid fire!

266 **sea-mark** the boundary or limit of the flow of the sea; a conspicuous object which guides sailors in navigation
  utmost farthest; last (*OED* 1, 3). Cf. *MM* 2.1.36, 'that's the utmost of his pilgrimage'.
267 **dismayed** appalled (stronger than today)
  lost groundless
268 **Man . . . against** use a mere rush as a weapon against. Cf. *KJ* 4.3.129–30, 'a rush will be a beam / To hang thee on'.
270 **ill-starred** ill-fated. A coinage, like 'star-crossed' (*RJ* Prol. 6). Perhaps alluding to Disdemona's name (= the unfortunate one, to which Cinthio drew attention: p. 386).
  wench Cf. 3.3.317n.
271 **Pale . . . smock** Cf. Dent, C446, 'As pale as a clout (= piece of cloth)'.
  compt the Day of Judgement ([ac]compt = account); cf. *AW* 5.3.57, 'the great compt'. This was a popular subject with Renaissance painters, who depicted the damned being hurled from heaven and seized in mid-air by devils: also found in bibles, stained-glass windows, emblem books, etc.

273–4 **Cold . . . chastity** Cf. Dent, I1, 'As chaste as ice (snow)'. Cf. 3.4.39, 'Hot, hot, and moist', 5.2.4.
274 **O . . . slave** He curses himself (or possibly Iago). Placed in the same line with *Even . . . chastity* in both Q and F (Q has only one *cursed*, = cursèd; F has two, = curs'd, curs'd). Some editors move the words down one line and print 'O cursèd, cursèd slave! Whip me, ye devils /'.
276 **possession** i.e. having, enjoying (he does not deserve to enjoy a 'heavenly sight': his rightful place is hell)
  heavenly a word associated with 'the divine Desdemona': cf. 4.3.65, 5.2.133
277–8 See LN.
277 **roast . . . sulphur** Cf. 3.3.332n.
278 **steep-down** precipitous (unique in Shakespeare)
  gulfs perhaps influenced by Luke 16.19ff.: the rich man, tormented by flames in hell, looks up and sees Lazarus in Abraham's bosom. Between them is a 'great gulf'.
  liquid fire Cf. Revelation 19.20, 'cast quick into a pond of fire, burning with brimstone'.

271 compt] *F;* count *Q*   274 ²cursed] *F; not in Q*   275 ye] *F;* you *Q*

O Desdemon! dead, Desdemon. Dead! O, O!

Enter LODOVICO, MONTANO, *Officers with* IAGO, *prisoner, and*
CASSIO *in a chair.*

LODOVICO
Where is this rash and most unfortunate man?   280
OTHELLO
That's he that was Othello? here I am.
LODOVICO
Where is that viper? bring the villain forth.
OTHELLO
I look down towards his feet, but that's a fable.
If that thou be'st a devil, I cannot kill thee.

                                        [*Wounds Iago.*]
LODOVICO
Wrench his sword from him.
IAGO   I bleed, sir, but not killed.   285
OTHELLO
I am not sorry neither, I'd have thee live:
For in my sense 'tis happiness to die.

---

279 Like Lear's 'Never, never ...'
(5.3.309), this line can be spoken in
many ways. F's punctuation is not
likely to be Shakespeare's.
   O, O! probably a single prolonged
moan or cry: cf. 195n.
281 **That's ... Othello** Some editors
take this as a statement. I prefer a
question (*That's* = that's to say):
'You mean – he that was Othello?'
He is on the verge of disowning himself. Cf. the *he–I* switch at 353–4,
and, in a different context, *TN*

1.5.234, 'such a one I was this
present'.
283 **his** Iago's. Othello means the fable
that the devil has a cloven foot
(Tilley, D252).
285 **Wrench** Others hold Othello now;
he probably surrenders his sword
without a struggle.
   I ... killed sarcastic: 'I bleed (like a
human being), but I'm not killed
(therefore I may be a devil).
287 for one who feels as I do would
think it happiness to die

279] *F; O Desdemona, Desdemoua, dead, O, o, o. Q*   279.1–2] *Enter* Lodouico, Montano, Iago, *and*
Officers, Cassio *in a Chaire. Q; Enter* Lodouico, Cassio, Montano, *and* Iago, *with Officers. F; ...* Cassio
led in wounded, Montano, *and* Iago *Prisoner, with Officers. Rowe*   280 unfortunate] *F;* infortunate
Q   281 Othello?] *this edn;* Othello, *Q;* Othello: *F*   282] *as Q; F lines* Viper? / forth. /   that] *F;*
this *Q*   284 If that] *F;* If *Q*   SD] *Rowe; not in QF*   285 Wrench] *F;* Wring *Q*   286 live] *Q_c,*
F; loue *Qu.*

LODOVICO

    O thou Othello, that wert once so good,

    Fallen in the practice of a cursed slave,

    What shall be said to thee?

OTHELLO   Why, anything;   290

    An honourable murderer, if you will,

    For nought I did in hate, but all in honour.

LODOVICO

    This wretch hath part confessed his villainy.

    Did you and he consent in Cassio's death?

OTHELLO

    Ay.   295

CASSIO

    Dear general, I never gave you cause.

OTHELLO

    I do believe it, and I ask your pardon.

    Will you, I pray, demand that demi-devil

    Why he hath thus ensnared my soul and body?

IAGO

    Demand me nothing. What you know, you know.   300

---

288 **O thou Othello** a curious form of address, but common in this play, usually spoken to or by Othello: 'O thou foul thief', 'O thou weed', 'O thou public commoner', 'O thou dull Moor', 'O thou pernicious caitiff' (1.2.62; 4.2.68, 74; 5.2.223, 316). Less respectful than *you*.

289 **in the practice** through the treachery or intrigue
    cursed cursèd

290 **What ... thee?** What can we possibly say to you?
    anything anything you like; or perhaps a question, 'why (say) anything?'

292 **in honour** with honourable intent. Is he deceiving himself?

293 **part** partly

294 **consent in** agree in planning

296 **Dear general** Othello can inspire strong affection, not only in Desdemona.
    I . . . cause Cf. 3.4.158.

297 Cf. Hamlet's similar apology to Laertes, shortly before his death, 'Give me your pardon, sir. I have done you wrong' (5.2.226).

298 **demi-devil** apparently Shakespeare's coinage. Othello accepts that Iago bleeds, therefore is not a proper devil: cf. 284–5.

299 **and body** He foresees his own damnation. Cf. *Homilies*, 82, 'damnation both of body and soul', and 357; Matthew 10.28, quoted 31–2n.

---

288 wert] *Q*; was *F*   289 cursed] *F*; damned *Q*   290 shall] *F*; should *Q*   292 I did] *F*; did I *Q*   296 never gave] *F*; did neuer giue *Q*   297 your] *F*; you *Q*   298 I pray] *F*; pray *Q*

From this time forth I never will speak word.

LODOVICO

What, not to pray?

GRATIANO   Torments will ope your lips.

OTHELLO

Well, thou dost best.

LODOVICO

Sir, you shall understand what hath befallen,
Which, as I think, you know not. Here is a letter   305
Found in the pocket of the slain Roderigo,
And here another: the one of them imports
The death of Cassio, to be undertook
By Roderigo.

OTHELLO

O villain!

CASSIO   Most heathenish and most gross!   310

LODOVICO

Now here's another discontented paper
Found in his pocket too, and this, it seems,
Roderigo meant t'have sent this damned villain
But that, belike, Iago in the nick
Came in, and satisfied him.   315

301 For his refusal to explain, cf. Hier-
   onimo in *The Spanish Tragedy*,
   'Sufficeth I may not, nor I will not
   tell thee' (Revels, 4.4.182); 'I'll speak
   no more but "Vengeance rot you
   all!"' (*TA* 5.1.58). How does Iago
   bear himself from now on? Some
   actors make him 'switch off', as if he
   has lost interest; others make him
   gloat in triumph (see p. 98).
302 **Torments** tortures
303 Does he mean 'Thou dost best not
   to tell us'?
304ff. Such summaries of the action are
   common in plays of the period: cf.
   TA (as in 301n.) and Friar Lawrence
   in *RJ* 5.3.229ff. Here Shakespeare
   focuses less on events than on reactions to events.

304 **befallen** happened
305 **a letter** Letters that conveniently
   help the plot are a convention of
   comedy: *TGV*   4.4.121ff.,   *LLL*
   4.3.191ff., *TN* 5.1.330ff.
310 **gross** monstrous; obvious. Cf. J.
   Chamber, *A Treatise* (1601), C1a, 'so
   grosse & heathenish a superstition'.
311 **discontented** i.e. filled with grievances
313 **damned** damnèd
314 **belike** probably
   in the nick at that point. Colloquial
   and 'low', hence 'sophisticated' in F
   (where *interim* gives a long line) or
   revised by Shakespeare. Cf. Dent,
   N160, 'In the nick (nick of time)'.
315 i.e. arrived and gave a satisfactory
   explanation

304 Sir,] *as Q ; F lines* Sir, / befalne, /   308–9] *as F; one line Q*   313 t'] *F; to Q*   314 nick] *Q ;*
interim *F*

OTHELLO

O thou pernicious caitiff!
How came you, Cassio, by that handkerchief
That was my wife's?

CASSIO   I found it in my chamber,
And he himself confessed but even now
That there he dropped it for a special purpose   320
Which wrought to his desire.

OTHELLO   O fool, fool, fool!

CASSIO

There is besides in Roderigo's letter
How he upbraids Iago, that he made him
Brave me upon the watch, whereon it came
That I was cast; and even but now he spake,   325
After long seeming dead, Iago hurt him,
Iago set him on.

LODOVICO   [*to Othello*]

You must forsake this room and go with us.
Your power and your command is taken off
And Cassio rules in Cyprus. For this slave,   330
If there be any cunning cruelty
That can torment him much and hold him long,

---

316 **caitiff** scoundrel, villain
317 In some productions (Hankey, 239, 333) the handkerchief now bandages Cassio's leg (a good idea, or too obvious?). If no handkerchief is visible, we may prefer Q 'a' to F 'that', since Cassio was not present when Emilia explained its significance (223ff.). But the audience knows its significance, which may be enough.
319 *but Q *it* was 'caught by the compositor's eye' from 318 or 320 (so Malone). This is a QF 'common error' (*Texts*, 90), if Malone is right.
320 **special purpose** Cf. 4.2.241–3n.
321 i.e. which had the effect he wanted
   O ... fool He sees only the least of

his errors: contrast Roderigo, 'O, villain that I am!' (Heilman, 164–5). This cry is almost a reply to his own 'O, blood, blood, blood!' (3.3.454).
324 **Brave** defy
   whereon it came whereupon (or, for which cause) it happened
325 **cast** dismissed
325–6 **and ... dead** Cf. Desdemona (115–23).
328 **forsake** leave; i.e. he is under arrest
   room could = employment, appointment (*OED* 12; Hulme, 273)
329 **taken off** withdrawn
330 **For** as for
332 **hold him long** keep him alive a long time before he dies

---

316 thou] *F; the Q*   317 that] *F; a Q*   319 but even] *Capell; it euen Q; it but euen F*

It shall be his. You shall close prisoner rest
Till that the nature of your fault be known
To the Venetian state. Come, bring him away.   335

OTHELLO

Soft you, a word or two before you go.
I have done the state some service, and they know't:
No more of that. I pray you, in your letters,
When you shall these unlucky deeds relate,
Speak of me as I am. Nothing extenuate,   340
Nor set down aught in malice. Then must you speak
Of one that loved not wisely, but too well;
Of one not easily jealous, but, being wrought,
Perplexed in the extreme; of one whose hand,
Like the base Indian, threw a pearl away   345
Richer than all his tribe; of one whose subdued eyes,
Albeit unused to the melting mood,
Drops tears as fast as the Arabian trees

---

333 **You** (to Othello)
  close confined, shut up
  rest remain
336 **Soft you** See LN.
  word or two Note the understatement: *some service, unlucky, not wisely,*
  Perplexed, etc. He tries to 'rewrite the
  past'.
338 **No ... that** Cf. 3.3.337.
340 **Speak of** i.e. in writing (*OED* 11)
  extenuate lessen, tone down. The
  sense 'extenuate the guilt of' first recorded 1741: *OED* 7b.
342ff. **Of one** Is this *one* a way of shift-
  ing some of the blame? With repeated
  of, cf. 1.3.135–40.
342 **loved not wisely** So Ovid,
  Heroides, 2.27, 'non sapienter amavi'
  (I loved not wisely).
343 **wrought** agitated (hence 'over-
  wrought'), worked upon
344 **Perplexed** 'not so much "puzzled"
  as "distracted"' (Ridley). *We* know

that the stronger 'distracted' is ap-
plicable, but *he* may mean bewildered
by misleading evidence.
345 **base** lowly (with 'Indian'); depraved, despicable (if we read
  'Judean')
  Indian See LN.
346 **Richer** of more worth
  tribe could be the tribes of Israel or
  an Indian tribe
  subdued overcome
347 **unused** (unusèd, if *Albeit* is disyllabic). Not strictly true: cf. his weeping elsewhere, and p. 20.
348–9 **Arabian ... gum** Pliny (see p.
  5) wrote at length about trees and
  gums (bks 12, 13). J. O. Holmer
  thinks *Arabian trees* = not balsam but
  myrrh trees, since they alone cor-
  respond fully to Shakespeare's speci-
  fications (Arabian, medicinal uses,
  profuse 'weeping'): *SSt*, 13 (1980),
  145ff.

---

335 him] *Q*; *not in F*   336 before you go] *F*; *not in Q*   340 me as I am] *F*; them as they are
Q   341] *as Q*; *F lines* malice. / speake, /   345 Indian] *Q, F2*; Iudean *F*   348 Drops] *QF*; Drop
Q2

Their medicinable gum. Set you down this,
And say besides that in Aleppo once,   350
Where a malignant and a turbanned Turk
Beat a Venetian and traduced the state,
I took by th' throat the circumcised dog
And smote him – thus!   *He stabs himself.*

LODOVICO

O bloody period!

GRATIANO   All that's spoke is marred.   355

OTHELLO

I kissed thee ere I killed thee: no way but this,
Killing myself, to die upon a kiss.

                        [*Kisses Desdemona, and*] *dies.*

CASSIO

This did I fear, but thought he had no weapon,
For he was great of heart.

LODOVICO   [*to Iago*]   O Spartan dog,

349 **medicinable** medicinal
  Set ... this He asks for a written
  report; Lodovico speaks of an oral
  report (368–9).
350 **Aleppo** Not mentioned before,
  Aleppo reminds us that much of
  Othello's past remains a closed book.
  It was an important staging post for
  trade between Europe and the East:
  an English factor lived there (as in
  Venice).
351 **turbanned** A turban was a symbol
  of Islam (hence should not be worn
  by Othello himself: p. 17).
352 **traduced** *Malignant* and *traduced*
  refer obliquely to Iago, who slandered
  Venetian women. But Othello, stabbing himself, also identifies himself
  with the Turk: see p. 23.
353 **took ... throat** Cf. 3.3.362n.,
  5.2.200n.
  circumcised See LN.
354 **SD** This was one of Salvini's most
  sensational moments as Othello: see
  p. 96. N.B. Should Othello's fall here

remind us of his fit (4.1.43)?
355 **period** conclusion; appointed end
  of a journey (cf. 265–6). In some
  productions the curtain came down
  after *period* (Hankey, 339).
356 **I ... ²thee** If *Judean* is right and not
  Indian (see 345 LN), this line refers
  to the kiss and suicide of Judas (Matthew 26.49, 27.5).
  ere before
  no ... this Cf. Dent, W148, 'There
  is no way but one (i.e., death).'
357 **to ... kiss** For the conventional
  'last kiss', cf. also *RJ* 5.3.120, 'Thus
  with a kiss I die', *AC* 4.15.20.
358 **SD** Several Othellos 'died in attempting to reach the bed, or just
  after reaching it' (Sprague, 220–1,
  Hankey, 237–8), i.e. not 'upon a kiss'.
  But 'no way *but this*' seems to imply
  that he kisses her.
359 **great of heart** 'great-hearted' =
  high-spirited, proud (*OED*)
  Spartan dog See LN.

349 medicinable] *F;* medicinall *Q*   351 malignant ... Turk] *Malignant* and a *Turband Turke Q;*
malignant, and a Turbond-Turke *F*   354 SD] *Q; not in F*   355 that's] *Q;* that is *F*   357 SD] *He
dies. Q; Dyes F*   359 Spartan] *F (*Sparton*)*

More fell than anguish, hunger, or the sea,   360
Look on the tragic loading of this bed:
This is thy work. The object poisons sight,
Let it be hid. Gratiano, keep the house
And seize upon the fortunes of the Moor
For they succeed to you. To you, lord governor,   365
Remains the censure of this hellish villain,
The time, the place, the torture: O, enforce it!
Myself will straight aboard, and to the state
This heavy act with heavy heart relate.   *Exeunt.*

FINIS.

360 **fell** savage, ruthless
    anguish excruciating bodily or mental pain
361 This line suggests (cf. 358 SD n.) that both Desdemona and Othello lie on the bed.
362 **object** spectacle; the presentation of something to the eye. Cf. *Cor* 1.1.20, 'the object of our misery'.
363 **hid** i.e. by a sheet, or by pulling the bed curtains (thus concealing the actors' breathing)
    keep guard
364 **seize upon** take possession of
    fortunes possessions
365 **they ... you** pass to you by succession (as Desdemona's uncle: 199n.)

to F *on* is possible, but awkward after *upon*.
    lord governor He reminds Cassio, who is mildly ineffective when sober, to take charge firmly as governor; hence, too, *enforce it*, 367.
366 **censure** formal judgement; correction
367 **torture** i.e. to make Iago confess his motives (cf. 301n.). Notice how insistently the end of this scene focuses on motives: 292, 296, 298–9, 301–2, 317, 320, 341ff.
368 **straight aboard** immediately go on board ship
369 **heavy ... heavy** distressful ... sorrowful
    act action, deed

361 loading] *F;* lodging *Q*   362] *as Q; F lines* worke: / Sight, /   365 to] *Q;* on *F*   369 SD] *F; Exeunt omnes. Q*

LONGER NOTES

LIST OF ROLES 'The Names of the Actors' was printed in the Folio, at the end of the play, in two columns (*Texts*, 70). It is one of seven such lists in F and may have been compiled by Ralph Crane, who is thought to have transcribed other F plays which have similar lists (*Tem, TGV, MM, WT*: see *Texts*, 70–2). The embellishment below 'The Names of the Actors', consisting of brackets, colons and asterisks, resembles similar ones found in other Crane manuscripts, but I have not seen one that is exactly the same in Crane's work or elsewhere. Apart from changing the heading and printing the names in capitals, the Arden 3 list adopts the sequence and layout of the Folio, and therefore places female parts separately. All additions to F's list are in square brackets.

Dramatists would have found such lists useful when they wrote their plays, or even before they began to write (Honigmann, *Stability*, 44–6). Did Crane copy his list from Shakespeare's own papers? It is curious that his list for *MM* begins '*Vincentio: the Duke.*', for the text of *MM* never mentions the Duke's name. Shakespeare had a weakness for naming his characters even when names are not strictly necessary: the *MM* list could be authorial. So, too, the *Othello* list calls Montano '*Gouernour of Cyprus*', an authorial intention that we may deduce from the dialogue (see *Texts*, 71–2), though not one spelt out in F. In Q *Othello*, however, occurs the SD '*Enter* Montanio, *Gouernor of* Cypres' (2.1.0), and Crane might have taken these words from Q. It follows that we cannot tell whether Crane copied or tidied such lists from Shakespeare's papers or whether Crane alone was responsible for them. It should be noted, though, that Crane usually placed the play-world's ruler first whereas in *Othello* the Duke is placed sixth, and that the *Othello* list differs from Crane's lists in other ways.

In Cinthio Shakespeare found only one name, Disdemona. In the French translation of Cinthio (1583) this became Disdemone. While Shakespeare's 'Desdemona' and 'Desdemon' (3.1.55, 3.3.55, etc.) may indicate that he knew the Italian and French versions (see p. 368), feminine names ending in -a lose the -a at times in other plays (Helena in *AW*, Isabella in *MM*). It is just possible, in view of the not uncommon *e:i* confusion in *Othello* (*Texts*, 88–9), that Shakespeare actually wrote Disdemon(a) and that Desdemona was a misreading that stuck (compare Imogen–Innogen in *Cym*). The misreading 'Montanio' like-wise stuck in Q, where F has 'Montano', and the misreading 'Rodorigo' stuck in F, instead of Q's 'Roderigo'. As F adopted many 'common errors' from Q (*ibid.*, 95–8), 'Desdemona' for 'Disdemona' could be one as well.

On a different tack, how should we pronounce 'Othello'? The medial -th- in *Hecatommithi* must be sounded as -t-; Ben Jonson's 'Thorello' (*Every Man In*) derives from Italian 'torello', a young bull; 'Othoman' was an alternative spelling for 'Ottoman': it seems possible that Shake-speare wrote 'Othello' and meant 'Otello'. He might have heard of the Jesuit, Girolamo Otello of Bassano (1519–81); according to T. Sipahigil ('Othello's name, once again', *N&Q*, 18 (1971), 147–8), 'Jesuit histor-ians invariably speak of the notoriety of Girolamo Otello as an over-ardent spirit, quick to follow zealous impulses', i.e. he had something in common with Othello. But Otello was an out-of-the-way name; if Shake-speare knew it he might still want to change it, as also in the case of Disdemona.

Several of the play's names were probably invented or adapted by Shakespeare. (1) Othello: from Otello, or from Otho, Othoman or Thorello (see F. N. Lees, 'Othello's name', *N&Q*, 8 (1961), 139–41; R. F. Fleissner, 'The Moor's nomenclature', *N&Q*, 25 (1978), 143). (2) Desdemona: from Disdemona. (3) Brabantio: cf. Brabant Senior in *Jack Drum's Entertainment* (1601) and the Duke of Brabant in *The Weakest Goeth to the Wall* (1600). (4) Montano: the name reappears in Q1 *Hamlet* (1603): see p. 345. (5) Michael Cassio: the only person in *Othello* with two names. Compare Cassius in *JC*. The verb 'to cass' was 'a frequent form of our word "cashier"' (Hart).

Several of the names have curious associations. Both Iago and Rod-erigo are Spanish forms (and Iago's 'Diablo!', 2.3.157, unique in Shake-speare, is the Spanish form of this word). The most famous Spanish Iago was Sant'Iago (St James of Compostella), known as 'Matamoros' ('the Moor-killer') (see Bullough, 217; Everett, '"Spanish" Othello'). Iago's 'I know our country disposition well' (3.3.204) nevertheless ap-pears to refer to Italy (where Spain was a dominant power in the later sixteenth century).

Disdemona, said Cinthio (see p. 386), was 'a name of unlucky augury' (it meant 'unfortunate'). Bianca (= Blanche, white, i.e. pure), a name previously used by Shakespeare in *TS* for a less than perfect young lady, was the Christian name of the notorious Bianca Capello (1548–87), a Venetian courtesan whose story Middleton dramatized in *Women Beware Women* and Webster perhaps glanced at when he created his 'white devil'.

Iago is usually trisyllabic ('I-a-go'). Cassio is more often disyllabic, but can be trisyllabic (1.1.19). See *Texts*, 104.

1.1.8 **his lieutenant** The military ranks of an ancient (i.e. ensign, or

standard-bearer), a lieutenant and a general may confuse readers because 'Elizabethan field-grade officers had also a different company
rank' (Paul A. Jorgensen, *Shakespeare's Military World* (1956), 100–18:
in this note I am indebted to Jorgensen's helpful discussion). Cinthio's
'Cassio' is a corporal, but Shakespeare made him a lieutenant, apparently lieutenant of a company: as such he would be superior to the
ancient, though there would be 'a troublesome overlapping of the two
offices, and an occasion for friction'. A company-rank captain personally
chose his company's lieutenant, ensign and lower officers; Othello did so
and, it seems, gave Cassio accelerated promotion, therefore we should
recognize that Iago has 'what to him seem real grievances'. Yet when
Othello is replaced as general in command of Cyprus the Venetians
appoint 'Cassio in his government' and 'Cassio rules in Cyprus' as 'lord
governor' (4.1.236, 5.2.330, 365). Towards the end of the play Shakespeare appears to think of Cassio not as a lieutenant of a company but as
a staff officer, a lieutenant-general – two ranks that are incompatible
(unlike Othello's two ranks as captain of a company and as general of an
army). Shakespeare either forgot Cassio's junior rank as a mere company lieutenant or assumed that his audience would forget (just as he
probably assumed that the audience would not notice the double time
scheme). See also Julia Genster, 'Lieutenancy, standing in and *Othello*',
ELH, 57 (1990), 785–805.

1.1.20 Furness cites several pages of explanation, including the following:
'he is not yet *completely damned*, because he is not *absolutely married*'
(Steevens, referring to 4.1.124: but the later suggestion that Cassio is
expected to marry Bianca does not help at 1.1.20); 'a man almost de-
graded into a woman (through feminine tastes and habits) . . . as when one
says "A soldier wasted in a parson"' (Earl of Southesk); 'a fellow who is
willing to go to perdition . . . for a beautiful woman' (Crosby). Cf. Sisson,
Readings, 'he is given to women, practically married and likely therefore
to be uxorious and distracted from soldierly virtue' (2.246). I prefer
Johnson's candid admission that the line is obscure and/or corrupt.

1.3.322 **nettles** Pliny has a chapter 'Of the nettle' (22.13), which was cultivated for medicinal purposes. J. T. McCullen thinks each pair of herbs
here contains an aphrodisiac and an anti-aphrodisiac, a combination
used by physicians to treat love sickness. Ridley compared Lyly, *Euphues*
(1.187), 'good Gardeiners . . . mixe Hisoppe wyth Time as ayders the
one to the growth of the other, the one beeinge drye, the other moyste'.

2.1.12 **clouds** Perhaps an echo of Ovid, *Tristia*, 1.2.19ff., 'what vast mountains of water heave themselves aloft . . . you think, they will touch the
highest stars . . . you think they will touch black Tartarus' (T. Sipahigil,
'Ovid and the Tempest in *Othello*', *SQ*, 44 (1993), 468–71). But cf.
Psalms 107.25ff.: such poetical storms were widely copied.

2.1.15 **guards, pole** These stars gave navigators their bearings. Both *ever-
fired* and *-fixed* are possible: cf. *KL* 3.7.61, 'quenched the stelled fires',

where *stelled* = either 'starry' (from Lat. *stella*) or 'fixed' (from ME *stellen*). Cf. also *Oth* 3.3.466, 'you ever-burning lights above'.

2.1.26 **Veronessa** = from Verona. The feminine ending *-essa* (as in *contessa*) is wrong here: the Italian word is Veronese (four syllables, perhaps what Shakespeare wrote). Verona, though an inland city, had ships at the battle of Lepanto; Shakespeare may have meant 'a ship on the side of Venice, belonging to Verona'. QF punctuation (unlikely to be Shakespeare's) implies that *Veronessa* refers to Cassio!

2.1.155 **change** exchange; hence, 'to make a foolish exchange' (Ridley). Shakespeare no doubt knew that 'the taile-piece [of many fishes] is in greatest request' (Pliny, quoted Hart), and that the cod's head is worthless. Puns on *cod* (= penis) and *tail* (= pudenda). Balz Engler compared Tilley, H240, 'Better be the head of yeomanry than the tail of the gentry', and proverbs 'directed against foolish ambition' ('To change the cod's head for the salmon's tail', *SQ*, 35 (1984), 202–3).

2.1.173 **three fingers** i.e. one after the other. 'The kissing of his hand was a quite normal courteous gesture from a gentleman to a lady' (Ridley, citing *LLL* 4.1.146, 'To see him kiss his hand', *TN* 3.4.32, 'Why dost thou smile so, and kiss thy hand so oft?'). But both extracts refer to foppish, extravagant behaviour, as Iago does here.

2.1.301 *****trash** check a hound, hence, hold back, restrain. An easy misreading in Q (less easy in F), and agrees with Roderigo's later complaint that Iago has not advanced his cause (4.2.175ff.). F *trace* might = pursue, dog (*OED* 5), i.e. whom I dog in the hope that he will help me with quick hunting; or, 'whom I keep hungry so that he may hunt the more eagerly' (a hawking metaphor: Hulme, 254–6).

2.3.85ff. Iago's song is adapted from an early ballad known as 'Bell my wife' or 'Take thy old cloak about thee'. The ballad predated *Othello*, being quoted in Robert Greene's *Quip for an Upstart Courtier* (1592), 'it was a good and blessed time heere in Englane [*sic*], when k. *Stephen* wore a paire of cloth breeches of a Noble a paire, anf [*sic*] thought them passing costlye' (sig. C3b). A complete text was printed in Thomas Percy's *Reliques of Ancient English Poetry* (1765), eight eight-line stanzas, consisting of the words of Bell and of her husband. They have been together forty-four years; it is bitter winter weather, and she tells him to put on his old cloak and to go out and save the old cow. Her stanzas end 'man! put (or, take) thine old cloak about thee!', his – 'for I'll have a new cloak about me'. *He* wants to abandon his peasant life and seek advancement at court, *she* warns him against pride. Stanzas 6 and 7 leave us in no doubt that the ballad expresses impatience with privilege (appropriately for Iago: see pp. 35–7):

> O Bell my wiffe! why doest thou flyte?
> now is nowe, & then was then;
> seeke all the world now throughout,

> thou kens not Clownes from gentlemen;
> they are cladd in blacke, greene, yellow, & blew,
>   soe ffarr aboue their owne degree;
> once in my liffe Ile take a vew,* [*= ?give myself some licence]
>   ffor Ile haue a new cloake about mee.
>
> King Harry was a verry good K[*ing;*]
>   I trow his hose cost but a Crowne;
> he thought them 12^{d} ouer to deere,
>   therfore he called the taylor Clowne.
> he was King & wore the Crowne,
>   & thouse but of a low degree;
> itts pride *that* putts this cumtrye downe;
>   man! put thye old Cloake about thee![1]

We cannot be certain that Percy printed the ballad exactly as Shakespeare knew it: if he did, which is unlikely, Shakespeare introduced changes in every line, though apparently retaining the character of the original and its 'class' feeling. We may assume that Shakespeare's audience was familiar with the ballad, even if Italian Cassio seems not to be. The ballad tune associated with the song is found in Robert Bremner's *Thirty Scots Songs* (1770), reproduced in Sternfeld, 149, and below on p. 391. (See also the books on music in Shakespeare cited in the LN on 4.3.39ff.).

2.3.166–7 Cf. *MA* 3.4.57, 'and you be not turned Turk'; Dent, T609, 'To turn Turk'. To Elizabethans, Turks and Moors must have seemed much alike (see p. 341): 166–8 bring out Othello's 'otherness'. Chew (108) notes 'the well attested fact that Turkish soldiers, though they might bicker and squabble among themselves, never came to blows with each other'; see Rodney Poisson, 'Which heaven has forbid the Ottomites', *SQ*, 18 (1967), 67–70. That is, 'do we fight amongst ourselves, which the Turks are forbidden to do by their religion?' Walker glossed 167 'by destroying their fleet'. Cf. also *Homilies*, 456, 'Surely it is a shame that Paynims [pagans] should be wiser than we.'

2.3.304–5 **creature** 1 Timothy 4.1–4 warns against seducing spirits that 'abstain from meats which God hath created to be received with giving thanks . . . For every *creature* of God is good'. Intoxicating drink was called a *creature* (facetiously) before Shakespeare, as also later by Dryden, 'My master took too much of the creature last night' (*OED* 1d); but *creature* could = any created thing (including food and drink).

3.1.3–4 He refers to the Neapolitan (venereal) disease (cf. *TC* 2.3.18), which could eat away the nose (*Tim* 4.3.157). He means that the instruments snuffle or scrape instead of ringing out musically; they 'must have

1 Reprinted from *Bishop Percy's Folio Manuscript*, ed. J. W. Hales and F. J. Furnivall, 3 vols (1867), 2.320ff.

double reeds (like modern oboe reeds) which produce a nasal sound' (R. King, '"Then murder's out of tune": the music and structure of *Othello*', *SS*, 39 (1987), 155).

3.3.126 *delations accusations; narrations; Q *denotements* = indications. 'Delate' and 'dilate' were interchangeable (cf. *Ham* 1.2.38, Q2, F): see Patricia Parker, 'Shakespeare and rhetoric: "dilation" and "delation" in *Othello*', in *Shakespeare and the Question of Theory*, ed. P. Parker and G. Hartman (1985), 54–74. Kittredge glossed *dilations* as swellings, i.e. 'emotions that make the heart swell'.

3.3.159 **immediate** i.e. dearest; of a relation between two things: existing without any intervening medium or agency (*OED* 2). Cf. Proverbs 22.1, 'A good name is more to be desired than great riches', Ecclesiasticus 41.12 (Noble, 218); Dent, N22, 'A good name is better than riches.' Perhaps influenced by *Homilies*, 127, 'there cometh less hurt of a thief, than of a railing tongue: for the one taketh away a man's good name; the other taketh but his riches, which is of much less value' (T. W. Craik, private communication). Compare Iago at 2.3.258ff.

3.3.291 *SD See p. 48. It is not clear here whether he or she drops the handkerchief: but cf. 315. If she tries to bind his head from behind he can push her hand away without looking at the handkerchief; *let it alone* then = leave my headache alone. See 441n. and L. Hartley, 'Dropping the handkerchief: pronoun reference and stage direction in *Othello* III.iii', *ELN*, 8 (1970–1), 173–6.

3.3.364 **man's** (as opposed to a dog, which has no soul), i.e. he will consign Iago's soul to eternal damnation (375). Q may imply that Iago risks his soul, F that Othello risks his (because of what he will do to Iago); but 364 could be less specific, i.e. a vague oath. See also Matthew 26.24–5, 'woe unto that man by whom the son of man is betrayed: It had been good for that man if he had not been born. Then Judas . . . said, Master, Is it I?' Did Shakespeare think of Iago as a Judas figure?

3.3.406–7 **prime, hot, salt, in pride** all synonyms for lecherous, 'on heat' (Ridley). *Prime* is not recorded in this sense elsewhere. I suggest *primed* = ready to discharge (sexually). Cf. Dent, G167, 'As lecherous as a goat'; also *TC* 3.1.130, 'hot thoughts beget hot deeds, and hot deeds is love'; *Tim* 4.3.84–6, 'Be a whore still . . . Make use of thy salt hours'; *Luc* 438–9, 'Smoking with pride . . . to make his stand / On her bare breast.'

3.3.450 **hollow hell** Cf. Seneca, *Thyestes*, tr. Jasper Heywood, 'Where most prodigious vglye thynges, / the hollowe hell dothe hyde' (1560 edn, sig. E4: 4th scene, added by translator). Q *Cell* is not unlike *Ham* 5.2.364–5, 'O proud death, / What feast is toward in thine eternal cell', and *Luc*, 881–2. F *hollow hell* anticipates *Tem* 1.2.214–15, 'Hell is empty, / And all the devils are here'. Cf. also Tourneur, *Transformed Metamorphosis* (1600), B6b, 'blacke horrors cell', R. Armin, *Two Maids* (1609), E1b, 'Rouse the blacke mischiefe from thy ebben cell'. Both Q and F are possible.

3.3.458 *keeps It is possible that one *keeps* is a copyist's error, but which one? Editors who follow Q2 may have two errors in this line. Cf. a possible echo in T. Powell, *Virtue's Due* (1603), B6a, 'Her resolution was *Proponticke* right, / And forward stem'd against the Moones retreat', which suggests 'ne'er keeps retiring ebb but stems due on' (*stems* = heads, *OED v.* 3). But Shakespeare liked to repeat words in 'rhetorical' passages. Sisson thinks that the first *keeps* was an anticipation of the second (by Shakespeare or a scribe): 'we simply delete the first keeps, and read *ebbs* for *ebb*, no difficult misreading'.

3.4.47 i.e. we now give our hands (in marriage) without giving our love. Stressing *of old* and *our*, the actor can suggest 'a denial of Desdemona's assertion' in 45 (Capell).

　　'It is difficult . . . to escape from seeing here an allusion to the new order of baronetage instituted by King James in 1612, of which the badge was the addition of a hand gules to the coat of arms' (Ridley, from Warburton, etc.). But this would mean that the 'allusion' was later added to the Q and F manuscripts – unlikely. Others thought no allusion necessary. Dyce compared Warner's *Albion's England* (1596 edn, 282): 'My hand shall neuer giue my heart, my heart shall giue my hand'; Hart quoted Cornwallis, *Essays* (1600–1): people used to 'give their hands and their hearts together, but we think it a finer grace to look asquint, our hand looking one way, and our heart another'.

3.4.72–3 sibyl prophetess, as in ancient Greece and Rome. 'We say, *I counted the clock to strike four*; so she *numbred* the sun *to course*, to run . . . two hundred annual circuits' (Johnson); i.e. she had calculated that the sun would make two hundred (further) circuits, that the world would end in two hundred years (hence *prophetic*). Calculating the date of the end of the world was a Renaissance pastime.

4.2.60 fountain spring, well (Lat. *fons*). The imagery picks up from 3.3.274, and from Proverbs 5.15–18, 'Drink the water of thy cistern, and of the rivers out of the mids(t) of thine own well. Let thy fountains flow forth . . . let thy fountain be blessed, and rejoice with the wife of thy youth' (Genevan Bible, which heads the chapter 'Whoredom forbidden'; here *thy cistern, thine own well* = thy wife). Cf. also *Homilies*, 114: whoredom is 'that most filthy lake, foul puddle, and stinking sink, whereunto all kinds of sins and evils flow'.

4.3.39ff. Shakespeare adapted the Willow Song 'from a pre-existing text and probably intended that his version be sung to one of two pre-existing tunes' (B. N. S. Gooch and D. Thatcher, *A Shakespeare Music Catalogue*, 5 vols (Oxford, 1991), 2.1255). The song was printed from an old ballad in Percy's *Reliques* (1765), and reprinted with music by Furness, 278. We should not assume, however, that Percy's version gives the ballad verbatim as Shakespeare found it. If it did, Shakespeare changed the sex of the singer and adapted quite freely, as the following extracts show.

A poore soule sat sighing under a sicamore tree;
   'O willow, willow, willow!'
With his hand on his bosom, his head on his knee:
   'O willow, willow, willow!
   O willow, willow, willow!
Sing, O the greene willow shall be my garlànd.'
. . .
My love she is turned; untrue she doth prove:
   O willow, &c.
She renders me nothing but hate for my love.
   O willow, &c.
Sing, O the greene willow, &c.

The cold streams ran by him, his eyes wept apace;
   O willow, &c.
The salt tears fell from him, which drowned his face;
   O willow, &c.
Sing, O the greene willow, &c.

The mute birds sate by him, made tame by his mones:
   O willow, &c.
The salt tears fell from him, which softened the stones.
   O willow, &c.
Sing, O the greene willow shall be my garlànd!

Let nobody blame me, her scornes I do prove;
   O willow, &c.
She was borne to be faire: I, to die for her love, . . .[1]

The earliest version of the tune is to be found in a 1583 manuscript lute book in the library of Trinity College Dublin. The version reproduced below on pp. 392–3 is the contemporary setting in BL Add. MS. 15117, fo. 118 as reprinted in Sternfeld, 43–4. See also Sternfeld, 23–52, for further discussion and other facsimiles and transcriptions of the music; J. H. Long, *Shakespeare's Use of Music* (1971), 153–61; and Gooch and Thatcher, *op. cit.* For Q's omission of the song, see *Texts*, 10–11.

5.2 The original staging of 5.2 has been explained in two different ways. (1) L. J. Ross suggested that a curtained structure was placed on the main stage, in front of the tiring-house façade ('The use of a "fit-up" booth in *Othello*', *SQ*, 12 (1961), 359–70). The bed was concealed when the curtains were drawn (cf. 103, 363). The same structure would be useful elsewhere – e.g. for the 'discovery' of the Senate at 1.3.0.1, or as the *bulk* of 5.1.1. (2) R. Hosley held that 'the bed with Desdemona lying in it is

1 Reprinted from *Percy's Reliques*, ed. G. Gilfillan, 3 vols (Edinburgh, 1858), 1.158ff.

"thrust out" of the tiring-house by stage-keepers . . . the bed curtains are manipulated as called for by the dialogue; and when Lodovico says "Let it be hid" the bed, on which are now lying the bodies of Desdemona, Emilia, and Othello, is "drawn in" to the tiring-house through one of its doors' ('The staging of Desdemona's bed', *SQ,* 14 (1963), 57–65). Both kinds of staging were possible, and we must not suppose that staging at the Globe and, later, at the Blackfriars, was identical: but note the clear SD in *2H6* 3.2.146, '*Bed put forth*' (F). Othello's *light* (5.2.0.1) = a candle.

5.2.83 SD Q *stifles* could = throttles; F *Smothers* = suffocates (actors normally use a pillow). Cf. Marlowe, *Massacre* (1.400), SD, '*Now they strangle him*'; Dekker, *Old Fortunatus* (1600), where Andelocia is strangled on stage (1.191). In some productions Desdemona was smothered behind closed curtains (Rosenberg, 99, 113).

5.2.98–100 For supernatural manifestations before or after an important death, common in classical literature, cf. *JC* 2.2.13ff., *Mac* 2.4.1ff. Othello's apocalyptic vision here may be biblical in inspiration: 'lo, there was a great earthquake, and the sun was as black as sackcloth . . . and the moon waxed all even as blood. And the stars of heaven fell unto the earth' (Revelation 6.12–13).

5.2.141 **chrysolite** sometimes glossed as topaz; 'a name formerly given to several different gems of a green colour' (*OED*). Lynda Boose thinks that Shakespeare meant a 'translucent white' gem, as in the Genevan Bible, Song of Solomon, Revelation 21.20 ('Othello's "chrysolite" and the Song of Songs tradition', *PQ,* 60 (1981), 427ff.). Cf. also *Weakest Goeth to the Wall* (1600), C3a, 'walles of purest Chrysolyte'.

5.2.251 Spain was famous for its fine swords (e.g. Toledo blades). To *temper* = to strengthen metal by repeatedly heating and cooling it: *ice-brook* (a coinage) could refer to the cooling process. 'Spanish rivers, such as the Tagus, being fed by melting snows, were considered to be partly responsible for the quality of Spanish blades' (Sanders). Q *Isebrookes* has been seen as a misreading of Innsbruck (which exported fine metal to England), and would be an easy misreading (*Texts*, 83–4); but this would be a poor exchange for the evocative *ice-brook*, a word perhaps connected with the 'tempering' that Othello imagines in 275–8.

5.2.277–8 The 'torment of the damned in hell' was another popular subject in Renaissance art. It may be thought that to be blown about in winds would be a pleasant change for anyone roasting in sulphur – but cf. the similar vision of hell in *MM* 3.1.121ff., 'To bathe in fiery floods . . . To be imprison'd in the viewless winds / And blown with restless violence round about / The pendent world'.

5.2.336 **Soft you** *Soft* and *But soft* are common in Shakespeare (*Ham* 1.1.126, 1.5.58, 3.2.392); *soft you* (= not so fast) is rare. In this speech Othello's sense of his own unquestioned superiority shows through in his attitude to the *base Indian* and the *Turk*: he adopts a 'European' view of darker-skinned races. Surprisingly the only reference to Desdemona is as the *pearl* (but see LN, 5.2.345, below): his speech is largely self-centred.

5.2.345 **Indian** Both Q *Indian* and F *Iudean* have strong support from discerning editors. *Indian* has been more popular with editors, though *Iudean* was preferred by Johnson and Malone. I list some of the arguments for and against each. (1) For *Iudean*. Judas Iscariot is so called because he was the Judaean disciple, unlike the others, who were Galileans. The kiss of Judas as a token of treachery was a commonplace (Matthew 26.49), hence 356; betraying Jesus, Judas threw away a 'precious pearl' (Matthew 13.46; in the Genevan Bible, 'a pearl of great price': see Noble, 92, 273). Judas, like Othello, committed suicide. Others think that *Iudean* could refer to Herod, who killed Mariamne, his 'pearl' of a wife (J. O. Holmer, 'Othello's Threnos: "Arabian trees" and "Indian" versus "Judean"', *SSt*, 13 (1980), 145–67).

(2) Against *Iudean*. The word 'Judean' was not in use in Shakespeare's time (R. F. Fleissner, 'A clue to the "base Judean" in *Othello*', *N&Q*, 28 [1981], 137–8). The metre of 345 requires Júdean, not Judéan. These objections are not decisive, as Shakespeare often invented words or changed their stress.

(3) For *Indian*. The wealth of India, and the ignorance of Indians, unaware of the value of their gold and precious stones, were commented on by Renaissance and earlier writers. Pliny (34.17) mentioned Indians who barter and undervalue pearls. For Shakespeare's knowledge of these commonplaces, cf. 'as bountiful / As mines of India' (*1H4* 3.1.166–7) and 'Her bed is India, there she lies, a pearl' (*TC* 1.1.100). Such passages mostly refer to Indian Indians (e.g. Pliny), but Shakespeare could have meant American Indians.

A different kind of evidence also supports Q *Indian*: the fact that the second Folio (1632) switched from *Iudean* to *Indian*. In general F2 followed the first Folio (F) closely, introducing some corrections that are clearly unauthorized (i.e. are based on neither Q nor F). F2 *Indian* shows that a near-contemporary, who was far less interfering as an editor than the Q2 editor of 1630 (see *Texts*, 170), was dissatisfied with F *Iudean*: this was one of his most striking corrections of his copy. On the other hand, the F scribe corrected Q *Indian* to *Iudean*; although F also miscorrected Q (*ibid.*, 100), F's correction must carry some weight.

(4) Against *Indian*. The widely shared conviction that the Folio is the 'better text' has no doubt influenced those who argue for F *Iudean*. I have suggested that editors overrated F's reliability and underrated Q's (*ibid.*, 146), which leaves the balance finely poised.

Conclusion. The best analysis is, I think, Richard Levin's 'The Indian/Iudean crux in *Othello*' (*SQ*, 33 (1982), 60–7), which ends with a telling point. It is appropriate for Othello to compare himself with the Indian, whose action results from ignorance, and 'very inappropriate for him to compare himself to Judas, whose action was regarded as a conscious choice of evil'.

5.2.353 **circumcised** (?circumcisèd) Circumcision was a religious rite with Muslims, so Othello's contemptuous reference to it implies that he 'was not nor had ever been a Mohammedan' (Chew, 521n.). But it could be simply a term of abuse, like 'the uncircumcised' in the Bible. These lines may be influenced by 1 Samuel 17.26ff., 'what is this uncircumcised Philistine, that he should revile the host of the living God?' (David of Goliath); 'I caught him by the beard, and smote him, and slew him' (David to Saul); 'And the Philistine [Goliath] said unto David, Am I a dog . . .?'

5.2.359 **Spartan dog** a kind of bloodhound. Applied to men, bloodhound = a hunter for blood (*OED* 2). Envy, Iago's disease, was sometimes represented as a snarling dog; *Spartan* may = unmoved, impassive, inhumanely determined (like the Spartan boy who carried a fox under his tunic, was bitten, and gave no sign of pain). Cf. the hounds of Sparta that were used to hunt bears (*MND* 4.1.112ff.).

APPENDIX 1
DATE

Othello must have been written at some time between 1601 and 1604. Holland's translation of Pliny's *Historie of the World* (dated 1601 on the title-page; SR entry 20 May 1600) almost certainly supplied Shakespeare with much of the play's 'foreign' and exotic material (see p. 5); a performance at court on 1 November 1604 provides the *terminus ante quem*. Can we date the play more precisely? E. K. Chambers thought in 1930 that a 'production in 1604 is consonant with the stylistic evidence',[1] and others have felt that *Othello* is 'Jacobean'. Useful as it is in assigning Shakespeare's plays to an approximate period, stylistic evidence gives less help with precise dating; the 'Jacobean' feeling, moreover, expresses itself chiefly through Iago, and one could argue that the romantic hero and heroine are thoroughly 'Elizabethan'. We are back where we started.

Alfred Hart offered a new suggestion in 1935:[2] the 'bad' Quarto of *Hamlet* seems to echo *Othello*, just as it garbles lines from many other plays. The bad Quarto was published in 1603, and its text may have come into being some time before 26 July 1602, the date on which James Roberts entered *Hamlet* in the Stationers' Register. Some editors accepted Hart's dating, others ignored it. *Othello*, said the Cambridge 2 editors, J. Dover Wilson and Alice Walker, 'can hardly be later than early 1603, and may even belong to 1602'.[3] The reason why others continued to date the play as before, in 1603 or 1604, must be that some of Hart's 'echoes' from *Othello* in the bad Quarto (Q1) of *Hamlet* are not convincing, being phrases in general use. Some, but not all: at least two echoes have to be taken more seriously.

1   Chambers, *William Shakespeare*, 1.462.
2   Alfred Hart, 'The date of *Othello*', *TLS*, 10 October 1935, p. 631.
3   Cam², xv.

(1) 'To my unfolding lend your prosperous ear' (*Oth* 1.3.245) must be connected with 'to my vnfolding / Lend thy listning eare' (Q1 *Ham* C3b, C4a). (2) The adjective 'Olympus-high' appears in both texts (*Oth* 2.1.186; Q1 *Ham* I1b).

On their own these two echoes are arresting, though perhaps insufficiently so to qualify as proof positive that *Othello* influenced Q1 *Hamlet*. Hart, however, did not cite all the relevant echoes. More have now been added.[1]

(3) The unusual name Montano, which replaces Reynaldo in Q1 *Hamlet*. The only Montano in Shakespeare occurs in *Othello*. This looks like unconscious substitution, perhaps because the same actor played Montano in *Othello* and Reynaldo in *Hamlet*. (4) In the closing moments of the two tragedies almost the same thought is repeated: 'Look on the tragic loading of this bed' (*Oth* 5.2.361) and 'looke vpon this tragicke spectacle' (Q1 *Ham* I4a). Other echoes have also been located, but we need not waste time on them. Hart's case seems to me to have proved correct: *Othello* must have existed by early 1603, and probably before July 1602. As Holland's Pliny printed a prefatory epistle dated 'Iunij xij. 1601' I conclude that *Othello* was probably written at some point in the period from mid-1601 to mid-1602.

How does this fit in with the 'Shakespeare chronology'? *Othello* is always placed later than *Hamlet* (*c.* 1600) and earlier than *King Lear* (1605): the tragedies are so well spaced that any date from 1601 to 1604 seems possible for *Othello*. Again, *Othello* and *Measure for Measure* are sometimes seen as twin plays, being based on the same collection of stories, Cinthio's *Hecatommithi*, and are therefore dated close together, in 1603–4. Yet while editors believe that some plays based on the same source were written consecutively (e.g. *Antony and Cleopatra* and *Coriolanus*), we know that others must be years apart (e.g. *Julius Caesar* and *Antony and Cleopatra*). The date of *Measure for Measure*, itself far from certain, should not influence our dating of *Othello*; neither should the dates of other plays that may belong to the years immediately after the turn of the century (*Merry Wives*, *Twelfth Night*,

---

1   See Honigmann, 'Date of *Othello*', and J. C. Maxwell, 'Othello and the bad Quarto of *Hamlet*', *N&Q*, 21 (1974), 130.

Troilus, All's Well), for these too defy all efforts to date them precisely.

Twelfth Night, though, may give some help, being related to *Othello* in two ways. (1) *Casting*. The casting requirements of the two plays are remarkably alike. So many characters have an obvious counterpart in the second play that Shakespeare must have had the same actors in mind, intending to exploit their special talents. Thus: (a) Orsino–Othello (a specialist in passion, despair, poetic declamation); (b) Viola–Desdemona (a boy actor who excelled in gentleness, suffering, romantic love); (c) Sir Andrew Aguecheek–Roderigo (a comedian who played foolish young gentlemen who are lovers and cowards); (d) Maria–Emilia (a boy actor who was good in sharp exchanges and plain speaking; an unromantic attendant); (e) Feste–the Clown; (f) Sebastian–Cassio (the supporting romantic lead). It would follow that other parts, less obviously alike, were also intended for the same actor: (g) Sir Toby–Iago; (h) Olivia–Bianca; (i) Fabian–Duke of Venice; (j) Antonio–Montano. The only major character that fails to fit in as obviously as the rest is Malvolio. I think that Brabantio (and later Gratiano) might be taken by the Malvolio actor (k), an older man (a specialist in rebuke, anger, despair), or, just possibly, that the same 'star' (Burbage) played both Malvolio and Othello.[1] In that case some minor adjustments would follow in the casting lists: Malvolio–Othello; Orsino–Cassio; Sebastian–Montano. Even so, the special actor strengths of the two plays remain surprisingly close, closer than in *Othello* and the adjacent tragedies.

Sir Toby and Iago, less self-evidently written for one actor than most of the other parts, call for several similar talents. Actor (g) could sing, roister in a drinking-scene, use his sword, could play 'the smiler with the knife under the cloak'[2] and, partnering boy actor (d) in a number of scenes in each play, may have been the master to whom this boy was apprenticed. Charles Gildon recorded in 1694 that he had heard 'from very good hands, that the

---

1 I think it likely that the same actor (Heminges?) played Julius Caesar, Polonius, Malvolio and Brabantio. He seems to have been good as a performer of tiresome, self-important older men.

2 For the less favourable view of Sir Toby, see *Twelfth Night*, ed. E. A. J. Honigmann (The Macmillan Shakespeare, 1971), 13–14.

Person that Acted Jago was in much esteem for a Comoedian',[1] a piece of gossip that confirms my casting and also throws light on Shakespeare's conception of Iago. While all the plays performed by a professional company in the same season had to be put on by the same group of actors, new plays written by the company dramatist would naturally pay more attention to the special talents of these actors than one would expect in the case of revivals. This would apply particularly to the parts written for boy actors, who could only take leading roles for a very few years.

(2) *A singing boy actor.* The Willow Song, intended for a boy actor who could sing, appears in F *Othello* but not in Q. It was carefully removed from the Q text (which omits 4.3.29–52, 54–6, 59–62, and also 5.2.244–6) – why would any sensible person wish to cut this song, so beautifully expressive of Desdemona's mood? The usual explanation is that at the time of a later revival of *Othello* the leading boy actor could not sing.[2] As it chances, something similar happened to a song in *Twelfth Night*, except that it was not cut but transferred to a different actor.

> It is almost certain from the insistence on Viola's musical accomplishments at I.ii.57–58 that she was meant to be a singer, and from the awkward opening of II.iv that the song 'Come away, come away death' has been transferred from her to Feste. We must therefore suppose that when the play was originally produced the company had a singing boy who was no longer available on the occasion of some revival.
>
> (Greg, 297)

Greg stated a widely shared view. If, however, *Othello* has been postdated and was composed between mid-1601 and mid-1602, the very period to which many assign *Twelfth Night*,[3] a simpler

---

1 See Chambers, *William Shakespeare*, 2.261.

2 Chambers, *op. cit.*, 1.460.

3 *Twelfth Night* has sometimes been dated 1599 (see *Texts*, 175 n. 19). If the performance of this play witnessed by John Manningham on 2 February 1602 (Chambers, *op. cit.*, 2.327) was not the very first one, it would still be very close in time to the proposed first performance of *Othello*; that is, the same boy actor will have played both Viola and Desdemona at this time, and this will have been the time when his voice broke and he could not sing the songs in the two plays that were intended for him.

hypothesis now suggests itself. The boy actor of Viola and Desdemona lost his voice earlier than expected, when Shakespeare had recently completed the two plays, and adjustments were hurriedly made in both, at the same time. This hypothesis avoids a difficulty that Greg (358 n. 9) noticed and tried to explain away: if Q *Othello* derives from the author's foul papers, or rough draft of the play (see p. 354) – as Greg assumed and I have tried to corroborate – why should changes introduced in a later revival be marked in the author's foul papers? The alternative is to assume that the Willow Song and other proposed cuts were lightly marked in the foul papers when *Othello* was first prepared for performance, and that the Folio scribe was later instructed to prepare a version of the complete text, reinstating all cuts (see *Texts*, 101). On this hypothesis the Willow Song, so far from being a special case, fits into a general picture: the play's textual history, date and casting requirements all point to the same conclusion.

Boys able to sing and to take leading dramatic parts 'were not easily obtainable in the public theatres at the beginning of James's reign', observed Richmond Noble,[1] the author of *Shakespeare's Use of Song* (1923), citing the changes involving the songs in *Twelfth Night* and *Othello*. 'If more evidence were wanted, we could turn to *Cymbeline* and note in Act IV, scene 3 the clumsy device Shakespeare had to adopt because Guiderius and Arviragus could not sing.' He continued:

> I am convinced that the first performance of *Hamlet*, *Twelfth Night* (in its original form), and *Othello* (as in the Folio) were not widely separated in time. When these three plays were produced Shakespeare had at his disposal a boy who could take a leading part and also sing ballads or popular songs.

A boy fully trained to act and sing would be a competent performer 'perhaps for two years, but certainly not very much longer'. Boy actor (b), it seems, was capable of playing Ophelia in 1600; he was approaching the time when his voice would break, but Shakespeare hoped that it would last another season and

1 'The date of *Othello*', *TLS*, 14 December 1935, p. 859.

wanted to exploit his special gifts by creating two even more important roles for him, Viola and Desdemona. The likelihood that Desdemona's character was partly determined by a boy actor's ability to sing and to play gentle, vulnerable roles (unlike the boy for whom Shakespeare created Beatrice and Rosalind a season or two earlier) is as interesting as Gildon's story that Iago was first performed by a comedian – where, again, Shakespeare seems to have exploited the actor's gifts, making Iago something of a humorist (quite unlike Cinthio's Ensign).

If, then, *Othello* belongs to the winter–spring of 1601–2, very much the same time as *Twelfth Night*, its relationship with other contemporary plays needs to be reconsidered. Heywood's *A Woman Killed With Kindness*, for which Henslowe paid £6 in February and March 1603, should be seen as a reply to *Othello* rather than as the domestic tragedy (see pp. 73ff.) that prompted Shakespeare to move in this new direction. On the other hand, *Patient Grissel* by Dekker and others, probably first performed early in 1600, would be closer to *Othello* than has been supposed, and this could help to explain why Cinthio's Disdemona becomes a more pronounced 'patient Grissel' figure in *Othello*. Shakespeare added episodes in which Othello rages at Desdemona and she, not understanding his fury, reacts, some think, too patiently (the letter episode, when he strikes her, 4.1.240; the 'brothel' episode, 4.2.24ff.). A lost play about George Scanderbeg, entered in the SR in July 1601, may have influenced Shakespeare as well: Scanderbeg, a renegade Christian, led Turkish armies against Christians, and *Othello* could have been intended as a counter-attraction, with a Moor starring as a Christian general against the Turks.

James Roberts, who entered *Hamlet* in the SR on 26 July 1602, appears to have acted as the players' agent on a number of occasions.[1] After the publication of the 'bad' Quarto of *Hamlet* (Q1) in 1603, Roberts printed the 'good' Quarto of 1604–5 that replaced Q1. The SR entry of 1602, I deduce, was made to 'block' the publication of an unauthorized text, since Roberts allowed two years to pass before printing *Hamlet*, an immediately popular play.

1 This view of Roberts has been challenged, but seems to me the correct one of Roberts and also of Edward Blount, who succeeded Roberts as the players' agent: see *Texts*, 174 n. 15.

An unauthorized text, it seems, was known or rumoured to exist as early as 1602, and this text is likely (but not certain) to have been the one printed in 1603 – the one that contained echoes of many other plays,[1] including *Othello*. There are some steps in this reasoning that cannot be proved but, all things considered, the evidence suggests that *Othello* had been performed by mid-1602. I am aware of no compelling evidence for a later date.

It is usually assumed that the 'bad' Quarto of *Hamlet* was put together by a minor actor who had only a hazy recollection of the text as a whole and who interpolated many scraps of dialogue from other plays in which he had acted. When could he have had a part in *Othello*? The years 1601 and 1602 were free of the plague. In 1603 playing was 'restrained during the illness of Elizabeth on 19 March and probably not resumed', as plague broke out in April and continued for the rest of the year.[2] *Othello*, then, would have been performed not later than March 1603, a *terminus ante quem* that again points to 1602 as the probable year of the play's first performance.

---

1 For the echoes of other plays in *Hamlet* Q1 see G. I. Duthie, *The 'Bad' Quarto of 'Hamlet'* (Cambridge, 1941), and Alfred Hart, *Stolne and Surreptitious Copies* (Melbourne and Oxford, 1942).
2 Chambers, *Elizabethan Stage*, 4.349.

APPENDIX 2
THE TEXTUAL PROBLEM

Two early texts of *Othello* were published some years after Shakespeare's death in 1616: a Quarto (known as Q) in 1622, and a version included in the First Folio collection of 1623 (known as F). They differ in many hundreds of readings – in single-word variants and in longer passages, in spelling, verse lineation and punctuation. Ever since the second Quarto of 1630 (Q2) editors have conflated Q and F, that is, they have chosen readings from both, blending them together as they saw fit. Although I have not checked every recorded edition of the play, I think it probable that no two editions are exactly alike and that no edition prints the play exactly as Shakespeare wrote it.

Before I try to explain these extraordinary differences, here is a brief description of Q and F. Q collates A², B–M⁴, N², and contains forty-eight leaves. The title-page reads 'THE Tragoedy of Othello, The Moore of Venice. *As it hath beene diuerse times acted at the* Globe, and at the Black-Friers, by *his Maiesties Seruants. Written by* William Shakespeare. [Ornament] *LONDON*, Printed by *N.O.* for *Thomas Walkley*, and are to be sold at his shop, at the Eagle and Child, in Brittans Bursse. 1622.' After an epistle, 'The Stationer to the Reader', signed 'Thomas Walkley', the text follows on pages numbered 1 to 99. Walkley had previously entered his 'copy' in the Stationers' Register: '**Thomas Walkley** Entred for his copie vnder the hands of Sir GEORGE BUCK, and Master **Swinhowe** warden, *The Tragedie of OTHELLO, the moore of Venice* . . . vjᵈ.'[1]

The F text of *Othello* was placed near the end of the volume followed by only two more plays (*Antony and Cleopatra* and *Cymbeline*). It occupies thirty pages, printed in double columns; on

1 See Charlton Hinman, *Othello 1622*, Shakespeare Quarto Facsimiles, 16 (Oxford, 1975), v.

the last page, after 'FINIS', it adds a list of 'The Names of the Actors'.

According to Charlton Hinman's Through Line Numbering,[1] F consists of 3,685 lines, about 160 lines more than Q. F's additional lines include more than thirty passages of 1 to 22 lines (all recorded in the textual notes); amongst F's more interesting additions we may mention Roderigo's account of Desdemona's elopement (1.1.119–35), Desdemona's Willow Song (4.3.29–52, 54–6, 59–62, and 5.2.244–6) and Emilia's speech on marital fidelity (4.3.85–102). On the other hand, F's omissions 'are trifling', said E. K. Chambers, chiefly a few half-lines here and there, 'and doubtless due to error'.[2]

Both Q and F were press-corrected. Many of the corrections merely adjusted loose type or spacing, and these are not recorded by Arden 3. I have recorded all corrections that affect meaning: such press-corrections do not necessarily restore authoritative manuscript readings, since press-correctors did not always refer back to the manuscript. Each correction has to be judged on its merits.

More than fifty instances of 'profanity', printed by Q, were deleted in F or replaced by less offensive words (e.g. 1.1.4, 32, 85, 107). Editors once assumed that F was purged because of the Act of Abuses (1606), which prohibited profanity and swearing on the stage, yet we now know that some scribes and perhaps compositors omitted profanity for other reasons (*Texts*, 77ff.). The censor of *Othello* was unusually cautious if he deleted *Tush* (1.1.1) and worried about other harmless expletives (2.2.10, 4.1.239), yet he also overlooked some profanity; nevertheless the evidence of purging is clear enough. Editors think that the profanity was Shakespeare's (he wrote the play before 1606), and revert to Q's readings.

Q and F divide the play into acts and scenes. Q only numbers Acts 2, 4 and 5, and one scene (2.1); F numbers the acts and scenes as in Arden 3, except that F's 2.2 combines two scenes (2.2

1 See Charlton Hinman's Norton Facsimile of *Shakespeare's First Folio* (New York, n.d.), xxiv.
2 Chambers, *William Shakespeare*, 1.459.

and 2.3). Q, however, marked scene endings with the usual *Exeunt*, and in effect initiated the divisions adopted by later texts. As Q was the first of Shakespeare's 'good quartos' to be divided into acts, its act divisions – like F's – may have no authority.

Q stage directions are often fuller and more informative than F's (cf. 1.1.157; 1.3.0.1; 2.1.0.1; 5.2.195, 232), the opposite of what one would expect if F was printed from a prompt-copy, as was once supposed (Greg, 370). The Q directions, said W. W. Greg, (360), 'might all have been written by the author', i.e. though fuller than F's they do not look like the essential information sometimes added in prompt-books. In fact, both Q and F omit many necessary stage directions.

Aware of so many differences between Q and F, how should an editor proceed? He must try to account for the differences: examining the detail of each text, he must explain its provenance and transmission. 'Provenance' refers to the manuscript origin of the printed text: it could be the author's rough draft or 'foul papers', or an authorial fair copy, or a scribal copy prepared for the theatre or for a private patron or for the printer. Clearly 'provenance' already involves transmission; an editor, however, also wants to know how many scribes and compositors copied and set the text, and, if possible, their working habits. Both scribes and compositors normally changed spelling and punctuation at this time, and took other liberties with the texts they 'transmitted'. When William Jaggard, later to be the printer of the First Folio, produced a reprint of *The Merchant of Venice* in 1619, 'the total number of variants introduced [by Jaggard's men] is something like 3,200', about one per line, mostly changes of spelling and punctuation.[1]

The 1619 text of *The Merchant of Venice*, being a reprint, gives the editor a less baffling challenge than the two texts of *Othello*. All or almost all of its 3,200 variants can be explained as conscious or unconscious compositorial substitutions. In the case of *Othello* we have to ask whether Q and F derive from a single authorial arch-text or from two (e.g. foul papers and authorial fair copy); if from two, some QF variants could be seen as Shakespeare's first and second thoughts. Again, since Q preceded F by a year, could

---

1   D. F. Mackenzie, quoted *Texts*, 51.

F have been printed from a corrected copy of Q? Or could the F scribe or compositor have occasionally consulted Q, perhaps because the F copy was illegible, thus transplanting 'common errors' from Q to F? Editors agree that some weak or nonsensical readings found in both Q and F must be common errors: if so, other readings vouched for by both Q and F, even though not self-evidently corrupt, could also be Q mistakes taken over by F.

All the possibilities outlined in the preceding paragraph have been backed by recent editors, and each one accounts for the transmission of Q and F *Othello* in a different way. Every theory of transmission, again, has its own implications for editorial policy. It would not be easy to do justice to all the editorial problems and suggested solutions in this short appendix: instead of attempting the impossible, I have prepared a companion volume, *The Texts of 'Othello'*, where there is enough space for a systematic study of the textual detail. I propose, next, to summarize the conclusions of the companion volume, and then to indicate how they affect editorial decisions in Arden 3.

CONCLUSIONS

Soon after writing the foul papers of *Othello* (I call this version manuscript A), Shakespeare made a fair copy (manuscript B), changing some words and phrases but not undertaking large-scale revision; that is, the longer passages found in F and not in Q were not later additions, but were present in A and subsequently cut. Professional scribes copied out A and B, and their scribal manuscripts (Aa, Bb) were used as printer's copy for Q and F. The sequence of the six early texts of *Othello* can be shown as follows.

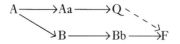

The broken arrow indicates that some Q readings also found their way into F.

EDITORIAL DECISIONS

Misreading

So many QF variants disagree in only one or two letters that misreading must account for the difference. Many such words would be easily confused in Secretary hand, which was used by Shakespeare in his six surviving signatures and, as all editors assume, in writing his plays.[1] A careful analysis of these variants suggests, further, that Shakespeare's hand was often almost illegible, much more so than in the three pages of *Sir Thomas More*, which were probably written eight or nine years earlier. The final letters of some words must have been an indistinct scribble, sometimes a superscript scribble (e.g. you^r = your), making it impossible to tell whether or not a letter was intended. Hence the frequent omission or addition of final *r* and *t* in *Othello*: you:your (1.1.79; 1.2.35; 3.3.40, 477; 5.2.262, 297); the:their (2.1.24, 45; 2.3.346; 3.4.146: viz. *their* spelt *ther*, as in *Sir Thomas More*, D, 260); worse:worsser (1.1.94), etc.; ouer:ouert (1.3.108); againe:again't (2.1.274); began:began't (2.3.213); of:oft (3.3.150); leaue ... keepe:leaue't ... kept (3.3.207); know:know't (3.3.340); loose:loose't (3.4.69); no:not (4.1.60), etc. Almost as commonly, initial and medial letters were omitted or confused, suggesting that Shakespeare's writing was difficult to read throughout and tailed off illegibly at the ends of many words.

Other letters often confused or misread in *Othello* include (1) minims (m, n, u, i, c, r, w); (2) a:minim; (3) e:d; (4) e:o; (5) o:a; (6) t:e; (7) t:c; (8) th:y; (9) h:th; (10) medial r; (11) the tilde, a suspension mark for m and n; (12) final y:e(e); (13) final s – the commonest cause of misreading, with more than one hundred variants in *Othello*. This is not a complete list, but gives some idea of the scale of the problem (for documentation, see *Texts*, ch. 8).

Since Q and F suffer from the same kinds of misreading we may deduce that Shakespeare himself was the source of the

---

1   See the reproductions of Secretary-hand minuscules and capitals in the Arden 3 *King Henry V* (ed. T. W. Craik), pp. 103–4, which show how easily letters could be confused and misreading could occur.

trouble. F has fewer obvious misreading errors, which is what one would expect if Q derives from foul papers and F from an authorial fair copy.

The Folio scribe

The hypothesis that it was Shakespeare's own writing that caused so much confusion is reinforced by the identification of the scribe who copied out manuscript Bb. A number of unusual spellings and his characteristic apostrophes, hyphens, colons, etc. make it as certain as such things can be that the scribe was Ralph Crane, who is generally accepted as the scribe responsible for five other Folio texts. Many dramatic and nondramatic manuscripts survive in Crane's hand, some with his signature: his spelling and punctuation were so distinctive that other printed plays are now recognized as 'Crane transcripts', apart from the five Folio texts (e.g. *The Duchess of Malfi*, 1623). For our purposes the all-important point is this: Crane, a professional scribe, wrote in a beautifully clear hand, therefore the misreading in F *Othello* cannot be blamed on an illegible manuscript (Bb) that defeated the Folio compositors. It was Crane, not the Folio compositors, who had to struggle to decipher a difficult manuscript – a manuscript that led to the same kinds of misreading as we find in Q. Again: the source of the trouble seems to have been Shakespeare's handwriting.

One arch-text or two?

Is it possible, though, that Q and F originated in the same manuscript, rather than in two different authorial manuscripts? Two reasons persuade me that we have to reckon with two autographs. (1) Short alternative passages in Q and F, too different to qualify as instances of misreading, are accepted by many editors as authorial revision. Such revision could conceivably survive in a single authorial manuscript, except for one factor. W. W. Greg, who analysed these passages and who did not subscribe to the 'two arch-texts' hypothesis, concluded in several instances that 'The impression is of deliberate revision in F rather than of corruption in Q', 'Everything therefore points to F's version having been reached by way of Q's, rather than Q's being a corruption of F's' (364ff.). Greg was impressed by the 'Shakespearian quality of both versions', with Q always the earlier and F the better one. Is this not strange? If Q and F both derive from a single authorial manuscript and it was obvious to the F scribe that one set of superior short passages replaced others that were inferior, why was it not obvious to the Q scribe? The simplest answer is that the Q scribe did not have access to the superior passages, because he copied from a different manuscript.

(2) F's inferior variants prompt a second argument on similar lines. Since the F scribe certainly had access to Q, as we know from common errors and common mislineation (*Texts*, 95ff.), why did he prefer inferior manuscript variants which look like corruptions, when Q supplied him with readings that later editors have thought undoubtedly superior? Had this happened just once or twice one might attach little significance to it, pleading in his defence that he need not have compared every word in the two texts. But it happened many times, and, as we have seen, he was copying a difficult manuscript, one that often forced him to resort to guesswork because he could not make out what Shakespeare had written: all the more reason, then, for checking Q's reading, if only to save himself time. Why should he waste his time attempting to decipher an illegible manuscript when the correct reading lay at hand in Q? The answer must be, I think, that Heminges and Condell had directed him to do so. Handing Crane manuscript B (Shakespeare's fair copy), they would have expressed their wishes roughly as follows. 'We need a clearly written manuscript of *Othello* for the Folio printer. Transcribe *this* manuscript. It is not easy to read – if you can make nothing of it, check the passage in this printed version [Q]. But keep in mind that the printed version is full of errors: it is a badly printed, unauthorized text [see *Texts*, 48–9]. Our manuscript has a much more reliable text. Follow the manuscript, as far as you can.' Crane did as he was told: when he thought that the scribble in the manuscript should be read as *worser* or *comes* (1.1.94, 114), not *worse* or *come*, as in Q, he preferred the manuscript reading. And, because the manuscript was so difficult, he sometimes thought he could make

out words, indistinctly written, that were not there (e.g. *tongued*, *chances*, instead of Q's *toged*, *changes*: 1.1.24, 71).

The 'better text'?

Assuming, as above, that Crane knew Q to be an inferior text and that he took some trouble to produce a better one, an editor may want to treat F as the 'better text', and therefore to follow F whenever Q and F readings are equally acceptable. Yet this is a dangerous policy, for several reasons. (1) Though he did his best, Crane clearly misread some words, some F variants being very unlikely (e.g. *super-vision*, 3.3.398, for Q *superuisor*). Consequently other words, which are not so self-evidently wrong, could be mis-readings as well. (2) If Crane transcribed from an authorial fair copy and Q was printed from a scribal copy of the foul papers, we are not entitled to assume that, when Q and F disagree, one or the other must be corrupt. Where there are variant readings Shake-speare could have written both: we know from Thomas Mid-dleton's holographs, and from other authorial texts, that many poets replace words when they transcribe their own work, either consciously or unconsciously. Even quite trivial changes were common, and many 'indifferent variants' in *Othello* may be in-stances of such authorial instability (1.1.16 chosen:chose; 42 be all:all be; 53 those:these). (3) Crane, and the Folio compositors, regarded some contractions and the uncontracted alternative as interchangeable, even when this appears to damage the metre (e.g. *Ile* and *I will*, *you've* and *you have*, *'t* and *it*). An editor who retains F's contracted or uncontracted form must warn readers that it may have to be lengthened or shortened or slurred, when spoken aloud, to suit the metre. I have in general chosen to follow F, not to correct the verse, because the alternative would be to force the verse into a metrical straitjacket. But when Q offers a variant that scans correctly (either the contracted or the uncon-tracted form), Arden 3 adopts the Q reading. In my view, Q rather than F is the 'better text' in some respects – in its punctuation, in retaining profanity, and in at least some of its stage directions and verbal variants.

Copy-text?

Yet F is better than Q in other respects – in its verse lineation, and in being marred by fewer 'manifest errors' than Q. Would it be possible, then, to modify the traditional editorial policy, and to treat F as copy-text for lineation, and to make Q the copy-text for profanity and punctuation? I believe that we should lean towards whichever text seems better at lineation when we consider lineation, whichever seems better at punctuation when we consider punctuation, and so on: lean towards but not follow slavishly, since both Q and F are sometimes self-evidently corrupt even in the textual department in which they seem generally better. Adopting this editorial position, Arden 3 is less committed to either Q or F than previous editions, exercising more freedom of choice. Nevertheless, because F transmits the later authorial version and corrects many Q errors, Arden 3 leans towards F rather than Q in some instances of genuine perplexity, particularly in dealing with indifferent variants (a preference shared with most other editions of *Othello*). We must acknowledge, however, that even this lesser reliance on F is dangerous. Arden 3 follows F twenty-two times in printing *hath* where Q prints *has*: yet there are good reasons for suspecting that the F scribe, Ralph Crane, substituted *hath* for *has* in *Othello* as in other texts (see *Texts*, 68), and was responsible for many other indifferent variants in F (including F's regular *handkerchief* and *murther* for Q's regular *handkercher* and *murder*). In the present state of knowledge we cannot be certain about indifferent variants but it seems likely that Arden 3, though far less committed to F as 'copy-text' than previous editions, still prints scores – or perhaps hundreds – of F variants that are scribal or compositorial substitutions, not the words written by Shakespeare.

Syllabic changes

In Elizabethan English a large number of words could gain or lose a syllable as the metre required. Some could be either monosyllabic or disyllabic (notably words with -er- and -en- syllables: heav(e)n, stol(e)n; nev(e)r, wheth(e)r, etc., and also others: dev(i)l, spir(i)t;

dear, fire, hour). Others had a variable syllable for the endings -(i)on, -(i)ous, -(i)an (e.g. jeal(i)ous, Venet(i)an). Arden 3 does not attempt to regularize, leaving it to the reader to try out the scansion and come to his or her own decisions, as with other contractions (p. 358 above, 'The "better text"? '). Readers may stumble here and there, as Shakespeare's actors no doubt did, yet at the same time they will learn an important lesson – that there is no single correct way of speaking Shakespeare's verse. The commentary offers help when this is needed.

Lineation

Arden 3 prints as verse a number of passages usually printed as prose. These are mostly short passages embedded in verse (preceded and/or followed by verse) which divide readily into lines consisting of ten or eleven syllables, Shakespeare's normal measure: e.g. 1.1.4–6; 3.3.316–19; 4.1.234; 5.1.121–3; 5.2.33–4, 68–70, 121–3. In a few cases the decision to print verse rather than prose is more problematic (3.1.32–41; 5.2.115, 138–9). It should be remembered, though, that Shakespeare experimented with verse-like prose and prose-like verse, that the difference between the two could be slight (2.1.178–80; 2.3.12, 61, 116; 4.2.175), and that, at the time of *Othello*, Shakespeare was capable of writing odd-looking verse lines (e.g. 3.1.48; 4.2.70; 5.2.279). In addition readers should note that expletives, vocatives and interruptions were often treated as extra-metrical (e.g. 1.1.4, 101; 1.3.173). The rules or conventions governing dramatic verse – I have only touched on a few – may be explored at greater length in specialist studies.[1]

Since Q mislines so many undoubted verse passages as prose and vice versa, wrongly divides verse lines and is exceptionally insensitive to the verse measure, the textual notes do not record Q's variant lineation in every instance. Where Arden 3 diverges from F's lineation, this is recorded.

1   See Abbott, or George T. Wright's more recent *Shakespeare's Metrical Art* (Berkeley, 1988).

Intended cuts?

Several 'good' texts of Shakespeare's plays print lines that were clearly meant to be deleted (sometimes they reappear in the same text in slightly altered form). Shakespeare's deletions, it seems, were marked very lightly or not at all. *Othello* includes lines and half-lines that are puzzling or metrically irregular, the removal of which does not damage the sense. They too could have been lightly marked deletions printed in error (e.g. 1.1.20; 1.3.17; 3.1.47). One four-line passage (4.3.63–6) looks like a false start immediately replaced by 4.3.67–9. If Q printed intended deletions, the F scribe could have copied them from Q.

Punctuation

On the evidence of Shakespeare's three pages in *Sir Thomas More* and of most of the 'good' quartos, editors believe that Shakespeare punctuated lightly, and very often omitted all punctuation. Both Q and F *Othello* punctuate more heavily than the 'good' texts published in Shakespeare's lifetime: Arden 3 repunctuates, distrusting the pointing of Q and F as post-Shakespearian (see *Texts*, ch. 11).

Modernization

Every Arden 3 text has been modernized – what does this mean? It does not mean that each text follows precisely the same principles of modernization. To take one example, modern texts almost certainly punctuate more heavily than Shakespeare did, yet punctuation is a notoriously personal matter, so it is unlikely that Arden 3 punctuation will be the same from play to play; indeed, the same editor may choose to punctuate more or less heavily in different passages of the same play. Punctuation is partly a matter of feeling; careful readers of *Othello* may feel – no, *should* feel – that, here and there, they disagree with the editor's pointing. And why not?

> The noise was high. Ha, no more moving?
> Still as the grave. Shall she come in? were't good?
> I think she stirs again. No – what's best to do?
> (5.2.92–4, Ard³)

> The noise was high. Ha! no more moving.
> Still as the grave . . . Shall she come in, were't good?
> I think she stirs again . . . ? – No. What's best to do?

Both are possible, and readers should remember that the editor's choice of punctuation often rests on grounds that could not be defended in a court of law.

Inevitably, the editor's modernized punctuation affects the 'feeling' of the whole play, in particular the flow of thought from sentence to sentence. It could be that we should not adopt the same pointing for dialogue and for soliloquy (where the thinking process, more elliptical, may need more dashes); or that the very different speech habits of Othello and Iago require different kinds of punctuation. Be that as it may, two things are clear. First, that the function of Shakespeare's dramatic words is often impossible to define with certainty. A question mark, in his texts, could indicate a question or an exclamation; the absence of a question mark, on the other hand, does not imply that no question is intended. There are questions and half-questions (as, perhaps, at 5.2.94, above), just as there are asides and half-asides:[1] Shakespeare's language breaks all the rules of grammar and precedent. Second, because he wrote performance scripts for actors, and because the actors must have spoken quickly, Shakespeare did not have to worry about the grammatical connections of words and sentences: in the theatre the verbal flow rushes past us like a fast-flowing river, and individual words are sometimes scarcely more identifiable than drops of water in a rippling current.

For these reasons a modernized text imposes a sharper focus than Shakespeare probably wanted – for example, by dividing dramatic speech into either prose or verse (see p. 360). A modern editor tidies the text, standardizing speech prefixes and stage directions, eliminating Shakespeare's first or second thoughts, normalizing his famously unstable spelling. Some editors even distinguish between 'Oh' and 'O' where, again, there is no evidence that Shakespeare did so (compare Othello's 'Oh, oh, oh' and 'O, o, o' in the Quarto at 5.2.195, 279). Such tidying introduces new difficulties: should we read 'O insupportable, O heavy hour!'

---

1 For half-asides see Honigmann, 'Stage direction', 119–20, and *Oth* 2.1.213–15.

(5.2.97) or 'Oh, insupportable! Oh, heavy hour!'? As with other forms of modernization, this question will seem more important to editors and readers than to actors in the theatre.

The editor of Arden 3 *Othello* modernizes reluctantly, with many reservations. Modern spelling and punctuation make Shakespeare more accessible, at a cost – namely, that we lose the Elizabethan flavour and suggestiveness of his language, making Shakespeare our contemporary even though his every word is around four hundred years old. It is like cleaning an old picture and slightly changing all the colours. In a few cases I refuse to modernize, since the modern form of some words will positively mislead. 'Count' now has different connotations and will not mean the Day of Judgement, therefore I retain F 'compt' (5.2.271); God is not an engineer, therefore remains an 'inginer' (2.1.65).

A sample passage

Having summarized the textual policy of this edition, I shall try to show how it affects editorial thinking in a sample passage, 5.2.0ff. (see pp. 364–5). (1) The opening stage direction differs in Q and F. Both texts omit essential information: Arden 3 reprints both, and adds one word to F, 'DESDEMONA *in her bed* [*asleep*]'. Q supplies one other stage direction, '*He kisses her*', opposite lines 19 and 20, omitted by F; Arden 3 expands this (see [8], p. 366). (2) Though Q and F sometimes agree in their punctuation, they frequently differ (six times in the first five lines). Arden 3 modernizes and repunctuates, on the assumption that both Q and F are more heavily pointed than Shakespeare's manuscripts would have been. (3) F, in line with its practice elsewhere, introduces many more 'emphasis capitals' than Q. Even if Arden 3 were not a modernized text, we would have to drop these capitals as post-Shakespearian.

Proceeding, next, to the verbal variants in the dialogue, we notice (4) that many are graphically related, i.e. would look very similar in Shakespeare's hand (see p. 355 above, 'Misreading') – e.g. (citing Q first, then F) returne:re-Lume (13), once:One (17, 19), when:where (22). (5) In two instances the variants are graphically alike but differ in their endings – cunning:cunning'st (11), *Desdemona:Desdemon* (25) – which may mean that

Enter Othello *with a light.*

Oth. It is the caufe,it is the caufe,my foule,
Let me not name it to you,you chafte ftarres :
It is the caufe,yet I'le not fhed her blood,
Nor fcarre that whiter skin of hers,then fnow,
And fmooth,as monumentall Alablafter ;
Yet fhe muft die,elfe fhee'll betray more men.
Put out the light,and then put out the light :
If I quench thee, thou flaming minifter,
I can againe,thy former light reftore,
Should I repent me; but once put out thine,
Thou cunning patterne of excelling nature,
I know not where is that promethian heate,
That can thy light returne : when I haue pluckt the rofe,
I cannot giue it vitall growth againe,
It muft needes wither ; l'le fmell it on the tree,
A balmy breath,that doth almoft perfwade
Iuftice her felfe to breake her fword once more,
Be thus,when thou art dead,and I will kill thee,
And loue thee after : once more,and this the laft,   *He*
So fweete was ne're fo fatall : I muft weepe,   *kiffes her.*
But they are cruell teares ; this forrowes heauenly,
It ftrikes when it does loue : fhe wakes.
    Def. Who's there,*Othello* ?
    Oth. I,*Defdemona.*
    Def. Will you come to bed my Lord?
    Oth. Haue you prayed to night,*Defdemona* ?
                        M

22 Quarto text of *Othello* 5.2.1–25

Shakespeare's writing tailed off into an indistinct squiggle, one
which might be misinterpreted (a) as standing for illegible letters;
or (b) as having no significance, even though the writer intended it
as one or two letters. Arden 3 adopts the F readings, taking Q's
'*Desdemona*' as an instance of (a) and 'cunning' as one of (b).

But should we ascribe all the variants to the misreading of a
difficult hand? (6) Some variants in both Q and F appear to be

> *Enter Othello, and Desdemona in her bed.*
>
> *Oth.* It is the Cause, it is the Cause (my Soule)
> Let me not name it to you, you chaste Starres,
> It is the Cause. Yet Ile not shed her blood,
> Nor scarre that whiter skin of hers, then Snow,
> And smooth as Monumentall Alablaster:
> Yet she must dye, else shee'l betray more men:
> Put out the Light, and then put out the Light:
> If I quench thee, thou flaming Minister,
> I can againe thy former light restore,
> Should I repent me. But once put out thy Light,
> Thou cunning'st Patterne of excelling Nature,
> I know not where is that *Promethean* heate
> That can thy Light re-Lume.
> When I haue pluck'd thy Rose,
> I cannot giue it vitall growth againe,
> It needs must wither. Ile smell thee on the Tree.
> Oh Balmy breath, that dost almost perswade
> Iustice to breake her Sword. One more, one more:
> Be thus when thou art dead, and I will kill thee,
> And loue thee after. One more, and that's the last.
> So sweet, was ne're so fatall. I must weepe,
> But they are cruell Teares: This sorrow's heauenly,
> It strikes, where it doth loue. She wakes.
>   *Des.* Who's there? *Othello?*
>   *Othel.* I *Desdemona.*
>   *Des.* Will you come to bed, my Lord?
>   *Oth.* Haue you pray'd to night, *Desdemon?*

23 Folio text of *Othello* 5.2.1–25

connected with other readings in the same text. Q's *it* and *doth* (15,
16) go together (third person), as do F's *thee* and *dost* (second
person). If Shakespeare revised these lines, perhaps he also
omitted Q *her selfe* (17) and added *one more* to the same line in
F. Or is it conceivable that the Q scribe or compositor misread

his manuscript, and was responsible for these and other Q variants?

(7) Not all of F's variants are clearly improvements. 'When I haue pluck'd *thy* Rose' (F) is less pleasing than '. . . *the* rose' (Q), and looks like final *e:y* misreading (*Texts*, 85). 'It *needs must* wither' (F) and 'It *must needes* wither' (Q) could both be right. '*Oh* Balmy breath' (F) may seem preferable to '*A* balmy breath' (Q) – until we recall that 'A' could stand for 'Ah', which again means that there is little to choose between Q and F.

(8) A more striking difference occurs at lines 17 and 19, where Q reads 'once more . . . once more', and F 'One more, [one more . . .] One more'. This is less likely to be revision than minim-misreading, common in both Q and F. Most editors have followed F, at the same time moving Q's '*He kisses her*' from line 19 to line 15. Yet there is no textual evidence for a kiss at 15, though Othello's words reveal that another action is needed at this point – 'I'll smell thee on the tree; / O balmy breath . . .'. 'Once more' refers back to this action, and to Othello's highly developed sense of smell (see p. 21). 'One more [kiss]' would be acceptable if a kiss had preceded, 'one more [smell]' or 'one more [sniff]' less so, for reasons that are not easy to explain. Here an editor may choose to move Q's stage direction, as editors do elsewhere in *Othello*, and read 'One more' (with F) or may prefer Q's 'once more'. Arden 3 follows Q and adapts the stage direction at line 19 to include smelling and kissing.

(9) It will be agreed, I think, that more of Q's variants are inferior than F's. Are all of Q's inferior readings corruptions, though, or could some be Shakespeare's 'first thoughts', which he improved upon when he prepared his fair copy? That is not so clear, and the question cannot be decided from a single passage, as other passages that may be revised occur in other scenes, and reinforce one another (e.g. 1.3.261ff., 277ff.; 5.2.217–18). All local decisions depend on other local decisions, and on the resulting 'editorial policy'.

The textual notes

As will now be obvious, many of the textual problems of *Othello* have not yet been solved. While we may think that we can explain some – the disappearance of profanity from F, 'Crane' spellings, anomalous lineation, misreading errors – we cannot always distinguish between authorial revision and scribal or compositorial substitutions: indeed, the more trivial the variants the more difficult it becomes to guess who was responsible and to make a reasoned choice (compare 1.1.4 you will:you'l, 16 chosen:chose, 26 the:th', 34 But:Why). Readers are therefore urged to pay special attention to the textual notes: these record all significant QF variants, and are printed conveniently below the text and commentary, on the same page. The editor has done his best, but editors are fallible. The small type at the foot of the page may after all transmit the best reading. Here, as elsewhere in this transitory life, the true men may lie low while impostors parade themselves more openly.

N.B. The textual notes include unusual spellings and other oddities that look like hangovers from the distinctive writing habits of Shakespeare and of Ralph Crane. These clues as to textual provenance are so numerous that it was not possible to explain each one in the commentary, but they are discussed in *Texts*, pp. 158ff. (Shakespearian spellings), 63ff. (Crane's spellings), and 68ff. (compositor E's retention of copy-spellings).

APPENDIX 3
CINTHIO AND MINOR SOURCES

The principal source of *Othello* is the seventh *novella* in the third decade of Giraldi Cinthio's *Hecatommithi* (1565). A French translation by G. Chappuys appeared in 1583, and the first extant English translation not until 1753. Chappuys kept close to the Italian version except for a few details, and Shakespeare could have read one or the other, or perhaps a lost English translation. The details that point to his acquaintance with the Italian text consist of unusual words or phrases not replicated in Chappuys, and are listed in the commentary at 1.3.350 (*acerb*), 2.1.16 (*molestation*), 3.3.363 (*ocular proof*), and in the notes on Cinthio in this appendix. Similar details, not found in the Italian text, suggest Shakespeare's possible acquaintance with Chappuys: 1.3.220 (*heart pierced*), 3.3.300 (*take out the work*), 4.1.196 (*touch*). The Italian words are more striking, and the *Othello* 'echoes' of Chappuys could be explained as coincidence.[1] Yet a lost English version, one that perhaps made use of both the Italian and the French texts, cannot be ruled out. Lodowick Bryskett's translations of various works of Cinthio were published before and after *Othello* was written,[2] and a translation of Cinthio's story of the Moor of Venice could have reached Shakespeare in manuscript. Not very long after composing *Othello* Shakespeare returned to the *Hecatommithi* for one of the sources of *Measure for Measure*.

M. R. Ridley said that 'there are a few verbal parallels which may be taken to suggest an acquaintance with the original [i.e. Cinthio], but I do not think that they are very significant' (Ard², xv). I

---

1 See Honigmann, '*Othello*, Chappuys and Cinthio', *N&Q*, 13 (1966), 136–7; and Naseeb Shaheen, 'Shakespeare's knowledge of Italian', *SS*, 47 (1994), 161ff., and below, p. 387.
2 See *Barnabe Riche His Farewell to Military Profession*, ed. Donald Beecher (New York, Publications of the Barnabe Riche Society, vol. 1, 1992), 50–1.

have to disagree: whether we consider Cinthio or Chappuys or a lost English version as Shakespeare's original, a surprising number of verbal parallels found their way into the play from Cinthio, with or without intermediaries – many more than Bullough listed in his translation. Their significance grows as we piece together the full jigsaw of borrowings – words, phrases, episodes, ideas – for then we see that, even though Shakespeare felt free to change whatever did not suit him, Cinthio's narrative supplied so much detail that in effect Shakespeare allowed it to guide his view of crucial events.

The translation of Cinthio that follows has been reprinted, with kind permission, from Geoffrey Bullough's *Narrative and Dramatic Sources of Shakespeare*, vol. 7, pp. 241–52. The footnotes, listing Shakespeare's verbal and other debts, are new. While, inevitably, some of these debts are less compelling than others, their cumulative weight seems to me considerable.

Cinthio's *Hecatommithi*, modelled on Boccaccio's *Decameron*, consists of a series of short stories about different kinds of love, chiefly married love. After an introduction (ten stories) there follow ten decades, each of ten stories, where the story-tellers explain how husbands and wives should be chosen. In the introduction one man argues that appetite should be ruled by reason (*Oth* 1.3.262–3, 'not / To please the palate of my appetite'; 327–9, 'If the balance of our lives had not one scale of reason to poise another of sensuality'), and that before marrying we should consider 'the quality, manners, life and habits' of possible partners (3.3.233, 'Not to affect many proposed matches / Of her own clime, complexion and degree'). He denounces women who, pretending to be virtuous, hide their ugly souls in 'singing, playing, dancing . . . and speaking sweetly' (3.3.186–8, ''Tis not to make me jealous / To say my wife is fair, feeds well, loves company, / Is free of speech, sings, plays and dances well'). Although these are commonplaces, I think it likely that Shakespeare glanced at Cinthio's introduction and at the pages that precede and follow the story of the Moor of Venice.

Cinthio's third decade revolves around the infidelity of husbands and wives (cf. *Oth* 4.3.85–102). In the sixth story a husband discovers his wife committing adultery, and revenges himself by arranging her 'accidental' death. The seventh story, which now follows, deals with a husband's revenge for supposed adultery and, again, the wife's 'accidental' death. In short, Cinthio's stories are interlinked: the account of the Moor, Shakespeare's immediate source, which he read with concentrated attention, no doubt led him to other parts of the *Hecatommithi*.

THE THIRD DECADE, STORY 7

A Moorish Captain takes to wife a Venetian lady, and his Ensign accuses her to her husband of adultery; he desires the Ensign to kill the man whom he believes to be the adulterer; the Captain kills his wife and is accused by the Ensign. The Moor does not confess, but on clear indications of his guilt he is banished; and the scoundrelly Ensign, thinking to injure others, brings a miserable end on himself.

The ladies would have had great pity for the fate of the Florentine woman had her adultery not made her appear worthy of the severest punishment; and it seemed to them that the gentleman's patience had been unusually great. Indeed they declared that it would be hard to find any other man who, discovering his wife in such a compromising situation, would not have slain both of the sinners outright. The more they thought about it the more prudently they considered him to have behaved.

After this discussion, Curzio, on whom all eyes were turned as they waited for him to begin his story, said: *I do not believe that either men or women are free to avoid amorous passion,*[1] *for human nature is so disposed to it that even against our will it makes itself powerfully felt in our souls.*[2] Nevertheless, *I believe that a virtuous lady has the power, when she feels herself burning with such a desire, to resolve rather to die than through dishonourable lust to stain that modesty which ladies should preserve*[3] as untainted as white ermine.

---

1 3.3.279, "'Tis destiny unshunnable, like death'.
2 2.1.231–3, 'very nature will instruct her in it and compel her to some second choice'.
3 4.3.60–1, 'Dost thou in conscience think . . . That there be women do abuse their husbands . . . ?'

And I believe that they err less who, free from the holy bonds of matrimony, *offer their bodies to the delight of every man*[1] than does a married woman who commits adultery with one person only. But as this woman suffered well-deserved punishment for her fault, so *it sometimes happens that without any fault at all, a faithful and loving lady, through the insidious plots* [tesele] *of a villainous mind,*[2] and the frailty *of one who believes more than he need,*[3] is murdered by her faithful husband; as you will clearly perceive by what I am about to relate to you.

There was once in Venice a Moor, a very gallant man, who, because he was *personally valiant*[4] and had *given proof in warfare*[5] of great prudence and skilful energy, was *very dear to the Signoria,*[6] who in rewarding virtuous actions ever advance the interests of the Republic. It happened that *a virtuous Lady of wondrous beauty called Disdemona,*[7] *impelled not by female appetite but by the Moor's good qualities, fell in love with him,*[8] and *he, vanquished by the Lady's beauty and noble mind,*[9] *likewise was enamoured of her.*[10] So propitious was their mutual love that, *although the Lady's relatives did all they could to make her take another husband,*[11] they were united in marriage and lived together in such concord and tranquillity while they remained in Venice, that never a word passed between them that was not loving.

It happened that the Venetian lords made a change in the forces that they used to maintain in Cyprus; and they chose the Moor as *Commandant*[12] of the soldiers whom they sent there. Although he was pleased by the honour offered him (for such high rank and

---

1 3.3.348–9, 'I had been happy if the general camp ... had tasted her sweet body'.
2 4.1.46–7, 'many worthy and chaste dames even thus, / All guiltless, meet reproach'.
3 5.2.342, 'Of one that loved not wisely, but too well'.
4 1.3.49, 'Valiant Othello' (It. *molto valoroso*; Fr. *fort vaillant*).
5 1.1.27, 'of whom his eyes had seen the proof' (Iago).
6 1.3.129, 'Her father loved me' (It. *caro a que signori*; Fr. *aymé des seigneurs*).
7 2.1.61–2, 'a maid / That paragons description'.
8 1.3.262–3, 'not / To please the palate of my appetite' (Othello).
9 1.3.253, 'I saw Othello's visage in his mind'; 266, 'to be free and bounteous to her mind'.
10 1.3.168–9, 'She loved me ... And I loved her'.
11 Brabantio in Act 1; 4.2.127, 'Hath she forsook so many noble matches?'
12 1.2.53, 'Come, captain' (It. *capitano*; Fr. *capitaine* and *chef*).

dignity is given only to noble and loyal men who have proved themselves most valiant), yet his happiness was lessened when he considered the length and dangers of the voyage, thinking that Disdemona would be much troubled by it. The Lady, who had no other happiness on earth but the Moor, and was very pleased with the recognition of his merits that her husband had received from so noble and powerful a Republic, could hardly wait for the hour when he would set off with his men, and *she would accompany him*[1] to that honourable post. It grieved her greatly to see the Moor troubled; and, not knowing the reason for it, one day while they were dining together she said to him: 'Why is it, my Moor, that after being given such an honourable rank by the Signoria, you are so melancholy?'

The Moor said to Disdemona: 'The love I bear you spoils my pleasure at the honour I have received, because I see that one of two things must happen: either I must take you with me in peril by sea, or, so as not to cause you this hardship, *I must leave you in Venice*.[2] The first alternative*must inevitably weigh heavily on me, since every fatigue you endured and *every danger we met would give me extreme anxiety*.[3] The second, having to leave you behind, would be hateful to me, since, *parting from you I should be leaving my very life behind*.[4]

'Alas, husband,' said Disdemona, hearing this, 'What thoughts are these passing through your mind? Why do you let such ideas perturb you? *I want to come with you wherever you go, even if it meant walking through fire*[5] in my shift instead of, as it will be, crossing the water with you in a safe, well-furnished galley. *If there really are to be dangers and fatigues, I wish to share them with you;*[5] and I should consider myself very little beloved if, rather than have my company on the sea, you were to leave me in Venice, or persuaded yourself that I would rather stay here in safety than be in the same

1   1.3.260, 'Let me go with him.'
2   1.3.256, 'if I be left behind'.
3   2.1.2; 46, 'I have lost him on a dangerous sea'; 16, 'never did like molestation view' (It. *estrema molestia*).
4   1.3.295, 'My life upon her faith.'
5   1.3.168, 'She loved me for the dangers I had passed'; 249, 'That I did love the Moor to live with him'.

danger as yourself. *Get ready then for the voyage in the cheerfulness*[1] that *befits the high rank you hold.*[2]

Then *the Moor joyously threw his arms round his wife's neck and said, with a loving kiss: 'God keep us long in this love, my dear wife!'*[3] Shortly afterwards, having donned his armour and made all ready for the journey, he embarked in the galley with his lady and all his train; then, hoisting sail, they set off, and with a sea of the utmost tranquillity arrived safely in Cyprus.

The Moor had in his company an Ensign of handsome presence but *the most scoundrelly nature in the world.*[4] He was in high favour with the Moor, who had no suspicion of his wickedness; for although he had *the basest of minds, he so cloaked the vileness hidden in his heart*[5] with *high sounding and noble words, and by his manner, that he showed himself in the likeness of a Hector or an Achilles.*[6] This false man had likewise taken to Cyprus his wife, a fair and honest young woman. Being an Italian she was much loved by the Moor's wife, and spent the greater part of the day with her.

In the same company there was also *a Corporal who was very dear to the Moor.*[7] This man went frequently to the Moor's house and *often dined with him and his wife.*[8] The Lady, knowing him so well liked by her husband, gave him proofs of the greatest kindness, and this was much appreciated by the Moor.

The wicked Ensign, taking no account of the faith he had pledged to his wife, and of the friendship, loyalty and obligations he owed the Moor, *fell ardently in love with Disdemona,*[9] and bent all his thoughts to see if he could manage *to enjoy her;*[10] but he did not dare openly show his passion, fearing that if the Moor

---

1   1.3.233, 'A natural and prompt alacrity' (It. *allegrezza*).
2   1.3.240, 'As levels with her breeding' (of Desdemona).
3   2.1.180; 191–3, 'But that our loves and comforts should increase'.
4   4.2.141–2, 'abused by some most villainous knave, / Some base notorious knave'.
5   3.3.110–11, 'some monster in thy thought / Too hideous to be shown'; 3.3.139, 'Utter my thoughts? Why, say they are vile and false?'
6   1.1.12–13, 'a bombast circumstance'; 2.1.221–2, 'bragging ... prating' (of Othello).
7   3.1.49, 'he protests he loves you'; 3.3.48.
8   3.3.58, 'Tomorrow dinner then?'
9   2.1.289, 'Now I do love her too'.
10 1.3.358, 'thou shalt enjoy her'.

perceived it *he might straightway kill him*.[1] He sought therefore in various ways, as deviously as he could, to make the Lady aware that he desired her. But she, whose every thought was for the Moor, never gave a thought to the Ensign or anybody else. And all the things he did to arouse her feelings for him had no more effect than if he had not tried them. Whereupon *he imagined that this was because she was in love with the Corporal*;[2] and he wondered how he might remove the latter from her sight. Not only did he turn his mind to this, but *the love which he had felt for the Lady now changed to the bitterest hate*[3] and he gave himself up to studying how to bring it about that, once the Corporal were killed, if he himself could not enjoy the Lady, then the Moor should not have her either. *Turning over in his mind divers schemes, all wicked and treacherous, in the end he determined to accuse her of adultery, and to make her husband believe that the Corporal was the adulterer.*[4] But knowing the singular love of the Moor for Disdemona, and his friendship for the Corporal, he recognized that, unless he could deceive the Moor with some clever trick, it would be impossible to make him believe either charge. Wherefore he set himself to wait *until time and place opened a way for him*[5] to start his wicked enterprise.

Not long afterwards *the Moor deprived the Corporal of his rank for having drawn his sword and wounded a soldier while on guard-duty.*[6] Disdemona was grieved by this and tried many times to reconcile the Moor with him. Whereupon the Moor told the rascally Ensign that his wife importuned him so much for the Corporal that he feared he would be obliged to reinstate him. The evil man saw in this a hint for setting in train the deceits he had planned, and said: 'Perhaps Disdemona has good cause to look on him so favourably!' *'Why is that?' asked the Moor.*[7] 'I do not wish',

---

1   3.3.362ff.
2   2.1.231; 285, 'That she loves him, 'tis apt'.
3   3.3.448–9, 'All my fond love thus do I blow to heaven . . . 'Tis gone' (Othello) (It. *acerbissimo odio*: cf. 1.3.349–50, 'acerb as coloquintida').
4   1.3.391; 2.1.310.
5   3.3.249, 'Leave it to time'; 2.3.294–5, 'the time, the place'.
6   2.3.147ff., 239.
7   3.3.179, 'why is this?'

said the Ensign, 'to come between man and wife, but *if you keep your eyes open you will see for yourself.*[1] *Nor for all the Moor's inquiries would the Ensign go beyond this:*[2] nonetheless his words left such a sharp thorn in the Moor's mind, that he gave himself up to *pondering intensely what they could mean.*[3] He became quite melancholy, and one day, when his wife was trying to soften his anger towards the Corporal, *begging him not to condemn to oblivion the loyal service and friendship of many years just for one small fault,*[4] especially since the Corporal had been reconciled to the man he had struck, *the Moor burst out in anger*[5] and said to her, 'There must be a very powerful reason why you take such trouble for this fellow, for he is not your brother, nor even a kinsman, yet you have him so much at heart!'

The lady, all courtesy and modesty, replied: 'I should not like you to be angry with me. Nothing else makes me do it but sorrow to see you deprived of so dear a friend as you have shown that the Corporal was to you. *He has not committed so serious an offence*[6] as to deserve such hostility. *But you Moors are so hot by nature*[7] that any little thing moves you to anger and revenge.'

Still more enraged by these words the Moor answered: 'Anyone who does not believe that may easily have proof of it! *I shall take such revenge* for any wrongs done to me *as will more than satisfy me!*[8] The lady was terrified by these words, and seeing her husband *angry with her, quite against his habit*[9] she said humbly: '*Only a very good purpose made me speak to you about this*[10] but rather than have you angry with me *I shall never say another word on the subject.*[11]

1 3.3.200, 'Look to your wife, observe her well'.
2 3.3.262, 362ff.
3 3.3.111, 'Thou dost mean something'; 157, 'What dost thou mean?'
4 3.3.18, 'My general will forget my love and service'; 64–6, 'his trespass . . . is not, almost, a fault'.
5 3.4.133, 'Is my lord angry?'
6 3.4.116, 'If my offence be of such mortal kind'.
7 3.4.30–1, 'the sun where he was born / Drew all such humours from him'.
8 3.3.446, 'my revenge'; 393, 'Would I were satisfied!'
9 3.4.125, 'My lord is not my lord, nor should I know him'.
10 3.3.76–80.
11 5.2.301, 'From this time forth I never will speak word' (Iago).

The Moor, however, *seeing the earnestness with which his wife had again pleaded for the Corporal,*[1] guessed that the Ensign's words had been intended to suggest that Disdemona was in love with the Corporal, and he went in deep depression to the scoundrel and *urged him to speak more openly.*[2] The Ensign, intent on injuring this unfortunate lady, after *pretending not to wish to say anything*[3] that might displease the Moor, appeared to be overcome by his entreaties and said: '*I must confess that it grieves me greatly*[4] to have to tell you something that must be in the highest degree painful to you; but since you wish me to tell you, and the regard that I must have of your honour as my master spurs me on, *I shall not fail in my duty*[5] to answer your request. You must know therefore that it is hard for your Lady to see the Corporal in disgrace for the simple reason that she takes her pleasure with him whenever he comes to your house. *The woman has come to dislike your blackness.*'[6]

These words struck the Moor's heart to its core;[7] but in order to learn more (although he believed what the Ensign had said to be true, through the suspicion already sown in his mind) he said, with a fierce look: '*I do not know what holds me back from cutting out that outrageous tongue of yours*[8] which has *dared to speak such insults against my Lady!*'[9] Then the Ensign: 'Captain,' he said, '*I did not expect any other reward*[10] for my loving service; but since my duty and my care for your honour have carried me so far, I repeat that the matter stands exactly as you have just heard it, and if your Lady, with a false show of love for you, has so blinded your eyes that you have not seen what you ought to have seen, that does

1 3.3.54; 3.4.89ff.
2 3.3.135–6, 'give thy worst of thoughts / The worst of words'.
3 3.3.147.
4 2.3.173, 'Honest Iago, that look'st dead with grieving'.
5 3.3.137; 197, 'To show the love and duty that I bear you'.
6 (Lit., to *tire* of your blackness; Fr., 'qui est déia ennuyée de vostre taint noir') 1.3.350–1, 'She must change . . . sated with his body'; 3.3.267, 'Haply for I am black'.
7 (It. *passorono il cuore*; Fr. *transpercèrent le coeur*) 1.3.219–20, 'But words are words . . . That the bruised heart was pierced through the ear'.
8 2.3.217, 'I had rather have this tongue cut from my mouth' (Iago).
9 3.3.362–6.
10 3.3.382, 'I thank you for this profit'.

not mean that I am not speaking the truth. For this Corporal has told me all, like *one whose happiness does not seem complete until he has made someone else acquainted with it.*[1] And he added: 'If I had not feared your wrath, *I should,* when he told me, *have given him the punishment he deserved by killing him.*[2] But since letting you know *what concerns you more than anyone else*[3] brings me so undeserved a reward, *I wish that I had kept silent,*[4] for by doing so I should not have fallen into your displeasure.'

Then the Moor, in the utmost anguish, said, '*If you do not make me see with my own eyes*[5] what you have told me, be assured, I shall make you realize that *it would have been better for you had you been born dumb.*[6] 'To prove it would have been easy', replied the villain, 'when he used to come to your house; but now when, not as it should have been, but for the most trivial cause, you have driven him away, *it cannot but be difficult for me,*[7] for although I fancy that he still enjoys Disdemona whenever you give him the opportunity, *he must do it much more cautiously than he did before,*[8] now that he knows you have turned against him. Yet I do not lose hope of being able to show you what you do not wish to believe.' And with these words they parted.

The wretched Moor, *as if struck by the sharpest of darts,*[9] went home to wait for the day when the Ensign would make him see that which must make him miserable for ever. But no less trouble did the Ensign suffer by his knowledge of the Lady's chastity, for *it did not seem possible to find a way*[10] of making the Moor believe what he had falsely told him, till, his thoughts twisting and turning in all directions, the scoundrel thought of a new piece of mischief.

1 4.1.25–9, 'knaves . . . [who] cannot choose / But they must blab'.
2 1.2.3–10.
3 4.1.195–6, 'if it touch not you it comes near nobody' (It. *appartiene*; Fr., 'ce qui vous touche plus qu'à aucun autre').
4 3.3.395, 'I do repent me that I put it to you.'
5 3.3.363, 'give me the ocular proof' (It. *vedere co gl'occhi*; Fr. *voir*).
6 3.3.365, 'Thou hadst been better have been born a dog'.
7 3.3.400–5, 'It were a tedious difficulty . . . To bring them to that prospect.'
8 3.3.422, '. . . "Let us be wary, let us hide our loves"'.
9 4.1.267–9, '[whom] shot . . . nor dart . . . Could . . . pierce?'
10 3.3.405, 'It is impossible you should see this'.

The Moor's wife often went, as I have said, to the house of the Ensign's wife, and stayed with her a good part of the day; wherefore seeing that she sometimes carried with her *a handkerchief embroidered most delicately in the Moorish fashion,*[1] *which the Moor had given her and which was treasured by the Lady and her husband too,*[2] the Ensign planned to take it from her secretly, and thereby prepare her final ruin. He had a little girl of three years old, much loved by Disdemona. One day, when the unfortunate Lady had gone to pass some time at the villain's house, he took the child in his arms and carried her to the Lady, who took her and pressed her to her breast. The deceiver, who had great sleight of hand, lifted the handkerchief from her girdle so warily that she did not notice it; and he took his leave of her in great joy.

Disdemona, knowing nothing of it, went back home and, being occupied with other thoughts, did not miss the handkerchief. But a few days later, she looked for it, and not finding it she became afraid that the Moor might ask for it, as he often did. The wicked Ensign, seizing a suitable opportunity, *went to the Corporal's room,*[3] and with cunning malice *left the handkerchief* at the head of his bed. The Corporal did not notice it till the next morning when, getting out of bed, he put his foot upon the handkerchief, which had fallen to the floor. *Not being able to imagine how it had come into his house, and knowing that it was Disdemona's,*[4] he determined to give it back to her. So he waited till the Moor had gone out, then went to the back door and knocked. *Fortune, it seems, had conspired with the Ensign*[5] to bring about the death of the unhappy lady; for just then the Moor came home, and hearing a knock on the door went to the window and shouted angrily: 'Who is knocking?' The Corporal, hearing the Moor's voice and fearing that he might come down and attack him, *fled without answering.*[6] The

1   3.3.300, 'I'll have the work ta'en out' (It., 'il qual pannicello era lauorata alla moresca'; Fr., 'vn mouchoir . . . ouuré à la Moresque').
2   3.3.297–300; 3.4.54; 5.2.48.
3   3.3.324; 3.4.188.
4   3.4.187–8, 'whose is it?' – 'I know not'.
5   5.2.223–4, 'that handkerchief . . . I found by fortune'.
6   3.3.30–40.

Moor ran down the stairs, and opening the outside door went out into the street and looked around, but could see nobody. Then returning full of evil passion, *he asked his wife who had knocked*[1] on the door below.

The Lady replied truthfully that she did not know. The Moor then said, '*It looked to me like the Corporal.*'[2] 'I do not know', she said, 'whether it was he or somebody else.' The Moor restrained his fury, though he was consumed with rage. He did not want to do anything before consulting the Ensign, to whom he went at once and told him what had occurred, praying him to find out from the Corporal all that he could about it. Delighted with what had happened, the Ensign promised to do so. Accordingly *he spoke to the Corporal one day while the Moor was standing where he could see them as they talked;*[3] *and chatting of quite other matters than the Lady, he laughed heartily*[4] and, displaying great surprise, he moved his head about and gestured with his hands, acting as if he were listening to marvels. *As soon as the Moor saw them separate he went to the Ensign to learn what the other had told him;*[5] and the Ensign, after making him entreat him for a long time, finally declared: '*He has hidden nothing from me. He tells me that he has enjoyed your wife every time you have given them the chance by your absence.*[6] And on the last occasion *she gave him the handkerchief which you gave her as a present when you married her.*'[7] The Moor thanked the Ensign and it seemed obvious to him that *if he found that the Lady no longer had the handkerchief, then all must be as the Ensign claimed.*[8]

Wherefore one day *after dinner,*[9] while chatting with the Lady on various matters, *he asked her for the handkerchief. The unhappy woman,*[10] who had greatly feared this, grew red in the face at the

---

1 3.3.37, 'Was not that Cassio?'
2 3.3.40, 'I do believe 'twas he.'
3 4.1.75, 93ff.
4 4.1.118, 169.
5 4.1.29, 168.
6 3.3.341, 'her stolen hours of lust'.
7 3.4.66–7, 'when my fate would have me wive, / To give it her'; 4.1.174.
8 3.3.443–4, 'If it be that, or any that was hers, / It speaks against her with the other proofs.'
9 3.3.284–5, 'Your dinner . . . attend[s]'; 3.4.52, 'Lend me thy handkerchief.'
10 3.4.103, 'I am most unhappy in the loss of it'.

request, and to hide her blushes (which the Moor well noted), she ran to the chest, pretending to look for it. After much search, *'I do not know', she said, 'why I cannot find it;*[1] perhaps you have had it?' 'If I had had it,' said he, 'why should I ask for it? But you will look more successfully another time.'

Leaving her *the Moor began to think how he might kill his wife,*[2] and the Corporal too, in such a way that he would not be blamed for it. And since he was obsessed with this, day and night, *the Lady inevitably noticed that he was not the same towards her as he was formerly.*[3] Many times she said to him, *'What is the matter with you?*[4] What is troubling you? Whereas you used to be the gayest of men, *you are now the most melancholy man alive!'*[5]

The Moor invented various excuses,[6] but she was not at all satisfied, and *although she knew no act of hers which could have so perturbed the Moor,*[7] she nevertheless feared that *through the abundance of lovemaking which he had with her he might have become tired of her.*[8] Sometimes she would say to the Ensign's wife, *'I do not know what to make of the Moor. He used to be all love towards me*[9] but in the last few days *he has become quite another man;*[10] and I fear greatly that I shall be a warning to young girls not to marry against their parents' wishes; and Italian ladies will learn by my example *not to tie themselves to a man whom Nature, Heaven, and manner of life separate from us.*[11] But because I know that he is very friendly with your husband, and confides in him, *I beg you, if you have learned anything from him which you can tell me, that you will not fail to help me.'*[12] She wept bitterly as she spoke.

1 3.4.85, 'It is not lost'.
2 3.3.391–2, 'If there be cords or knives, / Poison, or fire'; 4.1.168; 179, 'she shall not live'.
3 3.4.125–6, 'My lord is not my lord'; 4.1.268, 'He is much changed.'
4 4.2.100, 'what's the matter with my lord?'
5 4.2.43, 'why do you weep?'
6 3.3.288.
7 3.4.158, 'I never gave him cause'.
8 1.3.351–2, 'when she is sated with his body she will find the error of her choice' (Iago).
9 4.2.153, 'I know not how I lost him.'
10 4.2.125–6, 'My lord is not my lord'.
11 3.3.233–5, 'Not to affect many proposed matches / Of her own clime, complexion and degree, / Whereto we see, in all things, nature tends' (Iago).
12 4.2.151, 'What shall I do to win my lord again?'

The Ensign's wife, who knew everything (for *her husband had wished to use her as an instrument in causing the Lady's death,*[1] but she had never been willing to consent), *did not dare, for fear of her husband, to tell her anything.*[2] She said only: '*Take care not to give your husband any reason for suspicion, and try your hardest to make him realize your love and loyalty.*'[3] 'That indeed I do,' said Disdemona, 'but it does not help.'

In the meantime *the Moor sought in every way to get more proof*[4] of that which he did not wish to discover, and prayed the Ensign to contrive to let him see the handkerchief in the Corporal's possession; and although that was difficult for the villain, he promised nonetheless to make every effort to give him this testimony.

The Corporal had a woman at home who worked the most wonderful embroidery on lawn, and seeing the handkerchief and learning that it belonged to the Moor's wife, and that it was to be returned to her, *she began to make a similar one*[5] before it went back. While she was doing so, the Ensign noticed that she was working near a window where she could be seen by whoever passed by on the street. *So he brought the Moor and made him see her,*[6] and the latter *now regarded it as certain*[7] that the most virtuous Lady was indeed an adulteress. *He arranged with the Ensign to kill her and the Corporal and they discussed how it might be done. The Moor begged the Ensign to kill the Corporal,*[8] promising to remain eternally grateful to him. *The Ensign refused to undertake such a thing,*[9] as being too difficult and dangerous, for the

---

1 3.3.296–7, 'My wayward husband hath a hundred times / Wooed me to steal it'; 5.2.225–7.
2 3.4.24, 'I know not, madam'.
3 3.4.29, 'Is he not jealous?'; 3.4.100; 4.2.12, 'I durst, my lord, to wager she is honest'.
4 3.3.389, 'I'll have some proof.'
5 3.4.180, 'Take me this work out'; 190, 'I'd have it copied' (Fr., 'se mit à en faire vn semblable, *& en tirer le patron*'. The words in italics (= and take out the pattern) are not found in the Italian original).
6 4.1.156, 'By heaven, that should be my handkerchief!'
7 4.1.74, 'O, thou art wise, 'tis certain.'
8 3.3.475ff., 'let me hear thee say / That Cassio's not alive . . .' – 'But let her live.' – 'Damn her, lewd minx'; 4.1.198ff.
9 4.1.209 (Iago offers to kill Cassio).

Corporal was as skilful as he was courageous; but after much entreaty, and *being given a large sum of money,*[1] he was persuaded to say that he would tempt Fortune.

Soon after they had resolved on this, *the Corporal, issuing one dark night from the house of a courtesan with whom he used to amuse himself, was accosted by the Ensign, sword in hand,*[2] who directed a blow at his legs to make him fall down; and *he cut the right leg entirely through, so that the wretched man fell.*[3] The Ensign was immediately on him to finish him off, but the Corporal, who was valiant and used to blood and death, had drawn his sword, and wounded as he was he set about defending himself, while *shouting in a loud voice: 'I am being murdered!'*[4]

At that *the Ensign, hearing people come running,* including some of the soldiers who were quartered thereabouts, *began to flee, so as not to be caught there; then, turning back he pretended to have run up on hearing the noise.*[5] Mingling with the others, and seeing the leg cut off, he judged that if the Corporal were not already dead, he soon would die of the wound, and although he rejoiced inwardly, *he outwardly grieved for the Corporal*[6] *as if he had been his own brother.*[7]

In the morning, news of the affray was spread throughout the city and reached the ears of Disdemona; whereupon, being tender-hearted and not thinking that evil would come to her by it, *she showed the utmost sorrow at the occurrence.*[8] On this *the Moor put the worst possible construction.*[9] Seeking out the Ensign, he said to him: *'Do you know, my imbecile of a wife is in such grief about the Corporal's accident that she is nearly out of her mind!'*[9] 'How could you expect anything else?' said the other, 'since he is her very life and soul?'

---

1   3.3.472–3, 'I greet thy love . . . with acceptance bounteous'; 1.3.382, 'Thus do I ever make my fool my purse'.

2   4.2.235, 'He sups tonight with a harlotry'; 5.1.1ff., 'Wear thy good rapier bare'.

3   5.1.24ff.; 71, 'My leg is cut in two'.

4   5.1.27, 'Help, ho! murder! murder!'

5   5.1.26 SD; 45 SD; 48, 'Whose noise is this . . . ?'

6   5.1.56, 'O me, lieutenant!'

7   5.1.71, 'How is't, brother?'

8   5.2.72, 'my fear interprets'; 75, 'Alas, he is betrayed, and I undone'.

9   5.2.76, 'Out, strumpet, weep'st thou for him to my face?'

'Soul indeed!' replied the Moor, 'I'll drag the soul from her body,[1] for *I couldn't think myself a man*[2] if I didn't *rid the world of such a wicked creature.'*[3]

They were *discussing whether the Lady should perish by poison or the dagger,*[4] and not deciding on either of them, when the Ensign said: 'A method has come into my head that will satisfy you and that nobody will suspect. It is this: the house where you are staying is very old, and the ceiling of your room has many cracks in it. I suggest that we beat Disdemona with a stocking filled with sand until she dies. Thus there will not appear on her any sign of the blows. When she is dead, we shall make part of the ceiling fall; and we'll break the Lady's head, making it seem that a rafter has injured it in falling, and killed her. In this way nobody will feel any suspicion of you, for everyone will think that she died accidentally.'

The cruel plan pleased the Moor,[5] and they waited for a suitable opportunity. One night the Moor concealed the Ensign in a closet which opened off the bedchamber, and when the husband and wife were in bed, the Ensign, in accordance with their plan, made some sort of noise. Hearing it the Moor said to his wife:

> *'Did you hear that noise?'*
> 'Yes, I heard it', she replied.
> 'Get up', said the Moor, 'and see what it is.'[6]

The unfortunate Disdemona got out of bed, and as soon as she was near the closet, the Ensign came out and, being strong and muscular, he gave her a frightful blow in the small of her back, which made the Lady fall down at once, scarcely able to draw her breath. With the little voice she had *she called on the Moor to help her.*[7] But he, jumping out of bed, said to her, '*You wicked woman,*[8]

1 5.2.50, 'Sweet soul, take heed'.
2 4.1.65, 'Good sir, be a man'; 89–90, 'I shall say you're . . . nothing of a man'.
3 5.2.6, 'Yet she must die, else she'll betray more men'.
4 3.3.391–2, 'If there be cords or knives, / Poison . . . '; 4.1.202.
5 4.1.207, 'the justice of it pleases'; 5.2.247, 'she loved thee, cruel Moor'.
6 5.2.85, 'What noise is this?'
7 5.2.119, 'Help, help, ho, help!' (Emilia).
8 5.2.63, 'O perjured woman'.

you are having the reward of your infidelity. This is how women are treated who, pretending to love their husbands, put horns on their heads.'

The wretched Lady, hearing this and feeling herself near to death (for the Ensign had given her another blow), *called on Divine Justice to witness to her fidelity, since earthly justice failed;*[1] and *as she called on God to help her, a third blow struck her, and she lay still,*[2] slain by the impious Ensign. Then, placing her in the bed, and breaking her skull, he and the Moor made the ceiling fall as they had previously planned, and *the Moor began to call for help,*[3] that the house was falling. *Hearing his cries the neighbours ran in and found the bed, and the Lady dead*[3] under the rafters – which made everyone grieve, *for they knew what a good life she had led.*[4]

Next day Disdemona was buried, amid the universal mourning of the people. But God, the just observer of men's hearts, *did not intend such vile wickedness to go without proper punishment.*[5] He ordained that *the Moor, who had loved the Lady more than his life,*[6] on finding himself deprived of her should *feel such longing that he went about like one beside himself, searching for her in every part of the house.*[7] Realizing now that the Ensign was the cause of his losing his Lady and all joy in life, he held the villain in such abhorrence that he could not bear even to see him; and if he had not been afraid of the inviolable justice of the Venetian lords, he would have slain him openly. Not being able to do this with safety, *he took away his rank and would not have him in his company, whereupon such a bitter hatred sprang up between them that no greater or more deadly feud could be imagined.*[8]

---

1 4.2.82, 'By heaven, you do me wrong'; 88, 'What, not a whore?' – 'No, as I shall be saved'; 5.2.16–17, 'that dost almost persuade / Justice to break her sword!'
2 5.2.83, 'O Lord! Lord! Lord! [*(He) smothers her.*]'
3 5.2.162 (Emilia calls for help); 163 SD.
4 5.2.197, 'thou hast killed the sweetest innocent'.
5 5.2.365, 'To you . . . Remains the censure of this hellish villain'.
6 1.3.295, 'My life upon her faith'; 3.3.90, 'perdition catch my soul / But I do love thee'.
7 5.2.18, 'I will kill thee / And love thee after'; 97, 'O insupportable, O heavy hour!'
8 (This loss of rank perhaps suggested Iago's hatred when he is not promoted:) 1.1.5; 1.3.385, 'I hate the Moor'.

The Ensign, that worst of all scoundrels, therefore set all his mind to injuring the Moor, and seeking out the Corporal, who had now recovered and went about with a wooden leg instead of the one that had been cut off, he said to him, 'It is time you got your revenge for the leg you lost. If you will come to Venice with me, I shall tell you who the miscreant was, for here I dare not tell you, for many reasons; and I am willing to bear witness for you in court.'

The Corporal who felt himself deeply wronged but did not know the real truth, thanked the Ensign and came with him to Venice. When they arrived there the Ensign told him that it was the Moor who had cut off his leg because of a suspicion he had formed that he was Disdemona's lover, and that for the same reason he had murdered her, and afterwards made it known that the fallen ceiling had killed her. Hearing this, the Corporal accused the Moor to *the Signoria*,[1] both of cutting off his leg and of causing the Lady's death, and called as witness the Ensign, who said that both accusations were true, for the Moor had approached him and tried to induce him to commit both crimes; and that, having then killed his wife through the bestial jealousy that he had conceived in his mind, he had told him how he had killed her.

When the Signoria learned of the cruelty inflicted by *the Barbarian*[2] upon a citizen of Venice, *they ordered the Moor to be apprehended in Cyprus and to be brought to Venice,*[3] where with many tortures they tried to discover the truth. But enduring with great steadfastness of mind every torment, he denied everything so firmly that nothing could be extorted from him. Although by his constancy he escaped death, he was, however, after many days in prison, condemned to perpetual exile, in which he was finally slain by Disdemona's relatives, as he richly deserved.

The Ensign returned to his own country; and not giving up his accustomed behaviour, he accused one of his companions, saying that the latter had sought to have him murder one of his enemies,

---

1   1.2.18, 'the signiory' (= the Signoria).
2   1.3.356, 'an erring Barbarian'.
3   5.2.328–35, 'You shall close prisoner rest'.

who was a nobleman. The accused man was arrested and put to the torture, and when he denied that what his accuser said was true, *the Ensign too was tortured*, to compare their stories; and *he was tortured so fiercely that his inner organs were ruptured.*[1] Afterwards he was let out of prison and taken home, where he died miserably. Thus did God avenge the innocence of Disdemona. *And all these events were told after his death by the Ensign's wife, who knew the facts*[2] as I have told them to you.

[Story 8 is (as usual) prefaced by a linking passage commenting on the tale just heard:]

It appeared marvellous to everybody that such malignity could have been discovered in a human heart; and the fate of *the unhappy Lady*[3] was lamented, with some blame for *her father, who had given her a name of unlucky augury.*[4] And the party decided that since a name is the first gift of a father to his child, he ought to bestow one that is grand and fortunate, as if he wished to foretell success and greatness. *No less was the Moor blamed, who had believed too foolishly.*[5] But all praised God because the criminals had had suitable punishment.

No doubt Shakespeare's departures from Cinthio were carefully considered. Some were dictated by the exigencies of staging (Disdemona's death, the Ensign's 3-year-old daughter). Others resulted from Shakespeare's wish to compress and concentrate (the double time scheme, the accelerated ending) – the very opposite, be it noted, of what we find in *Hamlet* and *King Lear*. But Shakespeare's greatest effort went into his characterization, converting Cinthio's stereotype men and women, who exist only as plot mechanisms, into individuals interesting in themselves. Shakespeare's imagination also seized on many details, some of them barely hinted at by Cinthio, and conjured gold out of dross (the threat from 'the Turk', the imagery of sea and water, a generalized sexual antagonism). The handkerchief becomes a

1 5.2.302, 'Torments will ope your lips'; 367.
2 5.2.180ff.
3 1.1.161, 'O unhappy girl!'
4 Desdemona = (Greek) 'unfortunate'; 5.2.339, 'these unlucky deeds'.
5 5.2.340, 'Nothing extenuate'; 342, 'one that loved not wisely, but too well'; 159–60, 'O gull, O dolt, / As ignorant as dirt!'

crucial exhibit in the play's treatment of 'chance' (see pp. 72–3), and also brings with it glimpses of the Egyptian and sibyl, and of Othello's father and mother (3.4.57ff.). One can usually see good reasons for Shakespeare's changes (the development of Brabantio and the addition of Roderigo: see p. 68), or at any rate reasons (the addition of the Clown: the clown actor, a popular performer, had to have a part). Now and then, though, we may feel that Shakespeare might have tried harder to break free from Cinthio, as in the eavesdropping episode (4.1.93ff.). Readers will find it rewarding to compare the play and Cinthio in greater detail.

Apart from Cinthio, many other writers and 'sources' contributed to *Othello*. (I am not convinced that Shakespeare read Bandello in Italian, as has been suggested, since there are English sources for Desdemona's revival after being smothered.)[1] These are mentioned at various points in the introduction and commentary, and can be traced with the help of the index: John Leo, Pliny, Lewis Lewkenor (the translator of Contarini), Lyly, Marlowe, *Arden of Faversham*, *A Warning for Fair Women*, *Every Man in His Humour*, *Every Man out of His Humour*, Terence, Plautus, Ovid, Rabelais, the Bible, popular ballads, songs and proverbs, and the scenic form and characters in Shakespeare's own earlier plays, notably *Titus Andronicus*, *Much Ado* and *Twelfth Night*.[2] Anyone who thinks of *Othello* as a short story blown up beyond its capacity should keep in mind that Shakespeare packed into it much miscellaneous reading as well as something not far removed from research, his perusal of very recent books on the Mediterranean world, on north Africa and on Venice.

1 See Shaheen, as on p. 368 n.1, and p. 74 above.
2 See also Bullough, 195ff., for other posssible sources and analogues.

APPENDIX 4
EDWARD PUDSEY'S
EXTRACTS FROM
OTHELLO

Edward Pudsey, gentleman, from Tewkesbury, Gloucestershire, recorded extracts from several plays in notebooks which have survived. Most of the plays belonged to Shakespeare's company, and some of the extracts could have been written down during or just after a performance. Pudsey included passages from *The Merchant of Venice*, *Much Ado*, *Titus Andronicus*, *Romeo and Juliet*, *Richard 2*, *Richard 3* and *Hamlet*, and also from Jonson's *Every Man out of His Humour* and from a play called *Irus*. These were published by Richard Savage as *Shakespearean Extracts from 'Edward Pudsey's Booke'* (1888).[1]

Savage did not know Pudsey's will, which has now been printed.[2] The will, dated 8 January 1610, actually referred to his notebooks; administration was granted to his widow on 17 November 1613. Pudsey therefore could have quoted from the published versions of some plays, especially when his longer extracts are close to the quartos.[3] The extracts from *Romeo and Juliet* and *Hamlet*, on the other hand, two plays each of which reached print in two different quarto versions, could have been jotted down during a performance, for in these extracts he sometimes agrees with Q1 and sometimes with Q2 of the same play.

---

1 Stratford-upon-Avon Note Books, no. 1 (printed and published at Stratford-on-Avon by John Smith; London: Simpkin and Marshall). See also Peter Beal, *Index of English Literary Manuscripts*, vol. 1, part 2 (1980), 449.
2 See *Playhouse Wills 1558–1642: An Edition of Wills by Shakespeare and His Contemporaries in the London Theatre*, ed. E. A. J. Honigmann and Susan Brock (Manchester, 1993), 92–4.
3 For instance, see Savage, *Shakespearean Extracts*, 46 (*Much Ado*).

The extracts published by Savage were taken from papers now housed in the Bodleian Library (MS. Eng. poet. d. 3), but some leaves from Pudsey's notebooks found their way into the Shakespeare Birthplace Trust Record Office in Stratford-upon-Avon (MS. ER 82). The Stratford leaves contain short extracts from *Othello*, a play not printed until after Pudsey's death, and so transmit the earliest bits of text of the play now known. While we cannot tell whether Pudsey wrote them down in the theatre or later, they look like approximations, attempts to keep track of ideas rather than to record the exact words of the play.

I am grateful to Mairi McDonald of the Birthplace Trust for checking my transcription. I have added numbers in square brackets at the beginning of each of the four lines, have expanded contractions and included alternative and doubtful readings, also in square brackets.

[1] Dangerous to tell where a soldier lyes. [for] yf I shold say he lodge theer I lyed ther [or 'the^{c}r']

[2] Shee y^t is free of her tonng [or 'toung'] ys as frank of her lipps. An ey y^t offe^{r}s p[ar]le to p[ro]uocac[i]o[n]

[3] An equalitye of p[er]fections fit in mariage for when y^c act ys past theere wilbe

[4] a dulnes much needing y^c help of beauty youth loue & such lyke to p[re]uent loathing

[In margin, before line 3] A fit matc^h

Compare (1) and 3.4.1–13, (2) and 2.1.100–2, 2.3.21–2, (3) and 2.1.224ff., (4) and 2.1.224–31.

APPENDIX 5
MUSICAL SETTINGS FOR SONGS IN *OTHELLO*

Musical adviser: Helen Wilcox

All musical settings are reproduced from F. W. Sternfeld, *Music in Shakespearean Tragedy* (1963), by permission. Note that the wording in the settings may not be the same as that in this edition. A comprehensive listing of all musical settings, incidental music and operas associated with Shakespeare's plays may be found in *A Shakespeare Music Catalogue*, edited by Bryan N. S. Gooch and David Thatcher, 6 vols (Oxford, 1991).

'And let me the cannikin clink, clink' (2.3.65–9)

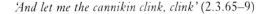

See note on p. 187. Reproduced from Sternfeld, 146.

'*King Stephen was and a worthy peer*' (2.3.85–92)

See notes on pp. 188, 336–7. Reproduced from Sternfeld, 149.

Willow Song (4.3.39–50)

I -land. Sing all a green wil-low; wil - low, wil-low, wil-low;
II   [stanza 2] [2]

I   sing all a green wil-low must be my gar-land.
II

1. [stanza 2, bar 16, singing interrupted:]
    Lay by these.

2   [stanza 2, bar 24, singing interrupted:]
    Prithee, hie thee; he'll come anon.

3   [stanza 3, bar 6, singing stops here:]
    Nay, that's not next. Hark! who is't that knocks? It is the wind.

4   [stanza 4, bar 14, singing stops here:]
    So get thee gone; good night. Mine eyes do itch. Doth that bode
    weeping?

See notes on pp. 291, 339–40. Reproduced from Sternfeld, 43–4.

ABBREVIATIONS AND REFERENCES

Unless otherwise stated, the place of publication is London.

ABBREVIATIONS

ABBREVIATIONS USED IN NOTES

	precedes commentary notes involving readings that are not found in either Q or F
as	substantively as in the edition cited (i.e. ignoring accidentals of spelling and punctuation)
cont.	continued
Fc	corrected state of F
Fr.	French
Fu	uncorrected state of F
It.	Italian
Lat.	Latin
lit.	literally
LN	longer note(s)
n.d.	no date
om.	omitted
opp.	opposite
Qc	corrected state of Q
Qu	uncorrected state of Q
SD	stage direction
SP	speech prefix
SR	Stationers' Register (see Arber)
subst.	substantially
this edn	a reading adopted for the first time in this edition
TLN	through line numbering in *The First Folio of Shakespeare*, ed. Charlton Hinman, Norton Facsimile (1968)
t.n.	textual notes at the foot of the page

SHAKESPEARE'S WORKS AND WORKS PARTLY
BY SHAKESPEARE

AC	*Antony and Cleopatra*
AW	*All's Well That Ends Well*
AYL	*As You Like It*
CE	*The Comedy of Errors*
Cor	*Coriolanus*
Cym	*Cymbeline*
E3	*Edward III*
Ham	*Hamlet*
1H4	*King Henry IV Part 1*
2H4	*King Henry IV Part 2*
H5	*King Henry V*
1H6	*King Henry VI Part 1*
2H6	*King Henry VI Part 2*
3H6	*King Henry VI Part 3*
H8	*King Henry VIII*
JC	*Julius Caesar*
KJ	*King John*
KL	*King Lear*
LLL	*Love's Labour's Lost*
Luc	*The Rape of Lucrece*
MA	*Much Ado About Nothing*
Mac	*Macbeth*
MM	*Measure for Measure*
MND	*A Midsummer Night's Dream*
MV	*The Merchant of Venice*
MW	*The Merry Wives of Windsor*
Oth	*Othello*
Per	*Pericles*
PP	*The Passionate Pilgrim*
R2	*King Richard II*
R3	*King Richard III*
RJ	*Romeo and Juliet*
Son	*Sonnets*
STM	*Sir Thomas More*
TC	*Troilus and Cressida*
Tem	*The Tempest*
TGV	*The Two Gentlemen of Verona*
Tim	*Timon of Athens*
Tit	*Titus Andronicus*
TN	*Twelfth Night*
TNK	*The Two Noble Kinsmen*
TS	*The Taming of the Shrew*

| VA | *Venus and Adonis* |
| WT | *The Winter's Tale* |

REFERENCES

EDITIONS OF SHAKESPEARE COLLATED

References to Shakespeare's works other than *Othello* are to the *Riverside Shakespeare* (Boston, 1974).

Alexander	*William Shakespeare: The Complete Works*, ed. Peter Alexander (1951)
Ard[1]	*Othello*, ed. H. C. Hart, Arden Shakespeare (1903)
Ard[2]	*Othello*, ed. M. R. Ridley, Arden Shakespeare, 7th edn (1958)
Bevington	*Othello*, ed. David Bevington, Bantam edn (1988)
Cam	*Othello*, ed. W. G. Clark, J. Glover and W. A. Wright, The Cambridge Shakespeare, 9 vols (Cambridge and London, 1863–6); revised W. A. Wright (1891–3)
Cam[2]	*Othello*, ed. Alice Walker and John Dover Wilson, The New Shakespeare (Cambridge, 1957)
Cam[3]	*Othello*, ed. Norman Sanders, The New Cambridge Shakespeare (Cambridge, 1984)
Capell	*Mr. William Shakespeare: His Comedies, Histories and Tragedies*, ed. Edward Capell, 10 vols (1767–8). For Capell's annotations see his *Notes and Various Readings to Shakespeare*, 3 vols (1779–83)
Collier	*The Works of William Shakespeare*, ed. John Payne Collier, 8 vols (1842–4)
Collier[2]	*The Works of William Shakespeare*, ed. John Payne Collier, 8 vols (1853)
Dyce	*The Works of William Shakespeare*, ed. Alexander Dyce, 6 vols (1857)
F	*Mr. William Shakespeares Comedies, Histories, and Tragedies*, The First Folio (1623)
F2	*Mr. William Shakespeares Comedies, Histories and Tragedies*, The Second Folio (1632)
F3	*Mr. William Shakespeares Comedies, Histories and Tragedies*, The Third Folio (1663)
F4	*Mr. William Shakespeares Comedies, Histories, and Tragedies*, The Fourth Folio (1685)
Folger	*Othello*, ed. Barbara A. Mowat and Paul Werstine, The New Folger Library Shakespeare (New York, 1993)
Furness	*Othello*, ed. Horace Howard Furness, New Variorum Shakespeare (Philadelphia, 1886; repr. New York, 1963)
Hanmer	*The Works of Shakespeare*, ed. Thomas Hanmer, 6 vols (Oxford, 1743–4)

Hart	See Ard[1]
Johnson	*The Plays of William Shakespeare*, ed. Samuel Johnson, 8 vols (1765)
Kittredge	*Othello*, ed. George Lyman Kittredge (Boston, 1941)
Knight	*The Pictorial Edition of the Works of Shakespeare*, ed. Charles Knight, 8 vols (1838–43)
Malone	*The Plays and Poems of William Shakespeare*, ed. Edmond Malone, 10 vols (1790)
Malone[2]	*The Plays and Poems of William Shakespeare*, ed. Edmond Malone, 21 vols (1821)
Muir	*Othello*, ed. Kenneth Muir, New Penguin Shakespeare (Harmondsworth, 1968)
Oxf	William Shakespeare, *The Complete Works*, ed. Stanley Wells and Gary Taylor (Oxford, 1986)
Pope	*The Works of Shakespear*, ed. Alexander Pope, 6 vols (1723–5)
Pope[2]	*The Works of Shakespear*, ed. Alexander Pope, 8 vols (1728)
Q	William Shakespeare, *Othello*, The First Quarto (1622)
Q2	William Shakespeare, *Othello*, The Second Quarto (1630)
Q3	William Shakespeare, *Othello*, The Third Quarto (1655)
Ridley	See Ard[2]
Riv	*The Riverside Shakespeare*, ed. G. Blakemore Evans and others (Boston, 1974)
Rowe	*The Works of Mr. William Shakespear*, ed. Nicholas Rowe, 6 vols (1709)
Rowe[2]	*The Works of Mr. William Shakespear*, ed. Nicholas Rowe, 6 vols (1709)
Rowe[3]	*The Works of Mr. William Shakespear*, ed. Nicholas Rowe, 8 vols (1714)
Sanders	See Cam[3]
Sisson	William Shakespeare, *The Complete Works*, ed. C. J. Sisson (n.d.)
Steevens	*The Plays of William Shakespeare*, ed. Samuel Johnson and George Steevens, 10 vols (1773)
Steevens[2]	*The Plays of William Shakespeare*, ed. Samuel Johnson and George Steevens, 10 vols (1778)
Steevens[3]	*The Plays of William Shakespeare*, ed. Samuel Johnson and George Steevens, 10 vols (1785)
Theobald	*The Works of Shakespeare*, ed. Lewis Theobald, 7 vols (1733)
Theobald[2]	*The Works of Shakespeare*, ed. Lewis Theobald, 8 vols (1740)
Walker	See Cam[2]
Warburton	*The Works of Shakespeare*, ed. William Warburton, 8 vols (1747)
Wilson	See Cam[2]

OTHER WORKS

Cited by author's name or short title. N.B. All quotations and translations from classical authors are taken from the Loeb Classical Library, unless another source is indicated.

Abbott	E. A. Abbott, *A Shakespearian Grammar*, 2nd edn (1870, etc.)
Adamson	Jane Adamson, *'Othello' as Tragedy: Some Problems of Judgment and Feeling* (Cambridge, 1980)
Arber	*A Transcript of the Registers of the Company of Stationers of London, AD 1554–1640*, ed. Edward Arber, 5 vols (1875, etc.)
Bible	Quotations from the Bible are from the 'Bishops' Bible' (1568, etc.), with modernized spelling, except when otherwise indicated
Bradley	A. C. Bradley, *Shakespearean Tragedy* (1904)
Bradshaw	Graham Bradshaw, *Misrepresentations: Shakespeare and the Materialists* (1993)
Bullough	Geoffrey Bullough, *Narrative and Dramatic Sources of Shakespeare*, 8 vols (1957–75), vol. 7 (1973)
Calderwood	James L. Calderwood, *The Properties of 'Othello'* (Amherst, 1989)
Chambers, *Elizabethan Stage*	E. K. Chambers, *The Elizabethan Stage*, 4 vols (Oxford, 1923)
Chambers, *William Shakespeare*	E. K. Chambers, *William Shakespeare: A Study of Facts and Problems*, 2 vols (Oxford, 1930)
Chew	Samuel C. Chew, *The Crescent and the Rose: Islam and England during the Renaissance* (Oxford, 1937, repr. New York, 1965)
Cotgrave	R. Cotgrave, *A Dictionarie of the French and English Tongues* (1611)
Dekker	*The Dramatic Works of Thomas Dekker*, ed. Fredson Bowers, 4 vols (Cambridge, 1953–8)
Dent	R. W. Dent, *Shakespeare's Proverbial Language: An Index* (1981)
ELH	*A Journal of English Literary History*
Elliott	Martin Elliott, *Shakespeare's Invention of Othello: A Study in Early Modern English* (1988)
ELN	*English Language Notes*
ES	*English Studies*
Everett, '"Spanish" Othello'	Barbara Everett, '"Spanish" Othello: the making of Shakespeare's Moor', *SS*, 35 (1982), 101–12
Fiedler	Leslie A. Fiedler, *The Stranger in Shakespeare* (1973)

Goddard	Harold C. Goddard, *The Meaning of Shakespeare*, 2 vols (1951, repr. 1965)
Greenblatt	Stephen Greenblatt, *Renaissance Self-Fashioning: From More to Shakespeare* (Chicago, 1980, repr. 1984)
Greg	W. W. Greg, *The Shakespeare First Folio: Its Bibliographical and Textual History* (Oxford, 1955)
GRM	*Germanisch-Romanische Monatsschrift*
Hankey	Julie Hankey, *Othello – William Shakespeare*, Bristol Classical Press: Plays in Performance (1987)
Heilman	R. B. Heilman, *Magic in the Web: Action and Language in 'Othello'* (Lexington, Kentucky, 1956)
HMC	Historical Manuscripts Commission
Homilies	*Certain Sermons or Homilies* appointed to be read in churches in the time of the late Queen Elizabeth (Oxford, 1844)
Honigmann, 'Date of *Othello*'	E. A. J. Honigmann, 'The First Quarto of *Hamlet* and the date of *Othello*', *RES*, 44 (1993), 211–19
Honigmann, *Myriad-Minded Shakespeare*	E. A. J. Honigmann, *Myriad-Minded Shakespeare: Essays, Chiefly on the Tragedies and Problem Comedies* (1989)
Honigmann, *Seven Tragedies*	E. A. J. Honigmann, *Shakespeare: Seven Tragedies. The Dramatist's Manipulation of Response* (1976)
Honigmann, *Stability*	E. A. J. Honigmann, *The Stability of Shakespeare's Text* (1965)
Honigmann, 'Stage direction'	E. A. J. Honigmann, 'Re-enter the stage direction: Shakespeare and some contemporaries', *SS*, 29 (1976), 117–25
Honigmann, *Texts*	E. A. J. Honigmann, *The Texts of 'Othello' and Shakespearian Revision* (1996)
Hulme	Hilda M. Hulme, *Explorations in Shakespeare's Language* (1962)
Johnson	Samuel Johnson, *Johnson on Shakespeare*, ed. Walter Raleigh (1908)
Jones	Eldred Jones, *Othello's Countrymen: The African in English Renaissance Drama* (Oxford, 1965)
Jones, *Scenic Form*	Emrys Jones, *Scenic Form in Shakespeare* (Oxford, 1971)
Jonson	*Ben Jonson*, ed. C. H. Herford and Percy and Evelyn Simpson, 11 vols (Oxford, 1925–52)
Lyly	*The Complete Works of John Lyly*, ed. R. Warwick Bond, 3 vols (Oxford, 1902)

Mack	Maynard Mack, *Everybody's Shakespeare* (1993)
Marlowe	*The Complete Works of Christopher Marlowe*, ed. Fredson Bowers, 2 vols (Cambridge, 1973)
Martial	*The Epigrams of Martial*, Bohn's Classical Library (1907)
Montaigne	*The Essayes*, tr. John Florio, Everyman's Library, 3 vols (1910)
MSR	Malone Society Reprints
Muir	Kenneth Muir, *The Sources of Shakespeare's Plays* (1977)
N&Q	*Notes and Queries*
Noble	Richmond Noble, *Shakespeare's Biblical Knowledge and Use of the Book of Common Prayer* (1935)
OED	*The Oxford English Dictionary*, ed. James A. H. Murray and others, 13 vols (1933, repr. 1977)
Partridge	Eric Partridge, *Shakespeare's Bawdy* (1947, repr. 1961)
PQ	*Philological Quarterly*
RD	*Renaissance Drama*
RES	*Review of English Studies*
Revels	The Revels Plays (Manchester University Press)
Rosenberg	Marvin Rosenberg, *The Masks of Othello* (1961, repr. 1994)
RQ	*Renaissance Quarterly*
SEL	*Studies in English Literature 1500–1900*
Sisson, Readings	C. J. Sisson, *New Readings in Shakespeare*, 2 vols (Cambridge, 1956)
SJW	*Shakespeare Jahrbuch West*
Snyder	Susan Snyder, *The Comic Matrix of Shakespeare's Tragedies* (Princeton, 1979)
Sprague	Arthur Colby Sprague, *Shakespeare and the Actors: The Stage Business in his Plays (1660–1905)* (Cambridge, Massachusetts, 1945)
SQ	*Shakespeare Quarterly*
SS	*Shakespeare Survey*
SSt	*Shakespeare Studies*
Sternfeld	F. N. Sternfeld, *Music in Shakespearean Tragedy* (1963)
Texts	See Honigmann, *Texts*
Tilley	Morris Palmer Tilley, *A Dictionary of the Proverbs in England in the Sixteenth and Seventeenth Centuries* (Ann Arbor, 1950)
TLS	*The Times Literary Supplement*
Vickers	Brian Vickers, ed., *Shakespeare: The Critical Heritage vol. 1 1623–1692* (1974); *vol. 2 1693–1733* (1974); *vol. 3 1733–1752* (1975); *vol. 4 1753–1765* (1976); *vol. 5 1765–1774* (1979); *vol. 6 1774–1801* (1981)
Walton	J. K. Walton, *The Quarto Copy for the First Folio of Shakespeare* (Dublin, 1971)
Wotton	Logan Pearsall Smith, *The Life and Letters of Sir Henry Wotton*, 2 vols (Oxford, 1907, repr. 1966)

INDEX

This index covers the Introduction, Commentary and Appendices. It omits Honigmann, *Texts*; *Othello*; William Shakespeare; and all *OED* entries except those listed as Shakespeare's coinages or 'first here' or 'first recorded' in a particular year.

Index

Leavis, F. R. 24
Lees, F. N. 334
Leo, John 4, 23, 387
Lepanto, Battle of (1571) 8
Levin, Richard 342–3
Lewkenor, Sir Lewis 5–8, 127, 387
Lieblein, Leanore 73
lineation (see also prose and verse) 351, 360
Little, Arthur L. 27, 69
Livy 266
Lloyd, W. Watkiss 63
location 11, 88, 115, 128, 135, 208, 227, 251, 272, 288
London 4, 8–9, 12, 16, 20, 29, 60
Long, J. H. 340
Look About You 257, 321
Lucas, F. L. 50
Luchese, Paulo Marchi 138
Lust's Dominion 160
Lyly, John 167, 171, 187, 210, 212, 231, 248, 258, 335, 387

McCullen, J. T. 335
McDonald, Russ 75
McGee, Arthur 69
MacGregor 292
Machiavelli, N. 33, 61, 116, 207
Mack, Maynard 23, 38, 53, 61, 153
Mackenzie, D. F. 353
MacLiammóir, M. 90
McNeill, W. H. 9
McPherson, D. C. 8–9
Macready, W. C. 68, 99, 101
Mahood, M. M. 85
make-up 15, 175, 234
malcontent 33, 41
Mallett, M. E. 9
Malone, Edmond 5–6, 144, 151–2, 195–7, 212, 231, 236, 238–9, 241, 249, 255, 266, 270–1, 295, 322, 329, 342
Manningham, John 347
Markham, F. M. H. 37
Marlowe, Christopher 108, 115, 166, 184, 230, 236, 238, 240, 312, 321, 341, 387
Marston, John 185, 239, 267, 276, 334
Martial 263
Mason, Robert 156

Massinger, P. 299
Maxwell, J. C. 41, 345
melodrama 40
Mendonça, B. H. C. de 75
Meyerstein, E. H. W. 146
Middleton, Thomas 59, 277, 282, 334, 358
Miller, Jonathan 90
Milton, John 56, 104, 157
miscegenation 27, 30–1
misreading 2, 115, 131, 138, 143, 151–2, 156, 162–3, 178, 186, 190, 195, 212, 217, 235–6, 238, 259–60, 263, 270, 290, 299, 307–8, 333–4, 336, 341, 355ff., 363ff.
modernization 131, 361–3
Moffett, T. 245
Money, J. 305
Montaigne, M. de 233, 286
Moors 2–4, 12ff., 22, 28–9, 33, 123
morality, moral 29, 58–60
Morozov, M. 79
Morrison, Toni 85
motives 19, 26, 33–5, 41, 160, 250, 306, 332, 335
Mucedorus 155
Muir, Kenneth 5, 25, 27, 166, 245
Munster, Sebastian 6
Muslim 2, 22

Nabokov, V. 28
narrative 23–4
Neill, M. 52, 86
night-scenes 86–7
Noble, Richmond 2, 22, 199, 202, 221, 279, 283, 338, 348

OED (only Shakespeare's coinages and 'first recorded' words are included) 116–17, 124–5, 133, 136–7, 140, 144–6, 149–55, 158–9, 164–7, 173–4, 193–4, 201, 211, 214–16, 218–21, 225–6, 229, 231–5, 237–9, 250, 259, 261, 263, 267–9, 271–2, 275–7, 281, 283, 285–6, 310, 317, 321, 325, 327, 330
Olivier, Laurence 21, 28, 31, 38, 50–1, 90, 96–9, 101, 239
Otello, G. 334
otherness 20, 27–9, 31, 337

405